Financial Innovation in Retail and Corporate Banking

NEW HORIZONS IN MONEY AND FINANCE

Series Editor: Mervyn K. Lewis, *University of South Australia*

This important series is designed to make a significant contribution to the shaping and development of thinking in finance. The series will provide an invaluable forum for the publication of high quality works of scholarship on a breadth of topics ranging from financial markets and financial systems to monetary policy and banking reform, and will show the diversity of theory, issues and practices.

The focus of the series is on the development and application of new original ideas in finance. Rigorous and often path-breaking in its approach, it will pay particular attention to the international and comparative dimension of finance and will include innovative theoretical and empirical work from both well-established authors and the new generation of scholars.

Titles in the series include:

Banking Reforms in South-East Europe
Edited by Zeljko Sevic

Russian Banking
Evolution, Problems and Prospects
Edited by David Lane

Currency Crises
A Theoretical and Empirical Perspective
André Fourçans and Raphaël Franck

East Asia's Monetary Future
Integration in the Global Economy
Suthiphand Chirathivat, Emil-Maria Claassen and Jürgen Schroeder

Reforming China's State-Owned Enterprises and Banks
Becky Chiu and Mervyn K. Lewis

Financial Innovation in Retail and Corporate Banking
Edited by Luisa Anderloni, David T. Llewellyn and Reinhard H. Schmidt

An Islamic Perspective on Governance
Zafar Iqbal and Mervyn K. Lewis

Financial Innovation in Retail and Corporate Banking

Edited by

Luisa Anderloni

Professor of Banking and Finance, Department of Economics, Business and Statistics, University of Milan; Researcher, Carefin, Bocconi University, Milan, Italy

David T. Llewellyn

Professor of Money and Banking, Department of Economics, Loughborough University, UK; Visiting Professor, CASS Business School, London, UK, Vienna University of Economics and Business Administration, Austria, and Swiss Finance Institute, Zurich, Switzerland

Reinhard H. Schmidt

Professor of International Banking and Finance, Department of Finance, Goethe University, Frankfurt am Main, Germany

NEW HORIZONS IN MONEY AND FINANCE

Edward Elgar

Cheltenham, UK • Northampton, MA, USA

Published by
Edward Elgar Publishing Limited
The Lypiatts
15 Lansdown Road
Cheltenham
Glos GL50 2JA
UK

Edward Elgar Publishing, Inc.
William Pratt House
9 Dewey Court
Northampton
Massachusetts 01060
USA

A catalogue record for this book
is available from the British Library

Library of Congress Control Number: 2008943834

PEFC
PEFC/16-33-111
CATG-PEFC-052
www.pefc.org

ISBN 978 1 84844 040 1

Printed and bound in Great Britain by MPG Books Ltd, Bodmin, Cornwall

Contents

Contributors

Luisa Anderloni Professor of Banking and Finance, Department of Economics, Business and Statistics, University of Milan, Milan; Researcher, Carefin, Bocconi University, Milan, Italy.

Francesca Arnaboldi Assistant Professor, Department of Economics, University of Milan, Milan, Italy.

Rym Ayadi Senior Research Fellow and Head of Financial Institutions and Prudential Policy Unit, Centre for European Policy Studies (CEPS), Brussels, Belgium.

Mascia Bedendo Assistant Professor, Department of Finance, Bocconi University, Milan, Italy.

Patrick Behr Assistant Professor, Department of Finance, Goethe University, Frankfurt am Main, Germany.

Paola Bongini Associate Professor, Department of Business and Economic Sciences, University of Milan – Bicocca, Milan, Italy.

David Bounie Assistant Professor, École Nationale Supérieure des Télécommunications, Département Sciences Économiques et Sociales, Paris, France.

Brunella Bruno Assistant Professor, Department of Finance, Bocconi University, Milan, Italy.

Santiago Carbó Valverde Professor of Economics, Department of Economic Theory and History, Facultad de Ciencias Economicas y Empresariales, Universidad de Granada, Granada, Spain.

Giuseppina Chesini Associate Professor, Department of Business Studies, University of Verona, Verona, Italy.

Peter Claeys Grup AQR IREA, Facultat de Ciències Econòmiques I Empresarials Universitat de Barcelona, Barcelona, Spain; Marie Curie Intra-European Fellow.

Pierre Gazé Assistant Professor, University of Orléans, Laboratoire d'Économie d'Orléans, Orléans, France.

David B. Humphrey Professor, Department of Finance, Florida State University, Tallahassee, Florida, USA.

Robert M. Hunt Senior Economist, Research Department, Federal Reserve Bank of Philadelphia, Philadelphia, USA.

David T. Llewellyn Professor of Money and Banking, Department of Economics, Loughborough University, Loughborough, UK; Visiting Professor, CASS Business School, London, UK, Vienna University of Economics and Business Administration, Austria, and Swiss Finance Institute, Zurich, Switzerland.

Caterina Lucarelli Associate Professor, Department of Economics, University Politecnica delle Marche, Ancona, Italy.

Camilla Mazzoli Assistant Professor, Department of Economics, University Politecnica delle Marche, Ancona, Italy.

Paolo Mottura Professor of Financial Markets and Institutions, Department of Finance, Bocconi University, Milan, Italy; Carefin, Bocconi University, Milan, Italy.

Merlin Rothfeld On Line Trading Academy, Irvine, California, USA.

Reinhard H. Schmidt Professor of International Banking and Finance, Department of Finance, Goethe University, Frankfurt am Main, Germany.

Samuli Simojoki Attorneys at Law Borenius & Kemppinen Ltd, Helsinki, Finland.

Tuomas Takalo Research Supervisor, Monetary Policy and Research Department, Bank of Finland, Helsinki, Finland; Professor of Economics, School of Business and Economics, University of Jyväskylä, Finland.

Monica Tamisari Senior Covered Bond Analyst, Cassa depositi e prestiti S.p.A., Rome, Italy.

Acknowledgements

The authors wish to thank anonymous referees.

The research project has been promoted by Carefin – Centre for Applied Research in Finance – Bocconi University.

Carefin acknowledges support from:

Università Commerciale Luigi Bocconi
CAREFIN
Centre for Applied Research in Finance

ALETTI GESTIELLE
ALLIANZ S.p.A.
ARCA ASSICURAZIONI
ARCA SGR
ASSICURAZIONI GENERALI
AVIVA VITA
AXA I. M. ITALIA SIM S.p.A.
AXA MPS ASSICURAZIONI VITA
BANCA CARIGE
BANCA MONTE DEI PASCHI DI SIENA
BANCA POPOLARE DI LODI
BANCA POPOLARE DI MILANO
BANCASSURANCE POPOLARI
BNL VITA
CATTOLICA ASSICURAZIONI SOC. COOP.
CNP UNICREDIT VITA
DELOITTE CONSULTING
EURIZON CAPITAL SGR
EURIZON VITA
FONCHIM
GENERALI INVESTMENTS ITALY
INTESA SANPAOLO
INTESA VITA
MEDIOLANUM VITA
PIONEER INVESTMENTS MANAGEMENT
SWISS RE
UBI ASSICURAZIONI
UNIPOL GRUPPO FINANZIARIO
UNIQA PREVIDENZA – UNIQA PROTEZIONE
VENETO BANCA

Preface

Paolo Mottura

Financial innovation has by now become a permanent and irreversible phenomenon, which therefore deserves to be continuously studied in order to understand its origins and drivers, to analyse its various forms, to evaluate its positive and negative externalities at the macroeconomic level and finally to investigate the organic relationship with the competitive strategies of financial intermediaries.

The current and prospective context of financial globalisation – which involves both capital markets and financial intermediaries – is characterised by particularly intense competition, onto which financial regulatory authorities try to impose certain rules, without, however, imposing limits. Obviously the challenge lies in trying to achieve the dual objective of, on the one hand maximising positive externalities, in other words the benefits of innovation for the real economy itself, and on the other, limiting as far as possible the negative externalities that innovation inflicts on real economies and on the return/risk performance for stakeholders (financial intermediaries, firms, investors, public administrations and so forth).

As far as the strategy of financial intermediaries is concerned, innovation has now become an instrument or, as some would say, a crucial competitive weapon.

Process innovation, strongly supported and stimulated by new technologies, plays an essential role as a factor of differentiation between the single producer and his/her competitors. Process innovation is focused on obtaining results and levels of productivity and slashing the costs of production and distribution (cost leadership), as well as improving the quality and reliability of the procedures themselves for the benefit of the client, risk control and internal checks. This type of innovation contributes greatly in improving the reputation of those who are able to manage it. It is important to note that process technology is important for two different reasons: on the one hand, technology that produces cost savings through the substitution of technological investments *vis-à-vis* labour, increasing its productivity and favouring more-skilled jobs, and on the other, 'enabling' technology which allows for the creation and valorisation of activities, products, services and solutions which were unattainable with previous levels of technological know-how.

Product innovation also has an important competitive role, as it allows financial intermediaries to differentiate their offer from that of their competitors, improving their ability to provide solutions for the needs of their clients (customer satisfaction) as well as allowing for greater freedom of pricing, with the obvious benefits this entails for profit margins. It is important to note that the innovation of financial products and services triggers different effects that make its interpretation complicated. In principle, innovation – as an invention of effective and efficient 'financial solutions' for the continuously evolving needs of clients – is a symptom and a factor of progress, contributing in the medium to long term to making financial markets more efficient.

This should be interpreted as a factor of improvement for financial markets. Without doubt, this interpretation of the phenomenon cannot be denied. On the other hand, innovation produced by the financial intermediary could be seen – especially within the competitive dynamics in the short term – as a temporary factor of inefficiency or market imperfection that can be exploited by the same actors of innovation, such as banks. We are referring here to the well-known theory of financial intermediation according to which constant improvement of capital markets in the long term leads to the gradual limitation of the economic rationale of financial intermediaries, thereby reducing their operative *raison d'être*.

Looking closer, innovation – in the short term, but also continuously, as it is an ongoing process – creates new opportunities for intermediaries, which is demonstrated by the constant expansion of capital market and investment banking activities compared to the phenomenon of credit disintermediation. This is the essential characteristic of the 'evolution' of the bank as an institutional subject. Innovation creates both positive and negative externalities. The offer of a new product or service produces *in primis* a situation of opaqueness and greater information asymmetry to the detriment of potential buyers. Faced with innovation and change, the potential buyers suffer from seeing their knowledge becoming obsolete (experience plus professionalism) and see themselves forced into making the costly effort of learning which may not be immediately productive for the necessary skills of analysis, evaluation, selection and decision concerning the purchase. If we add that, in most cases involving the offer of new products and services, the producer is also a 'consultant' for the purchase, the emerging conflict of interest is clear. In other words, product innovation inevitably incorporates risks of pre- and post-contractual opportunism by the producer towards the buyer, in such a way as to be directly correlated with the informative disadvantage of the latter. Put more simply: financial innovation, although being beneficial in the long term, increases the probability of uninformed and suboptimal decisions.

It is important to add that, in order to achieve a realistic interpretation of the phenomenon of financial innovation, it needs to be remembered that it is something often associated with technological progress, even if such a notion should be considered in the widest possible terms. For example, even the 'legal techniques' used for drawing up contracts which involve complex financial relations are part of financial innovation. Project finance, private equity, and the securitisation of new financial products (derivative and structured) would be good examples of this.

Process and product innovation induces a metamorphosis or mutation effect not only of the business models of the financial intermediaries but also of their institutional models. This type of change, due to innovation, appears particularly insidious as it tends to modify the structure, organisation, economic–financial balance, risk and the solvency of the financial intermediary without its external configuration appearing to be substantially modified. Most people still have an idea or image of a bank that is far removed from reality. Perceptions and knowledge are constantly behind the times in terms of getting to know what banks are all about today. In brief: current knowledge (in particular that of retail banking customers) involves an idea of the bank which no longer corresponds to what it has now become.

Traditional or credit intermediation (collection of deposits in order to provide credit) is increasingly being overtaken by the activities of investment banking, in which the bank is not a direct producer and provider of financial resources, but represents an 'access point' for capital markets. The mutation of the banker from borrower/lender to financial adviser, private banker and corporate banker radically changes the required responses to the client's expectations, whose experience and knowledge of the bank's new 'way of working' has not yet been consolidated. If the expectations of the client are unrealistic, particularly in terms of the amount of risk involved, this may create a situation where the offer of the bank can generate false expectations and consequently disappointment. Proof of this is the often negative experience of selling investment products whose performance is related not to the solvency of the bank, but to capital markets and other third parties.

In general, the securitisation of illiquid assets is most typical. The bank transfers the function of asset holding to an external 'intermediation chain', namely specialised vehicles that create supposedly liquid liabilities (sometimes drastically altering the implied maturity gap). The latter are then underwritten by institutional investors who transform these financial structures and transfer them to final investors. This is one of the many ways of unbundling, and substantial change, of credit intermediation. The bank, traditionally an asset holder, becomes specialised in screening, origination and monitoring assets which are potentially weakened in their selective rigour by the fact that the credit risk gets transferred to third parties. It is obvious that 'agency problems' take shape in intermediation chains created by securitisation and unbundling. This is another typical example of the potential negative externalities deriving from financial innovation.

We need to remember, however, that financial innovation can and should be a non-zero-sum game. This is a complex phenomenon for which it is necessary to devote a dual level of attention. On the one hand, attention needs to be paid to research and knowledge. Innovation should be studied continually in order to improve its comprehension for the benefit of those who produce it, use it and eventually who regulate it, in the common interest of creating and allocating value properly. On the other hand, attention needs to be paid to watchdogs, which have the difficult task of planning and keeping a 'mechanism design' which maximises incentives for virtuous conduct and establishes the rules of the game in order to prevent opportunistic behaviour and protect those for whom innovation could be a factor of information asymmetry.

This Preface concludes with Carefin's grateful acknowledgement towards the editors of this project, to Luisa Anderloni (who deserves a special mention for her effective coordination activities), to David Llewellyn and to Reinhard Schmidt, and also to all those scholars who generously contributed to this volume.

Milan, December 2007

1. Financial innovation and the economics of banking and the financial system

David T. Llewellyn

Derivatives are financial weapons of mass destruction, carrying dangers that, while now latent, are potentially lethal to the financial system. (Warren Buffett, *Financial Times*, 4 March 2003, p. 16)

If risk is properly dispersed, shocks to the overall economic system will be better absorbed and less likely to . . . threaten financial stability. (Greenspan, 2002, p. 6)

Not everything that counts can be counted, and not everything that can be counted counts. (Albert Einstein, 1936, sign in Einstein's office, Princeton University)

1 THE CONTEXT

In many respects, financial innovation has become a defining characteristic of national financial systems. Two particular characteristics of the recent evolution of financial systems have been increased globalisation of financial markets, and the rapid growth of financial innovation, and in particular the development of structured instruments and credit derivatives. One of the features of the globalisation of financial markets is that financial innovation generated in one market can be easily and quickly transferred to others.

Notwithstanding recent interest in the topic, financial innovation is not a new phenomenon. What is new is the acceleration since the mid-1990s in the pace and range of financial innovation, and the emergence of several secondary markets in which new instruments are traded, and the emergence of credit derivatives that enable credit risk to be shifted and traded (see Partnoy and Skeel, 2007, for a survey). In most developed financial systems there has been a substantial growth in the range and issue volume of financial instruments and, in particular, derivatives instruments and contracts together with a much higher volume of secondary market transactions.

The purpose of this overview chapter is to consider how financial innovation is changing the underlying economics of banking and the financial system, and the emergence of new banking models. In particular, we consider the economics of financial innovation in general and its implications particularly with respect to four key issues:

1. how financial innovation might contribute to enhancing the efficiency of the financial system,
2. its implications for risk management,
3. how financial innovation is changing the underlying economics of banking, and
4. the implications for financial stability.

This review chapter considers the theory of financial innovation within a general analytical framework. The central theme is that financial innovation is not an arbitrary or random process but can be analysed systematically in terms of the factors that create supply and demand conditions for new facilities and markets. However, we argue that, in the process, financial innovation changes the underlying economics of banking and the financial system, and has the potential to enhance the efficiency of the financial system in the performance of its core functions. It is through the latter route that financial innovation potentially has real economic significance and value added. A central issue to consider is the contribution that financial innovation might have to two key issues in the financial system: its *efficiency* and its *stability*. As indicated in the quotations at the beginning of the chapter, opinion is divided on these issues. Later sections discuss various ways in which financial innovation has the potential to enhance the efficiency of the financial system in the performance of its core functions, and also implications for systemic stability.

The main focus in this chapter is on credit risk instruments and the increasing ability to shift and trade credit risk. Credit derivatives in particular enable credit risk to be shifted, traded, insured and taken by institutions without the need to make loans directly to borrowers. This in turn changes in an important way the underlying economics of banking. The traditional model of banking is challenged by the emergence of credit derivatives and other techniques for managing and shifting credit risk.

The structure of the chapter is as follows. The next section considers the nature and theory of financial innovation: the different types of financial innovation, a *functional* approach to innovation, and the main drivers of financial innovation. Section 3 focuses upon innovations that enable credit risk to be shifted with a detailed consideration of new instruments and techniques such as securitisation, and credit derivatives including collateralised debt obligations and credit default swaps. Section 4 reviews some of the implications of financial innovation: how financial innovation contributes to the efficiency of the financial system in the performance of its core functions, how innovation affects the underlying economics of banking; and how the emergence of new instruments for shifting credit risk might impact on the stability of the financial system. Section 5 reviews some of the problems and hazards associated with new instruments. An overall assessment concludes the chapter.

This overview chapter represents an introduction to the whole volume and opens the way to the chapters that follow.

The theoretical and empirical literature on financial innovation is further deepened by Anderloni and Bongini (Chapter 2), who investigate whether financial innovation still represents a relevant issue in the communication strategy of European banks. In particular, the authors analyse banks' attitudes towards innovation according to the level of information conveyed to market participants via annual reports; in addition the study evaluates whether different levels of communications are linked to financial performance and asset growth.

Schmidt (Chapter 3) focuses on the most recent wave of innovations: microfinance. Indeed, microfinance as we know it today represents the outcome of a combination of product and process innovations. Its most visible part is a product innovation: finance for the poor, in particular for poor self-employed people. However, what has made it possible is that small loans are now offered to millions of people and microfinance has even started to attract the interest of private and institutional investors, leading to a rapid succession of process innovations.

Finally, the eight chapters that follow discuss in analytical detail various examples of financial innovation and their implications with respect to five key issues:

1. How financial innovation might contribute to enhancing the efficiency of the financial system: Lucarelli, Mazzoli and Rothfeld (Chapter 11) on innovation in trading activity and Arnaboldi and Claeys (Chapter 5) on financial innovation in online banking.
2. The implications of financial innovation for risk management: in particular, Bedendo and Bruno (Chapter 9) on credit derivatives versus loan sales in Europe.

3. How financial innovation is changing the underlying economics of banking with respect to ATMs and implicit pricing of network convenience: Carbó-Valverde and Humphrey (Chapter 4); and the challenges posed by internet payments to retail payments: Bounie and Gazé (Chapter 6).
4. The implications of financial innovation for financial stability: Hunt, Simojoki and Takalo (Chapter 7) on property rights and standard setting in the financial services industry.
5. The implications for regulation: Ayadi and Behr (Chapter 10) on the required regulatory support for credit derivatives markets; and Chesini and Tamisari (Chapter 8) on the regulatory and market developments with respect to covered bonds in Europe.

2 NATURE AND THEORY OF FINANCIAL INNOVATION

Financial innovation is a reflection, and partly a cause, of structural change evident in many financial systems since the early 1990s. In this period there has been a general trend towards securitisation (financial intermediation with a counterpart in tradable financial assets), the use of derivative instruments and contracts, the emergence of credit derivative instruments in particular, and a growing importance of off-balance-sheet business of banks. In line with this there has been a proliferation of new markets.

As will be demonstrated in later chapters of this volume, financial innovation can be categorised using a variety of different criteria. In this introduction, three particular ways of categorising financial innovation are identified: by *type*, by *function* and by *motive*.

Types of Innovation

With respect to the type of innovation, three dimensions are identified:

1. *Product innovation*: The creation of new financial instruments, contracts, techniques and markets.
2. *Risk-shifting innovation*: The unbundling of the separate characteristics and risks of individual instruments (such as credit risk and interest rate risk) and their reassembly in different combinations (Llewellyn, 1992; Pilbeam, 2005).
3. *Process innovation*: Process improvements typified by new means of, for instance, distributing securities, processing transactions, or pricing transactions.

A central feature of financial innovation is the unbundling of characteristics of different instruments and either keeping them separate or combining them in different ways (Llewellyn, 1992). This enables investors or borrowers to maintain those characteristics of an asset that they particularly want but give up those features that are not desired. This illustrates three central features of financial innovation: (i) it increases the range, number and variety of financial instruments; (ii) it combines characteristics in a more varied way and widens the combination of characteristics, thereby reducing the number and size of discontinuities in the spectrum of financial instruments; and (iii) it has the effect of eroding some of the differences between different forms of intermediation. In effect, financial innovation is about linking the different characteristics of financial instruments in various combinations. As part of this process, financial innovation often enables different risks within an instrument to be unbundled so that each can be priced separately and redistributed to, and held by, those who are most able and willing to absorb them. In this context, Llewellyn (ibid.) makes a distinction between 'instrument' and 'post-contract' innovation. In the former case, a new instrument is created with a particular set of characteristics. In the second case the same effect is achieved by various techniques that enable the characteristics of assets or liabilities to be changed after the event. An obvious example of this (discussed in detail in a later section) is a credit default swap, whereby a lender is able to hold an asset while shifting the credit risk on to a counterparty. In this way, many derivative instruments and other financial innovations enable different institutions to exploit their comparative advantages in different markets and to sell that advantage to others.

A Functional Approach to Financial Innovation

Financial innovation, and alternative financial instruments, can be categorised in various ways by adopting different criteria. In this chapter, we choose to apply a *functional* approach with a focus on the functions of the financial system. Adopting such a functional approach, financial innovation and instruments may be classified according to their contribution to the basic roles of the financial system:

1. Risk transference:
   (a) price risk (for example, swaps, options, forward and futures instruments);
   (b) credit risk (for example, securitisation, credit default swaps (CDSs), collateralised debt obligations (CDOs)).
2. The pricing of risk (for example, CDSs).

3. Liquidity enhancement (for example, securitisation has the effect of making bank loans more liquid).
4. Credit-generation enhancement (for example, CDSs, CDOs).
5. Equity generation (for example, debt–equity swaps).
6. Insurance (for example, CDSs).
7. Asset and liability management (for example, securitisation, CDSs, CDOs).
8. Funding of financial institutions (for example, securitisation).

This taxonomy extends that provided in BIS (1986) which emphasised 1, 3, 4 and 5 above and gave a useful set of examples of each at the time of the study.

- *Risk-transferring* innovations either reduce the risk inherent in a particular instrument, or alternatively enable the holder to protect against a particular risk. For instance, while an investor may be holding an asset or claim whose future value may be uncertain, a parallel CDS contract (while it does not reduce the probability of the risk) offers protection in the event that the risk materialises. Within this category a distinction is made between price risk (the price of an asset may change) and credit risk (the borrower may default).
- *Risk-pricing* instruments are designed to enhance the efficiency of risk pricing by, for instance, widening possible arbitrage channels and opportunities. A particular example is where a credit risk is embodied within, for instance, a CDO which can be traded in the secondary market. The market prices of such instruments effectively reflect the markets' view of risk. Similarly, the secondary market prices of asset-backed securities (ABSs) reflect perceptions of credit risk which would not be available had the underlying assets remained on the balance sheet of the originating bank. One aspect of financial innovation is to enable the various embodied risks in an instrument to be stripped out and priced, held and traded separately from the other risks within the same instrument.
- *Liquidity-enhancing* innovations have the effect of increasing the liquidity of instruments and assets. For instance, securitised assets enable loans to be sold in a secondary market which offers the lending institution the capacity to change the structure of its portfolio.
- *Credit-generating* innovations widen the access to particular credit markets and hence have the capacity to increase the total volume of credit. Such instruments have the effect of facilitating greater access to credit markets for borrowers. If, for instance, a bank securitises some of its loans, or becomes a buyer of credit protection, to the

extent that the risk is passed to others, its own lending capacity is increased either because it releases capital or because the transaction lowers the bank's exposure to a particular borrower or asset class.

- *Equity-generating* instruments have the effect of giving an equity characteristic (that is, where the rate of return is determined by the performance of the issuer) to assets where the nature of the debt-servicing commitment is predetermined. An example is the debt–equity swap whereby, under some circumstances, a borrower is able to transform a floating interest rate loan from a bank (a debt contract) into an equity-type liability. Convertible debentures are another example.
- *Insurance innovations*: some instruments enable risks to be insured in return for the payment of a premium. With respect to credit risk, an obvious example is a CDS where the protection buyer pays to the seller a stream of premium payments in return for which the protection seller undertakes to compensate the buyer in the event that a specified event occurs (see later section).
- *Asset and liability management*: in one way or another, virtually all instruments widen the scope for banks to manage their assets and liabilities by offering scope to manage risks, to widen lending opportunities, or to change the composition or risk structure of a bank's balance sheet.
- *Funding of financial institutions*: some instruments have the effect of widening the sources of bank funding. Securitisation, for instance, enables a bank to diversify its funding to a wider range of investors and to those who might be willing to invest in a particular class of bank assets (for example, mortgages) but not in the bank itself.

Drivers of Financial Innovation

There are several reasons why the pace of financial innovation in general, and the emergence of credit-risk-shifting instruments in particular, have accelerated in recent years. The BIS (2003) suggests a combination of: a greater focus in banks and other financial institutions on risk management; an increasing tendency to focus their credit-risk exposures on a portfolio basis; more rigorous approaches to risk–return judgements; the desire to increase fee and other off-balance-sheet income; the low interest rate environment which induced banks and investors to seek higher returns in different ways; and increased arbitrage opportunities associated with regulatory capital requirements.

The paradigm outlined in the last section is a *functional* approach to financial innovation where the focus is upon the different functions that various financial instruments perform in the system. Using a different categorisation (based on motives), Llewellyn (1992) identifies four categories of financial innovation: (i) *defensive* (in response to policy and regulatory changes); (ii) *aggressive* (financial institutions create instruments or new products they believe can be successfully marketed); (iii) *responsive* (when an instrument or service is developed in order to meet a change in portfolio requirements of customers); and (iv) *protective* (when institutions adopt techniques because of their own portfolio constraints). Financial innovation is not a random or arbitrary process but can be analysed in terms of portfolio preferences of the suppliers and demanders of financial products. Within this framework the impetus to financial innovation can be considered in terms of its broad determinants, and in particular wealth effects, portfolio behaviour and preferences of users, portfolio behaviour and preferences of the suppliers of financial services, portfolio constraints, changes in the market and economic environment, regulation, policy changes, technology, and competition (ibid.). This analysis is analogous to the approach of Silber (1983, p. 170) who argues that financial innovation responds to economic forces. His particular perspective is that: 'New financial instruments or practices are innovated to lessen the financial constraints imposed on firms'. In the same approach he argues: 'the stimulus to innovation can be interpreted as an increase in the cost of adhering to existing constraints'.

The role of technology in stimulating financial innovation has been particularly emphasised by Schmookler (1967), Bloomestein (2000) and White (2000). The development of technology in finance has had a powerful impact on financial innovation not least because it enables traders in new instruments (options being a good example) to immediately calculate arbitrage opportunities in complex situations. Technology also contributes to the design and pricing of new instruments, and facilitates the identification, measurement and monitoring of risks in portfolios containing complex instruments. It reduces trading costs in international markets, and has the effect of widening the market for new instruments to an international dimension. Several studies have noted that, through technological advancement, improvements in the ability to acquire and transfer information have made it easier to trade in assets that might otherwise be subject to asymmetric information problems and the potential 'lemons' problem (see, for instance, Gorton and Haubrich, 1990; Gorton and Pennacchi, 1995; and Greenbaum and Thakor, 1995).

Spectrum filling

The various drivers outlined above are specific and identifiable. A further factor is more general and emerges as a product of a competitive financial system. What might be termed 'spectrum filling' reflects the tendency for active financial institutions and markets to innovate by offering facilities to fill gaps or remove discontinuities in the full spectrum of financial intermediation facilities and financial instruments. It involves combining characteristics (such as yield, marketability, maturity) of different financial instruments so that the advantages of one instrument alleviate the disadvantages of another. In the process, the financial system inches towards the Arrow–Debreu world where financial instruments exist that combine (either explicitly or through a combination of derivatives) every possible combination of characteristics, and where any risk or combination of risks can be hedged or acquired according to taste.

3 SHIFTING CREDIT RISK

Instruments for the shifting and management of price risks have been widely used for decades (in some cases – such as forward instruments – even centuries) and have become a standard feature of banks' risk management. Instruments such as swaps, options, forward rate agreements, forward and futures instruments are used extensively to manage price, interest rate and foreign exchange risks. On the other hand, instruments for the shifting of credit risk are a recent development and raise different issues both of analysis and practicality.

There is a clear difference between a bank protecting against price rather than credit risk as the former is systemic in that the risk associated with a price movement is not influenced by the behaviour of the protection buyer: the probability is exogenous to the bank. Issues of asymmetric information, adverse selection and moral hazard therefore do not arise. The probability of these risks emerging is determined independently of the behaviour of the protection buyer. For instance, the probability of a currency depreciation or a rise in interest rates is not in any way determined by the fact that a bank might protect itself against these risks by, for instance, conducting forward transactions or buying option contracts.

Credit risk and its protection, on the other hand, raise different issues. The relationship between a credit-risk protection buyer and seller is fundamentally different from that between two counterparties in a swap or forward transaction. One of the features of credit risk is an asymmetric information dimension in that the lender has more information about the quality of loans than does a protection seller or a purchaser of the bank's ABSs. The traditional theory of banking is that this asymmetric information (and the potential for adverse selection and moral hazard) acts as a bar to credit insurance or the shifting of credit risk. As with standard insurance theory, there is a potential for banks to deliberately select high-risk loans to be insured (adverse selection) and to deliberately make high-risk loans or to fail to monitor borrowers (moral hazard) because the risk is passed to others through, for instance, a credit derivatives contract or securitisation. The implication is that, if an external agent (such as an insurance company) were to offer credit insurance to a bank, the premium charged would be excessive because of the greater element of uncertainty with respect to the probability of the insured risk occurring. This in turn means, according to traditional theory, that it is cheaper for a bank to develop insurance internally (by incorporating a risk premium in the loan interest rate for all borrowers) than to seek external insurance. As the latter premia would in turn be passed on to borrowers, the effective cost to the borrower of internal insurance would be less than that of external insurance. Overall, therefore, and unlike with price risk, the taking of external insurance may create incentives for behaviour that increases the probability of the risk occurring. This distinguishes in an important way price and credit risks and their protection.

However, the emergence of securitisation and, more recently, credit derivatives challenges this traditional paradigm. Notwithstanding the problems outlined above, it is now possible for a bank to shift credit risk either through asset sales of one sort or another or through an insurance contract such as a CDS. These recent innovations mean that credit risks can be shifted, traded and insured. Furthermore, they can also be used by a bank or other financial institution to acquire a credit risk without making a loan by, for instance, being a credit-risk protection seller. Thus, while Bank A may wish to shift a credit risk (perhaps because of an existing excessive exposure), Bank B might be willing to acquire such a credit risk (by, for instance, being a credit-protection seller in a CDS) because it might not have a relevant customer base or ability to make the relevant loans. This means that banks are able to develop credit-risk exposures of their choice without making loans. As with all derivative instruments, credit derivatives can be used either to shift an existing credit risk or to acquire one.

Several routes have emerged through which credit risks can be transferred from original holders (lenders). These can be categorised as follows:

1. guarantees;
2. credit insurance;
3. loan trading;
4. syndication of loans;
5. traditional securitisation: ABSs (homogeneous loans);
6. credit derivatives:
   (i) collateralised debt obligations
      - conventional (cash funded)
      - synthetic (unfunded)

(ii) credit default swaps
- single name
- portfolio.

As the focus of this chapter is on credit risks, the following sections outline the basic elements of these instruments and mechanisms.

Guarantees

A guarantee given by a third party is a bilateral contract where the guarantor (the risk taker) has an obligation to perform for the benefit of the risk shifter in the event of a loss incurred on, for instance, a loan.

Credit Insurance

Credit insurance is typically provided by specialist insurance companies to support, for instance, trade credit and is often used by the beneficiaries to obtain bank credit for its receivables.

Loan Trading

In secondary loan markets, single loans are sold by a lender (bank) to a counterparty wishing to acquire the specific credit risk being offered by the seller. Loans are often assigned in the form of participation where the original lender remains the only direct lender to the borrower though it contracts with other institutions to lay off part of the exposure.

Syndication of Loans

The oldest technique for banks to limit the size of credit exposures is to syndicate their loans. In order to maintain a good relationship with a customer, a bank might agree to a loan that is larger than it would be prudent for it to accept alone. In which case, the originating bank forms a syndicate of several banks which, between them, make the funds available on a joint basis when the total would be greater than any one of the banks could prudently accept. Such syndications have a management structure and various fees are paid to the lead bank.

Traditional Securitisation

The basic securitisation (ABS) model has been well established in banking markets for several decades (see Llewellyn, 1992 for a description of the mechanics). Securitisation has been a widely used technique by banks in the UK, especially in the mortgage market. The proportion of mortgage balances in the UK subject to securitisation rose from 10 per cent in 2003 to around 22 per cent (FSA, 2008). As a result, mortgage lending by banks has expanded at a faster rate than the supply of retail deposits.

In essence, the securitisation model involves a bank collecting together a large number of homogeneous loans (such as mortgages, credit card receivables, consumer loans and so on) that are on its balance sheet and selling the whole portfolio to a special purpose vehicle (SPV) which may be a subsidiary of the bank or some other organisation. It has become a major technique of bank management in three main respects: (i) an alternative funding mechanism, (ii) a technique for asset and liability management, and (iii) a route to manage credit risks and banks' capital. In essence, it is an 'originate and distribute' model whereby a bank originates loans but does not hold them (or the credit risk) on its own balance sheet. In 2006, securitised loans outstanding in the US amounted to $28 trillion compared with less than $5 trillion in 1990. Around 60 per cent of mortgage loans and 25 per cent of consumer debt in the US is securitised.

An SPV issues ABSs in the market, the proceeds of which are used to buy the selected portfolio of assets from the bank. The bank pays the interest from the assets to the SPV which in turn uses the proceeds to service the securities. There is usually some form of credit enhancement to the securities either from a third party or through 'oversecuritisation' whereby the initial value of the assets transferred is greater than the initial value of the securities issued. The securities are rated by a rating agency which is a crucial part of the securitisation model. In the process, securitisation protects the seller (the bank) from the risk of the assets and protects the investors in the securities from the risks of the bank. The assets are isolated from the bank so that the rate of return on the securities depends on the performance of the portfolio of assets rather than the bank itself.

The ABSs are attractive to several types of investors: those who wish to invest in the specific credit risks being securitised; those who prefer a subset of the assets of the bank rather than an investment in the bank itself; those who prefer this type of security; and investors for whom the type of asset being securitised fits their own asset and liability management requirements.

In the standard securitisation, there are four key characteristics of the assets: internally diversified within the same asset class, homogeneous (that is, within the same asset class), they have a statistical history of losses that can be calculated, and have similar terms (for example, fixed or floating interest rate loans). Four main motives for banks to securitise loans have been identified in Llewellyn (1992): (i) *asset transformation motive*: enabling the bank to increase the liquidity of loan assets, or to change the structure of assets on the balance sheet; (ii) *balance-sheet constraint motive*: to enable a bank to ease a capital constraint in that, while securitisation does not in itself generate equity capital for the bank, it raises the capital ratio to the extent that assets are removed from the balance sheet; (iii) *funding motive*: to the extent that investors prefer to invest in securities backed by a subset of the assets of the bank rather than to invest in the bank itself, it widens the source of funding for bank loans; and (iv) *fee income motive*: as the SPV usually pays fees to the selling bank, there is an additional source of income independent of assets. This in turn can raise the bank's rate of return on equity independent of loans maintained on the balance sheet.

A key motive for securitisation is to shift credit risk from the bank to an SPV and hence to the investors in the securities issued by the SPV. For this to work in full, the SPV needs to be 'bankruptcy-remote' from the bank itself. However, the experience of the financial turmoil in the second half of 2007 is that, while formally a securitisation vehicle might be bankruptcy-remote from the bank, the bank might nevertheless choose to protect its reputation by supporting the vehicle by, for instance, extending loans in the event of a funding problem or by buying back the securitised assets. This could be a chosen option in cases where a bank plans to securitise more assets in the future as part of an ongoing securitisation strategy.

Credit Derivatives

Credit derivatives are financial instruments whose pay-offs are linked to a change in credit quality (such as a default) of an issuer or issuers. Credit derivatives are flexible instruments that enable users to isolate and trade credit risk, and can be used to transfer credit risk of loans and other assets. They can be used either to shift risk away from the holder or to acquire credit risk without holding the relevant asset such as a loan or bond issued by a borrower. The underlying asset can be either a single asset or a pool of assets either by the same issuer or by a mix of different borrowers.

Credit derivatives (and unlike derivatives such as swaps, forward, options and so on) are a comparatively recent feature of financial innovation and have developed significantly only since 2003. The first credit derivative transactions took place between a small number of banks in the early 1990s. Since then the market has developed substantially in terms of the range of instruments available, the volume of transactions, the number of banks participating in the market, and the number and range of counterparties. The main credit derivatives are single CDSs, credit-linked notes, and CDOs. Although there is now a wide range of credit derivative instruments, the BIS (2005) notes that they can be distinguished in terns of two dimensions: single name versus portfolios, and funded versus unfunded.

Collateralised debt obligations

CDOs are a more complex development of the basic securitisation model except that the portfolio is a mix of different assets such as loans and/or bonds. CDOs are securities issued by an SPV which are backed by a mixed portfolio of ABSs which are bought either in the market or from a bank (Figure 1.1). The SPV can be created by an initiating bank, by another bank, or by any other type of institution. The CDO is a structured fixed-income security with cash flows linked to the performance of various types of debt instruments. A collateralised loan obligation is a CDO backed by bank loans, whereas a CDO backed by bonds is termed a collateralised bond obligation. Even when the underlying assets are all bank loans, and unlike the conventional securitisation model described above, they need not be homogeneous in that different types of securitised loans (for example, commercial mortgages or consumer loans) can be included in the same CDO package. They are, in effect, an aggregation of securitised assets.

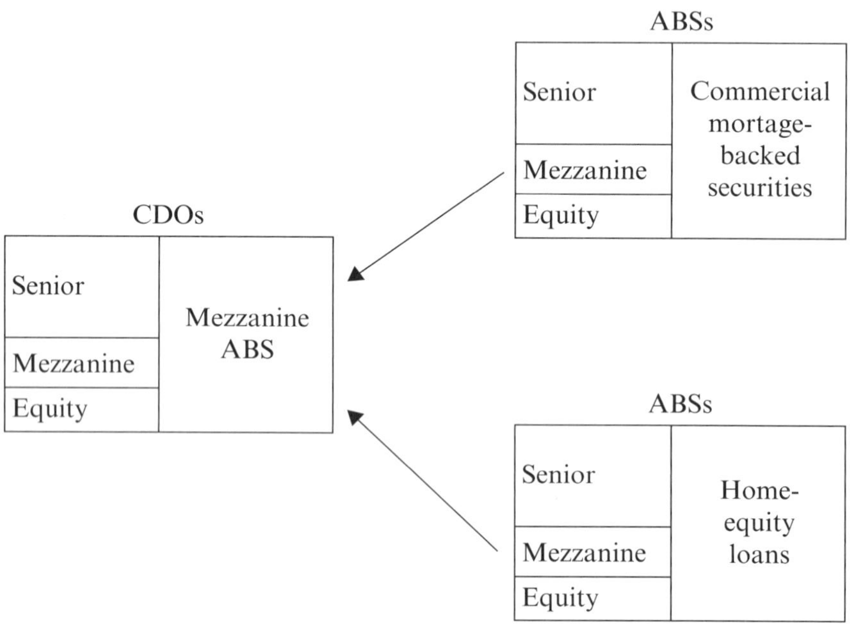

Source: Bank of England (2006).

Figure 1.1 A CDO structure

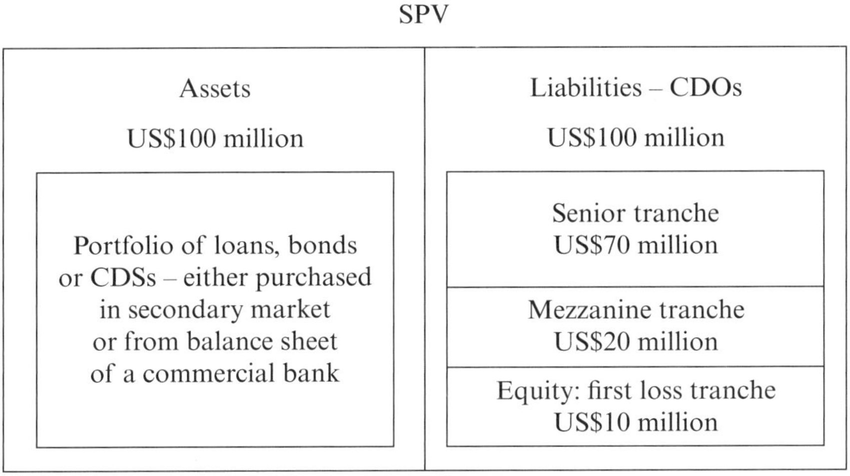

Source: Rule (2001).

Figure 1.2 Collateralised debt obligation

A yet more complex form is the CDO-squared which are CDOs of CDOs and which add yet another layer of potential leverage for investors.

A CDO is issued in tranches of varying risk and seniority (colloquially known as 'slice-and-dice') which is backed by a portfolio of credit instruments such as loans or bonds issued by governments, companies or banks. CDO securities take risk tranches from several existing ABSs and repackage the risks into new securities of different seniority and risk characteristics. In the funded version of CDOs, investors pay the SPV the principal amount of their tranches and any defaults on the underlying assets cause a write-down of principal and hence create a loss for the investor. The first losses are taken by investors in the equity tranche.

A key feature of CDOs is the ability to convert high credit-risk securities into new securities that contain very low credit-risk components. The assets and liabilities of a typical CDO are given in Figure 1.2. In other words, a CDO is a pool of debt contracts housed within an SPV whose capital structure is sliced and re-sold based on differences in credit quality. In the conventional CDO, the SPV purchases a portfolio of outstanding debt issued by a range of issuers (companies, banks and so on), and finances its purchase by issuing its own financial securities including debt and equity.

The basic structure of a CDO is given in Figure 1.2, which shows the assets and liabilities of the SPV issuing CDOs. The three tranches of liabilities shown (*Senior*, *Mezzanine* and *Equity*) are in rising order of risk and, therefore, declining order of seniority in the event of credit default by the

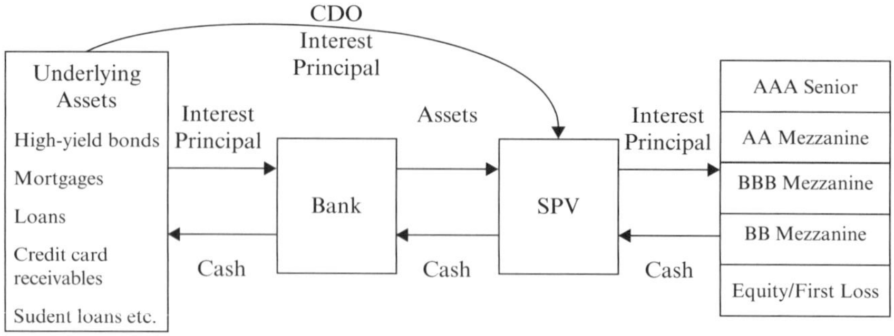

Source: Benfield Group (2002).

Figure 1.3 Collateralised debt obligations: flows

issuers of the underlying assets. Thus, in the event of a 'credit event' the first few percent of losses are allocated to the equity (first loss) tranche and then to the mezzanine tranche. It is only in the event that the losses exceed the combined percentage of these two tranches that losses are allocated to the senior tranche.

The pattern of flows in a conventional CDO is shown schematically in Figure 1.3. The SPV issues securities (CDOs) the proceeds of which are used to purchase a range of diverse assets from a bank (or from the market). The CDO is structured (risks are sliced) according to the risks of the assets purchased, and each segment of the CDO is sold to different types of investors. Interest and principal are received by the bank from the underlying assets which in turn are paid to the SPV in order to pay to the various investors according to the particular slices of risk in which they have chosen to invest.

The ongoing pricing of CDOs is complex not the least because, in practice, they are often not traded in secondary markets and hence there is no continuous pricing of the securities. In practice, they tend to be valued by the holders on the basis of complex mathematical models whose accuracy can often be questioned. This also adds to the lack of transparency in that there is no continuous market revaluation of the securities.

The return to an investor in the securities issued by an SPV depends upon the tranche held. The equity tranche pays a higher yield than the others in order to compensate for the higher expected risk. The holders receive an upfront fee and a fixed annual spread. Different tranches appeal to different types of investor dependent upon their risk appetites. The equity tranche is often bought by hedge funds. Private asset managers are also significant investors in the equity tranches of CDOs. Other investors include monoline insurers.

In many cases, however, the equity tranche is held by the originating bank or the CDO manager (which might be a hedge fund). This is designed, in part, to solve the adverse selection potential due to asymmetric information, and the moral hazard that because credit risk has been shifted an incentive might be created to cease monitoring the borrowers. In this way, investors will find the CDO a more attractive proposition given that the first line of risk is retained by the issuer. In fact, the equity tranche bears a substantial share of the CDO's risk but only a small share of the notional amount of exposure. In other words, when a bank transfers credits from its own balance sheet into a CDO but retains all or part of the equity tranche, it transfers virtually all of the notional exposure (the total amount less the bank's retention) but a low proportion of the risk.

One of the advantages of CDOs is that they contain different levels of risk and enable different degrees of risk to be taken by those who are willing and able to absorb them. In this sense they have a systemic benefit of spreading risk. Furthermore, they are also diversified instruments in that they contain a wide portfolio of underlying credits and ABSs. Thus, holders of CDO securities (and unlike the case of investment in standard ABSs) are less subject to idiosyncratic risks of particular ABSs and their issuers. A CDO is often given an AAA rating because, while one tranche (the equity tranche) is judged to be risky, it is mixed with low-risk assets. However, in some cases risks of different components may prove to be correlated especially because a downturn in the economy might adversely affect the value of all assets in a CDO portfolio.

There are three general motives for investors in CDOs: (i) to diversify their exposure to various credit risks, (ii) to capture higher yield, and (iii) to acquire a specific credit exposure that they cannot obtain directly by their own lending.

Synthetic CDO There are two basic types of CDO: *conventional* (cash funded) and *synthetic* (where instead of assets being the basis of the security, the basis is a portfolio of CDS premiums). Synthetic CDOs are based on CDSs as an alternative to underlying assets. CDSs are used to transfer credit risk to the SPV as the SPV becomes the proximate protection seller in a CDS contract. The SPV issues and sells CDOs to the end-sellers of protection and uses the proceeds of the sales to invest in high-quality collateralised securities (Figure 1.4). In this way the bank (protection buyer) has a potential claim on the SPV through the CDS which in turn is backed in the SPV by the securities it has invested in. As with the conventional model above, the CDOs are sliced according to the risk characteristics of the securities purchased by the SPV. The protection buyer pays premiums to the SPV (the protection seller) which in turn compensates the buyer if

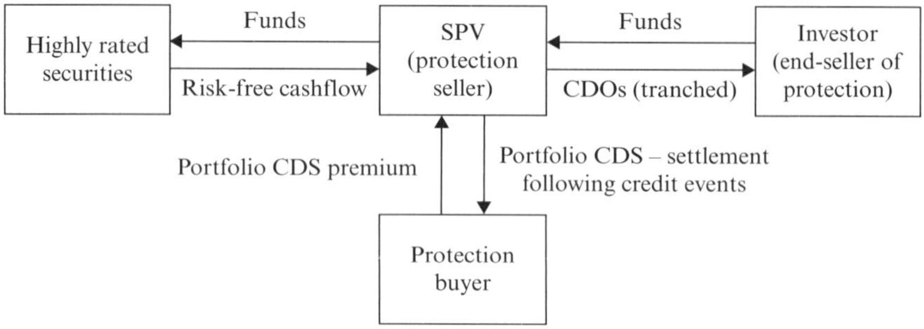

Source: Rule (2001).

Figure 1.4 Synthetic CDO

and when a 'credit event' occurs. The SPV also receives the income from the securities in which it has invested. In the case of a credit event that triggers the payment of compensation, the SPV is only able to pay less to the investors (who are the end-sellers of protection): this is the risk that the end-sellers of protection take. The end-sellers (the buyers of the CDOs) receive the return on the collateral securities purchased by the SPV plus the premium payments in the CDS.

Unlike the conventional CDO, in the synthetic model assets are not transferred by the protection buyer although the default risk is. The pay-off to the protection buyer is the difference between the initial notional value of the CDS (the sum insured) and the market value of the protection buyer's debt following the credit event.

A particular advantage of the synthetic CDO is the reduction in counterparty risk to both the bank and the ultimate sellers of protection. Both have potential claims on the SPV which are backed by the SPV's holdings of securities. To be effective as an insurance mechanism, the SPV must be bankruptcy-remote from the purchaser of protection (a bank) and the ultimate sellers of protection (investors in the CDOs).

One of the motives for a bank (or other entity) engaging in a credit derivative transaction is to shift credit risk away from itself. However, this raises the issue of counterparty risk, that is, the risk that the protection seller defaults on its obligations in the event that a relevant credit event occurs. Thus, while a bank may shift a credit-risk exposure, it opens itself up to a counterparty-risk exposure. Clearly, the less correlated are the risks attached to the counterparty and the underlying assets, the safer the transaction is for the protection buyer. Another dimension to the effectiveness of risk shifting relates to the relationship between a bank and its SPV subsidiaries. In principle, the two are bankruptcy-remote: the failure of one does not affect the other. In practice, however, this may not always be the case when a bank may wish to protect its reputation by supporting an SPV which has either liquidity or solvency problems. This was the case, for instance, early in 2007 when Bear Stearns supported its failing subsidiaries.

Credit default swaps

CDSs have emerged recently as an instrument to offer protection to a lender against, for instance, a default on a loan by a borrower. More generally, a CDS offers protection to the buyer against losses derived from defined credit events. This is, in effect, a form of insurance against credit risks that, in the traditional model of banking, is not feasible because of the asymmetric information problems outlined above. A CDS can be issued against bonds or bank credits. They have expanded substantially since 2004 and, at the end of 2006, the amount outstanding is estimated as being 10 times the size of tangible cash bonds on which they are often based.

The credit default structure is close to that of a guarantee but with three key differences: (i) the range of credit events that can trigger payment is wider, (ii) the protection buyer does not need to demonstrate an actual loss through the credit event: only that it occurred, and (iii) CDSs are based on standardised contracts so that they can be traded in secondary markets.

CDSs have two roles. First, they effectively offer insurance against a credit event (such as defaults on loans by borrowers). Second, they can be traded in secondary markets and such trading can be an alternative to trading in corporate bonds. As is the case with all credit derivatives, they can be used either by a lender or holder of a loan or bond to shift risk away from itself (the holder buys credit protection), or can be used to acquire a credit exposure/risk (by selling credit protection through a CDS). In the latter case, the selling of a CDS enables the seller to acquire a credit exposure against an entity without the necessity of making a loan to it. This implies access to credit risk without funding a loan and can therefore be used by (for instance) a bank to acquire credit exposure even in the event that it does not have a facility to make loans to borrowers. This effectively widens the source of funds to borrowers in that a bank making a loan can pass on the credit risk thereby freeing resources for other loans. With respect to a CDS against a tradable security (such as a bond issued by a borrower), the sale of a CDS by a protection buyer is equivalent to buying a bond, and the purchase of a CDS has the same effect as the alternative of selling the bond.

A bank is able to separate the funding of a loan from the risk taking. Thus a lending bank finances a loan while, through the purchase of CDS protection, it passes the risk to the seller. Conversely, the seller of the CDS acquires the credit risk without funding it by making the loan itself. This is outlined in Table 1.1. The potential for derivatives to enable a credit risk to be acquired without the necessity of making loans is discussed in ECB (2004). The CDS is activated (that is, payments made) when a specified credit event occurs: this might be, for instance, the default on a loan by a borrower or a delay in servicing a debt obligation.

Table 1.1 Risk taking versus funding

	Buyer of CDS protection	Seller of CDS protection
Funding of a loan	Yes	No
Risk taking	No	Yes

A further refinement of the CDS market is the recent emergence of CDS indexes such as iTRAxx in Europe and CDX in the US. These are traded as indices of large baskets of different companies' debt. These indices have contributed substantially to the liquidity of credit derivative instruments. As noted in BIS (2005), the indices provide a standard benchmark against which other more customised pools of exposures can be assessed and priced.

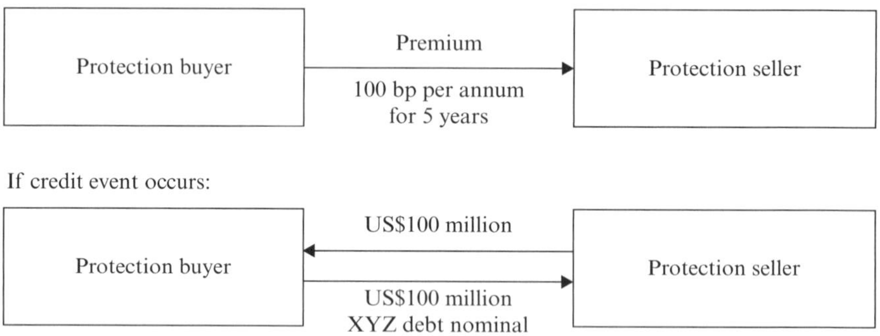

Source: Rule (2001).

Figure 1.5 Single name CDS: 5 years $100 million for XYZ company price at 100 bp per annum

A simplified representation of the mechanics of a single-name CDS is given in Figure 1.5. The protection buyer (for example, a bank that has made a loan) pays a regular premium to the protection seller (for example, another bank, a hedge fund and so on) over the duration of the loan. This is usually based on a number of basis points on the value of the loan. If the credit event (as specified in the contract) materialises, the CDS seller compensates the buyer in one of two ways: (i) physical settlement: the seller takes over the asset from the lender at its current estimated value while paying to the buyer the full nominal amount of the loan/bond (this is the nature of the 'swap'), or (ii) cash settlement: the seller of the CDS pays to the buyer the difference between the nominal amount of the debt that has been 'insured' and the estimated current value. A key issue, therefore, is how the current value of the debt is determined.

CDSs can subsequently be traded in a secondary market through which an original CDS seller can sell the contract within the maturity period in much the same way as can a holder of a futures contract. As always, such transactions are conducted at market prices which in turn are determined largely by market judgements about the risk of holding CDS obligations.

As with most derivatives, CDSs can be bought and sold for purposes of hedging of risks, speculation or arbitrage. One of the efficiency characteristics of CDSs is that they can be bought or sold to create almost any desired risk profile chosen by the buyer or seller. The mix of buying and selling different CDSs can create for the transactor a wide variety of overall risk exposures. For instance, through carefully constructed transactions a transactor can acquire a risk exposure to a particular borrower (firm within an industry) while at the same time removing the risk of the firm's industry as a whole. This enables an investor to make separate judgements about a particular firm within an industry and the industry itself if the investor judges that a firm is likely to out- or underperform the industry as a whole. Because of their flexibility, credit derivatives can be structured according to end-users' needs, for example, for the whole of the life of the underlying asset or for a shorter time, and the transfer can be complete or partial.

Summary

In sum, and on the basis of the analysis outlined in this section, the key characteristics of the different credit risk-shifting mechanisms and instruments are summarised in Table 1.2.

4 IMPLICATIONS OF FINANCIAL INNOVATION

Having outlined some of the key characteristics of instruments that have emerged through financial innovation (especially those related to credit risk), the focus turns to a discussion of some of the implications of financial innovation in general, especially as they relate to the efficiency and stability

Table 1.2 Credit risk shifting instruments

	Instruments								
	Credit guarantee	Credit insurance	Loan trading	Syndication	Securitisation (ABS)	Conventional CDO	Synthetic CDO	Single-name CDS	Portfolio CDS
Characteristics									
Funded	–	–	✓	✓	✓	✓	–	–	–
Unfunded	✓	✓	–	?	–	–	✓	✓	✓
Asset transfer	–	–	✓	–	✓	✓	✓	–	–
Insurance	–	✓	–	–	–	–	–	✓	✓
Tradable	–	–	✓	–	✓	✓	✓	✓	✓
Risk transfer	✓	✓	✓	?	✓	✓	✓	✓	✓
Single name	✓	✓	✓	✓	–	–	–	✓	–
Portfolio	–	–	–	–	✓	✓	✓	–	✓
Counterparty	✓	✓	–	–	–	–	–	✓	✓

of the financial system and the economics of banking. In particular, we consider the implications for:

1. the efficiency of the financial system in the performance of its core functions,
2. the economics of banking, and
3. the stability of the financial system.

A key issue is the extent to which financial innovation confers benefits on the real economy (for example, through its impact on resource allocation) as opposed to simply creating convenient instruments for the suppliers of financial services. In the final analysis, the financial system is designed to serve the interests of an economy as a whole. This analysis begins with a consideration of how financial innovation impacts on the core functions of a financial system. In the process, implications emerge for the underlying economics of banking and a possible trade-off between efficiency and stability in the financial system.

Financial Innovation and Efficiency

A central theme of the chapter has been that financial innovation has the potential to enhance the efficiency of the financial system in the performance of its core functions. Views vary on this issue as noted in the quotations at the outset. Greenspan (2004, p. 4) has argued: 'Credit derivatives and other complex financial instruments have contributed to the development of a far more flexible, efficient and hence resilient financial system'. The BIS has argued:

> [T]he development of credit risk transfer [CRT] has a potentially important impact on the functioning of the financial system. It provides opportunity for more effective risk management, promises the relaxation of some constraints on credit availability and allows more efficient allocation of risk to a wider range of entities. The pricing information provided by new CRT markets is also leading to enhanced transparency and liquidity in credit markets. (2003, p. 7)

This dimension to financial innovation can be summarised by considering in general terms the benefits of financial innovation that accrue to the financial system. A further discussion of this important dimension is given in Masala (2007). The potential benefits can be summarised briefly as they are implicit in much of the previous discussion:

- *Costs of financial intermediation* The costs of financial intermediation can be reduced in two ways: by giving borrowers access to a wider range of markets and facilities, and in some cases by allowing different institutions to exploit their comparative advantages. Securitisation enables a bank which has a comparative advantage in initiating loans (but not necessarily funding them or holding them on the balance sheet) to effectively pass on the loans to others who have a comparative advantage in funding and holding loans. A second example, in the case of CDSs, is where loan originators are able to keep the asset while at the same time pass the credit risk to others who have a preference for such risk but who are unable to initiate loans. There is a presumption that an increased variety of instruments increases the efficiency of saving and borrowing. Furthermore, to the extent that new instruments enhance competition in the financial system, the cost of financial intermediation might be expected to decline.

- *Matching portfolio preferences and optimal portfolio selection* By the same argument, innovation is presumed to increase efficiency as the wider range of facilities and instruments increases the probability that different portfolio preferences are met. New instruments facilitate a greater ability to unbundle transactions so that various parties are able to construct the risk–return structure most appropriate to them (Italian Bankers Association, 2008). To the extent that financial innovation widens the range of actual or synthetic assets and liabilities available to end-users and the suppliers of financial services, it facilitates agents selecting efficient portfolios of assets and liabilities to meet their particular requirements and preferences. Overall, such innovation has the effect of widening the range of risk–return trade-offs.
- *Responsiveness* Equally, to the extent that new instruments are created to reflect changes in portfolio preferences, the financial system becomes more responsive to consumer requirements and those of the suppliers of financial services.
- *Pricing of risk* Some instruments allow risks to be more accurately priced. Accurate pricing of risk enables the financial system to contribute to greater resource efficiency in an economy.
- *Allocate funds to their most efficient use* There is also a presumption that, to the extent that some innovations enable component risks to be identified, separated and accurately priced, funds are allocated more efficiently in the economy. One of the key functions of the financial system is to allocate resources on the basis of accurately priced risk–reward calculations, and risk-adjusted rates of return in particular. In general, if some risks are underpriced while others are overpriced, the allocation of resources in an economy becomes

suboptimal to the extent that excessive resources are allocated to the former while insufficient are allocated to the latter. This argument regarding the contribution to financial system efficiency assumes that particular instruments and innovations do in fact correctly price risks.

- *Arbitrage potential* New instruments facilitate arbitrage between markets in different countries which, in principle, erodes pricing anomalies, and reduces market imperfections through greater integration of markets. An earlier section also suggested that, through the use of credit derivatives, anomalies in the pricing of credit risk may be eroded. If an investor judges, for instance, that a particular credit risk is overvalued, (s)he can earn premium income as a protection seller in the CDS market.
- *Risk transfer and management* As has been noted in the analysis of the instruments discussed above, financial innovation enables various types of risk to be managed and shifted optimally to those who have a greater ability and/or willingness to absorb risk. The wider range of financial instruments now available has become an integral part of risk management both for the suppliers of financial services and their customers, and financial innovation widens the range of instruments available for risk management.
- *Risk more dispersed* One of the properties of some new financial instruments is that they enable risks to be dispersed optimally throughout the financial system and reduce the concentration of, for example, credit risk on a particular type of financial institution. This may have the effect of enhancing the stability of the financial system.
- *Limit exposure* By the same token, some instruments enable a bank to maintain a customer relationship without incurring an excessive credit-risk exposure to the customer. Credit derivatives offer an attractive mechanism for managing exposure concentrations.
- *Liquidity in credit risk* The traditional model of the bank is that loans are not marketable and hence the lender is effectively locked in to the borrower for the maturity of the loan. This limits the ability of a bank to change the composition of its loan portfolio if it is constrained in expanding the overall balance sheet. Many instruments (securitisation, CDOs and so on) remove this constraint and effectively create liquidity for loans that have traditionally been illiquid. Some instruments create a market in credit risk.
- *Information efficiency* Many financial instruments have the potential to increase informational efficiency through the market prices of derivative contracts and instruments including indexes.

- *Wider access to credit* As discussed in Masala (2007), many of the arguments outlined above can equally be applied to the issue of access to credit. For instance, by enabling banks to shift credit risk to others, financial instruments enhance the lending capacity of both credit-risk shifters (because they ease capital and risk constraints on further lending) and credit-risk absorbers. Securitisation widens the source of funding of loans initially made by banks. Although not a happy example, Northern Rock was able to expand its lending very sharply for several years because, through securitisation, it became less dependent on the flow of retail deposits. Equally, a bank may be more inclined to make loans if it knows that the risk can be shifted. All this implies that borrowers are less dependent upon the particular position of their bank. More specifically, some of the instruments discussed (such as CDSs) enable a bank (or any agent) to acquire a credit-risk exposure even though it may not have the capacity to make loans. In this case the function of originating loans, administering them and managing a customer relationship are performed by one institution while the credit risk is held by another. This is a further example of the process of 'deconstruction' (Llewellyn, 1999).
- *Portfolio management* In addition to the risk management potential noted above, to the extent that innovations create secondary markets they facilitate the management and adjustment of portfolios. Furthermore, in many ways, and for some investors, the cost of creating a CDO can be less than the cost of assembling a portfolio of loans and/or bonds to achieve the same risk–return objectives.
- *Unbundling of risks* Many instruments allow various risks to be unbundled, separately priced and 'sold'. Any financial instrument (whether it be complex or comparatively simple – such as a bank loan or deposit) is an embodied collection of a wide range of characteristics and risks. By allowing different risks within a given instrument to be separated and priced and held separately, agents are able to choose the particular combination of risks that suits their requirements and to change the combination of risks they are subject to. The ability to unbundle transactions means that various parties are able to acquire risk–return structures that are most appropriate to them (Masala, 2007).

By increasing the range of financial instruments, the process of 'spectrum filling' offers a wider range of choice with the presumption that the requirements of users are met more readily and efficiently. In principle, the process of spectrum filling moves the financial system closer to the Arrow–Debreu

(1954) ideal where all transactors can ensure for themselves delivery of goods and services in all future contingencies, and the system moves closer to approximating the number of 'states of nature'. In this regard, the creation of new instruments and facilities makes it possible to combine different characteristics in a more varied way and, in the process, widens the available combination of characteristics thereby reducing the number and size of discontinuities in the spectrum of financial instruments.

These, and other properties of credit derivatives are discussed further in Ayadi and Behr (Chapter 10 in this volume). As argued there, credit derivatives offer a wider range of risk profile and investment opportunities, and increase the liquidity of credit and bond markets. In these several and interrelated ways, therefore, financial innovation has the capacity to significantly enhance the efficiency of the financial system in the performance of its core functions.

The Economics of Banking

A central theme of this overview chapter is that, in some important respects, financial innovation (and most especially the emergence of credit derivatives) has changed the underlying economics of banking and the financial system. Earlier sections have outlined how new financial instruments have the potential to enhance the efficiency of the financial system in the performance of its core functions. In this subsection, an outline is offered of how the economics of banking has also been changing in part due to financial innovation. For illustrative purposes, a distinction is made in Table 1.3 between the traditional model of the bank (originate and hold), the securitisation variant (originate and sell), and the use of credit default swaps (originate, hold and externally insure).

It is instructive to begin with a stylised review of the traditional model of the banking firm (see Llewellyn, 1999 for a fuller discussion). Banks traditionally have information, risk analysis, and monitoring advantages which enable them to solve asymmetric information problems and hence mitigate adverse selection and moral hazard. In this standard model, banks accept deposits from one group of customers, and utilise their comparative advantages to transform deposits into loans. In this model, the bank accepts the credit (default) risk, holds the asset on its own balance sheet, monitors its borrowing customers, and holds appropriate levels of capital to cover unexpected risk. It also internally insures its loans through the risk premia incorporated into the rate of interest on loans. This is described in the *traditional* model in Table 1.3. In this process, the bank offers an integrated service in that it performs all functions in the financial intermediation process.

Table 1.3 Alternative bank models

		Traditional	Securitisation	CDSs
(1)	Accept deposits	✓	(✓)	✓
(2)	Originate loans	✓	✓	✓
(3)	Utilise comparative advantage:			
	Information	✓	✓	✓
	Risk analysis	✓	✓	✓
	Monitoring	✓	–	–
(4)	Transform into loans	✓	✓	✓
(5)	Accept risk	✓	–	–
(6)	Hold on balance sheet	✓	–	✓
(7)	Capital backing	✓	–	–
(8)	Insurance	Internal	Shift	Insure

Note: Traditional: Originate and hold; Securitisation: Originate and sell; CDSs: Originate and insure.

Furthermore, in this traditional model the bank is not able to shift credit risk to other agents because of its asymmetric information advantages: a potential buyer of a loan from a bank might judge that, because of the bank's information advantage, there is an adverse selection and moral hazard problem in that the bank might select low-quality loans to pass on and, if it knew that it could pass on risk, it might be less careful in assessing the risk of new loans and would conduct less-intensive monitoring of borrowers after loans have been made. For the same reason, the traditional view of the bank is that it is unable to externally insure its credit risks and instead holds capital as an internal insurance fund. The reason for this is that, given the uncertainties outlined above, an external insurer would reflect this uncertainty in the insurance premia charged to the bank. In this traditional view of the bank, therefore, credit risk cannot be shifted or insured, there is no liquidity to bank loans, and banks are locked into their loan portfolios.

However, as noted in earlier sections, many aspects of this traditional model are now questioned. In the *securitisation* model in Table 1.3, the process of securitisation (including via CDOs) means that the bank is able to sell loans (which the traditional model denies) and hence the bank does not hold the loan asset on its own balance sheet, does not absorb the credit risk, and therefore does not need to hold capital against the credit risk. As noted earlier, however, this depends upon precisely how the securitisation is conducted and most especially whether the SPV is truly bankruptcy-remote from the bank and vice versa.

The *CDS* model is similar to the securitisation model except that, while the credit risk is passed to the protection seller, the asset remains on the balance sheet of the originating bank. Furthermore, in this model there is explicit external insurance of bank loans.

The two simple examples of financial innovation in Table 1.3 related to credit risk illustrates that the traditional model of the banking firm needs, at best, to be modified. In particular, the examples of financial innovation considered in this chapter (and many others that have not) mean that the bank is no longer required to perform all the functions in the bank intermediation business: accept deposits, initiate loans, hold the loans on the balance sheet, absorb the credit risk, hold capital against the risk and so on. Furthermore, in an example of what was earlier termed 'process innovation', banks are also able to outsource some of their other activities such as loan administration, credit assessment through credit scoring models of other banks and so on. This further challenges the traditional view of the integrated bank. Banking is, therefore, no longer a totally integrated process whereby banks conduct all the functions in the loan process.

Credit-risk transfer facilities and instruments change the relationship between borrowers and lenders and create different incentive structures from those contained in the traditional model of the banking firm. In particular, the shifting of credit risk may create adverse selection and moral hazard in that the bank may have less incentive to monitor borrowers.

Efficiency versus Stability

An earlier section considered the efficiency characteristics of financial innovation and financial instruments in terms of their contributions to the efficiency of the financial system in performing its core functions. The main (though not only) efficiency benefits were found to derive from the risk-shifting characteristics of financial instruments. However, a trade-off often exists between efficiency and stability characteristics in the financial system, and some analysts judge this to be the case with financial innovation and especially with respect to credit derivatives.

The impact of financial innovation for stability is ambiguous. Until 2007, financial innovation (particularly with respect to credit risk) developed in a largely stable and benign economic environment of strong growth in the world economy, reasonably stable growth, strong profitability of banks, and low and reasonably stable rates of inflation. This benign combination meant that credit risks were low and required low pay-outs on credit instruments and credit insurance. In essence, the new credit-risk-shifting instruments had not been tested in a more demanding market environment. However, circumstances changed with the financial market turmoil that began in the summer of 2007 when banks around the world began to report substantial losses (and the need for re-capitalisation) on some of their derivative instruments.

Two views have surfaced regarding the stability characteristics of financial innovation. One school argues that, because they enable risks to be shifted optimally, they enhance the stability of the financial system. Against this, others argue that they have the potential to undermine financial stability not the least because it facilitates substantial leveraging of risk. A possible resolution of this apparent conflict focuses on the nature of shocks in that the increased use of derivative instruments (notably with respect to credit risk) may enhance the stability characteristics of the financial system in the face of small and low-correlated risks, while they may make the system more vulnerable to large systemic shocks such as the drying-up of liquidity in international markets as in the summer of 2007. Rajan offers the following perspective: 'Have these undoubted benefits [of financial innovation] come at a cost? Have we unwittingly accepted a Faustian bargain, trading greater welfare most of the time for a small probability of a catastrophic meltdown?' (2005, p. 14). The Financial Stability Forum report (BIS, 2005) identifies three issues with respect to the stability characteristics of credit derivatives: (i) whether they create a clean and total risk transfer, (ii) whether all participants understand the full nature of the risks involved in derivative transactions, and (iii) whether they produce a concentration of risks either inside or outside the financial system.

Some of the issues regarding the potential impact of financial innovation on systemic stability are briefly outlined in this subsection more with the objective of highlighting issues for further research rather than offering a detailed examination. There are several potential routes through which financial innovation might enhance the stability characteristics of the financial system, and through which structured finance may make financial systems more resilient to shocks:

- To the extent that financial instruments spread risks more widely within the system (and to those that are more willing and able to absorb them), stability is likely to be enhanced.
- In many ways, such credit-risk-shifting instruments enable banks to respond more easily to certain types of shocks. Greenspan (2002, p. 6) suggests that '[these episodes] suggest a marked increase over the two or three decades in the ability of modern economies to absorb unanticipated shocks. . .this has doubtless been materially assisted by the recent financial innovations that have afforded lenders the opportunity to become considerably more diversified and borrowers

to become far less dependent on specific institutions or markets for funds'.
- A further dimension and perspective has been offered by the BIS: 'The ability to switch smoothly between balance sheet financing and market-based financing contributes to the robustness of a financial system and improves its ability to deal with strain' (Knight, 2004, p. 6).

The overall assessment of the former Chairman of the Federal Reserve is that 'these increasingly complex financial instruments have especially contributed to the development of a far more flexible, efficient, and resilient financial system than existed just a quarter-century ago' (Greenspan, 2002, p. 4).

On the other hand, there may be a degree to which the instruments that enhance efficiency might under some circumstances threaten financial stability. Such instruments may both increase and decrease financial stability to the extent that the characteristics of different types of shock may be relevant to the stability/instability characteristics of financial innovation. Only a cursory review of some of the key issues is offered. The negative stability characteristics of financial innovation may be summarised as follows:

- The introduction of multiple layers between borrowers and lenders may increase new channels for the transmission of shocks within financial markets.
- To the extent that financial innovation has accentuated the market-centric nature of financial systems, shocks in one market may spread to a wider range of markets than before. The experience of 2007 and 2008 illustrates how this can occur. Globalisation coupled with financial innovation means that markets have become more closely linked and shocks can be spread more widely. In general, the potential for crises to be generalised through markets is greater than that between institutions, and we have observed that financial innovation has the effect of enhancing yet further the market-centric nature of financial systems.
- The enhanced leverage potential of some credit derivatives may increase the vulnerability of the financial system to certain types of shock.
- Credit derivatives tend to be inherently pro-cyclical in an economy through accentuating credit growth in the upswing of an economic cycle but equally accentuate the opposite trend in the downswing.
- Financial innovation has a general effect of enhancing competition in the financial system as all suppliers of financial facilities face

competition from a wider range of channels. While this is generally a beneficial outcome, competition can sometimes have the effect of inducing financial institutions into hazardous and risky behaviour as they strive to maintain market share.
- The experience of the financial turbulence in 2007 and 2008 was that in practice, credit risk is not always shifted as much as might be thought through the use of securitisation and credit derivatives. This in itself can introduce a higher element of potential instability in the system to the extent that, in the event that risk has not been shifted, banks may need to take back on to their balance sheets risks they thought had been shifted. This in turn may introduce capital problems for banks.

These considerations suggest a tentative conclusion regarding the stability implications of financial innovation. It seems that financial instruments that enable risks to be shifted, and which enhance the market-centric mature of financial systems, make the financial system less vulnerable to small shocks and enable such small shocks to be handled more easily. In this sense the stability characteristics of the financial system are enhanced by financial innovation. On the other hand, it may make the system more prone to large and systemic shocks and make it more difficult for them to be handled. One such event would be the type of systemic liquidity shock experienced in financial markets during 2007. Rajan (2005, p. 16), for instance, concludes that: '[while] the financial system is more stable most of the time, we may also have the possibility of excessive instability in really bad times (as well as higher probability of such tail events)'. He argues further that 'The linkages between markets, and between markets and institutions, are now more pronounced. While this allows the system to diversify across small shocks, it also exposes the system to large systemic shocks – large shift in asset prices or changes in aggregate liquidity'. A further dimension is that in some complex credit derivative instruments, correlations which are zero or even negative in normal times can turn out to be positively correlated in abnormal times (see Chan et al., 2005).

This is not the place to offer any detailed analysis of the financial market turmoil that erupted in international banking and financial markets in the summer of 2007. The Financial Services Authority (2008, p. 62) has argued that:

> Structured finance and the way in which firms have used associated finance vehicles, such as SIVs and conduits, are central to the instability that affected financial markets and financial institutions in the second half of 2007 . . . Liquidity more or less disappeared from the asset-backed commercial paper market after several years of unprecedented growth . . . The lack of liquidity caused significant

> problems for many products, most notably SIVs [Structured Investment Vehicles], ABCP [Asset-Backed Commercial Paper] conduits, CDOs and CLOs [Collateralised Loan Obligations].

In effect, all credit derivative markets were badly affected and to an extent that led some commentators to doubt their long-run viability (Llewellyn, 2009).

5 PROBLEM AREAS

A key issue is the extent to which credit derivatives achieve a genuine transfer of credit risk. In this regard, the issue arises whether this risk shifting simply replaces credit risk by counterparty risk: the risk that a counterparty becomes unable to honour its obligations in a credit derivative transaction. This is avoided in some cases where, for instance, the transaction is funded up-front through the issuance of securities so that the counterparty risk is mitigated.

A further issue is the extent to which complex instruments are fully understood by the transactors. New complex products might have consequences that are not fully understood by the initiators, users, or regulators (Masala, 2007). The full risk implications of some instruments are sometimes determined by the application of complex mathematical procedures, and these have to be appreciated as much by the users as by the institutions and regulators. The full risk and other implications of new instruments have not been tested in all circumstances. The FSA has argued (2002, 2008) that complexity and the lack of transparency of many credit derivative instruments (and notably CDOs) make it difficult for investors to determine precisely how exposed they are to particular risks. In particular, losses may be determined by the correlations of the risks within the portfolio and these are in practice difficult to calibrate. Furthermore, banks have also become less transparent in that it is difficult to know to what extent credit risks have been shifted or bought in the market through, for instance, CDSs.

The true extent to which risks are shifted through the various instruments discussed in previous sections may also be brought into question, especially at times of systemic crisis as in the second half of 2007 (Llewellyn, 2008). In practice what appears to be a risk-shifting instrument may have limitations. Thus, in the turbulence of 2007, many banks found that, in practice, risks had not been shifted because, for instance, they had committed lines of credits to their SPVs and conduits which, because of funding difficulties, were subsequently called upon. Furthermore, because of funding problems, several banks were induced either to take back securitised assets onto their balance sheet, or were unable to securitise loans they had made in anticipation of securitisation.

Difficult valuation problems also arise with some instruments. Because they are not always traded in secondary markets, it becomes difficult for accurate market valuations to emerge. The alternative that is commonly used is for valuations to be made by investors on the basis of complex mathematical formulae which, as noted in Ayadi and Behr (Chapter 10, this volume), may not always account for the true risk and which may apply oversimplistic methods to assess the risk profile (see also BIS, 2003). In particular, as noted in Masala (2007), there is uncertainty about how new products, instruments and markets might interact in the face of extreme stress and shocks. The familiar 'tail problem' (low-probability–high-impact risks) has, from time to time, caused severe difficulties for some institutions trading in complex derivative instruments.

In some respects, and as a result of the development of complex instruments, the financial system has become more opaque. The lack of transparency of some instruments (notably those involving credit-risk shifting) came to the surface during the financial turmoil of the summer months of 2007. In particular, some markets (such as the CDO and securitisation markets) virtually closed altogether, while conditions in some others (such as the inter-bank market in London) weakened considerably largely because of the difficulty of transactors in assessing counterparty risk exposure to mortgage-backed securities and CDOs. Banks began to report substantial losses in these instruments and it became difficult for market participants to assess with any degree of accuracy who was holding what risks. The failure of Northern Rock (and the serious difficulties of many other banks) demonstrates that excessive reliance on some risk-shifting instruments may cause a bank to become exposed to a particular funding risk: the bank became dependent on securitisation and the issue of very short-term securities.

Credit-risk shifting can also be undermined to the extent that a seller of credit-risk protection itself becomes insolvent, or in any other way unable to honour its obligations. This is particularly the case with unfunded risk-transfer instruments. In this sense, while a bank may be able to shift a credit risk, it becomes exposed to a different counterparty risk. In this event, the original credit risk reverts to the protection buyer. This arose in 2007 with respect to bond monoline insurers in the US which had been guaranteeing structured bonds backed by mortgages which subsequently lost value.

Credit-risk shifting has become an important feature of the new model of banking. However, the extent of such risk shifting should not be exaggerated. First, credit-risk shifters are often required to maintain some of the risks themselves, for example, through holding at least part of the equity tranche in a CDO. Second, the most actively traded names in the credit derivatives market in practice have investment-grade status and therefore are comparatively low-risk entities. However, the experience of 2008 indicates that this cannot be relied upon in times of stress. Third, a substantial proportion of the transactions in the markets are conducted between traders/dealers in the instruments which means that 'much of the notional amount of credit derivatives outstanding represents inter-dealing trading, not actual risk transfer' (BIS, 2005, p. 84). In any case, the amount of true credit risk transfer is small in relation to banks' total credit exposure.

Asymmetric Information Risks

There are several asymmetric information risks attached to the change in the banking model discussed in an earlier section with both adverse selection and moral hazard consequences. The underlying basis is that the initial lender is likely to have more information about borrowers and a greater capacity to conduct post-loan monitoring. Several problems in particular arise from this:

- The initiating bank may have an incentive to shift the risk on its existing low-quality loans (Pennacchi, 1988; De Marzo and Duffie, 1999).
- A potential moral hazard arises to the extent that a bank is able to shift credit risk as it has less incentive to accurately assess risk. This problem surfaced in the US sub-prime mortgage market during 2007.
- There is less incentive to subsequently monitor the borrower (Gorton and Penacchi, 1995; Morrison, 2005) and it is unlikely that a seller of credit risk protection (or buyer of CDOs) is able to monitor borrowers because they do not have the information or relationship advantages possessed by the initiating bank. This amounts to a new banking model which, to some extent, abrogates two of the fundamental roles of a bank: assessment of risk and *ex post* monitoring. There is some empirical evidence for this in that Mian and Sufi (2008) find that default rates tend to be higher on securitised mortgages than those which are held on the initiating bank's balance sheet. Keys et al. (2008) also find that securitisation tends to weaken screening of borrowers before loans are made.
- A lemons problem can emerge in some credit-risk transfer arrangements in that a lender buys protection on low-quality assets which may drive up the cost of protection on high-quality assets (Duffee and Zhou, 2001). The standard lemons problem is that, in the presence of asymmetric information, a market may eventually break

down as only low-quality assets are offered for protection (Akerlof, 1970).

- In some cases, either the borrower or the credit-risk protection buyer may be able to influence the probability of a relevant credit event.
- If contracts are incomplete (in that they do not specify the rights and obligations of all parties in all circumstances) there may be scope for one of the parties (often the risk-protection buyer) to act opportunistically against the interests of the risk taker.
- The risk shifter may retain a relationship with the borrower after the credit risk has been shifted as an agent of the risk taker. As noted in BIS (2003), this gives rise to a potential principal–agent problem. In whose interest is the bank working?
- Under some circumstances, there is an incentive for a buyer of credit protection through a credit derivative to trigger a default prematurely by, for instance, refusing to make further loans that it might otherwise have done had it not been for the terms of the CDS contract. It is often the case that the buyer of protection has the power to determine when a default occurs.

Some derivatives may be deliberately used to conceal information from markets and to make business less transparent. Enron, for example, used CDO technology to transfer assets to an SPV in order to overstate earnings and hide debt from the company's balance sheet.

While these potential moral hazards exist, the extent is likely to be limited by five considerations: in some contracts, the protection is not total and a protection buyer takes the first tranche of losses (the classic way of protecting against moral hazard in any insurance or insurance-like contract) and, if the buyer of protection plans for protection to be a continuing (rather than a one-off) game, it needs to consider its own reputation in the market. Also, in some contracts, the risk shifter selects loans for the portfolio at random. In the case of credit insurance, the insurer may require the risk shifter to disclose any material facts about the creditworthiness of the borrowers with the insurance becoming void in the event of a failure to disclose.

6 CONCLUSION

Financial innovation has become a defining characteristic of financial systems over recent years. In the process it has contributed, in some countries more than others, to major structural change in national financial systems and to more integration between systems. Knight (2004) has argued that the transformation of the financial landscape has altered the nature of risk. The reverse causation can also be argued: that financial innovation, and new instruments, have themselves been a force in the transformation of the financial landscape.

The process of financial innovation contributes to four specific functions of a financial system: (i) it increases the variety of financial instruments for both borrowers and lenders by offering various combinations of standard characteristics; (ii) it increases the liquidity of the system to the extent that tradable assets and markets are created; (iii) it enables particular risks to be more efficiently priced and transferred; and (iv) it may give borrowers access to particular markets from which they were hitherto excluded. These may be viewed as some of the basic 'functions' of financial innovation.

Financial innovation in general has had the effect of increasing the integration of markets, including between financial centres as many instruments straddle different types of markets, and markets in different countries. In many ways, new financial instruments (especially those focused on shifting credit risk) have changed in a fundamental way the underlying economics of banking. As part of this, the traditional formal distinction between bank and capital market intermediation has tended to become less pronounced.

The regulatory implications of financial innovation have been assessed succinctly by the Financial Stability Forum as follows:

> Credit risk transfer has the potential significantly to change institutions' risk profiles and their role in the financial system. From a financial stability perspective, it is important that these changes be addressed in regulation and disclosure standards, as well as in the behaviour of individual firms. Banks may in the future have less credit but more legal and operational risk. Liquidity risk might also become more important, created either by contingent liabilities within securitisation structures or by increased dependence on these transactions as a funding device. These risks are more difficult to measure than credit and market risk, and it may be more difficult to deal with them in quantitative capital rules and disclosure standards. A more qualitative approach, focussing on risk management, may be needed. (BIS, 2003, p. 94)

On the other hand, Santomero has raised doubts about some aspects of the use of financial derivatives, especially with regard to transparency. He has argued as follows:

> Perhaps recent events . . . suggest that, while we have made assets more tradable, we have not necessarily made their value more transparent. Indeed, the added complexity associated with current asset portfolios drawn from various types of credit and credit derivatives cries out for better transparency and better reporting. This ought to be the agenda for the next decade. (2007, p. 71)

Over the past decade, banks have considerably enhanced their risk analysis and management systems, and financial innovation has contributed to this in a significant way. For a decade or more, such innovation developed in a scenario of strong growth in the world economy, a fairly stable economic and monetary environment, low credit risks, and stable and low interest rates. The experience of the financial market turmoil in 2007 indicated that techniques and instruments to shift credit risk in a stable environment may become problematic when the market environment becomes more volatile and uncertain, and when there are systemic shocks, especially when they involve low-probability–high-impact risks. In the final analysis, many instruments have the effect of shifting rather than reducing risk. The question arises as to whom these risks are shifted and what impact various shocks have on those counterparties, and their ability to honour commitments in the face of various shocks. Perhaps some risk-shifting innovations are 'fair weather' friends. This has been amply demonstrated in the financial crisis of 2007 and 2008.

REFERENCES

Akerlof, G. (1970), 'The market for lemons', *Quarterly Journal of Economics*, **84**(3), August, 488–500.

Arrow, K. and Debreu, G. (1954), 'Existence of an equilibrium for a competitive economy', *Econometrica*, **22**, 256–90.

Bank of England (2006), *Financial Stability Review*, London, July.

Bank for International Settlements (BIS) (1986), *Recent Innovations in International Banking*, BIS, Basel.

Bank for International Settlements (BIS) (2003), Committee on the Global Financial System, *Credit Risk Transfer*, BIS, Basel, January.

Bank for International Settlements (BIS) (2005), Basel Committee on Banking Supervision/The Joint Forum, *Credit Risk Transfer*, BIS, Basel, March.

Benfield Group (2002), 'Water to Wine: Collateralised Debt Obligations', London, December, www.benfieldgroup.com, accessed 2006.

Bloomestein, H. (2000), 'The Changing Nature of Risk and the Challenges to Sound Risk Management in the New Global Financial Landscape', OECD, Paris, March.

Chan, N., Getmansky, M., Haas, S. and Lo, A. (2005), 'Systemic Risk and Hedge Funds', National Bureau of Economic Research, Cambridge, MA, Working Paper, 11200.

De Marzo, P. and Duffie, D. (1999), 'A liquidity-based model of security design', *Econometrica*, January, 65–99.

Duffee, G.R. and Zhou, C. (2001), 'Credit derivatives in banking: useful tools for managing risk', *Journal of Monetary Economics*, **48**, 25–54.

European Central Bank (ECB) (2004), *Credit Risk Transfer by EU Banks: Activities, Risks and Risk Management*, Frankfurt am Main, May.

Financial Services Authority (FSA) (2002), *Cross-sector Risk Transfer*, FSA, London, May.

Financial Services Authority (FSA) (2008), *Financial Risk Outlook*, FSA, London.
Gorton, G. and Haubrich, J. (1990), 'The loan sales market', in G.G. Kaufman (ed.), *Research in Financial Services: Private and Public Policy*, Vol. 2, JAI Press, Greenwich, CT, pp. 81–7.
Gorton, G. and Pennacchi, G. (1995), 'Banks and loan sales: marketing non-marketable assets', *Journal of Monetary Economics*, **35**, 389–411.
Greenbaum, S.I. and Thakor, A.V. (1995), *Contemporary Financial Intermediation*, Dryden Press, Harcourt Brace College Publishers, Fort Worth, TX.
Greenspan, A. (2002), 'International Financial Risk Management', Remarks to the Council on Foreign Relations, Washington, DC, November.
Greenspan, A. (2004), 'Economic Flexibility', Speech to HM Treasury Enterprise Conference, London, March.
Italian Bankers Association (2008), 'Recent Financial Innovations and their Implications for Risk and its Management', Report of XIV European Banking Report Board Meeting, Rome.
Keys, B., Mukherjee, T., Seru, A. and Vig, V. (2008), 'Did Securitisation Lead to Lax Screening? Evidence from the Sub-prime Loans 2001–6', http//ssrn.com/abstract=1093137, January.
Knight, M. (2004), 'Markets and Institutions: Managing the Evolving Financial Risk', 25th Societe Universitaire Europeenne de Recherches Financieres (SUERF) Colloquium, Bank for International Settlements, Basel, October.
Llewellyn, D.T. (1992), 'Financial innovation: a basic analysis', in H. Cavanna (ed.), *Financial Innovation*, Routledge, London, pp. 17–33.
Llewellyn, D.T. (1999), *The New Economics of Banking*, SUERF Study, No. 5, Societe Universitaire Europeenne de Recherches Financieres (SUERF), Vienna.
Llewellyn, D.T. (2008), 'The failure of Northern Rock: a crisis waiting to happen', *Journal of Financial Regulation and Compliance*, March, 35–58.
Llewellyn, D.T. (2009), 'Financial Innovation and the Global Financial Crisis', South African Reserve Bank, Monetary Policy in South Africa, SARB Institute, forthcoming.
Masala, F. (2007), 'Recent Financial Innovations and their Implications for Risk Management', Report for 2007 Advisory Board Meeting of the European Banking Report Observatory, Italian Bankers Association, Rome, November.
Mian, A. and Sufi, A. (2008), 'The Consequences of Mortgage Credit Expansion: Evidence from the 2007 Mortgage Default Crisis', http//ssm.com/abstract=1072304, January.
Morrison, A.D. (2005), 'Credit derivatives, disintermediation and investment decisions', *Journal of Business*, **78**, 621–48.
Partnoy, F. and Skeel, D. (2007), 'The promise and perils of credit derivatives', *University of Cincinnati Law Review*, June, 3–48.
Pennacchi, G.G. (1988), 'Loan sales and the cost of bank capital', *Journal of Finance*, **43**, 375–96.
Pilbeam, K. (2005), *Finance and Financial Markets*, Palgrave, London,
Rajan, R.G. (2005), 'Has financial development made the world riskier', International Monetary Fund, Washington, August.
Rule, D. (2001), 'Credit derivatives market: its development and possible implications for financial stability', *Financial Stability Review*, Bank of England, London, June, 16–40.

Santomero, A. (2007), 'Loan Portfolio Management: Good News or Bad News for Financial Stability', European Banking Report Board, Italian Bankers Association, Rome, November.

Schmookler, J.A. (1967), *Invention and Economic Growth*, Harvard University Press, Cambridge, MA.

Silber, W. (ed.) (1975), *Financial Innovation*, Lexington Books, Lexington, MA.

Silber, W. (1983), 'The process of financial innovation', *American Economic Review, Papers and Proceedings*, May, 16–32.

White, L.J. (2000), 'Technological change, financial innovation, and financial regulation in the US: the challenge for public policy', in D. Harker and S. Zenios (eds), *Performance of Financial Institutions*, Cambridge University Press, Cambridge, pp. 80–91.

2. Is financial innovation still a relevant issue?

Luisa Anderloni and Paola Bongini

1 INTRODUCTION

Financial innovation has regularly been regarded as one of the major drivers for the radical changes underwent by international and domestic financial markets in particular during the 1980s and 1990s. The approach adopted in the literature on financial innovation has typically focused on: (i) the concept of innovation, its features and forms; (ii) the determinants of financial innovation; and (iii) the effects generated by innovation.

The term 'financial innovation' has a broad range of both implicit and explicit definitions. Roger (1995, p. 11) defines 'innovation' as 'an idea, practice, or object that is perceived as new by an individual or other unit of adoption. It matters little, so far as human behavior is concerned, whether or not an idea is objectively new as measured by the lapse of time since its first use or discovery. The perceived newness of the idea for the individuals determines his or her reaction to it. If the idea seems new to the individual, it is an innovation'. Specifically with regard to the financial sector, Silber (1975, p. 1), in outlining the scope of his work, states:

> This book is devoted to studies of innovation in the financial sector. It focuses on the innovation of new financial instruments, institutions, markets, and practices. Innovation means change. It usually implies progress as well, although this need not always be the case. While most economists have reserved the term for a discussion of technological improvements, it has been broadened by economic historians to include institutional change. The studies included in this book fall within this expanded framework.

He then moves on to discuss the question of welfare gains generated by innovation: 'The issues how to measure the welfare gain of any innovation in the financial sector, or how to determine whether a new financial instrument, market, institution or practice deserves the appellation "innovation" with the implication of welfare are crucial' (p. 2).

The literature continues to confirm the indeterminate nature of financial innovation as a concept. Frame and White (2004, p. 118), after having analysed the basic functions of the financial system,[1] including financial intermediaries and 'financial facilitators', view financial innovation as representing 'something new that reduces costs, reduces risks, or provides an improved product/service/instrument that better satisfies participants' demands'. This definition appears to be widely shared and is the one that will be used in this work. On this basis, innovation can be broken down into the following categories: product or service innovation; innovation in production technologies; and organisational innovation. Innovation makes a direct contribution to reducing negative elements (costs or risks) as well as to enhancing positive ones (products, services, instruments equipped to better satisfy the demand side). Van Horne (1985) draws a pertinent distinction between 'true' and 'presumed' innovation in which the former is able to make markets more efficient and more complete. Llewellyn (1992; Chapter 1, this volume) specifies that innovation is both the creation of new financial instruments, techniques and markets and the unbundling of the separate characteristics and risks of individual instruments and their reassembly in different combinations; he also underlines that any financial innovation should be considered as such according to the extent to which it increases the overall efficiency of the financial system.

Turning to the question of what motivates financial innovation, the literature has focused on the following drivers, both common to the manufacturing and service industries:

- availability of new technology;
- competition;
- evolving customer needs;

and specific to the financial sector:

- rising levels of interest and exchange rate volatility and market uncertainty that generate new customer needs on the one hand, and new management solutions adopted by financial intermediaries, on the other (Miller, 1992);
- 'regulatory dialectic', namely innovative processes adopted as a way of reducing or avoiding regulatory constraints, for instance in the areas of monetary policy, supervision, tax and accounting. On this subject, see Greenbaum and Haywood (1974); Silber (1975, 1983), who developed the theory of constraints; Kane (1984), who proposes the idea of circumventing innovation within the framework of the regulatory dialectic; as well as Miller (1986).

The effects produced by these drivers tend to differ. In particular, the 'regulatory dialectic' may lead to short-term innovations that will not bring long-term operative improvements to the financial system in terms of improved efficiency or market completeness Therefore, it will simply raise satisfaction among single-market participants (on either the supply or demand side), while incurring negative effects on the objectives sought by regulation. Clearly, such circumventing innovation has come in for criticism (Van Horne, 1985). Some authors have hoped or asked for a greater use of market discipline so as to reduce the possibilities of opportunistic behaviour (ibid.; Anderloni, 1999).

Although comparatively smaller than the literature focusing on the manufacturing sector, studies addressing the issue of innovation within the financial system continue to grow. At this stage of the analysis, rather than providing an overview of the empirical literature – useful contributions in this area are provided by Silber (1975), Molyneaux and Shamroukh (1999) and Frame and White (2004) – we shall seek to identify, on the one hand, the specific forms of financial innovation present in the market and examined in the literature and, on the other, try to outline the limits that ongoing research on financial innovation have faced so far.

As to the first point, there is a lack of recent, wide-ranging studies able to offer a map of current trends in financial innovation; as a matter of fact, research attention has been placed on specific individual phenomena.[2] In their work on financial innovation, Frame and White (2004) review 24 studies, which can be summarised in the table below:

Area of innovation	Number of studies	Years in which studies were made
Instruments of payments and ATMs	5	1984, 1987, 1995, 2000, 2001
Securities: issuance and trading	5	1978, 1989, 1990, 1996, 2000
Internet and financial services	4	2000, 2001, 2001, 2002
Credit scoring	4	2001, 2001, 2001, 2002
Structure, management and diversification of banking groups (bank holding companies)	4	1998, 1999, 1999, 2002
Wide-ranging, yet undefined	2	1977, 2002

These studies test single hypotheses and provide specific answers to the questions raised above about innovation and its value, the models of application and their extent, and the ensuing effects. However, they represent pieces in a jigsaw that are difficult to put together owing to the variety of approaches adopted and the lengthy time periods concerned. For the most part, the studies focus on the United States and analyse phenomena relating to different time periods and diverse regulatory and competitive environments so that generalisations are difficult to make.

With regard to the second question – that is, which areas of research about financial innovation are the most neglected – we have to point out the relative lack of both theoretical and empirical studies on financial innovation relative to the comparative abundance of similar papers available for other sectors of the economy.

Among the factors that may explain this situation is the peculiarity of the financial industry itself, characterised by an absence of patent laws. In fact, until recently, financial innovations were generally not considered eligible for patent protection (Kumar and Turnbull, 2006). The US Court decisions in 1998 (see Lerner, 2006b), allowing business methods to be patentable, have opened the way for patenting and licensing financial innovations. Indeed a growing number of both US and EU banks have already taken initial steps in order to obtain trademarks or service marks for their products and services. This would confirm the implicit commercial value attached to these forms of protection and exclusiveness, and may contribute to promote the development of empirical studies.

The limited number of empirical studies on financial innovation can also be explained by the difficulties that researchers face in distinguishing between true innovators and imitators. In the financial industry, imitators can develop solutions in shorter periods of time in comparison with other sectors of the economy (Molyneux and Shamroukh, 1999) and reduce development costs[3] in a range of 50 to 75 per cent of total costs in comparison to first movers (Tufano, 1989).[4]

Another reason for the lack of empirical evidence regarding the impact of financial innovation may stem from the fact that the benefits deriving from the rapid development of financial innovation are substantially intangible such as, for example, reputation effects among customers and national or international competitors, whereas short- and medium-term economic returns for intermediaries, which are easier to measure and evaluate, would be marginal (Drew, 1995). However, this is a point on which empirical evidence lacks consensus. Indeed, several studies highlight the potential for innovators to enjoy excellent opportunities for profit thanks to the possibility of applying high commissions on new products even when these entail limited levels of innovation. For instance, Van Horne (1985, p. 626) argues:

> [T]he eagerness of financial-service consumers for almost anything new has allowed investment banks and other financial institutions to propose things lacking in the foundation of making the financial markets more efficient operationally and/or more complete . . . and . . . alleged innovations continue to be

sold with handsome fees to the promoters and, in mirror image, costs to the other parties involved.

Third, there is also a lack of business studies that analyse the cultural, strategic and organisational factors underpinning innovation in banks and financial intermediaries as a whole. While research and development (R&D) structures are well established in manufacturing firms and continue to evolve, they are largely unexplored in the banking sector. As previously indicated, there is a systematic informational deficit, arising from rigorous empirical studies, as to how banks organise their R&D activities to promote innovation and which of these organisational choices successfully sponsor financial innovation. This information gap is considerable if we take into account the contributions that theoretical and empirical studies made in the manufacturing sector, while less so with regard, specifically, to the service sector. In the banking and financial sector, the focus of research continues to be placed on the marketing of products and services rather than on addressing the question of which organisational solutions are the most appropriate for the successful promotion and management of innovation across all phases. An example of this is given, among others, by Johne and Storey (1998) who, focusing on the issue of 'new service development',[5] pay particular attention to the financial services sector, although limiting their analysis to marketing issues.

Numerous studies underline, at the theoretical level, the importance of organisational factors in determining the success of innovation in services, including those in the financial sector. In fact, crucial factors for the effective and efficient management of projects aimed at developing new services include excellence (for instance, knowledge of the market and not only skills in the areas of product development and launch), interpersonal and interdepartmental cooperation, and effective leadership (Johne and Harborne, 2003).

Considering financial innovation that originates and develops within a firm's organisation rather than within a dedicated organisational unit (for instance, specific R&D units in manufacturing industries), the most frequently adopted solution for the development of new products is the setting up of multidisciplinary work groups. Vermeulen and Dankbaar (2002) identify different types of teams: (i) teams with a fixed number of participants; (ii) teams with a number of participants that vary according to the requirement of the project phase; (iii) informal project teams with no official organisational design; and (iv) 'groups of people' providing support to the innovator. The authors report that most of the organisations under examination (32 out of 39), which were incidentally the biggest organisations, use teams in developing new products, with types (i) and (ii) being the most frequently adopted. The decision to create multidisciplinary groups is, however, not problem free in the areas of communication and collaboration.[6] Furthermore, in the service sector, the simultaneousness of production and consumption heightens the difficulties of developing new services and brings front-office staff into the decision-making process, thanks to their direct contact with customers.

All in all, research on financial innovation is still in its early days and there is a lack of systematic empirical evidence with unique and universally accepted results.

Given the scarcity of knowledge just described, our research seeks to contribute to the debate on financial innovation by addressing two main questions: first, whether financial innovation still has an important role to play in the decisional processes of European banks; and second, which business areas are involved and what are the implications for management processes.

The chapter is organised as follows: Section 2 illustrates our research questions and presents the methodology adopted; Section 3 discusses the results of the qualitative analysis; while Section 4 analyses the links between financial innovation, asset growth and bank profitability. The chapter ends with some concluding remarks.

2 THE EMPIRICAL ANALYSIS

Our empirical study seeks to identify banks' attitudes towards innovation according to the level of information conveyed to market participants in annual reports. In particular we want to ascertain first, whether financial innovation represents a relevant aspect in the business communication policies of European banks; and second, which business areas are most involved in such a communication strategy.

To provide answers to the questions raised above we analysed the annual reports of a sample of European banks[7] searching for indications of product and process innovations.

Studying corporate culture via text analyses is a relatively recent method of research. It has already provided us with interesting results, particularly in the areas of organisation, market reporting and the presentation of strategies adopted and performances/results achieved (Lord, 2002; Bexley and Hynes, 2003; Hynes and Bexley, 2003). In the light of these insights, the same approach has been adopted in the present study with respect to financial innovation.

Our analysis reveals that sample banks show differing attitudes towards innovation. On this basis we were able to draw up an initial ranking of banks in terms of both their interest in innovation and the pervasiveness of this interest. In parallel, in order to provide an answer to the second question, we sought to identify the areas of banks' products and services or management in which innovation is most significant. We then investigated possible links between the strategic importance of innovation and company performance.

The following phases made up the empirical research:

- choice of a sample of banks from major Western European countries;
- analysis of annual reports and identification of references to innovation;
- weighting of these references on the basis of the specific context where the references are made (for example, chairman's statement; business overview; risk management); in addition, the communication's effectiveness is also taken into consideration;
- definition of an innovation index, calculated both for each year of the sample period and as a sample period average;
- ranking of the banks and identification of bank clusters on the basis of the innovation index's distribution;
- analysis of the qualitative profiles and areas of significant innovation for those clusters of banks putting more emphasis on communicating financial innovation; and
- study of possible links between a commitment to innovation and company and market performances.

The banks sampled are large financial institutions in major EU15 countries. In particular, given the predominance of group structures, the sample comprises banking groups rather than stand-alone banks. As we refer to consolidated data, large national banks belonging to other transnational groups are not included in the sample. Furthermore, we focused on major players adopting the universal banking model.[8] Consequently, we had to exclude banks which, though leaders in terms of operating size and total assets, have a specialist vocation (for example, investment banks asset managers).

Total asset volumes of the banks selected (see Table 2.1) cover a broad range, reflecting the heterogeneity of European banking systems in terms of operating size and structure. None of the groups, however, had assets amounting to less than €100,000 million in 2006.

Such diversity almost meant that the number of banking groups per country was not fixed, ranging from five each for the United Kingdom and France, four for Italy and Spain, three for Germany, Belgium and the Netherlands, two for Ireland, Sweden and Norway, to one bank/banking group in Denmark.

Table 2.1 Sample composition

Country	Bank	Total assets, 2006 (€)
Belgium	Fortis	775,229,000
Belgium	Dexia	566,743,000
Belgium	KBC	325,400,000
Denmark	Danske	367,399,726
France	BNP Paribas	1,440,343,000
France	Credit Agricole	1,380,666,000
France	Société Générale	956,841,000
France	Groupe Caisse d'Epargne	539,711,000
France	Credit Mutuel	339,025,000
Germany	Deutsche	1,571,768,000
Germany	Commerz bank	608,339,000
Germany	Dresdner	497,287,000
Ireland	AIB	158,526,000
Ireland	Bank of Ireland	188,813,000
Italy	Unicredit	823,284,188
Italy	Banca Intesa	576,784,000
Italy	San Paolo IMI	158,743,797
Italy	MPS	158,555,703
Norway	DnB NOR	160,137,340
Norway	Nordea	107,749,812
Netherlands	ING	1,226,307,000
Netherlands	ABN AMRO	987,064,000
Netherlands	Rabobank	556,455,000
Spain	Santander	833,872,688
Spain	BBVA	411,916,313
Spain	La Caixa	209,123,203
Spain	Caja Madrid	136,952,406
Sweden	SEB	213,976,611
Sweden	SHB	198,000,273
UK	Barclays	1,485,729,593
UK	HSBC	1,412,873,549
UK	RBS	1,298,885,630
UK	HBOS	880,939,735
UK	Lloyds	512,139,220

The annual reports were studied and innovative features were highlighted in order to construct a ranking of banks on the basis of the importance given to innovation in their reports. The features were then quantified and weighted according to the importance assigned to the mention of financial innovation in the context of the annual report.

Annual reports were searched for the occurrence of any reference to financial innovation: for instance we looked for references to:

- the concept of 'innovation(s); innovating; innovator';
- the development and/or the launch of new products, services or processes;
- R&D activities and investments concerning financial innovation;
- organisational solutions such as the set-up of specific committees devoted to promoting, approving and monitoring financial innovation.

A subjective score was then attributed to such references according to the following criteria:

- a score equal to 1 if there was a *generic reference to innovation.* This category includes slogan-like messages not supported by a specific mention to the content of the innovation itself (such as new products and/or processes). Banks are thereby weakly communicating their interest in innovation;
- a score equal to 1.2 if the *reference is contextualised.* This category includes references which, though still not providing details or specific examples of the innovation itself, place it within a specific management or market context. The communication mode is therefore more articulated than the previous one: banks provide further information on the business area involved by the innovation;
- a score equal to 1.4 when a *precise and specific reference* to financial innovation can be uncovered. This category includes detailed references to the innovation developed and/or launched, such as the description of new products/services, the explanation of newly implemented processes, and the mention of new organisational solutions to promote financial innovation;
- a score equal to 1.5 when the reference to financial innovation is *located in strategic sections of the annual report.* Reporting in this category underlines the strategic importance of innovation for the bank. The relevance of financial innovation is communicated in the bank's mission statement, or in the business proposition, or in the chairman's statement or in other high-impact sections of the annual report, typically placed at the very beginning of the document. References here include paragraphs dedicated to the topic of innovation, which provide details of measures implemented by the bank, the target market, the economic impacts as well as any information regarding units or committees set up to manage and/or

monitor innovation, or referring to specific procedures developed in the area of innovation.

Following the above-mentioned approach, we were then able to construct an innovation index, as a sum of any score assigned, for each bank in each year under study. The adopted methodology undoubtedly presents some critical aspects relating to the fact that we concentrate on business communication via annual reports. Indeed, each year the bank management can choose which message should be emphasised in the annual report. Therefore, it may be that a very innovative bank chooses not to focus on financial innovation because it prefers to call attention to other issues. A second weakness relates to the potential for discriminating between 'true innovation', for example, creating new instruments, or 'imitating innovation', for instance, applying new instruments innovated by others . Annual reports are not informative on such issues, and any reference to innovation was considered as a reference to 'true innovation'.

Notwithstanding such potential biases, we believe that our index is adequately constructed to answer our research question, that is, whether financial innovation represents a relevant issue in banks' activity, at least in their business communication.

3 RESULTS OF THE QUALITATIVE ANALYSIS

Banking groups' annual reports for the years 2003, 2004, 2005 and 2006 were thoroughly examined to find evidence of interest in innovation. The analysis revealed main differences regarding the importance given to innovation in this form of market reporting.

Figure 2.1 shows the position of the sample banks in relation to the innovation index average for the 2003–06 period. As mentioned above, a variety of positions can be seen which range from those banks for which financial innovation is undoubtedly important, with references made for instance in the chairman's statement, the presentation of results for the period, the description of organisational structures of dedicated committees or work groups, to those which make only a passing reference to innovation such as at the launch of a product or on the introduction of new product delivery solutions.

By analysing the distribution of the innovation index, we are able to classify our sample banks into four main groups or clusters:

1. *banks strongly communicating innovation* (that is, banks with an innovation index equal or higher than the 85th percentile);

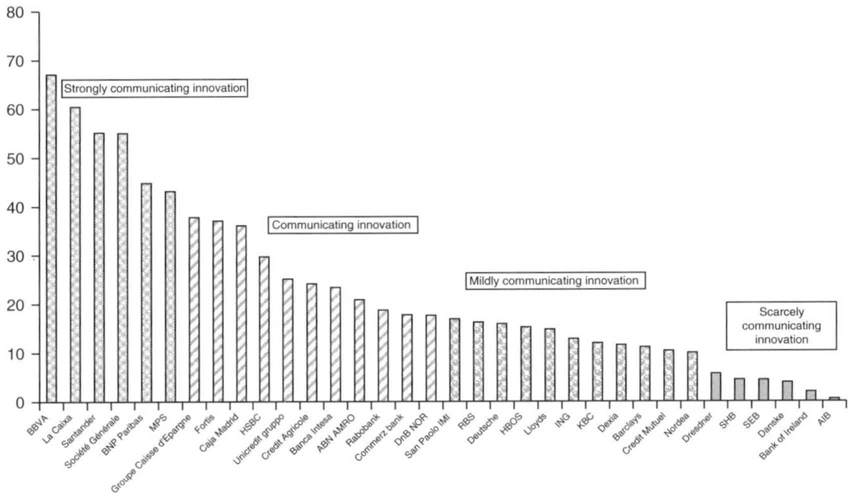

Figure 2.1 Innovation index distribution

2. *banks communicating innovation* (that is, banks with an innovation index between the 85th percentile and the median value);
3. *banks mildly communicating innovation (*that is, banks with an innovation index between the median value and the 15th percentile); and
4. *banks with scarcely any interest in communicating innovation* (that is, banks with an innovation index below the 15th percentile).

A first characteristic that emerges when analysing the composition of these clusters is the strong link between the nationality of the bank and its communicative strategy about its innovation activity. The dimension of the bank (measured by total assets in 2006) does not appear to be relevant (see Figure 2.2). Cultural elements, therefore, appear to be the primary factor in determining the attention given by banks to the issue of financial innovation in their annual reports. In particular, the two clusters particularly prone in communicating innovation mainly comprise banks from Mediterranean countries (Spain, France, Italy), while banks from the UK, Germany and Northern Europe in general make up the groups that are showing least interest in innovation.

At this stage, however, a logical doubt arises: does the handling of the issue of innovation in banks' annual reports accurately reflect its real role in groups' strategies or management policies, or is the emphasis on the value of innovation a mere window dressing aimed at raising levels of customer satisfaction? In fact, if 'innovation' is regarded as good, a bank

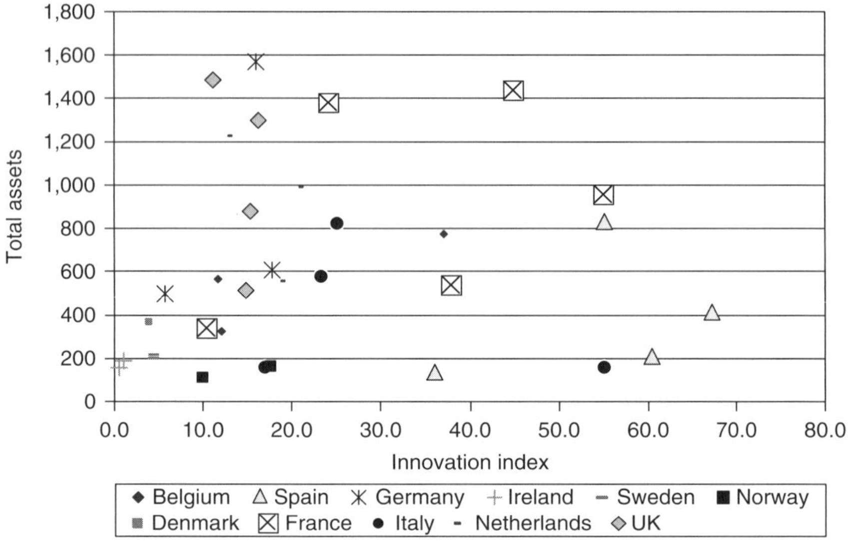

Figure 2.2 *Relationship among innovation index, total assets, and geographical factors*

may deliberately make many references to it even though it is not truly innovative at all.

Such a reasonable doubt appears unfounded since a large majority of 'strong communicators' have actually implemented measures that are consistent with their ranking. These measures include a range of organisational solutions such as: committees for the study of new products; work groups for evaluating innovation; committees for the evaluation, monitoring and management of banking risks with specific focus being devoted to innovation-related questions; manuals and procedures providing guidelines and support for the handling of innovation and change; human resource programmes designed to raise awareness among employees of the role of innovation and to encourage innovative proposals on the part of staff. BBVA, Santander and Société Générale[9] in particular are examples of banking groups that have implemented the organisational solutions listed above.

With regard to the areas targeted for innovation by banks belonging to the strong innovator segment, our research shows that attention to innovation is given in one form or another across all areas, thereby proving the strategic importance assigned to innovation. Some areas, nevertheless, appear to be given priority: in lending (mortgages, consumer credit, personal loans and credit cards); in asset management (savings management solutions, mutual funds and to a lesser extent pension funds). Innovation is also visible in banks' attempts to bolster deposit volumes with, for example, dedicated current account packages for certain market segments such as migrants, along with heightened attention to the value of customer relations.[10]

With regard to banks' corporate business, while traditional lending activities appear least affected by innovation, small and medium-sized enterprises (SMEs) have been the focus of innovation, particularly in the areas of payment services and risk management, the latter including hedging solutions for adverse changes in commodity prices. Overall, the most frequent targets for innovation appear to be retail customers and, to a lesser degree, SMEs. This does not apply, however, to French banking groups, some of which[11] are strongly focused on innovation in the areas of structured products and risk-management instruments.

Perhaps surprisingly, references to technology tend to be limited and e-banking solutions appear today to be an accepted part of banking activities even among technological pacesetters (Scandinavian banks, in particular) and are no longer viewed as being particularly innovative.

A further element that appears to confirm our finding that references to innovation do not solely serve as a marketing ploy can be found in the analysis and comments accompanying banks' income statements. In most cases a bank's competitiveness in terms of innovation is rewarded by higher productive volumes and increased profits, although higher R&D investments tied to the launch of new profits inevitably have an impact on costs.

Another element to be taken into account is reference to any industry awards a bank has received in recognition of its commitment to innovation. Such awards are more frequently mentioned by French banks, and to a lesser extent by banks from Spain and Italy, that is, from countries where, as previously stated, innovation is valued more. This confirms the importance assigned by Mediterranean countries to the communication of their policies towards innovation.

4 FINANCIAL INNOVATION, ASSET GROWTH AND PROFITABILITY: IS THERE A LINK?

In this section we investigate whether banks with an intense communicating activity in the area of financial innovation are better off in terms of performance and asset growth. The empirical research contained in the financial innovation literature has analysed the consequences of innovation both in terms of payoffs to the innovators and in terms of its impact on society as a whole. While the latter question has attracted a large number of studies (see Frame and White, 2004 for an excellent review), the empirical literature identifying gains from financial innovation in terms of operating or market performance for the 'innovating' financial institution is limited due to the absence of accessible data (see Tufano, 1989, 2003; Herrera and Schroth, 2003; Dew, 2006; Kumar and Turnbull, 2006; Lerner, 2006a, 2006b). While Tufano's results identify long-term payoffs in terms of cost advantages that allow innovators to capture more market share, according to Herrera and Schroth and Kumar and Turnbull, the innovating institution typically earns profits not by grabbing the entire market, but by expropriating the most profitable segments through a first-mover advantage based on expertise. In particular, Herrera and Schroth, studying the first-mover aspects of financial innovations in derivative markets, argue that innovators possibly enjoy a sustainable first-mover advantage as they learn how to structure a particular type of deal; repeating deals provides the innovator with more experience and the innovator can earn rents for a period before imitators learn how to structure similar deals eroding spreads. Similarly, Lerner suggests that the introduction of innovations is associated, on average, with increased profitability in the years after the product or process introduction, while Dew finds a positive link between innovative tendencies in financial intermediaries and their long-term market yields.

All empirical studies agree that innovators are able to enjoy a reputation for innovativeness which can produce capital gains through reputation effects.

The novel contribution of this study is the use of a unique dataset that identifies banks' attitudes towards innovation across time, and the level of information conveyed to market participants in order to understand to what extent an innovating attitude translates into greater asset growth and/or higher profitability and whether market participants discriminate between banks publicising their innovativeness and banks with a limited interest in communicating innovation.

As explained above, an innovation index is constructed which reflects the level of innovating behaviour as declared by our sample of banks in their annual reports.

By analysing the distribution of the innovation index, we are able to classify our sample of banks into four main groups or clusters (see Table 2.1).

Table 2.2 provides some accounting and financial description of our sample during the 2004–06 period.[12]

Banks strongly communicating innovation are better off in terms of operating performance: their return on assets (ROA) is well above that

Table 2.2 Clusters of banks and accounting information (mean values)

Cluster	Innovation index: cluster average	Change in total assets 2006–04 (%)	Change in ROA 2006–04 (% points)	ROA: average 2006–04 (%)	ROE: average 2006–04 (%)	Total assets: average 2006–04 (€m)	Cost–income: average 2006–04 %	Net interest revenue to operating income: average 2006–04 %
Strongly communicating innovation	54	13.94	0.34	0.79	15.02	590,368	59.63	49.76
Communicating innovation	26	19.75	0.08	0.66	14.20	609,167	62.50	53.32
Mildly communicating innovation	13	15.72	0.09	0.69	17.12	678,782	58.34	48.62
Scarcely communicating innovation	4	14.06	0.17	0.70	16.52	246,132	59.15	57.77

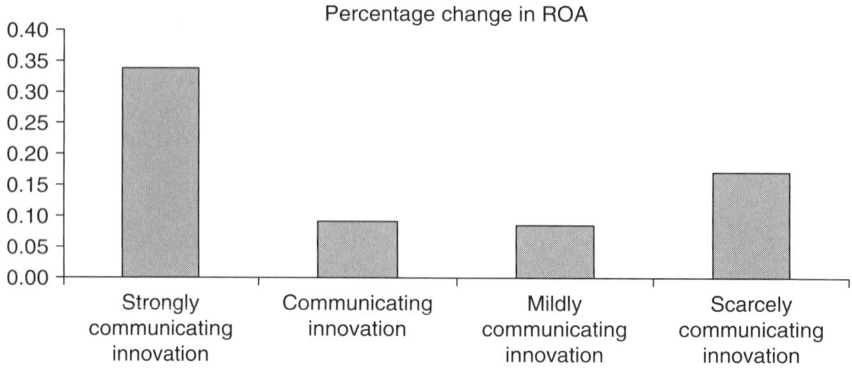

Figure 2.3 Clusters and profitability growth, 2004–2006

of other clusters and it grows at a faster rate (see Figure 2.3). The same does not hold true when measuring profitability with respect to equity. However, return on equity (ROE) is influenced by gearing and a bank's capital management policy. As a matter of fact, though not exempt from criticism,[13] ROA is the typical preferred measure of profitability which allows companies with different levels and types of gearing to be compared without having to consider the impact of balance-sheet and capital management.

As already highlighted, there is a weak association between size and the innovation index, although the least communicative cluster strikingly comprises the smallest banks in the sample. The result is in line with Dew's findings (2006) that it is not institutional size that matters in driving innovation. However, there is evidence of a positive link between an innovating tendency of individual banks and their asset growth, with the only exception being the strongly communicating cluster.

Innovations are expensive for the innovator, involving costs not incurred by imitators (Tufano, 1989, 2003), a tendency confirmed by the higher level of the cost–income ratio for the clusters of banks putting more emphasis on innovation.

To find out whether the relevance of innovation in the communication strategy is linked to operating or market performance, we run the following panel regression:

$$\text{Performance}_{i,t} = \alpha_i + \beta\,\text{II}_{it} + \delta\,\text{Controls}_{it} + u_{it}, \qquad (2.1)$$

where performance is either a bank's ROA or a bank's price to book value (P/BV) ratio; II is our innovation index and the control variables are the ones that are usually suspected of being connected to a bank's performance

Table 2.3 Innovation propensity and bank performance

	Dependent variable ROA	Dependent variable P/BV
Innovation index	0.003	–0.003
	(0.001)***	(0.003)
Log total assets	–0.09	–0.03
	(0.039)**	(0.10)
Cost–income ratio	–0.021	–0.04
	(0.003)***	(0.01)***
Net interest revenue to operating income	–0.001	–0.003
	(0.002)	(0.005)
Constant	3.08	4.99
	(0.58)***	(1.48)***
No. of observations	102	78
R^2	54.21%	26.94%
Hausman test (GLS estimator is consistent and efficient) Prob > χ^2	0.6916	0.1171

Note: Random effects generalised least squares (GLS) regression. Standard errors are in parentheses. ***, ** and * denote that the coefficient is statistically significant at the 1, 5 or 10 per cent levels, respectively.

and have proved significant in explaining the cross-sectional and time-series variation in ROA:

1. bank size, proxied by the logarithm of total assets;
2. cost structure, defined by the cost–income ratio; and
3. diversification, captured by the ratio of net interest revenues to operating income.

The sign and the significance of the coefficient β will highlight the existence, if any, of an association between a communication strategy of financial innovation and performance. A limited variability of each bank's innovation index across time, complemented by the result of the Hausman test, lead us to run a random effects panel regression. Table 2.3 shows the results of our investigation.

Along with a diversification strategy and a policy of cost control, levering on financial innovation brings about positive effects on ROA: the ratio is positively and statistically linked to our index of financial innovation.

Interestingly there is no positive (at least not statistically significant) relationship between market performance (as measured by the P/BV ratio) and the innovation index. The result is in line with previous literature which found that a weak association existed between innovation and the capitalisation of the market's perceived value of such innovation into the innovator's stock price (Tufano, 2003; Dew, 2006). In particular, Tufano finds that financial institutions' capital gains from innovation accrue over long periods, and therefore short-term measures of profitability, such as price movements at the innovation announcement or P/BV ratios, are unable to capture the investors' views about the value associated with the announced innovation. In sum, using Dew's words (2006, p. 10): 'the market is chary of awarding rents to announcements of financial innovation'.

5 CONCLUSIONS

Our empirical study analysed financial innovation by means of a unique measure of financial innovation that identifies banks' attitudes towards innovation according to the level of information conveyed to market participants in annual reports. On the basis of an 'innovation index', this study suggests that European banks put a different emphasis on financial innovation both in their strategies and in their operations.

Country-specific cultural factors are seemingly the best explanatory factors for such a diverse propensity in promoting a reputation for financial innovativeness and, in particular, a reputation as drivers of innovation in the real sector.

In Spain, France and to some extent Italy, a bank's aptitude towards financial innovation is deemed to positively drive its strategies and operations and, as such, it is often publicised in annual reports.

In Belgium and the Netherlands the results are mixed, with a preference for a modest transfer of information about financial innovation to stakeholders; in the other northern countries, communicating financial innovation is deemed irrelevant.

In light of the high banking automation and the widespread use of information and communication technology that these countries have long attained, it can be argued that financial innovation, in particular process and technology innovation, is included so much in banking operations and lending relationships that it no longer is an issue worth mentioning.

Another point of interest is the case of the Anglo-Saxon and German banks, which tend to reside in the cluster of banks 'mildly communicating innovation': their annual reports would rather mention 'growth', both on a national and international perspective, along with management soundness and cost control than linger on innovation issues. As a matter of fact, the terms 'growth', 'soundness' and 'cost control' are also frequently included in the mission and values of those banks more innovation-oriented;

however, German and British banks, so parsimonious in mentioning financial innovation, seem to regard innovation as an element of instability detrimental to their customers' interests.

Lascelles (2005) underlines the fact that British banks have moved too fast, thereby leaving their stakeholders behind. As a result, they are now more likely to face a problem with their reputations, which can be transformed into communication difficulties:

> [D]espite their new brashness, though, [British] banks still seem uncertain of their place in the world. There is a lack of sureness in their touch, a recurring insensitivity to customers' needs and public opinion which suggests that they are still, to an extent, inward-looking, more concerned with their internal process than their relationships with the outside world. They think of themselves – and want to be seen – as full-blooded commercial organisations, but their message is not really coming across. Their stakeholders – customers, government and even employees – still see them in mid-20th-century terms, as public duty-driven organisations who work for nothing. (p. 231)

Nonetheless the banking sector remains an industry where safety and stability are prized.

In fact, even the cluster of banks 'strongly communicating innovation' frequently refers to financial innovation in those sections of the annual report dedicated to risk management.

As already highlighted, several banks in the sample have set up organisational protections in the form of committees and procedures that are specifically finalised at *ex ante* evaluating and *ex post* monitoring the inherent risk associated with the supply of new products and services.

Past history and recent financial crises confirm that, notwithstanding the protections set up, flaws in the control systems and violations are always potentially possible; in addition, 'overstretched' financial innovations are an inherent part of the dynamics conducive to creating a crisis as the recent 'subprime crisis' clearly tells us. Hence, this often motivates the promotion of a business culture more oriented to operation and financial soundness than to innovation.

With regard to the effects that communication strategies related to financial innovation have on performance and asset growth, our results are mixed. While operating performance (ROA) is strongly associated with a bank's communicating attitude, market performance (P/BV) is not significantly linked to our innovation index. Two explanations stand out.

First, banks in general, and our sample banking groups in particular, are multiproduct firms competing for diverse market segments; these banks have also been major bidders in recent national and international merger and acquisition operations within the financial industry. Therefore, operating results, market performances and asset growth depend on a variety of factors hardly referable to the sole propensity towards financial innovation as declared in their annual reports.

Second, Dew's hypothesis (2006) that 'only internal innovations [that is, those not fully explained to the market] provide economic rent' could be confirmed. As the author points out, 'valuable innovations are hidden'. '[As such,] for outside observers, the secrecy leaves no direct way to determine whether these remaining innovations, completely internal to the institutions themselves exist' (p. 3).

In fact it is widely acknowledged that one of the major barriers to the study of financial innovation is the paucity of data on which to develop measures evaluating financial innovation. The abundant literature on manufacturing innovation is explained by the possibility of focusing on R&D spending and patenting as proxy of a firm's innovative attitude. On the contrary, financial institutions rarely report their R&D spending; similarly, up until very recently, financial patents have been rare.

As Frame and White (2004, p. 117) suggested, 'financial innovation is all around us – the plastic in our wallets, the new financial instruments listed in the daily financial pages, the now-ubiquitous automatic teller machines (ATMs)'; the most difficult thing to capture, however, is a multifacet phenomenon in one single measure. Our study represents an initial step towards the possibility of filling this gap in the financial innovation literature.

NOTES

1. This follows Llewellyn's (1992, p.15) approach which considers that 'The starting point to any analysis of financial innovation must be the financial system and its basic functions, for two reasons'. First, financial innovation is closely linked to how a financial system specifically works. Second, a financial innovation is such that it is able to increase the efficiency of the financial system as a whole.
2. For a map of the principal innovations and related drivers, see Anderloni (2004).
3. That is: (a) legal, accounting, regulatory and tax consultancy fees; (b) training of issuers, investors and traders; (c) dedicated pricing and trading information systems; (d) capital and human resources for market making activities; and (e) remuneration of groups set up to develop new financial products.
4. On the basis of interviews carried out with investment bankers responsible for the development of new products, Tufano estimates that first movers' development costs relating to new financial products range from $50,000 to $5 million, in addition to a fixed cost of $1 million in remuneration for the groups or units set up for product development.
5. Defined as 'the development of service products which are new to the supplier', that is, a relative concept has been adopted.
6. For further details and a review of the literature discussed, see Vermeulen and Dankbaar (2002).
7. For an overview of the literature on annual reports, see Lord (2002).
8. Regardless of ownership form, that is, private or cooperative.

9. However, the recent scandal involving Société Générale and its top management teaches that inappropriate behaviours can circumvent the lines of protection that an organisation can set up to deal with new risks and products.
10. Spanish banks tend to stand out in this area, Monte dei Paschi di Siena (MPS) is another example from Italy.
11. In particular, Société Générale and BNP-Paribas.
12. Longer time-series information is not available due to the introduction of the International Financial Reporting Standards (IFRS) in 2005.
13. In fact, ROA is influenced by the degree of a bank's off balance sheet activities (OBSAs), which may vary greatly from one bank to another.

REFERENCES

Anderloni, L. (1999), 'Tendenze evolutive nel sistema dei controlli', in Anderloni, L., Basile, I. and Schwizer, P. (eds), *L'innovazione finanziaria. Scenari, mercati, strumenti e implicazioni gestionali per gli intermediari*, Bancaria Editrice, Rome, pp. 13–16.

Anderloni, L. (2004), 'Introduzione. L'innovazione finanziaria: una tematica d'attualità?', in Anderloni, L. (ed.), *L'innovazione finanziaria. Corporate, investment e retail banking. Gestione del risparmio, mercati finanziari e previdenza,* Bancaria Editrice, Rome, pp. 19–37.

Bexley, J.B. and Hynes, G.E. (2003), 'Improving the understanding of banks' annual reports: a tool for improving investor relations', Proceedings of the 5th Association for Business Communication European Convention, Lugano, Switzerland, 29–31 May.

Dew, K. (2006), 'Why is the profitability of financial innovation so difficult to identify? Innovation clusters and productive opacity', Networks Financial Institute 2006-WP-12, Indiana State University.

Drew, S.A.W. (1995), 'Accelerating innovation in financial services', *Long Range Planning*, **28**(4), 11–21.

Frame, W.S. and White, L.J. (2004), 'Empirical studies of financial innovation: lots of talk, little action?', *Journal of Economic Literature*, **42**, March, 116–44.

Greenbaum, S.I. and Haywood, C.F. (1974), 'Secular change in the financial services industry', *Journal of Money, Credit and Banking*, **3**(2), May, 571–89.

Herrera, H. and Schroth, E. (2003), 'Profitable innovation without patent protection: the case of derivatives', ITAM Working Paper, Centro de Investigacion Economica, Av. Camino a Santa Teresa, 10700 Mexico.

Hynes, G.E and Bexley, J.B. (2003), 'Understandability of banks' annual reports', Proceedings of the 68th Association for Business Communication Annual Conference, Albuquerque.

Johne, A. and Harborne, P. (2003), 'One leader is not enough for major service development: results of a consumer banking study', *The Service Industries Journal*, **23**(3), 22–39.

Johne, A. and Storey, C. (1998), 'New service development: a review of the literature and annotated bibliography', *European Journal of Marketing*, **34**(3/4), 184–251.

Kane, E.J. (1984), 'Microeconomic and macroeconomic origins of financial innovation', in Federal Reserve Bank of St. Louis (ed.), *Financial Innovations, Their Impact on Monetary Policy and Financial Markets*, Papers from the seventh

annual economic conference, 1–2 October 1982, Federal Reserve Bank of St. Louis, Kluwer Academic, Boston, MA, pp. 3–20.
Kumar, P. and Turnbull, S.M. (2006), 'Patenting and licensing of financial innovations', Working Paper, CT Bauer College of Business, University of Houston, July, available at http://ssrn.com/abstract=917874.
Lascelles, D. (2005), *The Revolution in High Street Banking. Others People's Money*, Institute of Financial Services, London.
Lerner, J. (2006a), 'The new new financial thing: the origins of financial innovations', *Journal of Financial Economics*, **79**, 223–55.
Lerner, J. (2006b), 'Where does state street lead? A first look at finance patents, 1971–2000', *Journal of Finance*, **57**, 901–30.
Llewellyn, D. (1992), 'Financial innovation: a basic analysis', in Cavanna, H. (ed.), *Financial Innovation*, Routledge, London, pp. 15–51.
Lord, H.L. (2002), 'Annual reports: a literature review (1989–2001)', *Journal of Technical Writing and Communication Strategy*, **32**(4), 367–89.
Miller, M.H. (1986), 'Financial innovation: the last twenty years and the next', *Journal of Financial and Quantitative Analysis*, **21**, 459–71.
Miller, M.H. (1992), 'Financial innovation: achievements and prospects', *Journal of Applied and Corporate Finance*, Winter, 12–22.
Molyneaux, P. and Shamroukh, N. (1999), *Financial Innovation*, John Wiley, Chichester.
Roger, E.M. (1995), *Diffusion of Innovations*, 4th edn, Free Press, New York.
Silber, W. (1975), 'Towards a theory of financial innovation', in Silber (ed.), *Financial Innovation*, Lexington Books, Lexington, MA, pp. 1–3, 53–85.
Silber, W. (1983), 'The process of financial innovation', *American Economic Review*, May, 89–95.
Tufano, P. (1989), 'Financial innovation and first-mover advantages', *Journal of Financial Economics*, **25**, 213–40.
Tufano, P. (2003), 'Financial innovation', in Constantinides, G., Harris, M. and Stulz, R. (eds), *Handbook of the Economics of Finance*, North-Holland, Amsterdam, pp. 307–36.
Van Horne, J.C. (1985), 'Of financial innovation and excesses', *Journal of Finance*, **40**, 621–31.
Vermeulen, P. and Dankbaar, B. (2002), 'The organisation of product innovation in the financial sector', *The Service Industries Journal*, **3**, 77–98.

3. Microfinance, innovations and commercialisation

Reinhard H. Schmidt

1 THE MOTIVATION AND THE STRUCTURE OF THE CHAPTER

The Nobel Peace Prize of 2006 was awarded to the Grameen Bank in Bangladesh and its founder Professor Mohammad Yunus. What Yunus and his Grameen Bank – as well as a number of other microfinance institutions (MFIs) and their leaders – have achieved over the past 30 years not only deserves great respect for its political ambitions and its social and economic effects, but also has to be regarded as one of the most important and most interesting innovations in finance. Its hallmark is making credit and other financial services available to people who have so far not had access to formal finance. To use the expression coined by J.D. Von Pischke, these microfinance pioneers succeeded in 'shifting the frontier of finance' to territories into which formal financial institutions had so far not ventured to go.[1]

This chapter discusses microfinance as a financial innovation. A common classification distinguishes between product innovations, that is, doing new things, and process innovations, that is, doing certain things in a way not known or at least not used before. Microfinance as we know it today is the outcome of a combination of product and process innovations. Its most visible part is a product innovation: finance for the poor and especially for poor self-employed people.[2] However, a rapid succession of process innovations has made it possible for small loans to be offered to millions of people and for microfinance to now even attract the interest of private and institutional investors.

This chapter describes how microfinance has emerged over the last 30 years and highlights the innovations that have made this development possible. Section 2 provides some background information on microfinance that helps to put recent developments into perspective. Section 3 discusses those innovations of the 1990s that have shaped how MFIs operate today. Section 4 describes the most recent wave of innovations and the concerns these may raise. These innovations are summarised under the label of an increasing 'commercialisation of microfinance'. One particularly important aspect of commercialisation is the increasing role that debt and equity capital from purely commercial sources have recently started to play in microfinance. Some observers and experts who emphasise the social aspects of microfinance fear that what was formerly aid activity governed primarily by developmental considerations, may soon become the exclusive domain of commercial enterprises and be governed by purely commercial considerations.

2 SOME BACKGROUND ON MICROFINANCE

Definition and Illustrations of Microfinance

'Microfinance' is the generic name for all activities that are undertaken with the intention of improving the access of poor people to financial services. Apart from this, there is no generally accepted definition. This lack of a more formal definition is not surprising since the field has continuously undergone far-reaching transformations. Two decades ago, defining microfinance was easier than it is today. At that time, there were only a small number of specialised organisations that offered small and very small loans to poor borrowers whom the banks in the respective region would not consider as bankable, and the concept of microfinance corresponded largely to what these small MFIs were doing and how they were set up.

The early microcredit programmes were typically motivated by social and political considerations; they were often created and almost always funded by foreign public and private donors; they depended on subsidies; and not least for this reason, microfinance was clearly distinct from the activities of the banking sectors of the respective countries.

Some of the early microfinance programmes were successful in demonstrating that poor people needed small amounts of credit and were willing and able to repay their small loans; that these poor self-employed people could be identified and reached; and that small loans can have big effects on the situation of those who are fortunate enough to obtain a microloan. In view of the experience of the old development banks, these were important, new and certainly encouraging lessons.

Today, the boundaries between microfinance and conventional finance are blurred. The target population of MFIs has expanded to include not only the poor and even destitute and the owners of very small ('micro') businesses, but also those of small and even not so small businesses, so that it would be more precise to speak of small business finance or even neighbourhood finance. Moreover, since the costs of microlending are now much lower than they used to be, the institutions that now provide microfinance services include ones that have the formal status of a bank and cover the full costs of their operations. Microfinance methods are now even used by some banks that have traditionally not considered small businesses as their clientele.

In view of these transformations, it would not make sense to define microfinance on the basis of the features of what once was the dominant organisational form. Any narrow definition based on the characteristics of the institution that provides the services in question (for example, 'non-bank lending' or credit-granting by non-governmental organisations: NGOs), or on certain characteristics of the clients (for example, poverty-oriented lending or micro-enterprise lending), or on the services that are provided (for example, working capital finance) would create the wrong impression that small business lending by other than NGOs, or other financial services than lending, or the provision of financial services to persons other than poor self-employed people should not be covered by the definition of microfinance.

However, the difficulty of a precise definition does not imply that it would be misleading to let one's intuition be guided by the cases that are still typical for microfinance – a specialised institution providing small loans to relatively poor self-employed people – as long as one keeps in mind that this characterisation is not meant to draw a dividing line between something that is microfinance and something that is not.

The Origins of Microfinance and Its Place in Development Finance

As microfinance was first created as a tool of development policy, it is appropriate to show where it is located in the broader context of development finance, a concept referring to policies of foreign development aid institutions that aim to strengthen the financial systems of developing countries. Such policies have been devised and implemented since the early 1950s. In this subsection, we distinguish three phases of development finance and discuss how they are related to microfinance.[3]

In its first phase, which lasted until the mid-1970s, development finance consisted mainly in large-scale transfers of capital to developing countries to spur investment and growth. The underlying idea was to fill the presumed dual gap of insufficient local savings that could fund investment and of foreign exchange that could be used to buy machinery from industrialised countries. The providers of capital were international and national development organisations, and the local partner organisations were government-owned development banks that had been set up with the sole purpose of distributing the foreign funds to public and private investors.

Even though this approach to development finance was meant primarily to fund large-scale investment projects in industry and infrastructure, it was believed that it would also benefit the general public: the funding of large projects was assumed to increase ordinary people's incomes and thereby also induce small business investment, and thus to lead to a broad-based development. This is the concept of 'trickle down'. However, these indirect effects rarely materialised. Instead, economic dualism increased and social tensions mounted. The political and social effects of the first phase of development finance were largely negative.

In 1973, World Bank President Robert McNamara acknowledged the deficiencies of this approach and proclaimed 'the end of trickle down'. This started the second phase of development finance. Like the first one, it mainly consisted in a transfer of funds. However, it was now intended to channel development funds directly to the people whom they were supposed to benefit, that is, to poorer strata of the population of developing countries and even to really poor people and to the 'entrepreneurs of the informal sector'.

Transferring capital directly to poorer target groups required having suitable channels through which funds could flow and be distributed. They were not easy to find. Commercial banks were generally considered as not being suited for this role. They were not familiar with poor clients and their ways of doing businesses, and they were also not interested in serving this clientele since in most countries banks were not allowed to charge interest rates that would cover the presumed high costs of microlending. State-owned and government-related organisations were also not considered as appropriate channels since they were corrupt, inflexible and dependent on the dominant political powers that were all too often not fond of the new approach to development finance imposed by foreign donor organisations.

Around 1990, a consensus emerged that the best channel for development aid funds would be NGOs. The ideal NGOs seemed to be those organised and managed by socially conscious business people, since they were regarded as development minded and at the same time sufficiently business minded to understand the needs of the new clientele. Moreover, since NGOs are by design not profit oriented, many development experts expected that NGOs would not exploit the 'micro-entrepreneurs' but could rather support them in many respects and would even be capable of doing all of this in an efficient way.[4]

An additional factor that greatly facilitated new, seemingly fruitful, beginnings was a wave of measures to reform the financial systems in some parts of the world, especially in Latin America: capital flows were liberalised, interest rate restrictions were abolished and government influence was curtailed. These developments made it possible to try to implement the new policy on a large scale.

One of the main supporters of microfinance in Latin America was the Interamerican Development Bank (IDB), which had set up a huge programme to fund local credit-granting NGOs. However, the enthusiasm with NGOs did not last very long. A study commissioned by the IDB analysed the efficiency of those credit-granting NGOs that this bank regarded as its best partner institutions. The findings of this study were depressing.[5] With one exception, none of the NGOs that were analysed was able to cover its costs. Even for those NGOs which portrayed themselves as being efficiency oriented, total costs per year were almost as high as their outstanding loan volumes. Moreover, with loan portfolios of less than US$3 million even the largest NGO credit programmes were so small that cost coverage could hardly be achievable and their impact was minimal at best. The financial and developmental performance of NGO credit programmes was in no way better than that of government-related programmes and the earlier microfinance programmes.

These findings suggested that merely using NGOs as a channel for development funds would not solve the problem of how poor people and the owners of small businesses could be given access to financial services. This insight was the starting-point of the third phase of development finance, which still dominates policies and practices in microfinance. What was needed and looked for were ways of transforming NGOs and other MFIs into efficient and financially viable institutions, of making them independent of permanent foreign subsidies, and of allowing them to grow considerably. Institution building and an astute commercial orientation of MFIs were to become the highest priority and the hallmark of the third phase of development finance that came into full force in the 1990s. However, in spite of this reorientation on a practical level, it was always maintained that the ultimate objective of microfinance is to improve the economic and social conditions of 'ordinary people'. Institution building and a strict 'commercial approach'[6] are not more than means to achieve this developmental objective.

Microfinance as a Network of Incentive Problems

By the middle of the 1990s, it was already clear what the most important building blocks of successful microfinance were. At least on a conceptual level experts were well aware that:

1. the core business of MFIs is lending to people who have so far not had access to formal financial institutions and their services;
2. microfinance presupposes the existence of MFIs that are financially stable and efficient organisations; and
3. MFIs need to have owners in the sense of people who are responsible for the operations and the survival of the MFIs and who subscribe to the concept of a 'dual bottom line', that is, the coexistence and equal importance of financial and developmental objectives.

But it had also become increasingly evident that behind each one of these building blocks a serious incentive problem was hidden. If they really wanted to have a lasting and beneficial effect, MFIs would have to understand and solve these incentive problems. Moreover, they would have to understand how the three incentive problems are related to one another.

The first building block refers to lending, and the first incentive problem is grounded in the fact that nobody who has borrowed money would 'like' to repay the loan, and the legal means of enforcing loan repayments from poor borrowers are weak or even non-existent in most developing countries. That makes small business lending difficult, risky and costly. The challenge for any MFI therefore consists in finding ways of lending to poor people at terms that ensure high repayment rates and allow for cost coverage of the MFI. Therefore, MFIs must provide strong incentives for their borrower clients to repay their loans fully and on time. Appropriate lending techniques and great caution in defining credit terms that avoid overborrowing and putting too much of a burden on the clients are necessary but not sufficient to make them repay their loans. In addition, an MFI must demonstrate to its clients that prompt and full repayment is also in their own interest because it allows them to maintain a good standing with the MFI as their 'house bank'. This requires that the MFI strictly insists on repayment, sanctions non-repayment and payment delays and rewards good repayment performance with better terms for repeat loans. Even more important, an MFI must make it crystal clear that it will still be there to grant future loans if a client later comes back and asks for a second or third loan. Thus financial viability and even profitability and a strict commitment to the same target group and to the dual objectives of financial and developmental success are essential for repayment discipline.

The second building block refers to the current operations of an MFI. Because of the specific difficulties of lending to small businesses that conventional banks do not consider as bankable, loan officers need to have a great deal of freedom to make decisions and at the same time they have an enormous responsibility for their decisions and actions. To do their difficult job well, they need to be given strong incentives. One instrument to create incentives can be performance-based pay in accordance with a fair and transparent reward system that makes bonuses conditional on the repayment of the loans which the loan officer has originated and for which she or he is responsible. But there must be more. Loan officers also need the assurance that the lending policy of the MFI is such that if they do their work carefully and diligently they can count on being paid well, enjoying long-term employment and possibly also gaining promotion within the MFI. This in turn requires that it is clear and visible to everybody, including the borrower-clients and the loan officers themselves, that the MFI is not only a temporary creation born out of the illusions of some development bureaucrats working in an office in Washington, London or Frankfurt. Loan officers must see that their MFI is stable and profitable and able to grow, to offer employment and advancement opportunities for them and repayment incentives for the borrowers. This message can only be conveyed credibly if the MFI is indeed stable, profitable and growing.

In an MFI that is likely to break down under the burden of its costs and loan losses, borrowers will very soon stop repaying on time or repaying at all, and loan officers will start granting loans as favours to their friends and relatives and not care about the punctual and full repayment of the loans they have granted.

The third building block refers to the ownership of the MFI. The crucial question here is who 'owns' an MFI in the sense of being responsible for its stability and its continuing existence and growth as well as its lasting target group orientation. This economic ownership role may be connected with the legal status of being an owner, but this need not be the case; there are also de facto owners without an ownership title in the legal sense. They may have a formal role of a trustee or a board member, or they may be the founder and leader of an MFI.

Here we also encounter a serious incentive problem, since it is far from evident who should have the incentives – and the competence – to perform the difficult and burdensome functions of acting as a responsible owner. It may be the most urgent problem in microfinance that in many MFIs there is a lack of ownership. In the case of a donor-funded credit-granting NGO this problem is particularly acute because strictly speaking NGOs do not have owners and at the same time those who have the role of leading an NGO are expected to use other people's money, namely that of donor institutions, to provide services in the interests of yet another group of stakeholders, namely the clients of the MFI. The incentives for abusing power are strong and those for properly using it are weak. Proper use means in particular to ensure that an MFI is sufficiently cost-conscious and profit oriented to survive as an economic organisation and at the same time sufficiently developmentally and socially oriented to serve and benefit its clients. There are reasons to fear that de facto owners coming from development bureaucracies such as a donor institution or from the 'civil society' might not feel sufficiently responsible for the commercial success. This would argue for private ownership. However, there is also the fear that private owners might merely follow their own financial interest and disregard the social and developmental mandate of microfinance. As recent developments that will be discussed below illustrate, an answer to the question of who the ideal owner of an MFI would be, has so far not been found.[7]

The incentive problems concerning loan repayment by the borrowers and the work ethic of loan officers, and the incentive problem that no individual and no institution might have a sufficiently strong motivation to perform an ownership function and to use an ownership role for working towards achieving the dual objective of financial and developmental success, are intimately intertwined. A lack of responsible and competent ownership is a source of problems not only because it leads to a lack of control of the MFI management, but also because it soon becomes visible to anyone who has eyes to see, and then undermines the repayment incentives of the borrowers and the work incentives of the loan officers and other staff members. At the same time, declining repayment rates and increasing problems with staff members may negatively affect the incentives of those who have, for whatever reasons, agreed to perform some of the owner function.

However, there can also be a positive feedback: good repayment and a dedicated staff can strengthen the incentives of those in an ownership role to like this role and to perform their function with dedication, and good leadership and dedicated owners tend to strengthen repayment and work incentives for the reasons explained above.

3 INNOVATIONS IN MICROFINANCE: THE LONGER-TERM PERSPECTIVE

As pointed out in the introduction, the development of microfinance has been shaped by a sequence of innovations. This section provides a short overview of the most important innovations that have occurred in the 1990s and have largely determined how microfinance organisations and projects are now operating. These innovations refer to almost all aspects of the business of MFIs. The section starts by briefly discussing innovations in the core activity, which is still lending, and then covers innovations in the fields of product design and product range (of MFIs), project design and institutional design. Innovations concerning the financing of MFIs are dealt with in the next section.

Innovations in Microfinance Lending

Lending money to borrowers who have no balance sheets to present and no conventional loan collateral to pledge, and who often pursue business activities that are difficult to understand poses formidable problems. The unfortunate experience of the traditional development banks[8] made experts fear that loan default rates in microfinance might be very high and make it simply impossible to keep a microfinance project or programme alive for a long time. The reasons seem obvious: lenders find it difficult to assess the creditworthiness of poor borrowers, borrowers have a strong motive not to repay their loans, and all in all microlending is very costly. The first challenges for the new MFIs consisted in finding ways to overcome these information, incentive and cost problems of microlending. Innovations of the 1980s and the 1990s helped to solve this problem. They consisted in devising new lending technologies.

The best-known credit technology in microfinance – and the one that less well-informed observers still consider to be the hallmark of microfinance – is group lending. It is a method that relies on the mechanisms of social cohesion and social pressure. In a group lending programme, the MFI and its staff first establish groups of people who know and are socially close to one another, who need small loans, who trust and support one another and who might even provide guarantees for the loans granted to the other group members.[9]

Group lending adapts certain elements of informal finance. Its use by an institution that is part of the modern economy of its country was clearly an innovation when it was first introduced by Grameen Bank in rural Bangladesh and by others who tried to replicate the model in different parts of the world. Among others, the influential microfinance support organisation ACCION seems to have encouraged its affiliates for years to use what they call the 'solidarity group approach' for lending to borrowers from the slums of big cities in Latin America.

In principle, group lending is suited to overcoming the problems of lending to poor people described above, and it seems to function well in certain environments that are characterised by strong social cohesion and limited mobility. For some time, it was even advocated so strongly that one could have believed that group lending was the only feasible microcredit technology for really poor borrowers, and in any event group lending was the dominant approach to microlending until the mid-1990s.

However, the dominance of group lending was challenged early on by MFIs which believed that it would be better to lend to individuals and not to groups, and that forcing potential borrowers to join a credit group is an objectionable policy. One of the dissenters was Unit-DESA, a large

MFI in Indonesia that was set up as a division of a big state-owned bank;[10] others included a number of MFIs that were associated with Internationale Project Consult (IPC), a German consulting firm that has been specialising in microfinance support since the mid-1980s.

When it was introduced into microfinance in Latin America in the early 1990s, individual-based lending to equally small business clients as those served by the ACCION affiliates also appeared to be a bold and risky innovation. Of course, MFIs that employed individual-based lending also had to find ways of overcoming information, incentive and cost problems. They did this, among other things, by developing new methods of credit assessment and of rewarding good repayment performance, and by making their institutions strong, reliable and attractive partners for their clients with whom they wanted to remain in good standing.

For some time, the controversy between the advocates of group and individual-based lending seemed to be a matter of faith and almost religion, reflecting very different approaches to development finance and microfinance. Today, this 'battle' is almost over. Even most of ACCION's affiliates have by now adopted the individual-based lending technology which seems to be more in line with the commercial approach advocated by ACCION than group lending. There are still a number of MFIs that rely on group lending, and Grameen is still their flagship,[11] but they are now a clear minority. Which technology prevailed was something like a market test. It was won by the individual-based lending technology, not because the cost and repayment figures achieved by the really good MFIs that use different credit technologies differ a great deal, but rather because the clients have a clear preference for being treated as responsible individuals and not merely as members of a group.

Innovations in Product Design and Product Range

Almost all MFIs started by only offering credit to their clients. Once they had learned that long-term lending was too risky and that the preferred target group indeed needs short-term or working capital loans more than longer-term loans, they started to offer a standard type of a small and short-term loan with frequent repayment intervals. By now, the format of available loans for small and very small businesses is much more variable.

Loans are not the only financial product that poor people need and demand. In fact, it seems almost self-evident that many of them need and want facilities to save money and to transfer resources from one time period to another even more than they want loans. This is why savings are no longer 'the forgotten half' of microfinance.[12] The provision of deposit and savings facilities has by now become a second service offered by most

MFIs to their clients, at least of those that have the licence to take client deposits.

In the mid- to late 1990s, many MFIs greatly expanded the range of products they offered, reflecting the fact that poor people also demand housing improvement loans, agricultural loans, 'micro-insurance' and payment facilities. The widening of the scope of services offered by MFIs is another important innovation that goes hand in hand with the transformation of former credit-granting organisations into real small people's banks.

Innovations in Project Design

We now turn to innovations in the way foreign support for microfinance is organised. Seen from the perspective of a donor organisation, development aid activity has always taken the form of 'a project'. A project comprises all those measures deemed necessary and used to reach a certain well-defined objective. By definition, a project is temporary; it has an end, or it should at least have an end, whereas the outcome of a project may be, and often also is, something permanent. For example, for the IDB and the German development agency GTZ, the activities with which these organisations supported the creation of the Bolivian MFI Caja Los Andes in the early 1990s were projects. As such they ended about 10 years ago. In contrast, the MFI that has been created is by now Bolivia's largest. Innovations in project design consist in devising and implementing new project types.

Before 1985, the available set of project types in the area of development finance was limited. There were financial assistance projects that consisted in granting one or two lines of credit to a so-called partner institution, and technical assistance projects which meant in most cases that an expert in some technical matter would be sent to the partner institution for a limited time and with a precise mandate. In the early years of microfinance, this narrow concept of 'a project' still prevailed. But this was soon to change – and in a fundamental way.

The first important innovation in project design occurred in the early 1990s. At that time, the conventional support of credit-granting NGOs had already lost much of its appeal to some development aid organisations. These organisations had reconsidered their former verdict of banks and had come to the conclusion that it might be good to create entities that would serve the target group of microfinance, use the strengths of an NGO and also have some of the positive aspects of a 'real bank'. Inspired by some external advisers[13] the aid agencies started to devise a new type of microfinance project called 'upgrading'.

Upgrading is a two-stage project. During the first stage, an existing NGO is strengthened and reformed in such a way and to such an extent that it can, in the second phase, be transformed into a licensed finance company or a bank that specialises in providing a broader set of financial services to many more clients of the type the NGO has formerly served. The second step, that of institutional transformation, includes activities such as finding shareholders that will contribute equity for the new institution, founding a corporation as the legal entity that will run the banking business, obtaining a banking licence from the relevant authorities, transferring assets and staff to the new legal entity, and much more. The characteristic feature of an upgrading project is that the two steps are closely coordinated. In other words, institutional strengthening is a precursor of institutional transformation.

Upgrading is a complex project type and the results of using it are mixed in practice. Even though some of the most successful MFIs in Latin America have grown out of upgrading projects, the total number of former NGOs that have been transformed to become formal financial institutions is surprisingly small[14] and certainly much smaller than advocates of the concept of upgrading had originally assumed. One reason for the limited success of this innovation in project design is that the number of NGOs that would be suitable for being upgraded is small. There are also only very few support or advisory organisations that have the expertise to implement an upgrading project.[15] Moreover, some of the institutions that could be promising candidates for upgrading are dominated by leaders who do not want a transformation of 'their' institution for very personal reasons: it would deprive them of their status and power since they might not qualify as a top manager or president of a licensed bank or they would have to share power and prestige with others.

The next innovation in project design was in part a reaction to the limited potential of upgrading as a new project type. Based on the insight that banks have certain advantages over NGOs and given that an appropriate lending technology for micro and small business lending had been sufficiently tested in the early 1990s, development aid agencies in America and Europe[16] started to design and support yet another innovative project type called 'downscaling'. A downscaling project consists in supporting the introduction of micro and small business lending at existing banks that have so far not served micro, small and medium-sized enterprises.[17] It typically involves a (foreign) donor agency, an experienced consultant with expertise in microlending and institution building, and a set of local partner banks. It functions like this: the development agency hires a competent consultant to identify existing banks that are suited and willing to develop a capacity in small and micro-business lending. The consultant then teaches the banks and their staff how to grant very small, small and mid-sized loans successfully and helps them to set up small business departments. In addition, the development agency offers attractive lines of credit to the participating banks to refinance their small business loans, so that they can adopt and test the new financial technology with limited risk and limited investment.

Some downscaling projects in Eastern Europe and Asia have been surprisingly successful. However, the problem with this project type is that the new clients, the owners of small businesses, have never been regarded as particularly important clients by the top management of the banks that participate in a downscaling project. Therefore, the newly created micro and small business units have rarely had a lasting effect and almost never enjoyed the full support from top management that they would have needed and that they might get in a specialised bank.

Even though upgrading and downscaling projects are ultimately meant to expand the supply of small and very small loans and other financial services to a clientele that has so far not had access to formal financial services, in practice these two project types are mainly focused on strengthening existing partner institutions. Much time and effort needs to be spent on overcoming the resistance from within these partner institutions. Since time and energy are limited, they cannot be dedicated to working directly towards the ultimate objective of expanding the scale and scope of the services supplied to the clients and of building an institution that is exclusively designed for this purpose. First transforming existing institutions and putting those dominating these institutions at ease may appear like a detour if it is regarded from the viewpoint of the target group.

The insight gained acceptance in the late 1990s and led to yet another innovative project type, namely that of so-called 'greenfield investments' in micro- and small-business banks. A greenfield project consists in directly creating a formal, licensed bank for 'small people' from scratch without first taking the often cumbersome and time-consuming steps of strengthening an existing institution.

In a typical greenfield project, a so-called project sponsor first determines whether there is a need for a small and micro-finance bank in a given country and whether there is a chance of achieving financial self-sufficiency of such a bank within a time span of two to four years. Then three groups of partners that are necessary for such a project need to be identified.

These three partners are: (i) potential investors and future shareholders, (ii) a so-called technical implementer, that is, a consultant or a support organisation that would have the role of creating the bank and of getting it up and running, and (iii) aid organisations that would provide some start-up assistance in the form of a subsidy for the first years and offer lines of credit to start the lending operations. In most practical cases, the set of investors includes development aid agencies such as the International Finance Corporation (IFC), the private sector arm of the World Bank, and the EBRD, national aid agencies such as Germany's Kreditanstalt für Wiederaufbau (KfW) and the Dutch FMO, and possibly also private investors. Start-up subsidies and lines of credit are in most cases also provided by some of the aid agencies or by others such as US-AID, that consider the creation of small and micro-business banks as part of their development mandate.

The two most important roles in any greenfield investment project are (a) that of the project sponsor who has to find the necessary partners and make them agree to join forces, and (b) that of the technical implementer who has to get the bank up and running. The project sponsor can in principle be one of the aid organisations. However in most cases, this role has been taken on by the technical implementers, that is, by private microfinance support and advisory organisations. Thus, the innovations in project design described in this subsection reflect a continuous process of a shift of initiative from the public development agencies to private actors.

4 COMMERCIALISATION AS THE RECENT FOCUS OF INNOVATIONS IN MICROFINANCE

Aspects and Forms of Commercialisation

The most recent wave of innovations in microfinance refers to various aspects of microfinance that are rightly discussed under the common label of 'commercialisation'. Indeed, there is now a trend towards commercialisation of microfinance that has three different aspects. Generally speaking, this trend should be welcomed since it offers the chance of making the services of formal financial institutions available to many more people than in the past. However, commercialisation is not as unambiguously positive as it may appear, and it is not even clear what the term really refers to. We therefore start this section by distinguishing and briefly discussing three concepts of a commercialisation of small and micro-enterprise finance.

The first concept is that of MFIs becoming more concerned about their costs and the financial results of their operations than they were in the past. Commercialisation in this sense has implications for how MFIs are designed and managed. This concept is not as new as it may seem. Already in the early 1990s, a few experts had pointed out that microfinance can only have the social and developmental effect its advocates expect if MFIs could reach a large number of clients and serve them over a long period.

This presupposes that they adopt a commercial orientation. Over the years, it has been increasingly accepted that this form of commercialisation is necessary and clearly welcome.[18]

In 2002, Deborah Drake and Elizabeth Rhyne from ACCION published *The Commercialisation of Microfinance*. In general, the book reflects a favourable view of commercialisation. But by adding the subtitle *Balancing Business and Development* its editors acknowledged that commercialisation not only offers opportunities but also raises concerns. One such concern is that too much emphasis on commercial success might make MFIs lose their focus on poverty alleviation and development. In their contribution to this book, the two leaders of ACCION at that time pointed out that it would be an important role of development-oriented institutions such as ACCION and of international financial institutions (IFIs) such as the IFC to make sure that such a loss of development focus does not happen. They argue that it is one of the reasons why these organisations should be shareholders in commercially oriented MFIs specifically in order to ensure a lasting developmental orientation of these MFIs.[19]

A second use of the term 'commercialisation' refers to the role of strictly profit-oriented financial institutions in microfinance and in particular to their entry into what was formerly the exclusive domain of specialised MFIs.

The positive examples of commercialisation in this sense are a number of banks in Eastern Europe, Latin America and Asia that have recently started to provide financial services to the target population of traditional MFIs, thus putting into practice what was described above as the intention behind the downscaling projects.[20]

However, not all cases of commercial bank entry into the market for small loans are as positive as they may appear. An early experience was that of Spanish and Chilean consumer finance organisations 'invading' the microfinance market in Bolivia. The aggressive consumer lending strategy deployed by these institutions undermined the educational work that a number of MFIs had successfully undertaken there with their consistent focus on micro-business lending and of insisting on repayment discipline. The 'invaders' followed a different business model that led to overindebtedness of borrowers, high default rates for themselves as well as for the established Bolivian MFIs, and ultimately to a violent revolt of the over-indebted borrowers.[21]

Current events in Mexico give reason to expect similar things happening there. As *Business Week* reported in a series of articles in 2007, new purely financially motivated players including some large international banks have recently entered the market for small and very small loans (see, for example, Epstein and Smith, 2007). They seem to 'sell' loans without taking borrowers' repayment capacity into account. This raises default rates, an effect that consumer lenders accept as part of their business model and which they compensate for by charging very high interest rates. Current interest rates on very small loans offered by commercial banks and others in Mexico are even higher than seems warranted by high default rates. That a loan default may imply severe personal hardship for a borrower and her or his family does not seem to bother these lenders. Nor does it seem to matter for them that their strategies make the operations of serious small business lenders all the more difficult since they are also affected by higher default rates. Therefore current events in Mexico should not be misunderstood as the late but welcome entry of commercial banks into the domain of small business lending, but rather need to be seen as an unhealthy mixture of irresponsible lending and plain and simple exploitation of poor people.

The third concept of commercialisation refers to an increasing role of private capital in the refinancing of MFIs and their operations and ultimately also in the ownership of MFIs. The successes of a small number of financially stable and profitable MFIs that were created in the late 1990s[22] lead a number of observers to believe that microfinance is also good for private and institutional investors from advanced countries, as Deutsche Bank Research has recently argued in its 'Microfinance: an emerging investment opportunity' (2007). Private investment in 'mature' MFIs[23] on a large scale is clearly an important innovation and it is going to be even more important in the years to come.

This concludes our overview of the three concepts and current trends of commercialisation. While the first is hardly controversial any more, and the second is likely to remain of limited importance for some time to come, the third concept of a 'liability-side-related commercialisation' is the most important innovation in microfinance. Therefore, in the remainder of this section we shall examine how the involvement of private capital changes the practice of microfinance. We begin by discussing commercial debt financing and then turn to commercial sources of equity.

The Refinancing of MFIs

In purely quantitative terms, the most important source of 'commercial' refinancing of those MFIs that have achieved full profitability, are local retail deposits. They have been important for UNIT-DESA, Bank Rakjat Indonesia's (BRI) highly successful microfinance division, since its very beginning in the early 1980s. Also for credit unions, deposit taking has always been important, not least as deposits can finance loans. For Grameen Bank and ASA, the two largest MFIs in Bangladesh, and the small and microenterprise banks in the ProCredit network, the role assigned to deposits as a source of financing has greatly increased over the past years. Correspondingly, the role of donor funding with grants and soft loans has decreased in relative terms.

In addition to local deposits, other forms of debt financing from commercial sources and on commercial terms have gained importance in recent years. The first step of using quasi-commercial funding consisted in MFIs taking out large loans from IFIs such as KfW, the EBRD or the IDB on purely commercial terms in contrast to the former soft loans. The subsidy element inherent in these quasi-commercial loans can be seen in the fact that at the end of the last century, purely commercial financing for MFIs from other sources would simply not have been available. The second – 'more commercial' – source is funding from other banks in the respective countries. A growing number of MFIs are now in a position to obtain interbank loans, and in a few cases, for example that of some ProCredit banks in Southeast Europe, MFIs have even been able to issue bonds on their local markets and in local currency that were bought by local institutional investors. A particularly noteworthy development are cases of securitisation of small and microloan portfolios, such as that organised by Deutsche Bank for ProCredit Bulgaria in 2006, the first true sale securitisation of its kind in Eastern Europe by that time.[24]

Because of the risk distribution between debt and equity, debt financing is the easier case. Commercial equity financing of MFIs constitutes the most recent and most fascinating innovation in the field discussed here. Since the more advanced MFIs are now no longer NGOs operating outside of the reach of banking regulation, they are subject to the normal capital requirements for banks according to the Basle Rules. As the loan portfolios of most MFIs grow at a rapid pace of around 30 per cent per year, capital requirements increase in parallel. Therefore, procuring equity is a serious problem and possibly a constraint to MFI growth.

From where do MFIs obtain equity, who are the owners or shareholders of MFIs, to what extent are they commercial investors, and what are the factors that attract private and institutional investors to microfinance?

Up to now, equity financing of modern regulated MFIs has in most cases taken place with the active involvement of both public and private investors. The public investors are the 'usual suspects' that have for a long time played an active role in supporting microfinance by providing technical assistance and lines of credit. They include international donor institutions such as the IFC, regional development banks such as the IDB or the EBRD and national development banks from industrialised countries such as Germany's KfW and US-AID. The 'private' side is typically composed of specialised microfinance investment vehicles (MFIVs) such as

ProFund or AfriCap or ProCredit-Holding. There are also a few examples of individual private investors in microfinance banks such as the German Commerzbank, but so far these are rare exceptions.

Typically, the private MFIVs have been set up by microfinance support organisations such as ACCION or IPC to help MFIs obtain equity and to strengthen their own influence on the MFIs they helped to create. ACCION has greatly contributed to the spreading of modern microfinance in Latin America since the late 1970s; IPC is a private consulting firm based in Frankfurt, Germany, that has played a similar role since the mid-1980s in Latin America, in Southeast Europe and recently in Africa. Disregarding the special case of the large Asian MFIs, these two institutions have for a long time been the industry leaders and the most influential innovators in the area of modern, commercially oriented microfinance. In most cases, these sponsors of the MFIVs are also important shareholders in the investment vehicles they have set up. Other private shareholders include development-oriented organisations with a religious affiliation, a few private banks and some specialised investment funds. In the next subsection, we shall present the case of ProCredit, the largest institution of its type,[25] in some detail.

A special case of drawing private capital into the microfinance business is the sale of profitable MFIs to a private bank. Three years ago, this occurred in Russia where KMB, a successful small and microenterprise bank, was sold by its public and presumably development-oriented owners to a private bank. KMB had been created by the EBRD in the course of the Russian debt crisis of 1998. Its original function had been to continue and in fact rescue the EBRD-supported activities of the so-called Russia Small Business Fund, a very large downscaling programme that had been operating in the entire country and come under pressure during the crisis, when many of its former partner banks defaulted and the Fund barely survived. In 2005, KMB was the single most active partner bank of the revived Russia Small Business Fund and the largest bank catering to small and very small businesses in the country. Its main shareholders were the EBRD and the Soros Development Fund. In 2002, these shareholders started to look for a buyer and finally decided to sell out to the Italian bank INTESA. It was rumoured that the price paid was 400 per cent of KMB's book value. One of the questions that this profit-driven sale raises is to what extent the new owner will stick to KMB's difficult-to-serve traditional target group of small and very small businesses or rather become a consumer lender. This concern seems even more relevant in the case of the recent sale of an MFI in Mozambique that had been built up with considerable donor funding during two decades. The MFI has been sold to a consumer lender organisation from South Africa.

Microfinance Investment Vehicles: the Case of ProCredit

ProCredit is a network of 22 micro- and small business banks in Latin America, Southeast Europe and Africa. It was created by IPC as a commercial corporation in the form of a joint stock company under German law in 1998. IPC itself is a private consultant firm specialised in creating and supporting MFIs in different parts of the world. It has set up a system of municipal savings banks in Peru in the 1980s, then helped to build up two of the best-known MFIs in Bolivia (formerly Caja Los Andes) and El Salvador (formerly Calpiá), which were later converted into formal small and micro-business banks and are now the largest organisations of their kind in the respective countries. In the mid-1990s, IPC managed several large downscaling projects in Russia and other countries in the former Soviet Union. Through these projects, IPC earned the reputation of being more concerned than probably any other development consulting firm to make its partner organisations achieve both scale and financial sustainability. Through its projects, IPC demonstrated that it is possible to meet the dual objectives of financial and developmental success and thereby contributed in an important way to the current wave of innovations and commercialisation.

The Dayton Peace Accord that ended the war in Bosnia-Herzegovina stipulated that a microfinance bank was to be created in this war-torn country. IPC was contracted by the designated shareholders of this bank to set it up. Some of the other investors requested that, as a means to strengthen its incentives, IPC also take over a share of the new bank's equity. This arrangement was successful, and this positive experience led to the idea of making the financial involvement of the consultant a model to be replicated in other countries of the region. However, IPC's own financial resources were not enough for the investment that seemed necessary. Therefore IPC and some other private organisations founded what is now ProCredit-Holding (PCH) as an MFIV. The second-largest investor besides IPC was the Dutch DOEN Foundation. The initial equity of PCH was only slightly more than €600,000.

IPC as the technical partner and PCH as the strategic investor soon created a number of other microfinance banks. With only a few exceptions, these were newly founded banks or greenfield investments and not upgrading cases or acquisitions. Initially, PCH held only a minority share in these banks. The other shareholders in the new banks were the usual set of IFIs. In several cases Commerzbank also became a shareholder. The newly created small and microfinance banks were managed by IPC staff under a management contract. The IFIs provided technical assistance funding and lines of credit, first on preferential terms and later on only on purely commercial terms. In most cases, the newly founded banks achieved cost coverage after two years and were profitable after their third year of operation. Interest rates were – and still are – at the lower end of those charged by professional MFIs, that is, in the range between 15 and 30 per cent. Average loans were – and still are – below €1,000 in Africa, around €1,000 in Latin America and €4,000 in Southeast Europe. Loan losses were – and still are – around 1 per cent per year.

The wave of investments undertaken by PCH required a considerable increase in its own equity. Around the turn of the century, several of the IFIs that were also shareholders in the banks also became shareholders in PCH. The capital and the equity investment portfolio of PCH grew rapidly, funded by a succession of capital increases at the level of both the individual banks and the holding company, and a strict policy of retaining profits to finance expansion. After two years, PCH started to be profitable, though no dividends have been distributed before 2007.

In 2005, PCH started to buy the equity positions of the IFIs in the individual banks in exchange for additional shares in the holding company. As a consequence, PCH is now the majority shareholder in the 22 banks. In 2005, all the banks adopted the common name of ProCredit Bank. Taken together, the banks have a loan portfolio of around €3 billion, a staff of 17,000, and more than 600 branches. At less than 1 per cent, default rates are as low as they have ever been, and average loan sizes have increased, but the fraction of loans below €1,000 and €10,000, respectively, have remained what they used to be. The return on equity (ROE) of the group stands at 12 per cent. This ROE is slightly below the 15 per cent target rate of return of the company as informally determined by the board of directors and considered appropriate by the owners of PCH.

There have been three recent developments on the way towards full commercialisation. In 2004, PCH received an investment grade credit rating from Fitch. This was a very pleasant surprise since there is not a single comparable enterprise which Fitch could have used as a benchmark. As a consequence of this rating, PCH received offers of large loans from several strictly profit-oriented international banks on terms that are much more favourable than those that the IFIs had formerly offered. The commercial loans are long-term loans that PCH can pass on to its affiliated banks, also on a long-term basis, so that the banks can use them as tier-2 capital to meet their capital requirements. Thus the rating has greatly eased the equity constraint. On the debt side, PCH by now has virtually unlimited access to the capital market.

The second noteworthy development is that PCH has taken on new shareholders. After a very careful analysis of the company and its prospects, the well-known American pension fund TRIF-CREF and another large institutional investor have bought non-voting shares in PCH at a price considerably above book value.

The third recent development is that PCH has made plans to go public and to issue non-voting shares in the course of 2008 or 2009. We will take up this point again at the end of the next subsection.

Going Public as an Institutional Innovation

The process of commercialisation is advancing rapidly. The successful innovations of the past years have set the stage for another innovation and the next step of commercialisation: that of MFIs or MFIVs going public and attracting new private commercially oriented shareholders. In a certain sense, undertaking a successful initial public offering (IPO) is the ultimate proof that microfinance has reached a high degree of maturity. A firm can only go public if a credible commitment can be made to prospective shareholders that they will earn an appropriate rate of return on the investment they make when they buy newly issued shares.

The first MFI to take this step is Compartamos, a large Mexican MFI. In the spring of 2007, 30 per cent of the Compartamos shares that were outstanding at that time were sold to American and Mexican investors in the course of an IPO, and the shares were listed on the Mexican Stock Exchange. The IPO was very successful in purely financial terms. The issue price was 12 times the book value. This means that the market value of all outstanding Compartamos shares were US$1.5 billion. In spite of the high issue price, the IPO was oversubscribed by a factor of 12 and after the IPO the share price has risen further by more than 50 per cent. Those who sold some of their shares included the microfinance support organisation ACCION, the IFC and some private investors. They had all bought shares (at the nominal value) when Compartamos was converted from a credit-granting NGO into a corporation in 2000.

In the years since 2000, Compartamos had been extremely profitable. It has achieved a rate of return of more than 50 per cent on the book value of its equity in every single year. The internal rate of return of the original investment of the shareholders between 2000 and the time of the IPO almost reached the astounding level of 100 per cent per year compounded over eight years.[26]

In spite of the evident success, the financial aspects of the Compartamos IPO raised concerns. However, these concerns had little to do with the fact either that Compartamos issued shares to the general public or that the whole process turned out to be very profitable for the original investors. These features of the IPO simply send positive signals concerning microfinance and its potential. Instead, the main concern referred to the extremely high level of profitability of Compartamos as a business enterprise in the past, that is, since it had been converted into a private corporation with the evident objective of being profitable, and the presumption of the buyers of the newly issued shares that this high level of profitability would be maintained for some time to come.

This remark requires taking a look at Compartamos business policy to understand where its past profits and its likely future profits come from. Shortly before 2000, Mexico experienced a boost of inflation with inflation rates jumping to almost 100 per cent. In accordance with established good practice of MFIs, Compartamos reacted by raising its interest rates in order to keep its real or inflation-adjusted interest rate positive. However, the inflation rate very soon dropped back to normal levels, and instead of lowering its interest rates in parallel, Compartamos kept its interest rates at the high level. This is what made it so profitable.

Interest rates of around 100 per cent are a problem for any MFI operating in a country with moderate inflation rates, especially if this MFI has received some start-up subsidies, as was the case with Compartamos. This level of interest rates and profits leads to an enormous shift of wealth from the clients of the MFI to its shareholders. Moreover, it has consequences for the selection of borrowers. It seems highly unlikely that small business people would continue borrowing money from Compartamos for business purposes at these high rates. Those who would still borrow would most likely be uneducated and therefore in need of some 'benevolent' protection exercised by the MFI and imposed on it by its development-oriented shareholders such as ACCION[27] and IFC, or they would borrow out of dire need or simply to finance consumption. It seems that under the self-imposed pressure to become very profitable, Compartamos has transformed itself into a consumer finance organisation that exploits its clients and may have ceased to be a microbusiness lender.[28]

There are good reasons to be critical of what has gone on in this case. It sheds a negative light on the entire microfinance industry and especially its strictly commercial variant. It seems that the financial interest of the private shareholders, the public shareholders and the self-proclaimed development-oriented shareholders has been more powerful than their commitment to developmental objectives. Since the shares that were issued are normal voting shares and since the high issue price constitutes a commitment to the new shareholder, it is unlikely that this lack of balance would soon be corrected.

For others such as PCH who are also considering undertaking an IPO, the controversy that surrounded the Compartamos IPO is a burden, though perhaps one that may not be all that heavy. PCH has in the past adopted a policy that limits the profitability of the banks that belong to the ProCredit network by setting a 15 per cent ceiling for the rate of return on equity for the group as a whole. Those who have always advocated this limit on profitability have decided not to issue voting shares since this would entail the danger that this limitation might be abolished under the influence of new shareholders. By planning to issue only non-voting shares, the original ProCredit shareholders attempt to retain power. This is meant to ensure that PCH will stick to its established policy of being commercially oriented and at the same time pursue a developmental mission. As they see it, this policy will not stand in the way of offering an attractive investment opportunity to new shareholders, and it should also make PCH shares attractive for those who want to be commercial investors in organisations with a 'double bottom line' that gives equal weight to financial and developmental success.

The preparations for the PCH IPO are by now well advanced. According to the assessment of investment banks which might act as underwriters in the IPO, it will not be a problem to find a sufficiently large number of interested buyers at the envisaged issue price in spite of the facts that the business model of PCH is completely unfamiliar, that the newly issued shares are non-voting and that the owners of the voting shares are determined to maintain their policy of balancing financial and developmental objectives and of observing a self-imposed profit cap.

NOTES

1. For many years, J.D. Von Pischke has been among the most reputable experts in development finance. The quote refers to the title of his seminal book from 1991.
2. The most comprehensive sources on microfinance are still Ledgerwood (1999) and Robinson (2001).
3. For a more extended history of development finance, see Chapter B of Krahnen and Schmidt (1994, pp. 9–27).
4. Towards the end of the 1980s, the combination of development-oriented and socially minded foreign donor organisations, business-minded local NGOs and small business owners started to be regarded as the new dream team on the development scene. This view is perfectly reflected in the title 'NGOs: Alchemists for the Poor' of ACCION Monograph No 6 (Drake and Otero 1992) and in the content of the proceedings volume of the first world microenterprise conference held in Washington in 1989 (Levitsky 1989).
5. The author of this chapter was one of the coordinators of the study. For details, see Schmidt and Zeitinger (1996).
6. Jackelin and Rhyne (1991) were the first to use the term 'commercial approach' in a publication. However, what they discussed under this label and what others advocated under the labels 'financial sector approach' and 'institution building approach' did not differ very much. For a comparison, see Schmidt and Zeitinger (1998).
7. Some time ago, I advocated that donors should regard themselves as owners of MFIs and behave accordingly. The idea behind this suggestion was that they would have a motive to act in the long-term interest of the so-called target groups of MFIs; see Schmidt and Zeitinger (1998). By now I have largely lost confidence in my former

suggestion. In Schmidt and Moisa (2005) I discussed the model of a public–private partnership in microfinance that implies a form of co-ownership of public institutions and private institutions and persons. The weakness of such an organisational design is that its viability depends on the lasting ability and willingness of the public and the private sides to play their respective roles and to respect that the other side is also playing its role.

8. See, for example, Adams et al. (1984) and Von Pischke (1991).
9. The details of how group lending functions vary considerably from case to case. For a description see, for example, Ledgerwood (1999, pp. 67–70). In contrast to what is commonly believed and to how the bank presents itself to the general public, Grameen Bank does not use group lending in the sense of granting loans to a group as a whole or of making individual group members liable for loans granted to other group members, but merely practises group-based lending in the sense of lending only to women who belong to a group that has been formed by a Grameen extension worker.
10. Although much less well known than Grameen, Unit-DESA is an MFI that is almost as old and almost as large and was financially self-sufficient and even very profitable much earlier than Grameen Bank. That Unit-DESA is financially more successful may be due to the fact that it always relied on a different, and possibly better, lending technology. That it is less well known may be because it never needed to make itself known in order to attract subsidies from donors. For a comparison, see Yaron (1992) and Robinson (2001).
11. Surprisingly, this is in spite of the lending technology applied by this bank. It seems that in his many public speeches, Professor Yunus creates the impression that his bank practises group lending, obscuring the fact that it does not really do this. The lack of clarity may have something to do with the two facts that Grameen Bank has for a long time been strongly dependent on foreign subsidies and that donors seem to appreciate group lending.
12. See Vogel (1984) for the often quoted critique that savings had been 'the forgotten half' of rural finance.
13. Among those who may have influenced the major donor institutions were certainly organisations such as ACCION and IPC and other development consulting firms which depended on contracts from these donors and were at the same time strongly motivated to really bring microfinance forward. Researchers such as those belonging to the Rural Finance Group at Ohio State University, for a long time the leading academic research centre in this area, have acted as catalysts of innovation.
14. Nair and Von Pischke (2007) provide up-to-date information that shows that after 2000, only very few upgrading projects have been successfully completed.
15. Among those who have been considered by donors as being able to carry an upgrading project through, are certainly the first two organisations mentioned in note 13.
16. These included the IDB and the European Bank for Reconstruction and Development (EBRD) as early adopters of this approach – and thus as innovators. Germany's KfW later started to fund this type of projects in a big way.
17. The name of this project type reflects the fact that the new clients are smaller firms than the existing corporate clients of the banks that participate in this kind of project.
18. In spite of its general acceptance among the vast majority of microfinance experts, this seemingly self-evident concept of commercialisation has been harshly criticised on moral or ethical grounds by some, and this criticism is still alive today. Interestingly, those who reject the commercial approach and therefore disagree with the requirement that MFIs should cover costs and keep the costs of their operations as low as possible often refer to the Nobel Prize winning Grameen Bank as a positive example of an MFI that is not following the commercial approach. For an extended discussion of the ethical dimension of the debate concerning the commercial approach to microfinance, see Schmidt (2008).
19. See Otero and Chu (2002, p. 231).
20. Moreover, there are now some banks, including large national and international banks, that have so far not directly addressed the traditional clientele of MFIs but instead sup-

ported MFIs by refinancing them. The most notable example to date is the huge Indian bank ICICI. For details, see Nair and Von Pischke (2007).
21. An insightful account of this episode of the years 1998 to 2000 is presented in Chapter 6 of Rhyne (2001).
22. Estimates are that around 150 MFIs have by now reached the stage of covering all of their costs including the cost of equity. See, for example, Deutsche Bank Research (2007) and Nair and Von Pischke (2007). Both sources use data provided by CGAP and MIX.
23. Mature MFIs are those that have reached the stage of profitability. Deutsche Bank Research calls them 'Tier 1 MFIs'.
24. The next category of almost commercial debt funds are loans granted by specialised investment funds in industrialised countries such as Blue Orchard. In most cases, the interest rates these investors demand from MFIs are very high. Moreover, these new investors often require some form of guarantee from a development organisation.
25. For a survey of these specialised providers of equity capital to MFIs, see Goodman (2006). According to the author, in 2004 ProCredit had a market share of more than 40 per cent.
26. All figures reported here are taken from Rosenberg's careful assessment of the Compartamos IPO (Rosenberg, 2007). The extensive documentation by ACCION (2007) provides no reason to doubt Rosenberg's figures.
27. See the statement by ACCION spokespersons Otero and Chew (2002).
28. This assessment is largely in line with the critical analysis provided by Rosenberg (2007). Even more critical assessments have been expressed by others, including Yunus. For this and other assessments, the reader is referred to the discussion on the Development Finance Network (DFN) on the internet. See also Cull et al. (2007).

REFERENCES

ACCION (2007), 'The Banco Compartamos Initial Public Offering', ACCION InSight 23, June.

Adams, D., Graham, D. and Von Pischke, J.D. (eds) (1984), *Undermining Rural Development with Cheap Credit*, Boulder, CO: Westview.

Cull, R., Demirgüc-Kunt, A. and Morduch, J. (2007), 'Microfinance and the market', forthcoming in *Journal of Economic Perspectives*.

Deutsche Bank Research (2007), 'Microfinance: an emerging investment opportunity', research study, Frankfurt.

Drake, D. and Otero, M. (1992), 'NGOs: Alchemists for the Poor', ACCION Monograph 6, Boston, MA.

Drake, D. and Rhyne, E. (eds) (2002), *The Commercialization of Microfinance: Balancing Business and Development*, Bloomfield, CT: Kumarian Press.

Epstein, K. and Smith, G. (2007), 'The ugly side of microfinance. How big Mexican banks profit as many poor borrowers get trapped in a maze of debt', *Business Week*, 13 December.

Goodman, P. (2006), 'Microfinance investment funds: objectives, players, potential', in I. Matthäus-Maier and J.D. Von Pischke (eds), *Microfinance Investment Funds*, Berlin and Heidelberg: Springer, pp. 11–46.

Jackelin, H. and Rhyne, E. (1991), 'Towards a more market-oriented approach to credit and savings for the poor', *Small Enterprise Development*, **2**(4), 4–20.

Krahnen, J.-P. and Schmidt, R.H. (1994), *Development Finance as Institution Building*, Boulder, CO: Westview.

Ledgerwood, J. (1999), *Microfinance Handbook: An Institutional and Financial Perspective*, Washington, DC: World Bank.

Levitsky, J. (ed.) (1989), *Microenterprises in Developing Countries*, London: ITDG.

Nair, A. and Von Pischke, J.D. (2007), 'Commercial banks and financial access', in M.S. Barr, A. Kumar and R.E. Litan (eds), *Building Inclusive Financial Systems: A Framework for Financial Access*, Washington, DC: Brookings Institution Press, pp. 89–116.

Otero, M. and Chu, M. (2002), 'Governance and ownership of microfinance institutions', in D. Drake and E. Rhyne (eds), pp. 221–45.

Rhyne, E. (2001), *Mainstreaming Microfinance: How Lending to the Poor Began, Grew and Came of Age in Bolivia*, Bloomfield, CT: Kumarian Press.

Robinson, M.S. (2001), *The Microfinance Revolution*, Washington, DC: World Bank.

Rosenberg, R. (2007), 'CGAP reflections on the Compartamos Initial Public Offering: a case study on microfinance interest rates and profits', CGAP Focus Note 42, Washington, DC.

Schmidt, R.H. (2008), 'Microfinance, commercialisation and ethics', Finance and Accounting, Working Paper 194, Goethe-University, Frankfurt.

Schmidt, R.H. and Moisa, N. (2005), 'Public–private partnerships for financial development in Southeast Europe', in I. Matthäus-Maier and J.D. Von Pischke (eds), *EU-Accession: Financial Sector Opportunities and Challenges for Southeast Europe*, Berlin and Heidelberg: Springer, pp. 251–76.

Schmidt, R.H. and Zeitinger, C.P. (1996), 'The efficiency of credit-granting NGOs', *Savings and Development*, 20, 353–85.

Schmidt, R.H. and Zeitinger, C.P. (1998), 'Critical issues in microfinance and the role of donors', in M.S. Kimeyni, R.C. Wieland and J.D. Von Pischke (eds), *Strategic Issues in Microfinance*, Aldershot: Avebury, pp. 27–51.

Vogel, R. (1984), 'Savings mobilization: the forgotten half of rural finance', in Adams et al. (eds), pp. 248–65.

Von Pischke, J.D. (1991), *Finance at the Frontier*, Washington, DC: World Bank.

Yaron, J. (1992), 'Successful rural finance institutions', World Bank Discussion Paper 150, Washington, DC: World Bank.

4. Technological innovation in banking: the shift to ATMs and implicit pricing of network convenience

Santiago Carbó Valverde and David B. Humphrey

1 INTRODUCTION

Automated teller machines (ATMs) and electronic payments have been two of the most important innovations in the banking industry over the last 20 years. Together, these two changes are strongly associated with the over 30 per cent reduction in the ratio of bank operating costs to asset value across 11 European countries from 1987 to 2004. Branch offices in many countries have declined absolutely and been replaced with ATMs while electronic payments have replaced more costly paper-based transactions. Overall, some €25 billion may have been saved, accounting for over 0.35 per cent of these countries' GDP (updated from Humphrey et al., 2006).

Convenient access to ATM and branch networks is an important aspect of non-price competition for loan and deposit market shares. It is especially important for depositors since the majority of point-of-sale payments in Europe are in cash (Snellman et al., 2001) and ATMs are a cheaper way to deliver it to depositors than continued reliance on branch offices.

Banks recoup part of their payment and other expenses using fixed fees, paying below market deposit rates, and (sometimes) per transaction prices. Institutions that provide greater convenience by maintaining relatively larger ATM and/or branch office networks in their market area may seek additional compensation by adjusting further their fees on priced services. Alternatively, banks with larger branch and ATM networks are more 'productive' since they generally have higher deposit/branch ratios. This generates greater loan/security output and revenues per branch/ATM capital investment (output/capital ratio).

Either response can contribute to profits. The first response reflects indirect price compensation for a higher level of service provided while the second reflects potential productivity and cost savings. The lower cost of

ATMs compared to branches permits banks to expand convenience and is an important innovation in delivering banking services, an innovation that can also affect pricing strategies. We attempt to separate and quantify these two possible effects of non-price competition.

Unfortunately, other than Spain, no European country has publicly available panel data on individual bank ownership of ATMs. Such information is needed to determine whether banks that provide greater ATM or branch convenience may offset this expense by adjusting deposit/loan rate spreads (indirect pricing) or by attracting a higher level of deposits and loans per capita and/or labour input (productivity effect). As European banks tend to adopt similar practices, determining this trade-off for Spain is expected to shed light on how similar trade-offs may be made elsewhere in Europe.

In what follows, the growth of ATMs and branch offices is outlined for 11 European countries in Section 2 and the apparent relationship between ATM convenience and the loan/deposit rate spread is illustrated for Spain. In Section 3, previous efforts to quantify non-priced aspects of banking services and changes in service delivery are briefly summarised prior to presenting the analysis used to determine the effects of branch/ATM convenience on operating cost, deposit rates, loan rates, and other service fees. Fourier functions are used as they permit greater curvature flexibility across different sizes of bank branch and ATM networks.

Section 4 contains our results and indicates that deposit rates as well as loan rates are both on balance somewhat higher for banks with larger ATM and branch networks. As the latter effect exceeds the former, we conclude that convenience is to a degree implicitly priced and raises bank net revenues. This result occurs even when an indicator of deposit market concentration is included in the analysis. Thus competition studies that exclude this effect may overstate the degree to which price differences among banks are related only to market concentration.[1] In other words, branch and ATM convenience are likely viewed by consumers as a benefit and the net 'adverse' effect it seems to have on observed prices should be accounted for when determining how market concentration is associated with market prices and competition. The final section concludes.

2 DELIVERING BANKING SERVICES IN EUROPE AND THE LOAN/DEPOSIT RATE SPREAD

ATMs versus Branches in Europe

In 1987, the 11 European countries shown in Table 4.1 had 154,279 bank branches and 45,244 ATMs. By 2004, the number of branches had

Table 4.1 Percent changes in operating cost and ATM and branch networks, 1987–2004

Country	Operating cost (2004, €m PPP)*	OC/TA	ATMs	Branches
France	66,694	0.02	280	1.4
Germany	62,184	−40	601	14
UK	51,497	−52	160	−25
Italy	40,414	−29	809	133
Netherlands	27,496	−33	1,593	−50
Spain	25,857	−50	858	22
Belgium	9,716	−23	802	−48
Sweden	4,538	−38	70	−33
Denmark	3,311	−39	522	−38
Finland	2,240	−59	11	−46
Norway	1,739	−60	70	−38
All countries		−34	434	9.8

Note: *Millions of 2004 euros, purchasing power parity (PPP) ($1 = 0.805).

Source: Bolt and Humphrey (2008, Table 3).

expanded by 9.8 per cent to 169,362 offices while ATMs expanded by 434 per cent to 241,611. This represents a major change in how banking services are delivered in Europe. While implementation of this innovation differed by country (Table 4.1), over this 18-year period the total number of ATMs per branch office went from one ATM to around 3.5 branch offices in 1987 to close to 1.5 ATMs per office by 2004, a substantial reversal of intensity. Since population in these countries grew by only 11 per cent over this period (partly due to German unification), banks clearly provided greater convenience and access to their services. At the same time, the share of electronic payments in all non-cash transactions in these 11 countries more than doubled, rising from 35 per cent in 1987 to 86 per cent by 2004. These two factors, along with input cost reductions in computer processing and telecommunications, were the major forces behind the 34 per cent reduction in the ratio of operating cost (OC – labour, capital, and materials expenses) to total assets (TA) – an indicator of bank unit operating costs.

The reduction in unit operating costs differed across countries in part because of differences in the intensity of the substitution of ATMs for branches. In seven of the 11 countries in Table 4.1, the number of branch offices declined absolutely while in France the number was effectively constant. Branches expanded in Germany due to unification while in Italy and Spain they rose because previous restrictions on branching were removed and banks took this opportunity to expand into proscribed markets during the transition.

Similar ATM/branch intensity differences exist across banks within the one country – Spain – for which panel information exists on bank ownership of ATMs. Operating cost to assets fell by some 50 per cent in Spain (Table 4.1) and there was one ATM for about six branch offices in 1987 but 1.4 ATMs for each office by 2004. This was a greater change in ATM intensity than seen in the rest of Europe. Thus Spain represents a unique laboratory to explore the relationship between changes and innovation in delivery channels and related changes in pricing strategy. Similar to the diversity in ATM intensity seen across countries, some banks in Spain expanded their ATM networks more intensively than others in order to attract a larger market share by providing greater convenience. The issue we investigate is whether greater relative convenience by some banks may affect deposit or loan rates (implicit pricing) or whether the extra costs may be offset by collecting more deposits per branch office, leading to greater loan/security revenues (productivity effect).

Loan/Deposit Rate Spread and ATM Network Size in Spain

In most countries commercial banks have the dominant market share. While deposit shares are about evenly split between commercial and savings banks in Spain, savings banks serve the majority of the population: they service 44 million deposit/loan accounts compared to 23 million for commercial banks and had more ATMs and branch offices.[2] The fitted cubic spline in Figure 4.1 illustrates the simple bivariate relationship between the loan/deposit rate spread (in percentage points) and the log of the number of ATMs owned by 46 savings banks and 31 commercial banks, averaged over 1986–2003.[3] The average loan/deposit rate spread initially falls to around 4 percentage points for sampled banks with less than 50 ATMs, then rises and remains above 4 percentage points for banks with 50 to 400 ATMs, and finally falls below 4 percentage points for those (few) banks with more than 400 ATMs.[4]

The fitted splines in Figure 4.1 indicate that the bivariate relationship between the rate spread and ATM network size is not a simple linear or quadratic specification and that some banks appear to lower their rate spread while others raise it as the size of their ATM network changes.[5] Consequently, we expect that the specified multivariate relationship presented would benefit from using a Fourier function which, similar to the cubic spline, is much more flexible than (say) the translog form. Also, although not easy to see, most of the sampled banks (55 per cent of commercial and 67 per cent of savings banks) lie within the 50 to 400 ATM

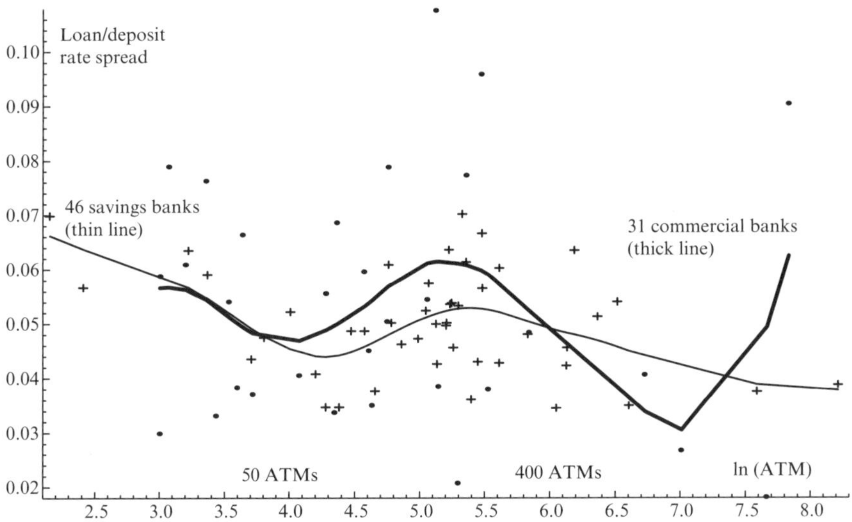

Figure 4.1 *Average loan/deposit rate spread and ATM network size, Spain, 1986–2003*

range where the loan/deposit rate spread first rises and then falls but exceeds 4 percentage points. Thus the mass of the data for both set of banks lies within this range and will primarily determine the effect, if any, of ATM (or branch) network convenience on deposit and loan rates.

3 ESTIMATING CONVENIENCE AND OTHER NON-PRICE EFFECTS ON LOAN/DEPOSIT RATES

Previous Analyses of Non-price Competition

Originally, non-price effects in banking focused on determining the 'implicit interest' paid for transaction and safekeeping services provided to depositors with funds in accounts that paid no explicit interest or a below market rate (Klein and Murphy, 1971; Santomero, 1979; Startz, 1983). For the US, this was facilitated by having cost accounting survey data for smaller banks (which is no longer available) to calculate the allocated underlying bank cost of providing non-priced transaction, savings account, and safekeeping services. This gave an estimate of the implicit interest being paid on deposits (Santomero, 1979).

As bank cost accounting data were not available for the UK, Heffernan (1992) regressed (unpublished) bank deposit and loan product interest rates on the market rate and certain non-priced deposit and loan account characteristics (such as the average real balance in an account, minimum balance requirements, the number of branches and ATMs a bank had, and other non-public information). That portion of the spread between the market rate and the interest paid (received) on a deposit (loan) account explained by the variation in non-priced account characteristics was taken to be the implicit price of the non-priced deposit/loan characteristics.

Focusing more directly on ATMs, Hannan et al. (2003) find that the probability of ATM surcharging in the US when depositors use another bank's ATM is an increasing function of bank size and ATM market share. Such a pricing strategy provides an incentive for depositors to remain with banks with large ATM networks since they are more likely to pay fewer surcharges. Also, Hannan (2006) finds that the positive relationship between deposit fees and market concentration for single-market (small) banks is attenuated when these markets contain multimarket (large) banks, indicating that ATM/branch competition affects deposit prices.[6]

While the development and deployment of ATMs represents the main innovation in bank service delivery, branches are also considered a strategic variable that affects market competition. Kim and Vale (2001) showed that loan demand in Norway is affected by the availability of a bank's own and a rival's branch network. Since a branch network approximates bank size, changes by one bank can lead rivals to respond (consistent with a local oligopoly).[7] Also, using conjectural variation, it was found that if a bank in Spain added one branch office, rivals responded by adding 1.4 offices to their own networks (Carbó et al., 2004).

Convenience and Other Non-price Effects on Loan/Deposit Rates

In this study, we use a balanced panel of 46 Spanish savings banks and 31 commercial banks observed every six months over 18 years (1986–2003), giving a sample of 2,772 observations, in a set of four equations.[8] These concern unit operating cost, interest cost, loan revenue, and deposit fee equations to determine how the differential provision of branches and ATMs, along with staffing (labour/branch ratio) and branch 'productivity' (deposit/branch ratio) indicators may affect the pricing of deposit and loan rates across banks. This illustrates the connection between innovations in how banks deliver services and corresponding innovations in pricing strategy. Although publicly available data for Spanish banks do not permit us to determine the rate paid on different subcategories of deposits or loans, we control for major differences in deposit, asset, and liability composition to help address this issue.[9]

Among the implications of technological innovation in any industry, cost savings and market power over price emerge as two of the most important. However, it is not easy to infer which one of these influences – cost efficiency or market power – has a greater effect on prices and/or profits. An earlier analysis by Berger (1995) distinguished between market concentration and cost efficiency as alternative explanations of profit differences among US banks. It turned out that both explanations were significant, with cost efficiency being slightly more important (but both together explained less than 20 per cent of the variation in profits). In our application, determining cost efficiency is not needed as we directly incorporate the influences that explain previously unexplained differences in cost efficiency across banks (Carbó et al., 2007). This concerns the level and mix of branches and ATMs – our primary indicator of non-price competition – as well as measures of internal bank productivity and the shift to electronic payments which are included in the analysis below.

The cost or shadow price effect of bank branch and ATM convenience is obtained from the operating cost component of a standard cost function. Bank operating and interest expenses are available separately and this permits more accurate local identification of the specified influences.[10] Operating cost (OC) divided by the value of deposits (Q_{dep}) is one component in setting a deposit rate, loan rate, or service fee and is the dependent variable of our operating cost function. Operating cost is a function of the size of a bank's branch and ATM network, the input prices of labour and physical capital being paid, the productivity of its branches in raising deposits given its staffing level, the bank's mix of liabilities and assets, as well as an indicator of technical change in banking (the share of electronic payments ELE).[11]

Operating cost function:

$$\begin{aligned}\ln(OC/Q_{dep}) = {} & \alpha_0 + \sum_{o=br}^{atm} \alpha_0 \ln Q_o + 1/2 \sum_{o=br}^{atm} \sum_{m=br}^{atm} \alpha_{o,m} \ln Q_o \ln Q_m \\ & + \sum_{p=l}^{k} \alpha_p \ln P_p + 1/2 \sum_{p=l}^{k} \sum_{n=l}^{k} \alpha_{p,n} \ln P_p \ln P_n \\ & + \sum_{p=l}^{k} \alpha_{p,br} \ln P_p \ln Q_{br} + \sum_{p=l}^{k} \alpha_{p,atm} \ln P_p \ln Q_{atm} \\ & + \alpha_{dep,br} (\ln Q_{dep} - \ln Q_{br}) + \alpha_{labour,br} (\ln Q_{labour} - \ln Q_{br}) \\ & + \sum_{mix=1}^{3} \alpha_{mix} Q_{mix} + \alpha_{ele} \ln ELE + 1/2(\alpha_{ele2}) \ln(ELE)^2 \\ & + \alpha_{merge} M + \alpha \ln HHI + Fourier \qquad (4.1)\end{aligned}$$

where:

OC/Q_{dep} = the operating cost 'shadow price' of deposits, expressed as operating cost (OC) composed of labour, physical capital, and materials expenses divided by the value of deposits (Q_{dep});

Q_{br}, Q_{atm} = the (o,m) number of banking offices (Q_{br}) and ATMs (Q_{atm}) owned by a bank;[12]

P_l, P_k = the (p,n) operating cost input prices – the average price of labour (P_l) and physical capital (P_k);

Q_{dep}, Q_{labour} = the value of deposits (Q_{dep}) and number of workers (Q_{labour}) which, along with the number of branch offices (Q_{br}) in (4.1), reflect the ln of the deposit/branch productivity and labour/branch staffing ratios;

Q_{mix} = three liability/asset mix variables (the ratio of loans to security holdings, the ratio of non-term transaction and savings deposits to term deposits, and the ratio of non-term plus term deposits to other bank funding);

ELE = share of non-cash payment transactions that are electronic;

M = a dummy variable equal to 1.0 when a bank merged with another bank;

HHI = the Herfindahl–Hirschman index of deposit market concentration (for savings and commercial banks together – only for this variable) where most banks service four regional markets while some are national in scope; and

Fourier = 18 Fourier functional form terms which increase the ability of (4.1), and the equations below, to fit the underlying data in more than just a quadratic (or translog) manner:

$$= + \sum_{o=1}^{2} [\tau_{1o}\sin(\ln Q_o^*) + \tau_{2o}\sin(2\ln Q_o^*) + \tau_{3o}\sin(3\ln Q_o^*)]$$

$$+ \sum_{o=1}^{2} [\tau_{4o}\cos(\ln Q_o^*) + \tau_{5o}\cos(2\ln Q_o^*) + \tau_{6o}\cos(3\ln Q_o^*)]$$

$$+ \tau_7\sin(\ln Q_o^* + \ln Q_m^*) + \tau_8\cos(\ln Q_o^* + \ln Q_m^*)$$

$$+ \tau_9\sin(2\ln Q_o^* + \ln Q_m^*) + \tau_{10}\cos(2\ln Q_o^* + \ln Q_m^*)$$

$$+ \tau_{11}\sin(\ln Q_o^* + 2\ln Q_m^*) + \tau_{12}\cos(\ln Q_o^* + 2\ln Q_m^*)$$

where: $o, m = br, atm$ as above.[13]

The two main components of technological innovation in banking are the substitution of ATMs for branch offices and the shift to electronic payments. Unlike ATMs, payment information is not available by individual bank so our indicator of the influence of electronic payments on operating cost uses the share of electronic payments in the national economy.[14]

Electronic payments cost from only one-third to one-half as much as their paper-based alternatives, such as checks or bills of exchange (Carbó et al., 2006). As the share of electronic payments in all non-cash transactions in Spain was 0.50 in 1986 but rose to 0.93 by 2003, this technological development lowered bank operating cost.[15]

Deposit interest cost (*IC*) divided by the value of deposits (Q_{dep}) is a second component in setting a loan rate. This ratio, which does not include non-deposit funding expense, is the dependent variable of our deposit interest cost function. The rate a bank pays on deposits is allowed to vary by the size of a bank's branch and ATM network, the concurrent market rate of interest, the productivity of its branches in raising deposits given its staffing level, the bank's mix of liabilities and assets, as well as an indicator of technical change in banking (the share of electronic payments *ELE*) so the specification is similar to (4.1):

Deposit interest cost function:

$$\begin{aligned}\ln(IC/Q_{dep}) &= \beta_0 + \sum_{o=br}^{atm} \beta_o \ln Q_o + 1/2 \sum_{o=br}^{atm} \sum_{m=br}^{atm} \beta_{o,m} \ln Q_o \ln Q_m \\ &+ \beta_r \ln P_r + 1/2(\beta_{r2})(\ln P_r)^2 + \beta_{r,br} \ln P_r \ln Q_{br} + \beta_{r,atm} \ln P_r \ln Q_{atm} \\ &+ \beta_{dep,br}(\ln Q_{dep} - \ln Q_{br}) + \beta_{labour,br}(\ln Q_{labour} - \ln Q_{br}) \\ &+ \sum_{mix=1}^{3} \beta_{mix} Q_{mix} + \beta_{ele} \ln ELE + 1/2(\beta_{ele2})(\ln ELE)^2 \\ &+ \beta_{merge} M + \beta \ln HHI + Fourier \qquad (4.2)\end{aligned}$$

where:

P_r = the market interest rate which helps to determine the rate banks decide to pay depositors on non-term (transaction, savings) and term accounts.

In addition to possibly altering deposit rates, the provision of non-priced services may affect bank revenues by attracting depositors with higher incomes who offer more (mortgage, auto, and small business) loan opportunities and/or place a higher value on non-priced services than others. Higher-income depositors typically hold higher average balances and, since deposits are a more stable and lower cost funding source compared to borrowed funds (depending on the interest rate cycle), this would enable a bank to hold a larger share of loans which typically earn higher returns than securities. As well, depositors that value greater ATM access, more convenient branch offices, and faster service may be marginally less concerned with the loan rates and service fees they may pay relative to depositors at other banks.

These potential influences may be determined from the following loan revenue function where loan revenue ($LREV$) is divided by the value of loans (Q_{loan}).

Loan revenue function:

$$\begin{aligned}\ln(LREV/Q_{loan}) = {} & \theta_0 + \sum_{o=br}^{atm}\theta_o \ln Q_o + 1/2\sum_{o=br}^{atm}\sum_{m=br}^{atm}\theta_{o,m}\ln Q_o \ln Q_m \\ & + \theta_{pdep}\ln P_{pdep} + 1/2(\theta_{pdep2})(\ln P_{pdep})^2 \\ & + \theta_{pdep,br}\ln P_{pdep}\ln Q_{br} + \theta_{pdep,atm}\ln P_{pdep}\ln Q_{atm} \\ & + \theta_{dep,br}(\ln Q_{dep} - \ln Q_{br}) + \theta_{labour,br}(\ln Q_{labour} - \ln Q_{br}) \\ & + \sum_{mix=1}^{3}\theta_{mix}Q_{mix} + \theta_{ind}\ln IND + 1/2(\theta_{ind2})(\ln IND)^2 \\ & + \theta_{merge}M + \theta \ln HHI + Fourier \qquad (4.3)\end{aligned}$$

where:

P_{pdep} = the bank's actual deposit rate, which is a primary component involved in setting the loan rate;
IND = the index of industrial production which can affect loan demand over the business cycle.

Finally, fees for priced deposit and loan services may also be adjusted to compensate banks for their provision of extensive branch and ATM networks. This may be reflected in the ratio of fee income to the value of deposits ($FeeIncome/Q_{dep}$) which approximates a composite 'price' for fee-based services.

Fee income function:

$$\begin{aligned}\ln(FeeIncome/Q_{dep}) = {} & \phi_0 + \sum_{o=br}^{atm}\phi_o \ln Q_o \\ & + 1/2\sum_{o=br}^{atm}\sum_{m=br}^{atm}\phi_{o,m}\ln Q_o \ln Q_m \\ & + \sum_{p=l}^{k}\phi_p \ln P_p + 1/2\sum_{p=l}^{k}\sum_{n=l}^{k}\phi_{p,n}\ln P_p \ln P_n \\ & + \sum_{p=l}^{k}\phi_{p,br}\ln P_p \ln Q_{br} + \sum_{p=l}^{k}\phi_{p,atm}\ln P_p \ln Q_{atm} \\ & + \phi_{dep,br}(\ln Q_{dep} - \ln Q_{br}) + \phi_{labour,br}(\ln Q_{labour} - \ln Q_{br})\end{aligned}$$

$$+ \sum_{mix=1}^{3} \phi_{mix} Q_{mix} + \phi_{ele} \ln ELE + 1/2(\phi_{ele2}) \ln (ELE)^2$$

$$+ \phi_{merge} M + \phi \ln HHI + Fourier \quad (4.4)$$

where the specification is the same as (4.1) and all terms have been defined above.

4 IMPLICIT PRICING AND PRODUCTIVITY EXPLANATIONS OF NON-PRICE COMPETITION

Results for the Average Bank

The four operating cost, interest cost, loan revenue, and fee income Fourier equations were estimated using (i) first differences of all logged variables and (ii) individual fixed effects for each bank in the separate savings and commercial bank panel data sets.[16] The elasticity results of interest are shown in Table 4.2.[17] Variation in the size of either ATM or branch networks, although adding to total operating costs, seem not to significantly affect average operating expenses per unit of deposits. This is after controlling for the value of deposits raised per branch office (deposit/branch ratio) and the staffing of these offices (labour/branch ratio), along with liability/asset mix, factor input prices, share of electronic payments, and market concentration influences on unit operating expenses specified in (4.1). In contrast, a higher deposit/branch ratio significantly reduces unit operating expenses while employing more labour per branch significantly raises these costs. Although the sign of these two relationships is expected, the similar level of these elasticities was not. In effect, one offsets the other for both savings and commercial banks while higher market concentration (HHI) is significantly associated only with higher operating costs for commercial banks.[18]

The effect of network convenience on the deposit rate in (4.2) is significant only for savings banks.[19] Here a larger branch network (given the size of the same bank's ATM network) is associated with a lower deposit rate while a larger ATM network (given the number of branches) is associated with a higher deposit rate. This suggests that banks with a relatively low ratio of ATMs to branches tend to pay a lower deposit rate while institutions showing a higher rate of innovation in service delivery (by having relatively more ATMs) tend to pay a higher rate. As savings bank branches expanded by 150 per cent over our 18-year period while their number of ATMs rose by a factor of 14, this suggests that the net effect has been for savings banks to pay a higher deposit rate, since this differential in network expansion

Table 4.2 Cost and revenue effects associated with non-price competition (Fourier form, 1st differences, fixed individual effects, 1986–2003)

Elasticities		Branch	ATM	Deposit/ Branch	Labour/ Branch	HHI	R^2	D–W
(4.1)	Operating cost/ deposits:							
	Savings banks	−0.002	0.010	−1.00*	0.983*	0.005	0.99	2.64
	Commercial banks	0.040	−0.186	−1.04*	0.867*	0.708*	0.77	2.12
(4.2)	Deposit rate:							
	Savings banks	−0.736*	0.298*	−0.740*	0.036	−0.009	0.35	1.89
	Commercial banks	−0.034	0.048	−0.718*	0.060	−0.049	0.15	2.15
(4.3)	Loan rate:							
	Savings banks	0.134	0.175*	−0.053	0.081*	−0.016	0.86	2.52
	Commercial banks	−0.056	0.037	−0.226*	0.063	−0.010	0.26	2.16
(4.4)	Fee income/ deposits:							
	Savings banks	−0.105	−0.081	−0.841*	0.937*	−0.014	0.46	2.78
	Commercial banks	−0.622	−0.239	−0.946*	0.609*	−0.016	0.33	1.95

Note: * (**) indicates p-value ≤ 0.05 (0.10).

exceeds the differential in the branch and ATM elasticities shown. The overall higher deposit rate paid by savings banks, with no significant effect for commercial banks, accords well with the fact that branching restrictions on savings banks were removed in 1989, leading to an expansion of their branch and ATM networks into existing and previously proscribed markets during the early 1990s to expand market share. This expansion of convenience, along with an aggressive strategy of offering more attractive deposit rates to current and new depositors, resulted in a more contestable banking market during the transition.[20]

Interestingly, the effect of having a higher deposit/branch ratio is associated with a significant reduction in the deposit rate and is not offset by having a higher staffing ratio. This suggests that the ability to raise more deposits per branch capital outlay – which also generates greater revenues per branch office – is not passed on to depositors. Indeed, the reverse occurs here as deposit rates appear to fall. Overall, with the lowest R^2 values in Table 4.2, it is clear that explaining the variation in the deposit rate (in first difference terms) has been the least successful even with a specification that includes the market interest rate.

More success is achieved in explaining the behaviour of the loan rate (4.3), at least for savings banks.[21] Here a larger ATM network and greater staffing per branch are significantly associated with a higher loan rate. In contrast, the only significant effect in Table 4.2 for commercial banks is a reduction in the loan rate for institutions with a higher deposit/branch ratio, suggesting that greater branch output productivity (and revenues) is passed on to borrowers in the form of a lower loan rate. This is the opposite of what occurred in (4.2) for commercial bank deposit rates, which fell.[22]

There appears to be no significant effect on fee income in (4.4) from differences in ATM/branch network size. And, although both the deposit/branch and labour/branch ratios significantly affect revenue from fees, these influences are opposite in sign and appear to largely offset each other as the elasticity values are rather similar. In other words, and in terms of average relative profitability over our time period, the highest profit quartile of savings banks generated 17 per cent more deposits per branch over our time period than did the lowest profit quartile but offset this advantage by having a 26 per cent higher staffing level per branch office.[23]

Net Effects of Non-price Competition on Bank Pricing

Due to the sometimes differential responses outlined above for the different equations, it is not easy to determine the likely net effect of ATM/branch network size on overall bank pricing behaviour. The same applies to the net

Table 4.3 Net effect of non-price competition on deposit/loan rates and fee income (predicted values from estimated equations)

	Using all parameters*			
	ATM/Branch		Productivity	
	%	€	%	€
(4.1) Operating cost:				
Savings banks	4.4	5,443	4.3	5,314
Commercial banks	5.1	8,663	2.2	3,706
(4.2) Interest cost:				
Savings banks	1.6	3,074	0.3	600
Commercial banks	0.3	1,243	1.0	4,402
(4.3) Loan revenue:				
Savings banks	6.0	18,235	6.3	19,063
Commercial banks	6.5	38,754	5.4	32,229
(4.4) Fee income:				
Savings banks	2.0	659	−1.5	−499
Commercial banks	−6.5	−6,069	−8.3	−7,788
Using all parameters				
Net effect:				
Savings banks		15,820		17,964
Commercial banks		31,442		20,039
Using only significant parameters				
Net effect:				
Savings banks		14,329		18,713
Commercial banks		0		20,160

Note: *Percentages are rounded and values are in thousands of euros.

effect of branch 'productivity' in generating deposits versus a tendency to incur greater staffing expenses (taken here to indicate more timely service although it raises labour costs). Our estimates of these net effects are shown in Table 4.3.

Concentrating on changes in delivery channels, we evaluate each estimated equation allowing only ATMs and branch offices to vary, holding all other variables (including the deposit/branch and labour/branch ratios) constant at their mean values in the sample panel. For the price of deposit equation (4.2), this gives the predicted value of the dependent variable in first differences of logs as $\ln[(IC/DEP)_t/(IC/DEP)_{t-1}]$. This can be re-expressed as $\ln[(IC_t/IC_{t-1})/(DEP_t/DEP_{t-1})]$ where IC = deposit interest expense and DEP = value of deposits, so the ratio IC/DEP is the average deposit rate paid by each bank for each time period. Expressing the mean value (*) of the predicted dependent variable as ln $[(IC_t/IC_{t-1})/(DEP_t/DEP_{t-1})]^*$, this value is first exponentiated and then multiplied by the mean value of $(DEP_t/DEP_{t-1})^*$. Subtracting 1.0 from this result gives $(IC_t/IC_{t-1})^* - 1$ which is the predicted mean percent change in interest costs, shown in Rows 3 and 4 of Column 1 for savings and commercial banks.[24] Multiplying this result by the mean value of interest costs (IC*) gives the estimated mean euro change in interest costs from the variation of ATM and branch network size, shown in Rows 3 and 4 of Column 2. Doing the same for the deposit/branch and labour/branch ratios, the other two non-price competition influences, gives Columns 3 and 4.[25] Thus Table 4.3 (excluding the last four rows) shows the results for each equation using all estimated parameters.

Using all parameters, operating cost is 4.4 to 5.1 per cent higher at banks that have larger ATM/branch networks and is from 2.2 to 4.3 per cent higher at institutions with higher deposit/branch and labour/branch ratios. This higher relative cost is not, however, compensated on average by banks lowering deposit interest rates. Indeed, interest costs at banks with larger ATM/branch networks, greater deposit/branch productivity and staffing levels are slightly higher (from 0.3 to 1.6 per cent higher). The extra operating expenses shown in (4.1) in Table 4.3 instead appears to be more than compensated for by higher loan rates, generating 5.4 to 6.5 per cent larger loan revenues. This positive benefit for banks, paid for by borrowers, is partially offset by lower fee income, which is generally reduced by 1.5 to 8.3 per cent at institutions with larger ATM/branch networks, and higher deposit/branch productivity and staffing levels.

As the percentage changes in Table 4.3 apply to different interest cost, loan revenue, and fee income bases, the implied values have been calculated (Columns 3 and 4, in thousands of euros). When properly summed, the overall net effect of our two forms of non-price competition – ATM/branch network size and branch deposit productivity/staffing levels – has been to raise deposit rates slightly, lower fee income, but raise loan rates to more than offset these benefits to bank customers. Higher bank interest expenses and lower deposit fees favours bank customers while higher loan rates favours the bank. Overall, the net benefit (shown in Rows 9 and 10) favours banks and is implemented through the loan rate, which is commonly viewed as being less transparent to borrowers than is the deposit rate and fees to depositors for deposit services.

Little is changed if, instead of using all parameters from the estimated equations, the predicted effects from ATM/branch network size and branch deposit productivity/staffing levels are recomputed using only the significant branch, ATM, deposit/branch, and labour/branch ratios in

Table 4.2.[26] The net effects from this recalculation are shown in the last two rows of Table 4.3. The only change is that the size of ATM and branch networks has no effect for commercial banks since the branch and ATM elasticities for these institutions in Table 4.2 were always insignificant (at the 90 per cent confidence interval).

5 CONCLUSIONS

Studies of banking competition typically focus on prices and priced services in assessing the degree of market competition. We focus on non-price aspects of this competition such as the provision of convenient branch offices, staffing levels, and ATM access. We find that innovations in the delivery of banking services – mainly, the substitution of ATMs for branches – represents an important influence on bank pricing so innovations in how services are delivered can also lead to innovations in bank pricing strategies. Although the costs of providing ATM and branch convenience to depositors is not directly priced, banks may seek implicit compensation by adjusting deposit and loan rates or service fees. And, as institutions with larger branch and ATM networks generally experience higher deposit/branch ratios, banks may rely on this greater deposit 'productivity' and loan revenue per branch/ATM capital investment to offset these network costs. Our analysis is applied to Spanish savings and commercial banks over 18 years (1986–2003) since Spain has the largest number of ATMs in Europe and is the only country with data on ATM ownership by bank. Our analysis suggests that: (i) banks obtain a positive net compensation for providing convenience through expanded ATM and branch networks; and (ii) these bank benefits are augmented by being able to raise more deposits per branch office as well as from higher office staffing levels. Overall, non-price competition affects banking prices with the net effect being that net revenues are expanded.

Analyses of priced services have been concerned with how deposit and loan rates vary with market concentration (the structure, conduct, performance paradigm), the mark-up of rates over marginal cost (Lerner index), the loan/deposit rate spread, and the degree to which changes in input prices are reflected in output prices (H-statistic). We show that differences across banks in their measured prices may also be affected by differences in bank branch/ATM convenience and not be solely due to market competition. This is similar to Brewer and Jackson (2006) who show that the negative relationship between deposit rates and a market concentration ratio is reduced by half (but still significant) when another explanation of deposit rate dispersion is included in the analysis.

NOTES

1. This point is similar to that of Brewer and Jackson (2006) who found that the negative relationship between bank deposit rates and a three-firm concentration ratio was substantially reduced when other plausible influences on deposit rates were considered.
2. Savings banks concentrate on providing consumer-based services rather than business-based products, although there is some competition between these two entities for both consumer and business customers.
3. These banks account for more than 90 per cent of total assets in the Spanish banking system.
4. These values are averages over 1986–2003 so, today, banks would have more ATMs than those illustrated in Figure 4.1. The 50 and 400 ATM reference points correspond approximately to ln ATM values of 4.0 and 6.0, respectively.
5. Although not shown, the average ratio of fee income to deposits is generally higher for banks with larger ATM and branch networks (and has increased for all banks over time).
6. In a related paper, Donze and Dubec (2006) illustrate theoretically that ATM interchange fees, which are currently chosen cooperatively by banks, should reduce deposit rate competition but increase competition to process ATM withdrawals. This supports the possibility that deposit prices are altered to compensate for ATM availability.
7. This is because the number of branches is a good indicator of the deposit, loan, or asset size of a bank. In Spain, for example, the R^2s between the number of branches and the value of deposits, loans, or total assets are, respectively, 0.78, 0.79, and 0.78 so branches are correlated with savings bank size. Commercial banks are less retail oriented and have a weaker relationship (0.72, 0.65, and 0.63).
8. While the raw data was observed every six months, all the 'flow' information (for example, interest expense, loan revenue, and so on) was multiplied by two to express the flow data in approximate annual terms. No manipulation was needed for the 'stock' data (value of deposits, loans, assets, number of workers, and so on).
9. More information is available on balance sheet composition than on corresponding revenue or expense flows.
10. For example, the statistical model does not have to use covariation among non-orthogonal variables to 'know' that the market rate of interest affects bank deposit rates rather than operating cost (which would be necessary if only total or average total cost were specified). Similarly, the variation of labour input prices would be restricted to affecting only operating costs and not interest expenses.
11. The standard translog symmetry and summation restrictions for homogeneity of degree 1.0 for input prices are imposed in our Fourier estimation.
12. Security holdings and off-balance sheet activities generate almost no operating costs while loan operating costs are relatively small. The main operating expenses are associated with deposit activities using branches and ATMs along with front- and back-office processing of cash and non-cash payments.
13. The new terms are $\ln Q^* = \ln Q \cdot YQ + ZQ$, $YQ = (0.8 \cdot 2\pi)/(\max \ln Q - \min \ln Q)$ $ZQ = 0.2\pi - \min \ln Q \cdot YQ$, and $\pi = 3.141593\ldots$, so that $\ln Q^*$ is essentially expressed in radians. See Mitchell and Onvural (1996) and Berger and Mester (1997).
14. Use of electronic versus paper-based payments does not importantly differ among regions in Spain. In addition, electronic payments are often processed centrally so our use of national data (which is all that is available) should be acceptable to reflect bank level usage as well.
15. Electronic giro payments (direct debits and credit transfers) accounted for 56 per cent of total non-cash transactions in Spain in 2003 while electronic debit and credit cards comprised 35 per cent. Cheques and bills of exchange (a special type of check used in business transactions) currently account for 9 per cent. Payment data are from the European Central Bank 'Blue Book'.
16. First differences were used since data in log levels form (with or without individual fixed

effects) generated Durbin–Watson statistics that were typically around 0.50, suggesting positive autocorrelation in the set of 36 six-month time series observations in the panel data set for both sets of banks.

17. Parameter estimates are shown in Appendix 4A. The LSQ subroutine in TSP 5.0 was used and a Wald test (ANALYZ) was applied to determine the overall significance of the branch and ATM variables in each equation. Other reported significance tests did not require this procedure.
18. The cost/price equations (4.1) and (4.2) were concave for both savings and commercial banks while equation (4.3) was concave for savings banks only. The estimated marginal effect of branches and ATMs in each of the four equations can be seen in the sign of the elasticities in Table 4.2 and can be positive or negative.
19. The only difference in RHS variables between (4.1) and (4.2) is the substitution of the market interest rate in (4.2) for the labour and capital input prices in (4.1). These latter two inputs will have almost no effect on deposit interest expenses while the market rate, of course, has a major impact.
20. Branching restrictions on commercial banks were removed prior to the start of our sample period.
21. The specification of RHS variables in (4.3) differs from (4.2) in the substitution of each bank's actual deposit rate for the market interest rate used in (4.2) to explain the deposit rate and the addition of a business cycle indicator (index of industrial production) in (4.3) to help explain the loan rate.
22. Although collinearity between the deposit/branch and the labour/branch variables in Table 4.2 may seem to be a problem, the R^2 here is only 0.15 for savings banks and 0.08 for commercial banks.
23. Other results indicated that the shift to cheaper electronic payment methods significantly reduced operating cost, deposit rates, and fee income at larger banks while the index of industrial production was a significant influence on the loan rate. All three balance sheet composition variables were significant in two of the four equations.
24. Applying the same procedure to the other three equations gives the other entries in Column 1.
25. Here only the deposit/branch and labour/branch ratios are allowed to vary, holding all other variables (including the number of ATMs and branches) constant at their mean values in the sample.
26. As the branch and ATM variables are specified to have more than one parameter (for example, own, squared, and cross terms as well as the Fourier parameters) these parameters are only used if the branch or ATM elasticities based on all of these parameters shown in Table 4.2 are significant at a p-value ≤ 0.10.

REFERENCES

Berger, A. (1995), 'The profit–structure relationship in banking – tests of market-power and efficient-structure hypotheses', *Journal of Money, Credit, and Banking*, **27** (2), 404–15.

Berger, A. and L. Mester (1997), 'Inside the black box: what explains differences in the efficiencies of financial institutions', *Journal of Banking and Finance*, **21** (7), 895–947.

Bolt, W. and D. Humphrey (2008), 'Payment network scale economies, SEPA, and cash replacement', *Review of Network Economics*, **6** (4), 453–73.

Brewer, E. and W. Jackson (2006), 'A note on the "risk-adjusted" price–concentration relationship in banking', *Journal of Banking and Finance*, **30** (3), 1041–54.

Carbó, S., J. Fernández de Guevara, D. Humphrey and J. Maudos (2004),

'Estimating the intensity of price and non-price competition in banking', Working Paper, IVIE, Valencia, October.
Carbó, S., D. Humphrey and R. López (2006), 'Electronic payments and ATMs: changing technology and cost efficiency in banking', in M. Balling, F. Lierman and A. Mullineaux (eds), *Competition and Profitability in European Financial Services*, Routledge, London, pp. 96–113.
Carbó, S., D. Humphrey and R. López (2007), 'Opening the black box: finding the source of cost inefficiency', *Journal of Productivity Analysis*, **27** (3), 209–20.
Donze, J. and I. Dubec (2006), 'The role of interchange fees in ATM networks', *International Journal of Industrial Organization*, **24** (1), 29–43.
Hannan, T. (2006), 'Retail deposit fees and multimarket banking', *Journal of Banking and Finance*, **30** (9), 2561–78.
Hannan, T., E. Kiser, R. Prager and J. McAndrews (2003), 'To surcharge or not to surcharge: an empirical investigation of ATM pricing', *Review of Economics and Statistics*, **85** (4), 990–1002.
Heffernan, S. (1992), 'A computation of interest equivalences for non-price characteristics of bank products', *Journal of Money, Credit, and Banking*, **24** (2), 162–72.
Humphrey, D., M. Willesson, G. Bergendahl and T. Lindblom (2006), 'Benefits from a changing payment technology in European banking', *Journal of Banking and Finance*, **30** (6), 1631–52.
Kim, M. and B. Vale (2001), 'Non-price strategic behavior: the case of bank branches', *International Journal of Industrial Organization*, **19** (10), 1583–602.
Klein, M. and N. Murphy (1971), 'The pricing of bank deposits: a theoretical and empirical analysis', *Journal of Financial and Quantitative Analysis*, **6** (2), 747–61.
Mitchell, K. and N. Onvural (1996), 'Economies of scale and scope at large commercial banks: evidence from the Fourier flexible functional form', *Journal of Money, Credit, and Banking*, **28** (2), 178–99.
Santomero, A. (1979), 'The role of transaction costs and rates of return on the demand deposit decision', *Journal of Monetary Economics*, **5** (3), 343–64.
Snellman, J., J. Vesala and D. Humphrey (2001), 'Substitution of noncash payment instruments for cash in Europe', *Journal of Financial Services Research*, **19** (2/3), 131–45.
Startz, R. (1983), 'Competition and interest rate ceilings in commercial banking', *Quarterly Journal of Economics*, **98** (2), 255–65.

APPENDIX 4A

Parameter estimates for equations (4.1) to (4.4) for savings banks using first differences of logs of all the variables are shown in Table 4A.1. Results for commercial banks are available from the authors by request. Standard errors were computed from a quadratic form of analytic first derivatives (Gauss) and determined from a heteroscedastic-consistent matrix (Robust-White).

Parameters refer to the variables as follows: A1, ln branch; A2, ln ATM; A11, $(\ln \text{branch})^2$; A22, $(\ln \text{ATM})^2$; A12, ln branch × ln ATM; APL, ln labour price; APL2, $(\ln \text{labour price})^2$; A1PL, ln branch × ln labour price; A2PL, ln ATM × ln labour price; ADEPBR, ln deposits – ln branch; ALABORBR, ln quantity labour – ln branch; AMIX1, AMIX2, and AMIX3 are the three balance-sheet composition mix variables; E1, ln share of electronic payments; E11, $(\ln \text{share of electronic payments})^2$; MDUM, dummy variable for past bank mergers; F1 to F18 are the 18 Fourier form variables; AIRATE and APDEP substitute the market interest rate (IRATE) and the actual price of deposits (PDEP) at each bank, respectively, for the price of labour (PL) above; and IND substitutes the index of industrial production (IND) for the share of electronic payments (ELE). All variables are in first difference form: for example, ln ATM represents $\ln \text{ATM}_t - \ln \text{ATM}_{t-1}$, and so on for the other variables.

Table 4A.1 Parameter estimates

(4.1) Operating Cost/Deposit Value		(4.2) Interest Cost/ Deposit Value		(4.3) Loan Revenue/ Loan Value		(4.4) Fee Income/ Deposit Value	
A0	0.371		22.4*		−8.86*		−16.8**
A1	11.5		−41.7		−4.80		−68.2
A2	−2.46		27.1*		−6.13		−45.7*
A11	−22.8		−107		58.7		138
A22	5.14		−50.7*		12.1		92.4*
A12	−0.085		72.1*		−14.2*		11.6
APL	0.915*	AIRATE	0.264*	APDEP	0.420*	APL	0.890*
APL2	0.003	AIRATE2	−1.08*	APDEP2	0.427*	APL2	−0.013
A1PL	0.170*	A1IRATE	0.509	A1PDEP	1.87*	A1PL	1.21*
A2PL	−0.090*	A2IRATE	−0.188	A2PDEP	0.004	A2PL	−0.281*
ADEPBR	−1.00*		−0.740*		−0.058		−0.841*
ALABORBR	0.983*		0.036		0.081*		0.937*
AMIX1	0.000		0.009		−0.032*		0.031*
AMIX2	0.005*		−0.004		0.005		−0.052*
AMIX3	0.000		0.000		−0.000*		−0.000*
E1	−0.254*	E1	−1.03*	IND1	−0.387*	E1	−2.65*
E11	12.1*	E11	167*	IND11	4.43	E11	69.0*
MDUM	0.002		0.146*		0.001		−0.096
AHHI	0.005		−0.009		−0.016		−0.014
F1	4.15		−17.9		−1.62		−28.4
F2	−1.26		−18.0**		9.02*		17.2
F3	−1.08		21.5*		−4.94**		−16.1**
F4	0.573		−14.5*		3.22*		6.52

Table 4A.1 (continued)

	(4.1) Operating Cost/Deposit Value	(4.2) Interest Cost/ Deposit Value	(4.3) Loan Revenue/ Loan Value	(4.4) Fee Income/ Deposit Value
F5	0.722*	1.55	0.156	−0.050
F6	−0.671	6.26	−0.150	8.71
F7	0.050	1.75*	0.242	−3.49*
F8	0.141	−5.30*	0.956*	2.68**
F9	−0.270	−16.9*	2.38**	−1.50
F10	0.218	−8.30*	2.51*	−2.33
F11	0.202*	0.386	0.679*	−1.79*
F12	0.229*	3.73*	0.198	−1.27**
F13	−0.084	−3.81*	0.469**	0.239
F14	−0.106**	0.702*	−0.603*	1.76*
F15	−0.092	0.923	−0.274	2.59*
F16	−0.261*	−1.33**	−0.004	0.995
F17	0.021**	0.043	0.025	0.148
F18	0.032	−0.381*	0.044	0.594*

Note: * value significantly different from zero at p-value ≤ 0.05; ** value significantly different from zero at p-value ≤ 0.10.

5. Financial innovation in internet banking: a comparative analysis*

Francesca Arnaboldi and Peter Claeys

1 INTRODUCTION

Internet banking has attracted increasing attention since the 1990s. Partly fostered by technological advance, banks started to use the internet as an innovative payment method and as a way to reduce costs, enhance profits and increase customer convenience. Online banks have been promoted basically by financial groups, organised by both banks and insurance companies. In some cases commercial incumbents decided to enter the market. In our study we have focused on financial groups since the market share held by incumbent competitors does not seem to be relevant.[1] Two main business models may be identified in the use of banking portals online. The first one consists in cross-selling bank products via a website, thus new clients are reached and distribution channels are diversified, as opposed to the original bank based one (mixed business model). A second model is the creation of a pure internet/online bank (IB), which implies the absence of physical branches (pure business model). Usually pure online banks are created by banking groups to target price-sensitive clients whom they would not be able to reach via traditional distribution channels (DeYoung, 2005). Nearly half of US banks were using transactional websites at the beginning of 2002.[2] However, only a few of them have adopted a pure online business model, gaining rather diverse results. Some exited the market via liquidation or acquisition; others developed a mixed model and opened physical branches. Only a few pure online banks were able to achieve profits and survive.

The growth of online banking raises two major questions. First, what is the success model of internet banking? Is it better to create a pure IB, part of a banking group but perceived by clients as an 'external', innovative bank, or to offer the same products via a website, thereby 'internalising' the distribution channel? Pure IBs face fewer costs, and can offer deposit-based services at lower cost all the time. Nonetheless they lack a face-to-face relationship, which prevents them from targeting particular groups of clients, interested in tailored products and less sensitive to variation of prices.[3] Click and mortar banks have a competitive edge over pure IBs because of the mix of distribution channels used. They can cross-sell different products to clients using the most appropriate distribution tool. Second, technological barriers hinder the full deployment of internet transactions. The adoption of online banking as a product or process innovation is driven by factors external to the banking industry. One might wonder whether economic features, such as the level of investment in technology, research and development (R&D) expenses, internet access, and the familiarity of end users with new technologies may influence in some way online banking development.

Much of the existing evidence on the development of online banking focuses on a specific bank market in a single country. The contribution of this chapter is to compare the performance of banking groups with pure IBs to mixed internet banks across countries. Two comparisons are possible in terms of performance and cost. First, pure IBs may be compared to mixed banks' internet websites. Bankscope does not allow distinguishing among costs in such detail. In order to have data of a similar standard, we chose another approach. We have compared data from banking groups internalising the offer via website, and banking groups externalising it, by creating their own IBs. We are aware that banking group performance and cost are influenced by many variables. Nonetheless, our analysis attempts to isolate those features specifically linked to internet banking.[4] We examine the situation of internet banking in four European countries, Finland, Italy, Spain and the UK, which have rather different banking systems and are at various levels of technological development. We first endeavour to group pure and mixed IBs according to certain performance criteria and bank characteristics. We then provide panel estimates of bank performance on the basis of these bank-specific characteristics. We finally relate performance to various country-specific banking structure characteristics and various aspects of new technologies. The chapter is structured as follows. In Section 2, we mention a few studies that have examined the performance of pure IBs relative to mixed banks. We argue, in Section 3, that differences in banking structure and macro/micro features of economies are decisive in the performance of online banks. Therefore we provide a descriptive analysis of banking structure and country-specific characteristics for Finland, Italy, Spain and the UK. In Section 4, we analyse the performance of pure and mixed IBs, and relate these to bank and country-specific characteristics. Our conclusions are set forth in Section 5.

2 DOES INTERNET BANKING ENHANCE BANK PERFORMANCE AND WHY?

The relevant literature on this topic may be divided into two groups: on the one hand some authors focus on the internet as an innovative delivery channel representing new challenges to the financial sector. These studies relate the adoption of internet websites to economic features, such as PC ownership and usage, technology changes, R&D investments and mostly use descriptive techniques. The second group of studies examines the consequences on bank performance of different strategic models of online banking. Pure online banking, the development of internet websites as a delivery channel, or traditional banking do not have the same implications.

Referring to the first group, Birch and Young (1997) argue that the internet may be exploited as a new delivery channel by the financial services industry to completely reorganise the structure of banks. The use of solely electronic channels (without physical channels) threatens traditional retail banks as pure IBs can compete with lower overheads. Moreover, non-bank competitors may use electronic channels to bypass retail banks completely.[5] Jayawardhena and Foley (2000) explore the internet as a new delivery channel, arguing that internet websites may help to overcome the inherent disadvantages of a traditional branch. The provision and the implementation of internet banking have been slow, probably due to the limited range of services offered at that time. However, the authors point out that the internet may act as a facilitator in payment systems as it provides a broader range of services at all times, and thus assists the growth of electronic commerce. Finally, the internet has been analysed as a substitute/complementary channel in delivering certain bank products, such as current accounts. Gondat-Larralde and Nier (2004) investigate the competitive process in the UK market for personal current accounts between 1996 and 2001. In particular, the authors examined the speed with which the distribution market shares have changed in response to price differentials by comparing traditional banks to 'direct banks' that operate via telephone and the internet. The results point to the importance of customer switching cost as a key determinant of the competitive process in this market.

Few studies attempt to assess the performance of IBs. Nearly all studies refer to the US banking system. Sullivan (2000) argues that traditional banks are not affected by the adoption of the internet as a distribution channel. In a comprehensive study, Furst et al. (2002) develop a statistical model to explain why banks choose to adopt internet banking and why they differentiate their supply of online products. The authors also investigate the effects of online banking on profitability. They find that bank profitability is strongly correlated with internet banking for all US national banks. The first to adopt the new system were large, profitable banks, located in urban areas and forming part of a holding company. These banks use internet services as an aggressive business strategy to gain market share rather than for making profits. Their study shows no relationship between the existence of internet banking and profitability but this could be due to the disproportion of customer use of internet banking in their sample. In a more recent study, DeYoung (2005) analyses the performance of a dozen pure IBs that started up between 1997 and 2001. This paper attempts to identify which features of the pure online banking model have been effective, why some banks have been able to deploy this model more successfully than others, and whether the 'internet only' business model could be economically sustainable in the long run. The empirical results confirm the low average level of profits at pure IBs. Nonetheless the study reveals that typical internet start-ups offer better prices than the average traditional banking start-ups and grow faster as well. The problem is that the expected reduction in overheads and other expenses does not materialise and hence reduces profits because of insufficient scale in the operations. Finally, the evidence shows the existence of some technology-specific scale effects, suggesting the need for a pure online competitor to grow larger in order to survive. The study concludes that the 'internet only' banking model is potentially viable but its market share is likely to be limited.

To our knowledge, there are few attempts to empirically investigate internet banking performance in Europe. Ciciretti et al. (2008) analyse the performance of multichannel commercial banks *vis-à-vis* traditional banks in Italy. Internet adoption seems to influence positively bank performance, measured in terms of return on average assets (ROAA) and return on average equity (ROAE). Hernando and Nieto (2007) examine the impact on bank financial performance in the Spanish banking market when a transactional website was set up. The authors conclude that the adoption of the internet as a delivery channel gradually reduces overhead expenses. This cost reduction boosts the performance of banks about 18 months after the adoption in terms of ROAA, and after three years in terms of ROAE. In line with DeYoung (2005), this study proves that the internet had been used more as a complement than as a substitute for physical branches, suggesting the dominance of a multichannel banking model.

3 ONLINE BANKING IN EU COUNTRIES

The development of online banking in European countries reveals some common traits. In recent years, the dominant industrial strategy in EU countries is for banking groups to own both pure IBs and more traditional banks with an internet portal, thus exploiting both business models. IBs that initially offered only online tools have gone over to a mixed model, using other channels as, for example, telephone banking, or financial advisors. Stand-alone IBs are rather rare.[6] The large majority of traditional banks have set up an internet portal to diversify their distribution channel. But in addition, many banking groups have set up separate IBs with their own brand that function as independent entities.

We examine the performance of banking groups that have set up internet banks (pure IBs) versus banks that offer a mix of distribution channels (mixed banks). We look into the development of online banking in four EU countries (Finland, Italy, Spain and the UK). This enables us to expand the dataset to produce clearer evidence regarding the performance of online banking. But in addition, it allows us to contrast different banking models. This makes the results more widely applicable than studies focused on a specific market. These four countries not only represent a variety of banking structures but also differ in their economic structure, and in particular in their adoption of new technologies. These external factors possibly affect the success of internet banking.

Table 5.1 shows the banks in Finland, Italy, Spain and the UK that we consider in this study. With the exception of eQ bank in Finland, there are no stand-alone IBs. We will not further consider this bank in the analysis. Several large banks and two financial groups held by an insurance company have established pure IBs within their holding. We consider all IBs in the four countries. There are relatively more bank groups that have created separate online banks in Italy and the UK. In Spain, only three IBs have been set up whereas in Finland, only the traditional banker Nordea has created a pure internet service. A similar number of banking groups offer online transactions alongside their traditional branch services. They are peers in terms of size, products and market mix. Basically, IBs develop simple, deposit-based products that clients perceive as commodities. Usually they offer current and savings accounts, money transfers and payment services (for example, bill payment). In Italy trading online has also been offered by some IBs. Practically the same services are offered via transactional websites. In summary, the sample of pure and mixed banks accounts for more than 70 per cent of all banking activities in these countries.

Data on these banks are taken from Bankscope, a Bureau Van Dijk database, which provides balance-sheet information on banks at comparable standards.[7] We measure bank profitability in terms of return on average equity, return on average assets, cost to income ratio and the overheads/profit before tax ratio. ROAA is the ratio of gross income to

Table 5.1 Traditional and online banks in four EU countries

	Spain	Finland	Italy	UK
Stand-alone internet banks	–	eQ bank	–	–
Pure internet banks (in group)	Caixa Catalunya (Banco de Europa) BBVA (Uno e-bank) BSCH (Open Bank)	Nordea (Luottokunta)	Unicredit (Xelion) MPS (Banca 121) Capitalia (Fineco) BPU (Banca Akros, IW Bank) BPM (Webank) Gruppo Ras (Rasbank)*	HBOS (Capital Bank) Cooperative (Smile) RBS (Coutts) Prudential (Egg)* Standard Life (Standard Life)*

Mixed banks/banking groups	CajaAhorro	OP Cooperative	Unicredit	Barclays
	Ibercaja	OKO	Intesa	Bradford & Bingley
	Pastor	Sampo	Monte dei Paschi	Alliance & Leicester
	Bancaja	Alandsbanken	San Paolo	Bank of Scotland
	Popular		Sella	Halifax
	Sabadell			HSBC
	BBVA			Lloyds TSB
	La Caixa			Natwest
	Caja de Ahorros del Mediterraneo			Northern Rock
	CajaMadrid			Scottish Widows
				Abbey National
				Ulster
				HFC
				Cheltenham
				AMC

Note: * Indicates financial groups held by insurance companies.

Table 5.2 Statistics on four performance criteria of pure and mixed internet banks

	Spain	Finland	Italy	UK
Criterion	ROAA			
Mixed banks	0.95	0.83	0.48	0.90
Internet banks	0.91	0.93	0.51	−0.22
Criterion	ROAE			
Mixed banks	13.91	14.24	9.59	17.83
Internet banks	13.99	16.44	8.86	8.86
Criterion	CI			
Mixed banks	57.20	61.11	70.95	45.58
Internet banks	60.53	54.13	71.57	94.41

average assets and ROAE is the ratio of gross or net income to average equity. Gross income is usually preferred to net income to avoid the differences in taxation among countries.[8] ROAA is a good overall indicator for banking performance showing the ability of a bank to generate profits from the assets at its disposal. Nonetheless, it has some disadvantages. The denominator does not account for off-balance-sheet activities. ROAE is an alternative measure of profitability designed to reflect the return to owners' investment. Its main disadvantage is that the denominator may vary across banks, due to the choices made by management as to the mix between equity and debt capital as well as the total amount of capital held by a firm.[9] On the cost side of bank operations, the cost to income ratio (CI) reflects the ability of the bank to generate revenue from its expenditures.[10] The ratio of overheads on profit before tax ratio gives similar information, but constitutes an improved check on costs.

Table 5.2 displays the mean performance of banking groups holding IBs versus mixed banks in the four countries being analysed. There is no statistically significant difference between these two types of bank. Both deliver a positive return on assets and equity. Only the UK IBs perform substantially worse than the UK mixed banks. In fact, the return on assets ratio is negative for IBs, and the return on equity is about half of that of mixed banks. Spanish and Finnish banks outperform the Italian and UK ones. Spanish banks deliver a higher return on assets, while Finnish banks perform better with respect to equity. Italian banks perform badly in comparison to their peers in the EU. Their average return is about half of that of banks in the other countries.

Table 5.2 shows that cost–income ratios are comparable across all countries. Groups with IBs have similar costs relative to the income that their assets generate with the exception of UK IBs. The inferior return on assets of UK IBs is due to much higher costs. Whereas UK mixed banks manage to have a really low CI in comparison to mixed banks in other countries, UK IBs have a much higher ratio as compared to their European peers. This indicates problems in their cost structure given the revenues that the activity of the IB generates. There are various reasons for the difference between UK and Continental banks. For example, UK banks may pay higher interest rates to clients in order to expand the deposit base. We shall now examine some structural differences across EU countries.

The four EU countries have a somewhat different financial market structure (Table 5.3). The banking sector in Europe has been undergoing a consolidation process since the end of the 1990s and this has led to a decline in the number of credit institutions. This consolidation was particularly pronounced in Italy and the UK (−6.6 and −8.6 per cent, respectively). On the other hand in Finland, the banking system has remained stable as to the number of banks and branches. These figures are the consequence of more numerous mergers and acquisitions (M&As) in Italy and in the UK. Spanish banks closed only two M&A deals in the same year, while there were none in Finland (ECB, 2005). The ongoing consolidation of the EU banking sector may have changed competitive conditions and led to the adoption of new business strategies and to the use of the internet as an innovative delivery channel.

Despite consolidation, the number of branches in the EU has increased on average, as shown in Table 5.3. This may suggest that internet websites, where adopted, have been a complement to and not a substitute for physical branches. Whereas in Italy and Spain the number of branches increases, the opposite tendency emerges in the UK (+5.7, +4.1, −3.8 per cent, respectively). One may ask whether the increase of branches has been followed by an increase in the number of employees. The answer is mixed: the total number of employees has decreased in Italy and in Finland, whereas it has increased slightly in Spain and in the UK. Nonetheless, the number of employees per bank has increased in every country except Finland. Thus the reduction in the number of banks seems not to be followed by a decrease in the number of branches and in the number of employees per bank. One explanation could be the difficulty of cost cutting after M&As in Europe, which may lead to excess capacity. Another view is that competitive markets have boosted the level of employment. Finally, specialised financial services may need higher-qualified and better-paid employees. The dense network of banks and ATMs as well as the high number of employees rather suggest an overcapacity of distribution channels. The internet could then be redundant in the delivery channel mix.[11]

Table 5.3 The banking system, 2001–2004

Characteristics	Year	Spain	Finland	Italy	UK	EU25
Number of credit institutions	2001	366	369	843	452	9,363
	2002	359	369	821	451	8,944
	2003	348	366	801	426	8,613
	2004	346	363	787	413	8,374
Growth rate in %		−5.5%	−1.6%	−6.6%	−8.6%	−10.6%
Number of branches	2001	39,024	1,571	29,267	14,554	206,265
	2002	39,021	1,572	29,948	14,392	202,483
	2003	39,762	1,564	30,501	14,186	199,426
	2004	40,621	1,585	30,946	14,001	199,606
Growth rate in %		4.1%	0.9%	5.7%	−3.8%	−3.2%
Number of employees	2001	244,781	26,733	343,812	506,278	3,177,776
	2002	243,429	27,190	341,584	501,787	3,134,816
	2003	243,462	26,667	338,288	500,656	3,075,993
	2004	246,006	25,377	336,979	511,455	3,057,528
Growth rate in %		0.5%	−5.1%	−2.0%	1.0%	−3.8%
Number of employees per bank	2001	669	72	408	1,120	339
	2002	678	74	416	1,113	350
	2003	700	73	422	1,175	357
	2004	711	70	428	1,238	365

Total assets of credit institutions (€m)	2001	1,247,998	163,416	1,851,990	5,830,158	24,685,988
	2002	1,342,492	165,661	2,024,156	5,854,355	25,296,181
	2003	1,502,861	185,846	2,125,366	6,175,244	26,462,180
	2004	1,717,364	212,427	2,275,652	6,970,009	29,009,982
Growth rate in %		37.6%	30.0%	22.9%	19.6%	17.5%
Loans of CIs to non-financial firms (€m)	2001	306,019	30,943	520,856	439,735	3,543,665
	2002	340,980	32,991	546,559	439,530	3,612,910
	2003	387,804	34,719	588,676	408,655	3,732,341
	2004	454,715	37,708	615,688	426,897	3,891,107
Growth rate in %		48.6%	21.9%	18.2%	−2.9%	9.8%
Total loans of CIs for housing purchase (€m)	2001	206,815	27,329	107,711	965,934	3,073,881
	2002	236,388	30,960	131,660	1,035,553	3,323,029
	2003	277,573	36,049	154,374	1,100,210	3,722,676
	2004	335,665	41,544	185,014	1,238,492	4,123,180
Growth rate in %		62.3%	52.0%	71.8%	28.2%	34.1%

Source: ECB (2005) and authors' computation.

Table 5.4 Competition in the banking system, 2001–2004

	Year	Spain	Finland	Italy	UK	EU25
Herfindahl index 0–10,000	2001	551	2240	260	282	506
	2002	529	2050	270	307	521
	2003	521	2420	240	347	549
	2004	482	2680	230	376	569
Share of big 5 in total assets (%)	2001	44.9	79.5	28.8	28.6	37.8
	2002	44.3	78.6	30.6	29.6	38.3
	2003	43.9	81.2	27.0	32.8	39.8
	2004	41.9	82.7	26.0	34.5	40.2
Number of branches of foreign banks	2001	56	18	110	202	850
	2002	59	19	106	190	827
	2003	57	18	90	181	807
	2004	61	20	104	175	831

Source: ECB (2005) and authors' computation.

Finally, if we look at the size of banks in the four countries from 2001 to 2004, the growth rate of total assets has been higher than the European average (17.5 per cent), almost double in Spain and Finland (37.6 and 30 per cent, respectively), 22.9 and 19.6 per cent in Italy and in the UK. The last two countries probably had a higher level of bank size on average in 2001, which could explain their lower growth rate. As for the mix of products, both loans to non-financial firms and for house purchase have been growing since 2001. In Spain and in Italy the mortgage sector reveals the highest rate of growth (62.3 and 71.8 per cent). This could be explained by the boom of the real estate sector, by the particular focus on core activities, especially on retail, as well as by cyclical developments such as low interest rates in the economic environment. However, the internet can hardly be used as a substitute delivery channel for physical branches on loan granting. Frequently, websites provide reliable information on loan conditions and may help in the customer acquiring phase. The final steps still require interaction with telephone and/or physical branches.

Table 5.4 gives more insight into market structure and competition in the banking sector. Finland is characterised by high concentration in the banking sector according to both the Herfindahl index and the share of the five largest credit institutions in total banking sector assets (C-5 ratio).[12] Italy and the UK show a lower concentration than the European average in both indicators. In Italy the low market concentration may be attributed to a dual banking structure, with both commercial and cooperative banks.

In the UK it may be due to the presence of many foreign banks not directly providing retail services to residents.[13] A concentrated market structure does not necessarily have a negative impact on competition (Martins et al., 1996; Nicoletti et al., 2000). It can be the consequence of economies of scale and scope: larger players tend to be more efficient and cannot exploit market power. As to foreign competitors, the UK seems to have the most open banking market with about half of all banks being non-UK based. In Spain and Italy, the percentage of foreign banks in terms of number of branches is about 20 per cent, but in Finland it is only about 5 per cent. Of course, this picture is slightly distorted as (i) we measure the number of registered banks, and not the assets held by these banks; (ii) we do not consider the attraction of the City as a financial centre; and (iii) we do not take into account service supply without the establishment of cross-border subsidiaries.

The adoption of internet banking depends much on the technological capacity of using online tools. Not all countries in our sample are at a similar level of technological advancement (European Commission, 2005). R&D expenditure gives an overall indication on the level of scientific headway (Table 5.5). In this respect, Finland stands out above the UK, and outpaces Italy and Spain by far. A similar order prevails in terms of the number of employees involved in R&D activities. The number of employees in R&D activities is relatively lower in the business and government sector, whereas higher education institutions employ the major share. In the banking sector, more investments are made on human resources in science and technology than in most other economic sectors. Financial intermediation can be considered as a knowledge-intensive sector in that respect.

Expenditure on communication technologies (installation of internet, broadband and so on) is fairly evenly spread across countries as are communication costs. Local calls are only slightly more expensive in the UK, but this is compensated by much cheaper national calls. Broadband technologies are more widespread in Finland than in the other countries, however. The largest difference across the countries derives from investment in information technology (IT). For both Italy and Spain, this is much lower as a share of GDP than in Finland or the UK.

Even if the total expenditure on new technologies is fairly uniform, the extent to which new communication technologies are used is quite different between the northern and southern countries (Table 5.6). Access to computers, and to the internet, is much lower in Spain and Italy. Use of the internet does not pose important security problems, such as fraudulent payments or the abuse of privacy, and virus problems are relatively limited (with the exception of Spain). Nonetheless, the security of the internet for carrying out transactions is perceived as problematic in Spain and Finland,

Table 5.5 Science and technology, 2004

	Spain	Finland	Italy	UK
R&D employment (% of total)				
All sectors	1.49	1.14	3.24	–
Business	0.52	0.37	1.72	–
Government	0.22	0.20	0.42	–
Science and technology employment (% of total)				
All NACE branches – total	36.2	32.6	45.5	38.5
Manufacturing sector	30.8	19.8	39.0	32.5
Services	44.0	41.7	51.7	41.8
Knowledge-intensive financial services	70.8	64.5	72.4	49.3
Other knowledge-intensive services employment (% of total)	72.8	75.1	59.2	58.4
Financial intermediation	70.8	64.5	72.4	49.3
Information technology				
IT expenditure as % of GDP	1.80	2.00	3.60	4.30
Communications expenditure as % of GDP	3.70	3.30	3.40	3.80
Price of local calls (in €)	0.28	0.25	0.24	0.44
Prices of national calls (in €)	0.88	1.15	0.90	0.44
Broadband penetration rate (%)	5.40	4.80	9.50	5.30

Source: Eurostat, European Innovation Scoreboard.

and it could possibly affect access to internet-based services. The use of online bank products is more widespread in Finland than in the UK, and much more than in the southern countries. Internet banking is predominantly used for basic deposit-based transactions roughly to the same extent as for buying goods and services. Specialised bank services are only a fraction of the total transactions carried out online.

4 A COMPARATIVE ANALYSIS OF INTERNET BANKING

We first describe the characteristics of different banking groups with pure or mixed IBs, and analyse the effect of the internet on the performance of both types of bank. We then examine the effect of country- and technology-specific characteristics on banking performance.

Table 5.6 Availability and usage of internet, 2005

	Spain	Finland	Italy	UK
Accessibility	% of households having access to			
Internet at home	34	51	34	56
A personal computer	55	64	46	65
Security	% of individuals who have, in the last 12 months, experienced the following security problem			
Fraudulent payment (credit or debit) card use	0.30	0.10	0.30	1.60
Abuse of personal information sent on the internet	7.40	2.10	1.40	2.20
Computer virus resulting in loss of information or time	22.90	23.10	14.60	26.00
	% of individuals who, in the last 12 months, haven't ordered goods or services over the internet, because of			
Security concerns	26	24	7	8
Privacy concerns	23	23	4	5
Usage of internet	% of individuals who used internet, in the last 3 months, for			
Financial services (internet banking)	14	56	8	27
Other financial services (e.g. share purchasing)	5	14	2	5
Purchasing/ordering goods or services	11	33	4	38

Source: Eurostat.

A Cluster Analysis

We examine whether there is a pattern in the performance of banks that choose different online strategies. Using fuzzy cluster analysis, we look into various characteristics of banks – various sets of performance and other bank-specific features – to distinguish different groups of banks. Fuzzy clustering is a simple descriptive technique to classify observations in groups with other observations that show the greatest similarity. It is an innovative statistical tool commonly used in pattern recognition techniques. Applications in economics have focused on grouping with similar business cycle movements (Artis and Zhang, 1998). It has been used in financial literature, by Sörensen and Puigvert (2006) to examine the degree of financial integration in the euro area banking industry, for example.

Let us assume that we have a dataset of n objects, and each object is characterised by some p variables denoted by $X_{n,p} = \{x_1, x_2, \ldots, x_n\}$, where each $x_i = \{x_{i1}, \ldots, x_{ip}\}$. The dissimilarity for a certain variable p is given by the (Euclidean) distance between two objects.[14] The total distance between different objects on all p characteristics is then given by (5.1).

$$d(i, j) = \sqrt{\sum_{k=1}^{p} (x_{ki} - x_{kj})^2}. \qquad (5.1)$$

The two observations that are most similar are classified in a first group. By repeating this procedure on this group and the remaining $n - 1$ objects, each object is eventually assigned to a particular group according to its closeness to one of the most similar groups. The highest coefficient indicates the group to which the unit n most likely belongs. The silhouette width indicates the degree of similarity within a group of observations. A value close to one means that the objects are well classified in the cluster. A value near zero indicates ambiguity in deciding which cluster the object might belong to. We select the optimal number of groups as the one that gives the highest average silhouette width. The normalised Dunn's partition coefficient indicates the existence of a partition in the structure of the panel, varying between 0 (complete fuzziness of the data) and 1 (well-partitioned data). Cluster analysis has some limitations. It may be difficult to determine (i) the correct number of clusters, and (ii) whether the clusters formed from the data significantly represent different groupings or are random concentrations of observations within an original distribution (Hair et al., 1998).

The primary goal of the analysis is to identify clusters among banks in the sample and find out whether pure and mixed IBs belong to two different groups. This would mean the existence of some common development of IBs regardless of country or other bank-specific features. Cross-country differences and other relevant variables (mix of products, type of client and so on) might play an important role, too, and this could mask clear classification.

We group banks according to each of the four performance criteria (ROAA, ROAE, cost to income and overhead to profit before tax ratio) discussed in Section 3, and some other bank-specific features. These bank features focus on both revenues and the costs side of the bank balance. Deposits to total assets ratio (*DEP*) refers to the amount of deposits and short-term funding (excluding bank to bank deposits). Usually, the wider the deposit base, the higher are the revenues. Pure IBs should have a higher ratio, since they need to reach a broader customer base to survive. Non-interest income to net operating revenue (*NII*) is an approximation for the amount of revenues generated by 'non-traditional banking activity'. The variable is expected to be significant and positively related to performance. Risk profile is provided by loan/loss provision to net interest revenue (*LOAN*), which shows the extent to which the bank has made provisions to cover credit losses. The higher this ratio, the larger the amount of expected bad loans on the books, and the higher are the risks for the bank. Pure IBs should have a lower ratio than multichannel banks since they do not usually provide loans to customers.[15]

As to cost-related variables, pure IBs should have lower labour expenses (*LAB*) compared to multichannel banks. We expect a significantly negative relationship due to the fact that if expenses increase, profitability decreases on average. A substitution effect may nonetheless be present. If banks employ more highly skilled workers to develop IT services, labour costs increase even if the number of employees decreases. Non-interest costs (*EXP*) are taken as an approximation for IT and marketing expenses. One of the reasons for implementing web-based services is cost reduction, which should lead to higher performance. Pure IBs should have lower expenses than multichannel banks. Nevertheless, costs could be higher after adopting the internet as a new distribution channel because of higher IT expenses in the short run. We scale both variables to total bank assets.

All data are taken from Bankscope; Table 5.7 summarises the variables we use. We apply the cluster analysis to the year 2004, for which we have the most complete set of data for the four different performance criteria and the bank-specific criteria. If we consider ROAA, ROAE and the overheads to profit ratio, we find that the observations can be optimally grouped in two different clusters (Table 5.8). These clusters are not clearly associated with a distinction between internet and mixed bank groups. Most of the banks classified in cluster 2 are indeed IBs, but a few mixed banks belong to this group as well. Conversely, there are also IBs that belong to the other group. Furthermore, the distinction between the two groups is not very strong. Banks in group 2 are often on the border of being in the first group. The silhouette width indicates that some banks are misclassified when we use the ROAA or the overhead/profit ratio. As a consequence, average silhouette width is low. The ambiguity in the classification is also indicated by the low normalised Dunn coefficient.

These results are slightly modified when we employ the cost–income ratio. The data are optimally divided into five different groups. There seems to be a classification of banks according to country basis. Nearly all Finnish banks belong to group 4; many UK-based banks form part of group 5; and most Italian and Spanish banks are located in group 3 (and often in group 2 too). But these are not exclusive sets. A few individual banks are often classified in different groups. IBs belong to each of these

Table 5.7 Description of variables

Variables		Description
DEP	Deposits and short-term funding	(deposit and short-term funding – deposits from other banks)/total assets
NII	Net interest income	(other operating income)/(other operating income + net interest revenue)
LOAN	Loan loss provisions	Loan loss provision/total loans
LAB	Personnel expenses	Personnel expenses/total assets
EXP	Overheads	Overheads/total assets
SIZE	Total assets	Total assets
R&D		Total expenditure on R&D (% of GDP)
		Employment in R&D, all sectors (% total)
		Human resources in science and technology, all sectors
		Human resources in science and technology, Knowledge-intensive financial services: NACE Rev. 1.1 codes 65, 66, 67
		Human resources in science and technology, financial intermediation
Banking structure	Herfindahl index	Sum of the squared market shares of the individual banks
	C-5 ratio	Market share of the five largest banks
	Competition of foreign banks	Ratio of foreign bank branches on total number of bank branches
Technology	Usage	Percentage of households having access to the internet at home
		Percentage of households having access to a PC
		Prices of telecommunication, local calls
		Prices of telecommunication, national calls
		Broadband penetration rate (%)
	Spending	Information technology expenditure (% of GDP)
		Communication expenditure (% of GDP)
Macroeconomic		Long-term interest rates
		Growth of labor productivity

Table 5.8 Fuzzy clustering on bank characteristics, 2004

	ROAA		ROAE		Cost income ratio		Overhead/profit before tax	
	Silhouette width	Cluster	Silhouette width	Cluster	Silhouette width	Cluster	Silhouette width	Cluster
HBOS holding	0.53	(1)	−0.29	(1)	0.37	(2)	0.60	(1)
RBS	−0.49	(2)	−0.15	(1)	0.66	(2)	0.54	(1)
Cooperative	0.68	(1)	0.58	(2)	0.56	(3)	0.71	(1)
Standard Life	0.60	(1)	0.79	(2)	0.76	(3)	−0.42	(2)
Prudential	−0.32	(2)	–	–	–	–	–	–
Barclays	0.38	(1)	−0.05	(1)	0.67	(2)	0.47	(1)
Bradford & Bingley	0.57	(1)	0.77	(2)	0.65	(5)	0.77	(1)
Bank of Scotland	0.64	(1)	0.79	(2)	0.56	(5)	0.71	(1)
Cheltenham	0.71	(1)	0.84	(2)	0.65	(5)	0.78	(1)
Halifax	0.69	(1)	0.85	(2)	0.67	(5)	0.78	(1)
HFC	0.03	(2)	−0.32	(1)	0.47	(4)	−0.02	(2)
HSBC	0.49	(1)	−0.09	(1)	0.55	(2)	−0.53	(2)
Lloyds TSB	0.51	(1)	−0.20	(1)	0.25	(5)	0.58	(1)
Natwest	0.47	(1)	−0.31	(1)	0.26	(5)	0.59	(1)
Northern Rock	0.70	(1)	0.80	(2)	0.66	(5)	0.78	(1)
Scottish Widows	0.68	(1)	0.76	(2)	−0.09	(5)	0.72	(1)
Ulster	0.72	(1)	0.79	(2)	0.67	(5)	0.77	(1)
Abbey National	−0.48	(2)	0.66	(2)	0.65	(5)	0.77	(1)
Alliance & Leicester	0.68	(1)	0.70	(2)	0.57	(5)	0.74	(1)
AMC	−0.33	(2)	0.58	(2)	0.53	(4)	−0.41	(2)
Unicredit	0.65	(1)	0.59	(2)	0.48	(2)	0.72	(1)
Akros	0.15	(2)	0.07	(1)	0.65	(4)	0.13	(2)

Table 5.8 (continued)

	ROAA		ROAE		Cost income ratio		Overhead/profit before tax	
	Silhouette width	Cluster	Silhouette width	Cluster	Silhouette width	Cluster	Silhouette width	Cluster
Capitalia	−0.65	(2)	0.73	(2)	0.46	(3)	0.74	(1)
MPS	0.63	(1)	0.79	(2)	0.56	(3)	0.72	(1)
Rasbank	−0.16	(2)	−0.34	(1)	−0.48	(1)	−0.30	(2)
BPU	0.71	(1)	0.83	(2)	0.76	(3)	0.79	(1)
BPM	0.69	(1)	0.82	(2)	0.79	(3)	−0.73	(2)
Intesa	0.64	(1)	0.69	(2)	0.12	(2)	0.72	(1)
San Paolo	0.67	(1)	0.72	(2)	−0.09	(2)	0.74	(1)
Sella	0.69	(1)	0.80	(2)	0.77	(3)	0.73	(1)
CajaAhorro	0.77	(1)	0.74	(2)	−0.50	(3)	0.82	(1)
BBVA	0.68	(1)	0.65	(2)	0.31	(2)	0.77	(1)
Santander	0.60	(1)	−0.50	(1)	0.66	(2)	0.68	(1)
Ibercaja	0.77	(1)	0.84	(2)	0.73	(3)	0.81	(1)
Pastor	0.76	(1)	0.83	(2)	0.67	(3)	0.80	(1)
Popular	0.62	(1)	0.80	(2)	0.36	(3)	0.80	(1)
Sabadell	0.77	(1)	0.84	(2)	0.77	(3)	0.82	(1)
Caixa	0.77	(1)	0.83	(2)	0.68	(3)	0.82	(1)
Cam	0.76	(1)	0.85	(2)	0.64	(5)	−0.60	(2)
CajaMadrid	0.77	(1)	0.86	(2)	0.74	(3)	0.82	(1)
Bancaja	0.77	(1)	0.83	(2)	0.70	(3)	0.82	(1)
Nordea	0.69	(1)	−0.67	(1)	0.60	(3)	0.74	(1)
OKO	−0.27	(2)	0.53	(2)	0.70	(4)	−0.38	(2)
Sampo	−0.58	(2)	−0.41	(1)	0.41	(3)	−0.62	(2)

OP	−0.24	(2)	−0.35	(1)	0.65	(4)	−0.31	(2)
Aland	−0.19	(2)	−0.37	(1)	0.63	(4)	−0.29	(2)
Number of clusters	2		2		5		2	
Silhouette width	0.29	(1)	0.76	(1)	0.09	(1)	0.73	(1)
	0.66	(2)	0.28	(2)	0.32	(2)	0.37	(2)
					0.64	(3)		
					0.59	(4)		
					0.51	(5)		
Average silhouette width	0.28		0.33		0.33		0.35	
Dunn's coefficient	0.50		0.54		0.45		0.52	
Normalized Dunn's coefficient	0.00		0.08		0.31		0.03	

Note: Bold names indicate internet banks, the others are mixed banks.

different groups, but are not specific enough to be identified as a separate group.[16] The silhouette width indicates that each of the groups is quite well defined, and so is the overall classification of the five sets of banks. Generally speaking the result indicates that some latent country-specific characteristics are important determinants in bank performance. The distinction between internet and mixed banks seems of secondary importance. Therefore the country-specific features we are going to add should help to better describe a bank's business model.

A Panel Analysis

The results from the fuzzy cluster analysis indicate that the distinction between pure internet and mixed banks cannot be fully assessed. Cluster techniques only detect a pattern in the unit observations, but do not give a structural explanation for the performance of banks. We therefore focus on a regression analysis of the performance $c_{i,t}$ of bank i by these bank-specific features $\overline{X}_{i,t}$:

$$c_{i,t} = \alpha_i + \beta \overline{X}_{i,t} + \mu_{i,t}. \tag{5.2}$$

The panel of 46 banks spans the 1995–2004 period. We use fixed effects panel estimates, as there is probably a lot of unobserved heterogeneity across the banks. The above-mentioned bank-specific features ($\overline{X}_{i,t}$) give an insight into the characteristics that are important in determining differences in performance.[17]

The estimation by fixed effects simply assumes any differences in bank-specific characteristics into the constant. These features could be related to the bank's choice to develop internet portals, or to a set of country-specific features. The similarity of online banking models in several countries with different banking structures, market organisation and level of technological progress suggests either that these different factors are only of secondary importance in the choice of online banking strategies, or that different characteristics offset each other. We check the effect of cross-country differences of some of the macro and micro characteristics discussed in Section 3. A spate of recent OECD studies relates aggregate economic performance to summary indicators of technology or regulation (Scarpetta and Tressel, 2002). We extend this literature in two ways. First, we look into a particular innovation (e-banking) and the performance of the financial sector. Second, we relate performance to a wider set of indicators.

We thus explain bank performance $c_{i,t}$ by both bank-specific features $\overline{X}_{i,t}$ and economy-wide characteristics $\overline{Z}_{i,t}$:

$$c_{i,t} = \alpha_i + \beta \overline{X}_{i,t} + \lambda \overline{Z}_{i,t} + \mu_{i,t}. \tag{5.3}$$

Information on the economic structure of the four countries considered is drawn from the ECB, the OECD, and Eurostat. We consider three different categories of variables.

The first set of indicators concerns the banking system of each country. We are particularly interested in the effect of competition on banking performance. The effect is not unambiguously clear. On the one hand, a competitive financial sector boosts individual bank performance but also skims any monopoly rents. On the other, oligopolistic industries are more competitive and innovative than fully competitive industries. IBs could be seen in both types of market as having a technological edge over competitors. That IBs are set up by larger bank holdings indicates perhaps that the oligopoly structure of financial markets is more relevant. We include both the Herfindahl index and the C-5 ratio, and expect its sign to be negative. Competitors from other EU member states have often used online strategies to attract some of the clients to traditional banks. We look into the effect of foreign entry on the performance of domestic banks (ratio of foreign bank branches on total number of branches).

With a second set of variables, taken from the European Innovation Scoreboard and Eurostat, we explore the importance of some microeconomic characteristics on the use of the internet. We consider the effect of increased use of computers and home access to the internet, the availability of broadband lines and telecommunication rates. An increased use at lower costs of online technologies should improve the performance of online banking.

A third group of variables concern aggregate technological indicators, such as R&D expenses, employment in R&D sectors, communication and technology and data on human resources investment (in all sectors, knowledge-intensive financial services and financial intermediation, respectively). Increasing expenditure in each of these categories would raise the viability of online banking as an alternative banking channel.

Finally, we look at some macroeconomic variables, such as the level of long-term interest rates, which control for the growth of the cost of deposits. The growth of labour productivity proxies aggregate economic growth.

Results

We run the panel estimates for the entire group of banks, and then compare results for the group of pure and mixed IBs. Table 5.9a displays the results of the fixed effects estimates for the entire panel of banks, and when the return on average assets and equity are taken as dependent variables, for pure and mixed IBs separately. Table 5.9b does the same for the cost to income ratio and the overhead/profit ratio. The results on the cost income

Table 5.9a Panel estimates of model (2), fixed effects, 1995–2004

	Return on average assets			Return on average equity		
	All banks	Internet banks	Mixed banks	All banks	Internet banks	Mixed banks
C	−0.77	−1.32	−1.02	−0.78	−17.09	16.32
	(0.24)	(0.12)	(0.32)	(0.96)	(0.35)	(0.58)
DEP	0.06	−0.14	0.15	8.45	10.82	−2.36
	(0.83)	(0.71)	(0.71)	(0.20)	(0.18)	(0.84)
NII	0.52	0.58	0.11	12.76	14.42	−1.44
	(0.00)***	(0.00)***	(0.78)	(0.00)***	(0.00)***	(0.90)
LOAN	0.40	0.44	22.31	2.87	4.20	102.62
	(0.00)***	(0.00)***	(0.00)***	(0.29)	(0.12)	(0.47)
LAB	63.56	28.53	107.34	988.82	280.41	1510.29
	(0.00)***	(0.26)	(0.00)***	(0.05)**	(0.60)	(0.13)
EXP	−20.53	−4.43	−48.11	−475.06	−152.66	−696.08
	(0.06)*	(0.74)	(0.02)**	(0.08)*	(0.59)	(0.20)
SIZE	0.10	0.16	0.13	0.47	1.88	−0.45
	(0.05)**	(0.02)**	(0.11)	(0.72)	(0.20)	(0.85)

Observations	301	136	165	310	136	174
R^2 within	0.19	0.23	0.19	0.30	0.19	0.13
R^2 between	0.09	0.10	0.50	0.16	0.10	0.02
R^2 overall	0.12	0.22	0.19	0.06	0.19	0.04
sigma_u	0.42	0.42	0.34	5.83	7.96	4.97
sigma_e	0.32	0.30	0.31	7.89	6.34	8.89
rho	0.64	0.67	0.55	0.35	0.61	0.24
F test that all u_i = 0	0.00	0.00	0.00	0.00	0.00	0.78
corr FE, X	−0.29	−0.46	−0.46	0.05	−0.41	−0.31

Note: */**/*** indicates significance at 1, 5 and 10%, respectively; *p*-values in parentheses.

Table 5.9b Panel estimates of model (2), fixed effects, 1995–2004

	Cost to income ratio			Overheads/profit before tax		
	All banks	Internet banks	Mixed banks	All banks	Internet banks	Mixed banks
C	119.92	145.34	68.35	−7.14	−3.77	−1.98
	(0.01)***	(0.10)	(0.00)***	(0.74)	(0.93)	(0.81)
DEP	23.33	78.73	−2.03	−3.14	−9.86	0.05
	(0.19)	(0.04)**	(0.76)	(0.71)	(0.61)	(0.99)
NII	−43.21	−55.32	11.13	−1.14	−0.82	−0.53
	(0.00)***	(0.00)***	(0.10)	(0.82)	(0.92)	(0.87)
LOAN	−14.08	−17.26	−119.98	1.27	1.22	−98.59
	(0.06)*	(0.19)	(0.15)	(0.72)	(0.85)	(0.02)**
LAB	−3,043.74	−1,851.65	−2,809.38	520.76	688.36	−31.09
	(0.03)**	(0.47)	(0.00)***	(0.43)	(0.60)	(0.91)
EXP	1,602.50	885.14	2,043.92	−175.69	−278.84	114.99
	(0.03)**	(0.51)	(0.00)***	(0.62)	(0.68)	(0.46)
SIZE	−5.80	−10.25	−1.82	0.98	1.13	0.31
	(0.11)	(0.15)	(0.19)	(0.57)	(0.75)	(0.64)

Observations	299	136	163	310	136	174
R^2 within	0.30	0.57	0.18	0.12	0.10	0.00
R^2 between	0.16	0.28	0.27	0.01	0.00	0.04
R^2 overall	0.12	0.16	0.32	0.00	0.01	0.05
sigma_u	18.89	20.39	7.90	3.23	5.09	2.03
sigma_e	21.37	30.61	5.19	10.29	15.43	2.58
rho	0.44	0.31	0.70	0.09	0.10	0.38
F test that all u_i = 0	0.00	0.02	0.00	0.81	0.95	0.00
corr FE, X	−0.27	−0.27	−0.29	−0.42	−0.57	−0.19

Note: */**/*** indicates significance at 1, 5 and 10%, respectively; *p*-values in parentheses.

ratio and the overheads/profit ratio confirm most results for the performance criteria. As these variables are related to costs, the coefficients obviously switch signs.

Let us first consider some aspects of the revenue side of banks' balance sheets. A larger fraction of deposits – relative to total assets – does not improve the performance of banks. A separate estimation for the panel of IBs does not show a positive effect; but nor does it for the group of mixed banks. We find a similar result if we take the return on equity as the performance criterion. Banks seem to earn fewer profits on basic intermediation. At the same time, more deposits do not entail higher costs for the income they generate in mixed banks. In contrast, IBs have trouble in keeping under control the costs of additional clients with deposit accounts. This would be a rather worrying development, as the handling of deposit accounts constitutes the core activity of IBs. The main source of revenue for IBs is interest generated by deposit-based products. An extension of the customer base to clients only via deposits seems not a very profitable strategy. As the core of banking revenues is nowadays generated by other operating income, a pure internet banking model does not seem feasible in the long run from this point of view.

If an online bank is to prove profitable it would appear necessary for it to reduce fixed costs on deposit accounts or to address itself towards more rewarding activities, such as supporting other bank products. As anticipated, non-interest income is an important factor in driving a bank's performance. Whether we measure performance in terms of return on average assets or on equity, there is always a significant positive impact on performance. Curiously, this effect can be entirely attributed to IBs. This may seem a bit counterintuitive as IBs mainly handle deposit-based products. However, groups that encompass IBs probably perform better on average than other groups that use the web as a mere delivery channel. Possibly banking groups that have set up IBs (i) are more advanced in their management, keeping an eye on client needs and being able to rapidly adapt to them; (ii) have at their disposal other resources from activities not related to intermediation, which makes it possible to invest in internet banking technologies; (iii) are able to acquire new clients via IBs or exploit synergies with IBs to attract more clients that stream into activities with higher value (cross-selling of products). As the effect of non-interest income is to raise the cost to income ratio, these three different rationales may be relevant.

Higher provisions for loans – relative to total outstanding loans – improve the performance of banks. This effect is positive and significant for all types of banks, but it is especially so for mixed banks. Since higher provisions shrink the asset base for additional loans, this would reduce the performance of bank activities. However, banks issue loans at a decreasing marginal rate. A rationale for the positive effect of loan provision clauses is that setting aside a fraction of loans effectively protects banks against granting loans of bad quality and partially prevents banks from incurring losses. IBs do not directly engage in loan activities, but may contribute to cross-selling them. Websites are a powerful and interactive way to give information on various products (for example, personal loans, mortgages). Pure IBs may then direct clients to the bank holding to complete the transaction. In addition, the information collected online may help banks to reduce credit risk exposure, since current account movements, money transfers and payments are currently tracked. This information may be an early warning on clients' repayment capacity. The effect of loan provisions on performance for the entire group suggests that the creation of an IB seems to be more likely if there is a large share of intermediation activities. Banking groups with few loan activities may consider IBs as a means of reducing costs on standard transactions.

We then consider some cost-related variables. A rather surprising finding is the positive sign on labour costs. Higher expenses on personnel – relative to total assets – would lead to higher performance and reduce costs. This effect is significant for banking groups with no internet subsidiary. Hence, internet banking groups seem to perform better in terms of personnel management than other banks. The latter do not exploit all opportunities to assign staff to highly specialised activities. IBs seem to be more successful in the substitution of low with highly skilled workers. This interpretation is endorsed by the significantly negative effect of other operating expenses on performance. The effect of other non-personnel-related costs on performance is much larger for mixed than for internet banks. The former may have higher expenses on IT, marketing, and new product development and start-up costs, but even a small reduction in these overheads would considerably improve performance.

Finally, if we consider the scale of bank operations we find evidence in favour of economies of scale. The larger the bank, the higher the performance. This effect is slightly more pronounced for IBs. An increase of total assets by 1 per cent would increase the return on assets by 1.16 per cent for IBs, and 1.13 per cent for mixed banks. Further increasing assets could be even more rewarding for IBs in terms of return to equity. The result, which is consistent with De Young's (2005) findings on IB size, might be explained by the specific features of online banking. Since its major activity is based on deposits and their related products, an increase in size would lead to higher revenues. Regarding costs, once the IT platform is set up and the basic system is working, personnel and other expenses increase less than proportionally as the dimension of the bank increases. We do not find a significant impact of scale on the cost/income ratio, however. This may be due to the relatively small size of IBs as compared to the overall banking group. A cost reduction in the IB may not be large enough to affect the balance sheet of the group as a whole.

The explanatory power of the model for both internet and mixed banks is in line with previous studies. However, we have presumably omitted some other explanatory factors behind bank performance in the four EU countries. We can usually reject that the fixed effects of each model are irrelevant, except if we use the overheads/profit ratio. The fixed effects model is not entirely satisfactory in some other aspects, either. There is still a significant (negative) correlation left between the fixed effects and the explanatory variables.

These baseline results still hold good if we add various economy-wide characteristics $\overline{Z}_{i,t}$. In order not to burden the evidence with additional tables, we summarise here the effect of these characteristics on bank performance.[18] First, competition in the banking sector affects only slightly the performance or cost structure of banks. We do not find a significant impact of the Herfindahl index on return or costs. However, we find that a larger market share of major banks reduces the profitability of mixed banks. We may read this finding in two different ways. On the one hand, higher concentration is associated with more competition as it reduces profits. On the other, high concentration may give rise to inadequate incentives to be cost efficient, hence reducing profitability too. As we examine both returns and cost income ratios, we can distinguish these two different models. For mixed banks, more competition does not reduce costs. Hence, mixed banks do not seem completely cost efficient and there may be little pressure from competitors.

One explanation may be that mixed banks in concentrated markets probably need to deliver higher-quality services over a broader range of clients at higher costs. In contrast, for IBs, high market power in the banking sector reduces the cost to income ratio but does not have an impact on returns. This indicates that banking groups with pure internet branches are more able to compete and are more cost effective, as they can expand their services in a more competitive market at lower cost. There seem to be somewhat diverse effects in different countries. For example, in the case of Finland there is a high degree of concentration which might account for the high profitability of banks. On the other hand, concentration is very low in the UK, and yet profitability is comparatively high. However, the concentration in the UK banking market is peculiar because of the role of London as a financial centre. Nonetheless, foreign entry, as measured by the ratio of foreign bank branches to the total number of branches, does not have an impact at all. Note that we did not consider the effect of entry of foreign pure IBs on the domestic market.

Second, as to internet-related activities, an increase in the percentage of households with home access to the internet improves the return for all banks, but reduces costs only for IBs. Increased internet access enhances the chance of profitable contact to new clients, and thus boosts the scale of the potential market for IBs. Each new access represents a possible cost reduction for online banks, since, for example, IT and start-up costs are distributed over a larger base of clients. This allows a substitution effect among physical and internet branches, since some transactions, originally only carried out at the bank, are now available online at home 24 hours a day. Nonetheless new clients accessing the website may entail higher personnel expenses for mixed banks.[19] The use of personal computers as such does not increase returns for IBs, albeit it does for mixed banks. It contributes to higher costs for IBs, however. A higher broadband penetration rate has similar positive effects for all banks, but also decreases costs for all banks. Curiously, higher prices of local telephone calls increase the returns to banks. More costly national calls reduce the cost income ratios of IBs, however. The high cost of calls and broadband penetration, which increases internet speed, may lead to a substitution among communication tools. Broadband allows more functionality at cheaper cost per unit at a higher speed. The next step could be fast access to online current accounts. Potential clients may start considering personal computers not simply as a working instrument but also for banking activities.

Other technology-related features at the macroeconomic level have a clear-cut implication. Spending on R&D employment in the economy as a whole or in the financial services sector has positive effects on the return to assets or equity of mixed banks, and reduces their cost–income ratios. IBs do not seem to reap any particular competitive advantages from R&D spending. The effect seems spread out among all banks, showing a generalised benefit from these investments. Expenditure on IT as a share of GDP does not lead to higher performance in the banking sector. On the contrary, it reduces returns as it boosts costs. However, outlay on communication technologies pays off for both internet and mixed banks.

Macroeconomic variables have little to no impact. Higher long-term interest rates decrease the return to assets of IBs without increasing their cost to income ratio. The growth of labour productivity has limited impact on the costs of mixed banks.

5 CONCLUSION

We compared the performance of different online banking models over the 1995–2004 period in Finland, Spain, Italy and the UK. Groups with

IBs are not performing worse in terms of average returns to assets (or equity), and do not seem to run higher operational costs for the little income they generate. From the fuzzy cluster analysis we found that IBs are hard to distinguish from banks that adopt both click and mortar strategies. Country-specific features appear to be more important in explaining differences across banks. We therefore explain the performance of banks by a group of selected bank-specific features, but also add country-specific macroeconomic indicators and IT-related ratios. We find that the strategy of banking groups to incorporate IBs reflects some competitive edge that these banks have in their business models. The management of these banks is generally more capable of handling personnel and other costs. The strategy of banking groups to incorporate IBs reflects some competitive edge in their business models. Personnel expenses are comparatively low, but the costs for IT are disproportionately high. Management has become more aware of the possibilities of online banking.

The success of internet banking depends on the structure of clients' deposits. By focusing mostly on bank deposits, these banks cannot gain benefits from more rewarding banking activities. Clients interested in value-added products still prefer interaction with a physical branch. IBs need to reach a minimum dimension in order to become profitable. Nonetheless, the fact that IBs have been started up with the support of larger bank holdings, shows that pure IBs are not as profitable as a simple cost/revenue comparison would suggest.

The adoption of online banking as a product or process innovation is largely driven by factors external to the banking industry. The percentage of households with access to the internet at home, a higher broadband penetration rate, and higher outlay on R&D employment are all factors positively influencing IB performance. But this technology effect should not be overrated: these effects are as important for traditional banks as for IBs.

Increasing competition does not have an immediate impact on bank performance. Yet, the creation of IBs may be a sign of more competitive banking markets, and their existence will probably increase transparency and product range. Clients oriented to cheap and quick deposit accounts would probably prefer IBs. Hence, such banks may cause innovation in the banking sector, and serve as a learning experience for mixed banks in terms of technology. In interpreting the data we should keep in mind that IBs are not widespread, and make up only a tenth of the overall banking market. We should expect that the impact of IBs may not be strong enough to affect the banking system as a whole. However, they certainly contribute to increasing transparency on specific products, such as current accounts, allowing for comparisons among banks that were previously more difficult.

NOTES

* Peter Claeys acknowledges support by a Marie Curie Intra-European Fellowship within the 6th European Community Framework Programme. The authors thank L. Anderloni, D.T. Llewellyn and B. Rossignoli for precious comments. All errors are ours. The chapter is the result of intense collaboration between the two authors. However, Sections 2, 3 and 4 (third subsection) are attributable to F. Arnaboldi, and Sections 1 and 4 (first two subsections) to P. Claeys. Section 5 is a joint effort.

1. For example we refer to Carrefour in France or Sainsbury's in the UK. The number and dimension of online banks promoted by such competitors are not relevant to the market formed by financial groups. Moreover, studying these banks poses problems in terms of homogeneity of the sample. Therefore we decided to limit our analysis to financial groups.
2. 'Transactional Websites' have been defined by DeYoung (2005) as websites which allow customers remote access to banking services. The most basic transactional websites allow a few operations such as money transfers, payments, and checking account balances. Some websites allow their customers to apply for mortgages and loans and manage clients' investments.
3. If clients have lower price sensitivity, they would be less attracted by an online bank. They would probably prefer to pay more to get better service.
4. Our analysis presumably omits some other explanatory factors behind bank performance. Obviously, an extension of the panel could make the analysis of bank performance by country-specific features more interesting from a macro perspective. In particular we have in mind a more detailed analysis of technology-specific factors, as well as the importance of various financial products (loans, mortgages, and so on) across countries. We have not considered the effects of experience in handling new IBs. As most IBs have been created recently, this does not necessarily mean that online banking is not a viable strategy. Learning economies, mainly technology learning, may be present. Also, the link of the IB to its mother holding could be more detailed. One could consider to what extent financial support is important for pure IBs. More evidence on IT expenses could show how established banks learn about various online technologies. This requires a more detailed insight into the balance sheets of IBs, however, which is not fully available at the moment.
5. This situation could be seen in embryo form where telephone companies issue prepaid phone cards. In the UK major retail chains have entered the market. For example, Safeway has created its own bank (Safeway Bank) which offers debit card services, consumer loans and grant access through website (Source: Corporate annual reports and websites).
6. As we said in the introduction, our sample is limited to financial groups with banks or insurance companies as holder.
7. We consider consolidated statements. Hence, IBs are part of banking groups. Bankscope does not provide information on subsidiaries' balance sheets.
8. 'Average' means that the item is averaged using the arithmetic mean of the value at the end of year t and $t-1$. See Bankscope Ratio definitions.
9. These choices are basically conditioned by regulation. However, management has some margin to influence the bank structure.
10. According to Bankscope definitions, cost to income is the ratio of overheads to operating income.
11. However, it should be noted that less densely populated countries, like Finland, may need more branches to cover the same number of customers or a more complete mix of distribution channels to satisfy clients' needs.
12. According to US competition authorities, a number higher than 1,800 indicates a concentrated market.
13. Thus the level of concentration of banking services to residents may be underestimated (ECB, 2005).
14. Each variable is standardised with mean zero and standard deviation one in order to treat them as having equal importance in determining the structure.

15. The success of online banking also depends on the characteristics of financial products offered in each market. For example, online banks are not able to provide mortgages as the client–bank relationship remains crucial in this case.
16. RasBank constitutes a group by itself. RasBank is part of a financial group held by an insurance company thus differing from other banks that belong to financial bank groups. Similar cases are Egg, which is owned by Prudential, and Standard Life. Few data were available for these banks. Nonetheless, in the case of ROAA, Egg belongs to the same cluster as RasBank; in addition, Standard Life belongs to cluster 2 in two out of four variables tested, confirming the particular features of these three IBs.
17. We did not use size in the cluster analysis, as we would simply classify banks according to the scale of operations. Note that total deposits are considered when the dependent variable is ROAA.
18. Detailed results are available from the authors on request.
19. It may depend on the size of the market and on the number of new clients. Nonetheless, new clients acquired by a mixed bank via website would presumably be targeted by other products, such as loans, mortgages and so on, which require a face-to-face relationship.

BIBLIOGRAPHY

Artis, M. and W. Zhang (1998), 'Business cycles, exchange rate regimes and the ERM: is there a European business cycle?', *International Journal of Finance and Economics*, **2**, 1–16.

Birch, D. and M. Young (1997), 'Financial services and the internet – what does the cyberspace mean for the financial services industry?', *Internet Research: Electronic Networking Applications and Policy*, **7** (2), 120–28.

Ciciretti, R., I. Hasan and C. Zazzara (2008), 'Do internet activities add value? Evidence from traditional banks', *Journal of Financial and Services Research*, July, DOI 10.1007/s10693-008-0039-2.

DeYoung, R. (2001), 'The financial performance of pure play internet banks', *Federal Reserve Bank of Chicago Economic Perspectives*, **25** (1), 60–75.

DeYoung, R. (2005), 'The performance of internet-based business models: evidence from the banking industry', *Journal of Business*, **78** (3), 893–947.

DeYoung, R. (2006), 'The limits of information technology: how much will the banking industry change?', in P. Heikkinen and K. Korhonen (eds), *Technology Driven Efficiencies in Financial Markets*, Helsinki: Bank of Finland, pp. 35–46.

European Central Bank (ECB) (2004), 'Outsourcing in the EU banking sector', Report on EU Banking Structures, Frankfurt am Main, November, pp. 25–32.

European Central Bank (ECB) (2005), 'EU banking structures', Frankfurt am Main, October.

European Commission (2005), 'Towards a European Research Area. Science, Technology and Innovation. Key Figures 2005', Directorate General for Research.

Furst, K., W.W. Lang and D.E. Nolle (2000), 'Special studies on technology and banking. Who offers internet banking?', *Quarterly Journal*, **19** (2), 29–48.

Furst, K., W.W. Lang and D.E. Nolle (2002), 'Internet banking: developments and prospects', Program on Information Resources Policy, Center for Information Policy Research, Harvard University, April.

Gondat-Larralde, C. and E. Nier (2004), 'The economics of retail banking – an empirical analysis of the UK market for personal current accounts', *Bank of England Quarterly Bulletin*, Spring, 153–9.

Hair, J., R. Anderson, R. Tatham and W. Black (1998), *Multivariate Data Analysis*, 5th edn, London: Prentice-Hall.

Hernando, I. and M. Nieto (2006), 'Is the internet delivery channel changing banks' performance? The case of Spanish banks', *Journal of Banking Finance*, **31** (4), 1083–99.

Jayawardhena, C. and P. Foley (2000), 'Changes in the banking sector – the case of internet banking in the UK', *Internet Research: Electronic Networking Applications and Policy*, **10** (1), 19–30.

Llewellyn, D.T. (2001), 'Technology and the new economics of retail financial services', The Annual Building Societies Association Lecture, Extended version, September, London.

Martins, J.O., S. Scarpetta and D. Pilat (1996), 'Mark-up ratios in manufacturing industries: estimates for 14 OECD countries', OECD Economics Department Working Paper 162, Paris.

Nicoletti, G., S. Scarpetta and O. Boylaud (2000), 'Summary indicators of product market regulation with an extension to employment protection legislation', OECD Economics Department Working Paper 226, Paris.

Scarpetta, S. and T. Tressel (2002), 'Productivity and convergence in a panel of OECD industries: do regulations and institutions matter?', OECD Economics Department Working Paper 342, Paris.

Sörensen, C. and J. Puigvert (2006), 'Euro Area banking sector integration using hierarchical cluster analysis techniques', ECB Working Paper 627, Frankfurt am Main.

Sullivan, R.J. (2000), 'How has the adoption of internet banking affected performance and risk at banks? A look at internet banking in the tenth Federal Reserve district', *Federal Reserve Bank of Kansas City Financial Industry Perspectives*, December, 1–16.

6. How do internet payments challenge the retail payment industry?*

David Bounie and Pierre Gazé

1 INTRODUCTION

Since the mid-1980s, the role of money and banks has been affected by various innovations. The rapid development of financial markets, new behaviours in terms of investments and new modes of financing and so on have transformed the financial sphere. These significant changes have taken place in a context of financial globalisation, an internationalisation of payments and a mutation of monetary systems which have gradually imposed new rules for payment systems. All these transformations have affected the orientation and control of monetary policy, which has become increasingly difficult to implement as the concept of money becomes harder to define.

In the context of a changing monetary system, the current electronisation of retail payment systems provides a new set of challenges for banking and monetary authorities. Faced with the ongoing transformation of the payment environment through the development of electronic face-to-face transactions (vending machines and so on) and electronic remote transactions (the internet, wireless networks), numerous product innovations have appeared, including electronic purses, electronic payment systems on the internet and mobile payments. Among these innovations, the development of electronic payment systems on the internet is probably at the origin of the most surprising developments. Numerous electronic payment systems have been conceived by institutions, other than banks, as a way of contesting the bank monopoly on payment instruments. Some innovative payment instruments are now competing with traditional payment instruments (for example, the payment card) for specific payment services.

In this context, the objective of this chapter is to try to understand why the development of some promising and innovative electronic payment systems on the internet, such as billing systems and person-to-person online payments for micro-payments, are competing with traditional payment instruments issued by banks. In other words, why are banks not able to compete with non-banks for such payment services? The main conclusion reached in this chapter is that inter-bank payment organisations induce high costs, which prevent banks from offering specific payment services, such as online micro-payments and person-to-person online payments, unless they make significant changes. At this stage, in the absence of competitive payment instruments, new electronic payment systems, backed by private closed systems, can develop. The latter are, in turn, backed by private payment networks whose simplified systems enable them to be free from inter-bank authorisation, clearing and settlement. The development of private closed systems consequently challenges the capability of the inter-bank retail payment industry to cope with these innovations. This issue is particularly important at a time when the European Union is attempting to build a Single European Payments Area (SEPA) and the Financial Services of the European Commission are endeavouring to create more competition between banks and providers in the payment card industry.

The remainder of this chapter is structured as follows. First, we present the main banking and monetary innovations that have taken place in the development of electronic payment systems. We briefly show that some electronic payment systems have been conceived of as a way of contesting the bank monopoly of outside and inside moneys as well as the bank monopoly of payment instruments. Second, we try to understand why some new payment instruments will be able to compete with existing ones by reviewing the main theoretical contributions on the topic of competition between payment instruments. We note that the main theoretical findings rely on a cost-based approach and predict that the costs, the network effects and the price structure of the payment instruments determine their market shares to a large extent. We therefore analyse the main empirical studies that have been undertaken on the costs of payments and go on to outline that the specific organisation of the retail payment systems involves high costs to process scriptural payments – verification, clearing and settlement – compared to cash and e-purse payments. These elements allow us to conclude that the inter-bank payment system that ensures the universality of the payments is not necessarily suited to all forms of payment and especially not to online micro-payments.

These observations basically explain the rise of innovative electronic payment systems such as billing and person-to-person online payments used in closed private systems and operated by non-banks. These electronic payment systems are three-party systems in which a platform has direct relations with end-users, and within which monetary transfers are directly carried out between consumers and merchants or between two consumers, and are directly cleared and settled within the system. To conclude, we discuss how the current four-party banking systems could adjust to change, in order to reduce the costs of retail payments. This could be done by reversing the kinematics of payment flows between card-holders, merchants and banks in order to lower payment costs.

2 THE RETAIL PAYMENT INDUSTRY FACING PRODUCT INNOVATIONS

The purpose of this section is to comment on the main implications of product innovations in the development of electronic payment systems on the internet.[1] To begin with, we present some stylised facts on contemporary monetary systems in order to gauge the effects of the development of electronic payment systems more accurately.

Contemporary Monetary and Banking Systems: Some Stylised Facts

Several stylised facts can be presented to characterise the organisation and functioning of the main contemporary monetary and banking systems:

1. Contemporary monetary systems are hierarchical. At the top of the structure, a central bank defines and issues the fiat money to the whole of the monetary system. This means of payment is legal tender.
2. At an intermediate level of the pyramidal payment structure, banks are the only institutions entitled to issue private liabilities redeemable at par and which are entitled to collect deposits from the public. The bank liabilities are primarily held as deposits in accounts (scriptural money).
3. The base of the payment structure is composed of non-banking agents that benefit from payment services. Deposits are transferable by multiple payment instruments issued by banks. In numerous European countries, banks have a monopoly on the management and the issuing of 'universal' payment instruments, that is, payment instruments accepted by institutions different from the issuer. Two main types of payment instruments are typically differentiated: means of payment and means of exchange (Goodhart, 1990). Means of payment (notes and coins) are the payment instruments of fiat money; they allow the immediate extinction of debts contracted during transactions. By contrast, means of exchange (cheques, payment cards and so on), that is, the payment instruments of scriptural money, simply constitute 'vehicles' for exchanging payment orders between consumers, sellers and banks, which will be settled within inter-bank payment systems.

Payment orders can be transmitted physically (cheques) or remotely (payment card) through telecommunications networks. The internet thus constitutes a new 'medium' for economic agents and banks to transfer payment orders.
4. The central bank is in charge of monitoring the payment systems since debts between banks are settled in central money. Two main types of payment systems exist: those intended for small value payments – the retail payment systems – and which result from transfers between consumers and banks through payment instruments and clearing systems; and those devoted to large value payments from inter-bank transfers or transfers between banks and financial intermediaries. Given the importance of payment systems in monetary economies, the agents taking part in the payment systems – mainly banks – are subject to prudential rules.

Starting from these stylised facts, we can now comment on the uniqueness of the electronic payment systems on the internet.

The Development of Electronic Payment Systems: Outline and Outlook

Bounie and Gazé (2007) have proposed a typology of the main electronic payment systems developed over the internet. These form a heterogeneous group articulated around electronic money systems (virtual and electronic purses) and scriptural systems (account-based systems). We use this typology hereafter to better assess how electronic payment systems challenge the contemporary banking and monetary systems summarised in the above-mentioned stylised facts.

Electronic payment systems: contesting bank monopoly on outside money

One of the unique attributes of the electronic payment systems is the manner in which it is able to produce private currencies such as QQ coins, therebucks, Everquest Platinum and Piece, which is unbacked or backed by private liabilities or commodities such as a metal (gold, silver, palladium and so on). In the E-gold system, for instance, users hold titles of a precise weight of a metal on non-bank accounts managed by private firms. Starting with these accounts, the users transfer their titles closer to the seller affiliated to the system. The intermediary in this case manages any transaction. In order to ensure users' confidence, the non-bank offers full coverage of the gold deposits, as has been expounded in theories on 'narrow banking' by Greenbaum and Thakor (1995). Similarly, numerous major 'Massively Multiplayer Online Role-Playing Games' (MMORPG) produce their own money that is used by several thousand people – and sometimes by several million people – to buy and sell in-game assets. For example, the game 'There' has therebucks that sell for US dollars. The currency in 'Entropia Universe', Project Entropia Dollars (PED), could be bought and redeemed for real-world money at a rate of 10 PED for one US dollar.[2] Tencent, China's largest instant-messaging service provider, which boasts more than 220 million users, issues the so-called 'QQ' coin which can be purchased with a bank, telephone or 'QQ' card at an official rate of 1 yuan (12.5 cents) per coin. These game moneys can be bought directly online, exchanged between gamers or purchased on online auction websites such as eBay. Some intermediaries such as 'IGE' allow gamers to buy, sell or trade several major virtual currencies; others, such as GameUSD, provide real exchange rates between major game currencies.[3]

These developments are interesting from a monetary point of view because they question the central bank's position as sole producer of outside money, as in the Hayekian theory on competitive monetary systems (Hayek, 1978). The development of such systems may appear improbable, unrealistic or even anachronistic; yet some central banks such as the Chinese Central Bank, for instance, have recently expressed their concern with the rapid development of game currencies. 'QQ coin', issued by Tencent, has become so popular that the central bank is worried that it could affect the value of the yuan, and has planned to draft regulations to govern virtual transactions (see Asia Times Online, 2007).

Electronic payment systems: contesting the bank monopoly on inside money

Another innovation of certain electronic payment systems is to allow exchanges of non-bank liabilities whose values derive from their being redeemable for central bank money, from non-bank accounts. Without questioning the central bank position as sole producer of outside money, these electronic payment systems can be seen as a way to deregulate 'inside money', that is, a way to compete with banks.

The best-known electronic payment system is PayPal, which was developed in the United States and has been established in some European countries. PayPal is a person-to-person online payment instrument designed for any type of monetary transfer such as auctions (eBay), gifts and so on between PayPal users. Monetary transfers are completed by e-mail. The funds received by the payee can be left in deposits on the PayPal account or transferred into a bank account. PayPal takes a two-part tariff (fixed and variable) on transactions received on their accounts and also manages the float of the system. PayPal organises an intermediation in payments by fulfilling all the traditional functions of a bank: it provides payment instruments, manages accounts and carries out the clearing and settlement between accounts. The PayPal account is thus designed as a substitute for the bank account: any payment between PayPal accounts no longer involves an entry into the bank account and a settlement in inter-bank payment systems. The only link with banks remains when PayPal accounts are credited or debited through credit and debit card systems.

Electronic payment systems: contesting the bank monopoly of payment instruments

Finally, some of the electronic payment systems are conceived of as a way of contesting not necessarily the outside and inside bank moneys but rather the bank monopoly on payment instruments. As outlined in the third stylised fact, the issuing of universal payment instruments is legally entrusted to banks in most developed countries, and this monopoly constitutes a strategic advantage for banks since revenues derived from payment activities are substantial. For instance, Rice and Stanton (2003) estimate that, on average, 16 per cent of the operating revenue of the top 40 American Bank Holding Companies is derived from payment-related activities. Moreover, the payment data collected on bank accounts are a formidable tool to monitor loans (Mester et al., 2005). For instance, a cheque cancellation can inform the bank of the nature of the difficulties encountered by borrowers. Consequently, when borrowers are also depositors, banks have a significant cost advantage in the monitoring of the granted loans. The question of the bank monopoly on payment instruments is therefore not without implication.

In addition to the PayPal system described above, two other classes of electronic payment systems can be presented.

The first class covers the payment protocols designed to secure online payment orders by debit and credit cards (mainly the online protection of the number of the debit/credit card). Several types of protocols are available even if the Secure Sockets Layer (SSL) has taken the lead on the market. SSL was conceived of by a non-bank (Netscape) and standardised by the Internet Engineering Task Force under the name of Transport Layer Security (TLS). Banks and non-banks within a competitive market today market SSL. The current version of this protocol in use does not ensure the complete security of payments in so far as the payer is not authenticated during the payment session. The seller is thus not guaranteed against attempted fraud by opportunistic consumers. The SSL protocol cannot be likened directly to a payment instrument and non-bank providers do not necessarily seek to contest the bank monopoly on payment instruments. However, in many European countries (such as France), banks also have a monopoly on the design and standardisation of payment protocols to ensure the security of the payment instruction transfers on the networks (bank, telephone networks and so on). In this case, a bank payment instrument, the payment card, can be used with a non-bank payment protocol designed to secure the payment card's instructions over the internet. A direct economic consequence of the development of such a protocol is the desegregation of the added-value payment chain between different bank and non-bank firms and, possibly, the development of online fraud.

The second class is concerned with billing systems for low-value payments. Some non-banks provide consumers with the possibility of buying goods and services during a determined period from sellers affiliated to them. The purchases are aggregated and paid for at the end of the period at the time of the reception of a bill, using a banking means of exchange such as a cheque, for instance. This system, which originally appeared with the 'Minitel kiosk' in France, is not limited to the internet. It is used to settle some debts in traditional trade (electricity, water and so on) and is also spreading today within mobile networks in the context of the invoicing of data services: NTT DoCoMo (I-Mode), Vodafone (Live) and Orange (World). Non-banks such as mobile operators and internet service providers then intermediate by collecting their customers' payments by means of bills and transferring to the sellers the incomes of the transactions minus a fee. The non-bank thus makes a pre-compensation of payer and payee positions. This has a direct consequence in the reduction of the number of entries in bank accounts and inter-bank payment systems. Instead of directly paying all the transactions to the merchants by way of bank means of exchange, the consumer settles only an aggregate of all consumptions with the non-bank. The billing system is nevertheless still conceived of as a complement to the bank account in so far as the ultimate payment of the bill (aggregate of consumptions) can only be made via a bank payment.

The development of electronic payment systems: synthesis

The electronic payment systems described above have three types of implications.

The first is monetary and deals with questions of competition between outside moneys – fiat moneys and online private moneys – and between online inside moneys. These questions are significant but not new, and are largely debated in monetary economics (see Martin and Schreft, 2006, for instance).

The second implication relates to banking and is concerned with the effects of increased competition over deposits, on the profitability of banks and on financial intermediation (Bounie and Gazé, 2007). For instance, could a decrease of deposits or information on bank accounts in the long term raise the costs of financial intermediation?

The third implication is industrial and relates to the bank monopoly on payment instruments. Billing and person-to-person payments (PayPal), for instance, are widely used for low-value internet payments. As a result, these electronic payment systems compete with traditional payment instruments, such as cash, payment cards, cheques and so on. In this context, a question arises: why do electronic payment systems compete with traditional payment instruments on the internet?

In the next section, we try to answer this and other questions.

3 INDUSTRIAL ORGANISATION OF RETAIL PAYMENTS: THE START OF A NEW TYPE OF COMPETITION

The theoretical literature on the economics of payment instruments provides interesting findings on the competition between current payment instruments such as cash, cheque and payment cards. In this section we provide a synthesis of the main theoretical findings to further our understanding of the development of new electronic payment systems and to gauge the major implications for the organisation of the retail payment industries more accurately.

The Economics of Payment Instruments: A Review of Selected Theoretical Models

During the past few decades, the considerable increase in the number of payment instruments has prompted economists to explain why people are likely to prefer to use one specific payment instrument over another. Inspired by the formal models of Baumol (1952) and Tobin (1956) on the consumer (individual) demand for money for transaction purposes, the theory has progressively evolved to integrate the strategic payment behaviour of all economic agents involved in the payment process, namely merchants and banks. In the following subsection we comment on the main findings of this theoretical literature.

A cost-based approach without strategic interactions: a theory of consumer payment behaviour

The Baumol (1952) and Tobin (1956) models have greatly influenced and oriented the major theoretical contributions that relate to the understanding of payment behaviour. In their approach, a cost-minimising consumer has to decide on the optimal stock of cash to be held for transaction purposes, given the cost of a withdrawal (a fixed fee per withdrawal) and the interest earnings forgone on the average money holding. The main result of this inventory theoretical approach is that the average cash holding is proportional to the square root of the value of transactions and inversely proportional to the square root of interest. Globally, this 'square root law' implies 'economies of scale' in the transaction balances.

Starting from this cost-based approach, Santomero (1979), Whitesell (1989, 1992) and Santomero and Seater (1996) have extended their analysis to include several payment instruments, such as the cheque, the payment card and the electronic purse. As in the Baumol and Tobin approaches, consumers are supposed to minimise their transaction costs (time, interest earnings forgone on money holdings). For instance, in Whitesell (1989, 1992), the consumer has already adopted an alternative payment instrument – a cheque and/or a payment card[4] – and each of them is attended by fixed and variable costs (which depend on the size of the transaction).[5] Given the size of transactions, the consumer has to realise that there is a trade-off between the different costs associated with the various payment instruments. The originality of Whitesell's approach is to show that each payment instrument has a transaction domain determined by its costs: since cash payments are attended by the lowest fixed costs and card payments by the lowest variable costs, consumers will use cash for low-value payments and a card for high-value transactions.

This first group of theoretical models is interesting because it provides a robust micro-founded framework to explain the diversity of multiple payment instruments in the economy. Mainly centred on consumer payment behaviour, the models predict that the market share of a new payment instrument depends to a very large extent on its cost structure. However, the existence of multiple payment instruments at the market equilibrium is not the only result of consumer payment decisions. The payment process implies the participation of many merchants who can also optimise between various payment instruments. A second strand of literature has consequently appeared that has focused on the role of merchants.

A cost-based approach with strategic interactions: the role of merchants

The specificity of a payment act is to gather two different economic agents who have their own strategies in terms of *adoption* and *use*. Sometimes, these strategies may differ and impact on the number of payment instruments at the market equilibrium, as well as their use. As a result, strategic interactions between merchants and consumers matter and must be taken into account.

The first theoretical contribution that deals with the role of merchants in explaining the adoption and the coexistence of payment instruments on the market is Berentsen's (1998). The starting-point of that simple framework is the existence of a generally accepted medium of exchange – cash

– used to pay for all purchases in the economy. At some point, a firm decides to launch a new payment instrument called the 'electronic purse'. The market is composed of two agents: one representative consumer and one representative merchant. The author assumes that there is only one transaction between the consumer and the merchant whose value is P. Both parties have to decide whether they want to use the old (cash) or the new (electronic purse) payment instrument to pay for the transaction. The use of the electronic purse requires from both parties an initial investment expenditure f (fixed cost) and a cost of use a_2. Likewise, the use of cash costs a_1 for the consumer and the merchant and, by assumption, the total cost are smaller when both parties use the electronic purse, that is, $a_1 > f + a_2$. At this stage of the game it is reasonable to wonder why consumers and merchants will agree to adopt and use the new payment instrument. The answer is clear: the profitability of the investment f will depend on whether the other party uses the new payment instrument. Thus, if the merchant decides to invest, the revenue associated with the transaction will depend on the consumer's decision to invest or not; in this case, the merchant will respectively earn $P - a_2 - f$ or $P - a_1 - f$ if the consumer chooses to invest or not. Using the assumption $a_1 > f + a_2$, three results can emerge according to the investment decision: $P - a_2 - f$, $P - a_1$, $P - a_2 - f$ with $P - a_2 - f < P - a_1 < P - a_2 - f$. Likewise, if the consumer decides to invest, the cost of the transaction will depend on the merchant's decision to invest or not. Once again, we have three possible results: $P + a_1 + f$, $P + a_1$, $P + a_2$ with $P + a_1 + f > P + a_1 > P + a_2$.

The author shows there are three Nash equilibria in this game. In the first, the electronic purse is *not used* even though it would be less costly to do so for both parties. Indeed, it makes sense that if consumers do not use the electronic purse a best response for merchants is not to accept the electronic purse either. Moreover, given that merchants do not accept cash, a consumer's best response is not to use cash either. In the second equilibrium, cash and electronic purse are used simultaneously. In the last equilibrium, only the electronic purse is used: if consumers use the electronic purse, a best response for merchants is to accept it as well, and given that merchants accept it, a consumer's best response is also to use it. This situation is preferable to all other situations for both consumers and merchants in so far as profits are maximal for merchants and costs are minimal for consumers.

The model clearly reveals that the rate of return of the investment depends on the investment decisions of all other agents. Thus, comparable to a telephone network, the incentive to participate will depend on the number of users. If only a few merchants accept electronic purses, why would a consumer acquire one? At the same time, if only a few consumers are using electronic purses, why would a merchant invest in equipment to process electronic money? In conclusion, since the behaviour of an agent is a function of the anticipated action of the other economic agents, users must be convinced of the positive rate of return on their investments.

By introducing strategic interactions between consumers and merchants, this approach proves to be very fruitful in explaining the coexistence of payment instruments. However, it relies on implicit assumptions regarding the pricing of payment instruments and tends to undermine the role of banks which actually help to explain the adoption and use of payment instruments. Payment instruments are, in fact, priced by banks on perfect or imperfect competitive markets which, in turn, affect the way consumers and merchants are likely to adopt and use payment instruments.

A cost-based approach with strategic interactions: the role of banks and payment card networks

In line with Baumol (1952), Tobin (1956), Whitesell (1989, 1992) and Santomero and Seater (1996), Shy and Tarkka (2002) have extended their research to include the role of banks (issuers of cards) in order to study the potential market share of electronic cash cards. In their model, there are four types of interacting agent: consumers, merchants, a payment card issuer and an electronic cash card issuer. Consumers and merchants bear some costs regarding the use of cash, payment cards and electronic cash cards, such as loss of time, forgone interest and so on. Each payment instrument has different costs for consumers and merchants, leading to both having some strict preferences between the multiple payment instruments. The electronic cash card issuer does not incur any significant transaction-specific costs since electronic cash card transactions are assumed to be anonymous (as are cash transactions); an annual fixed fee is consequently imposed on merchants and consumers. Conversely, a payment card issuer incurs a cost per transaction since payment card transactions require verifications; hence, the issuer can impose three types of fees on merchants and consumers (annual fees, fixed fees per transaction, and/or a proportional fee on a transaction of a certain size on both agents). In the absence of fees imposed on merchants and consumers, that is, the case where all cards are distributed for free by banks, Shy and Tarkka show that, at the equilibrium, the electronic cash card is preferred over cash for low-value transactions and that the payment card is preferred over cash and electronic cash cards for high-value transactions. Such transaction domains reflect some conflicting preferences between merchants and buyers due mainly to differences in losses of time. However, in the presence of fees imposed on consumers and merchants, the authors show that the transaction domains of the different payment instruments may change, especially if annual fees on electronic cash cards imposed by issuers are high. Similarly, high annual fees on the use of charge cards could eliminate them from the market.

The Shy and Tarkka model is an important step in capturing the role of banks in a model of coexistence of multiple payment instruments. However, its main shortcoming is that the choice of a payment card for consumers and merchants is independent of the number of cardholders and merchants in the economy. Henceforth, the model does not precisely account for the presence of indirect network externalities between cardholders and merchants in respect of the more current general theory on *two-sided markets*. Two-sided markets can be defined, in a first approximation,[6] as markets ruled by a payment card platform (payment card network) that is characterised by the presence of indirect network externalities in two distinct groups of users. According to this definition, payment instruments can be considered as network goods provided by a payment card platform where there are indirect network externalities between consumers and merchants. As a result, a new actor in the payment organisation becomes highly significant: the payment card network.

The literature on two-sided markets is interesting for our purpose as it shows that the payment card network may influence the price structure in order to attract and balance the demands on both sides (merchants and consumers). More precisely, one of the main results is to illustrate that an asymmetric pricing of users – between consumers and merchants – may be implemented in order to maximise the volume of transactions processed through the platform, so that the prices do not necessarily reflect the cost of serving them. The platform of the payment network may consequently heavily influence the process of adoption and use of payment instruments.

This rapid survey of theoretical contributions on the economics of payment instruments allows us to conclude that the cost and price structure of these instruments are important in explaining the competition between them.[7] In the next subsection we use these results to explain the reasons why electronic payment systems can compete with traditional payment instruments (cash, payment card, cheques) and, implicitly, the reasons for which traditional payment instruments cannot be used for such transactions.

An Empirical Analysis of the Use of Payment Instruments: From Transaction Domains to the Cost of Payment Instruments

The previous theoretical contributions allow us to conclude that costs are essential in explaining the use of payment instruments. But what is the empirical reality of such theories?

The traditional structure of transactions in trade is characterised by a

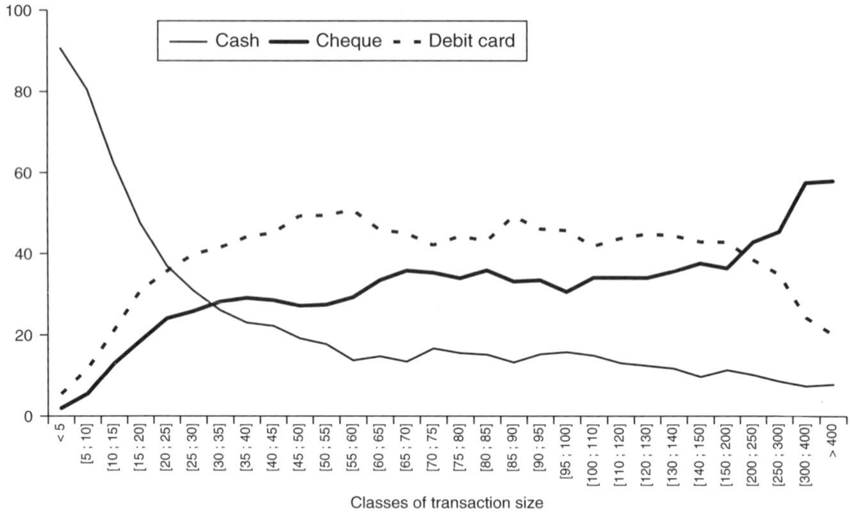

Source: Bounie and François (2006).

Figure 6.1 Distribution of the use of payment instruments by class of transaction size

high number of low-value transactions. In France, for instance, Bounie and François (2006) estimate that transactions below €5[8] account for 35 per cent of all transactions, but only 2 per cent of their total value. This specific structure of transactions seems to be corroborated in other European countries, such as Belgium (Steering Committee, 2005), and in the United States.[9]

Cash is the most frequent payment instrument used to pay for low-value transactions. For example, Bounie and François (2006) show that the cash market share for transactions of under €5 is about 90 per cent in France,[10] with debit cards and cheques being used for 8 and 2 per cent of transactions, respectively (Figure 6.1). But the cash market share quickly decreases when the price goes up. For example, when the transaction size is approximately €23, cash and debit card market shares are equal (35 per cent). Beyond that, debit card use increases up to values of approximately €60, and significantly decreases for values higher than €150.

The results of Whitesell's formal model, which predicts a high cash market share for low-value payments, are consequently confirmed. We can therefore conclude, first, that the fixed costs per transaction incurred by consumers are lower for cash compared to alternative payment instruments such as payment cards and cheques and, second, that the variable costs per transaction are higher for cash due to forgone interest.

From the consumer's point of view, the fixed cost per transaction for payment cards and cheques mainly consists of time to process the transaction – a payment card transaction, for instance, is costly in time since it requires a debit or credit verification of the buyer over a payment network.[11] From the merchant's point of view, a payment card transaction implies a direct charge that can be either a fixed fee for every transaction or a two-part tariff according to the type of payment network involved. In fact, two main types of payment card systems exist: closed- and open-loop systems. Closed-loop systems are three-party systems such as American Express, in which the platform clears and settles all payment card transactions among cardholders and affiliated merchants. Open-loop systems are four-party systems such as Visa and MasterCard and imply a further level made up of banks: an issuer bank (which provides the card to consumers) and an acquirer bank (which manages the merchant account) are at an intermediate level between the platform and the end-users (cardholders and merchants). In such payment card systems, one further level of price must generally be taken into account: the merchant's bank pays an 'interchange fee' to the consumer's bank for every payment card transaction[12] (and interaction).

From a theoretical point of view, this interchange fee is relatively well known since the pioneering contribution of Baxter (1983), and met renewed interest recently with the development of the 'two-sided markets' literature. According to Baxter, the role of the interchange fee in payment card systems is fundamental since its level may increase the volume of card payments and restore the social optimality.[13] Since this first contribution, the literature on two-sided markets has evolved considerably in its analysis of the effects of an imperfect competition between banks, heterogeneity between merchants and between consumers and so on. Globally, the results of this ongoing research are today controversial in so far as economists seem generally to accept the idea that such a fee could be a factor of efficiency, whereas the regulatory authorities claim: 'Overall, the inquiry has not confirmed the possible justifications for interchange fees which rely on economic efficiency arguments' (European Commission, 2006, p. vi).[14] More precisely, the interchange fee can be perceived, according to the European Commission, as a way of extracting profits on the most inelastic demand component, that is, the demand of merchants. The total demand of card payments is made up of the demand of cardholders and the demand of merchants and its level is determined by the minimum of both demands. For this reason, the payment network, through the interchange fee, may influence one of the two sides of the market.

Our intention is not to discuss these aspects in detail[15] but rather to stress that any means of exchange requires the use of sophisticated and interoperable payment networks, either to authorise the transactions or to transfer payment messages between banks through clearing and settlement systems. But these systems are costly for end-users and consequently dissuade low-value transactions. For instance, the levels of payment card fees for merchants are variable according to brands (Visa, MasterCard and domestic networks), payment cards (credit and debit cards) and use (point-of-sale, e-commerce and so on). The results of the Interim Report on Payment Cards of the European Commission (2006, pp. iv–v) points out, for instance:

> [M]erchant fees vary considerably across the European Union: (i) merchants in Hungary, the Czech Republic and Portugal have to pay an average fee of between 2.5% and 3.1% of the total transaction value to accept a MasterCard/Visa credit card. This is 3 to 4 times higher than in Sweden, Finland and Italy; (ii) businesses pay a far higher merchant fee on average to accept cards issued in international networks than cards issued in domestic networks; typically, businesses pay 30–40% lower fees on average for domestic debit card usage than for MasterCard (Maestro)/Visa debit; (iii) international payment systems make smaller businesses pay more than larger ones. This does not seem to be justified solely by transaction volumes, as smaller firms typically pay between 60% and 70% higher fees on average for MasterCard and Visa credit and debit card transactions than larger businesses do. In domestic card payment systems, however, the price difference between smaller and larger merchants is only 7% on average.

More generally, recent publications have tried to measure the social costs of payment instruments. The social cost of a payment instrument refers to the resources that society consumes in providing and using the payment service. It is calculated by adding up the private costs of all the payment agents (consumers, merchants, banks, the central bank and so on) and eliminating any transfer payments – in order to avoid double counting.[16] Two main contributions are available for European countries, which have also been partly commented on by Van Hove (2006). According to the studies led by the Dutch Central Bank (2004) and the National Bank of Belgium (2006), which relied on data for 2002 and 2003, respectively, the overall social cost of point-of-sale payments amounts to 0.65 and 0.74 per cent of the GDP, and 73 and 75 per cent of the total social cost is cash related.

According to the Dutch Central Bank, the average cost of the least expensive means of exchange (excluding the e-purse) is that of the debit card with €0.48 compared to that of the credit card, which is the most expensive and amounts to €3.58 (see Table 6.1). Moreover, the cost of one additional transaction[17] allows us to conclude that e-purse (0.03) and cash (0.11) are the cheapest payment instruments. Finally, if we disregard fixed costs and calculate a pure social marginal cost, the analysis puts forward three main

Table 6.1 Cost measures of the payment instruments in the Netherlands, 2002

	Cash	Debit card	E-purse	Credit card
Number of transactions (m) (1)	7,066	1,069	87	46
Average value (€) (2)	9.37	44.13	2.72	115.2
Total cost (€ m) (3)	2,122	520	81	165
Average cost (3)/(1) (€)	0.30	0.48	0.93	3.58
Cost of one additional transaction (€)	0.11	0.19	0.03	0.79

Source: Dutch Central Bank (2004).

points: first, the e-purse is the most economical for any transaction amount; second, the break-even sales amount between cash and the debit card comes out at €11.63, so that cash is more economical for paying small amounts (below €11.63) and the debit card more economical for high-value transactions; third, the credit card is always cost-dominated for any transaction amount.[18]

Also interesting is the analysis of the distribution of costs among the three types of actors involved, that is: (i) the retailer sector, (ii) banks, Interpay[19] and credit card companies and (iii) the central bank. The cost of banks, Interpay and credit card companies are partly due to the production and distribution of payment cards, the construction of the inter-bank computer network allowing such transactions to be processed and, finally, the maintenance of the network in order to guarantee its security. The analysis of the costs shows that banks, Interpay and credit card companies face relatively high fixed costs, while variable costs weigh in heaviest for the retail sector. Moreover, we note that mainly due to the absence of verification during transactions, the e-purse implies low variable costs for merchants (15 per cent) and banks (1.5 per cent) compared to the debit card (61 per cent for merchants and 21 per cent for banks) and therefore constitutes a socially optimal payment instrument to replace the use of cash in transactions.

To conclude this subsection, we can summarise the main points of our analysis as follows: first, the costs of payment instruments are central to their use by consumers and merchants; second, these costs determine the transaction domains of the payment instruments, that is, the market shares of the various payment instruments; third, the transaction domains are the result of a specific organisation of the retail payment systems, which

Table 6.2 Distribution of the costs of payment instruments in the Netherlands, 2002

	Cash	Debit card	E-purse	Credit card	Total
Costs to the retail sector	1,157	252	13	11	1,433
Fixed costs	43.0%	39.3%	84.6%	36.4%	42.6%
Variable costs	57.0%	60.7%	15.4%	63.6%	57.4%
Costs to banks, Interpay and credit card companies	895	268	68	154	1,385
Fixed costs	39.2%	78.7%	98.5%	72.1%	53.4%
Variable costs	60.8%	21.3%	1.5%	27.9%	46.6%
Costs to the central bank	70	0	0	0	70
Fixed costs	42.9%	0	0	0	42.9%
Variable costs	57.1%	0	0	0	57.1%

Source: Dutch Central Bank (2004).

involve high costs to process the scriptural payments – verification, clearing and settlement – in opposition to cash and e-purse payments. In the last subsection, we use these elements to discuss the challenges of some electronic payment systems.

The Challenges of Online Payments: the Competition of Closed Private Systems

The development of information technologies coupled with that of online markets has given millions of individuals the opportunity to purchase online. These markets are clearly attractive to consumers in terms of selection, availability and prices, compared to their physical counterparts, thereby explaining their rapid growth. Online retail sales in the United States reached $109 billion in 2006, up from $88,026 million in 2005 (an increase of 23.5 per cent). This trend is similar in Europe with €38 billion being spent in 2006 in the United Kingdom, €19 billion in Germany and €12 billion in France (+37 per cent compared to 2005) (eMarketer, 2006).

Apart from purchases, individuals are also becoming more motivated to sell their used goods on online markets through multiple auction websites (eBay, eBid and so on). A report of the Pew Internet and American Life Project (2005) reports that about 25 million people in the US have used the internet to sell something:

> Almost everything imaginable is currently for sale or has been for sale by individuals on various auction or classified ad sites. Tangible items like pink plastic Christmas trees, collectible coins, wedding dresses, automobiles, books, or CDs share web space with a myriad of intangibles including virtual weaponry and characters from online games (sold for real money) and services, including everything from finding a French tutor, a personal trainer or someone to clean your aquarium.

Consequently, more consumers become sellers on the internet. Recent empirical contributions point out that that these markets are constantly growing: 'Internet sales of used books made up an estimated 67% of all used-book sales in 2004. . . . This represents the highest Internet penetration for any physical product category that we are aware of, and compares to a penetration of only 12.7% for Internet sales of new books' (Ghose et al., 2006, p. 4).

Of all the characteristics of these electronic markets, two are of particular interest here: micro-payments and person-to-person online payments. Micro-payments are frequently, although arbitrarily, defined as purchases below five dollars or euros. They mainly concern information goods, that is, goods consisting of data, information, and knowledge content such as books, CDs, DVDs and so on. Person-to-person online payments such as those carried out through PayPal are between individuals. Micro-payments and person-to-person online payments are fascinating because of the way they challenge the retail payment industry. First, unlike physical markets where cash is the principal payment instrument used to settle transactions, cash will never be used in online low-value payments. Similarly, as the payment card is rarely accepted below €5, cards will rarely settle micro-payments. Furthermore, the payment card has been conceived of as a way of settling debts between consumers and merchants and not between two consumers; therefore, the payment card cannot be used to pay for such transactions even if the price of the transaction exceeds the marginal cost of the payment. Likewise, the cheque is not well suited to online payments, since it is mainly designed for domestic transactions and not intended for low-value transactions. Finally, the last possible solution, the credit transfer, is also unsuited to online payments since to transfer a monetary claim in favour of a beneficiary, consumers need the bank references (which is time-consuming).

These observations call for two major comments: first, there is no bank payment instrument designed to settle micro-transactions; second, there is no cost-effective solution allowing for the transfer of monetary values between individuals. Together, these two observations explain the development of closed systems operated by non-banks in order to decrease the cost of payments and provide scriptural person-to-person online payments. These systems, which we call 'closed private systems', are three-party systems in which a platform has direct relations with end-users, consumers and merchants. Monetary transfers can be directly carried out between consumers and merchants or between two consumers. The platform directly clears and settles within the system. An excellent description of person-to-person online payment systems is provided by Kuttner and McAndrews (2001). Online billing systems also work according to this principle. The customer can purchase online goods and pay the internet access provider, which serves as the platform, after the purchase (at the end of the month, for instance). The merchant, affiliated to the platform, will receive his or her monetary value directly from the platform. To proceed as a payment service provider, the platform needs to maintain accounts for both payer and seller in order to keep track of the monetary claims against the payer and due to the merchant. At the end of the month the platform will collect the payer's bill from his or her bank account and will transfer the amount due to the merchant.

These systems are extremely simple as the payment is made through a book-entry transfer and occurs almost immediately, unlike most existing four-party systems which require the exchange of information between the two account-maintaining banks. This simplification is interesting from a cost point of view since three-party systems involve neither inter-change fees between banks nor clearing and settlement instructions through dedicated networks. This simplification consequently induces decreasing costs for end-users. The main shortcomings of these systems are their sphere of acceptance: closed private systems are by definition non-universal, which means that consumers and merchants are constrained to hold several systems to pay or attract consumers. Several electronic payment systems are based on this model, such as network games (Massively Multiplayer Online Role-Playing Game) which adopted original pricing payment systems based on micro-payments (for instance Yohoho! Puzzle Pirates) and, more recently, video-on-demand services proposed by Google and based on the Google wallet.

4 CONCLUDING DISCUSSION: TOWARDS A NEW RETAIL PAYMENT ECONOMY?

The development of electronic payment systems on the internet shows that the monetary, banking and industrial implications are considerable. Actually, they challenge the nature of the organisation of the retail payment industry based mainly on four-party systems with payment networks dedicated to payment verification (payment card networks) and to the clearing and settlement of instructions. This organisation, well-suited to medium-sized transactions, is actually not appropriate in new forms of retail payment such as online micro-payments and person-to-person payments, and requires some adjustments to current trends. The inter-bank system, which was the forerunner up to now, can provide certain drawbacks when used with new forms of transactions because of the structural costs, the duration of the operations and the loss of differentiation between members associated with such a system. In this last section, we discuss how the current four-party banking systems could adjust to changes to reduce the costs of retail payments.

The payment card is today the main bank payment instrument used to pay online. Based on a four-party system, the organisation of the online payment process is strictly similar to an offline payment card. However, the internet makes it possible to reconsider the kinematics of payment flows between cardholders, merchants and banks and can thus lower the costs of the payments.

Let us first describe a payment card in the physical world[20] when the cardholder uses his or her payment card at a merchant's point-of-sale (POS) terminal. The card transaction goes from the POS terminal via a telecommunication network to the acquiring bank. The bank then sends an authorisation request through a payment network to the issuing bank. The issuing bank authorises the transaction after verifying whether the card has not been stolen or lost and whether sufficient funds are available on the cardholder's bank account to execute the transaction. The authorisation approval then goes from the issuing bank to the acquirer bank which routes the authorisation response via the telecommunication network up to the POS terminal at the merchant. The POS terminal then sends an acceptance acknowledgement via the telecommunication network to the acquiring bank. Finally, the acquiring bank forwards this message to an automated clearing house to obtain the payment at the cardholder's issuing bank.[21]

This specific organisation of card payments is the result of technical constraints related to POS payments where cardholders physically meet merchants. In this scheme, the card reader drives the operations by indicating the controls to execute, the authorisation requests and so on. In this organisation there is a specific kinematics of the payments piloted by the merchant and the acquirer bank. However, while a POS payment card imposes such a technical system, the internet is challenging this equation. More precisely, the constraints which required relying on the acquirer bank are no longer needed. Since there are no more physical relations between merchants and cardholders, the card reader disappears from the equation. As a result, the entire payment card system is called into question with a decreasing importance given to the acquirer function. With the disappearance of the card reader function it is thus no longer necessary to preserve the same kinematics of card payments.

A new kinematics can thus be adapted to online payment card specificities. More precisely, it is no longer necessary to delegate to the merchant and the acquirer bank the controls of security and so on. The latter function can be assumed directly by the cardholder and the issuer bank. In this case, an inversion of the payment flows can be envisaged. For instance, we can imagine that after the commercial negotiation between the merchant and the consumer, the latter accepts the offer and sends an electronic message to his or her issuer bank, along with the merchant bank references, in order to proceed to the payment. In this case, there are no more authorisation requests between banks and only the clearing and settlement instructions prevail. However, these technical developments have significant economic repercussions since the mechanisms of interchange fees must be redefined to the disadvantage of the acquirer bank and, *in fine*, to the merchants. This development is probably minimal when it comes to questions of micro-payments and person-to-person payments, but it opens the way to a new retail payment economy for four-party banking systems.

NOTES

* This work has benefited from the support of the Centre National de la Recherche Scientifique (CNRS) under the programme 'ATIP Jeunes Chercheurs'.

1. In the rest of the chapter, 'electronic payment systems' will stand for all the vehicles and procedures which allow payment orders to be exchanged between economic agents over the internet.
2. On 14 December 2004 an island in Project Entropia was sold for US$26,500.
3. To allow the gamers to get a clear view of the market trend, Game Money Price Research recently published 'Price Trend Charts: First Half 2005' for 12 major games (see http://www.gameusd.com).
4. The question of the adoption of the payment instruments is outside the scope of these studies.
5. The fixed cost of cash is considered as nil in Whitesell (1989) and negative in Whitesell (1992).
6. Rochet and Tirole (2004) provide a more precise definition: a market can be considered as two-sided if the total volume of transactions going through the platform depends on the relative prices paid by the two groups of users.
7. Empirical studies dedicated to payment economics highlight the role of further determinants such as individual characteristics (income, age, education and so on) and transaction characteristics (size of transaction, type of good purchased, type of location visited and so on) in explaining the choice of payment instruments. See Bounie and François (2007) for a recent survey of these contributions.
8. Although arbitrary, the threshold of 5 dollars or 5 euros is a standard amount, cited frequently for distinguishing micro-payments from conventional transactions.
9. According to TowerGroup, micro-payments of less than $5 accounted for more than $1 trillion in consumer spending in 2003 at the point of sale, across 400 billion transactions (see McGrath, 2006).

10. Similarly in Belgium, cash was reportedly still used in 81 per cent of point-of-sale transactions in 2003 (Steering Committee, 2005).
11. The fixed cost of the cheque may be associated with the time needed to fill it out.
12. Several pricing methods exist. The French payment card system 'CB', for example, uses a two-part tariff which involves a fixed multilateral part and a variable bilateral part. The first element of the variable part depends on the transaction volume, and the second on another bilateral part which is calculated according to the relative number of cards from each bank used fraudulently. See Weiner and Wright (2005) for a detailed review of the systems. Note, however, that some payment card networks do not use this pricing (for example, Finland, Luxembourg).
13. Baxter (1983) showed that socially optimal payment card transactions could sometimes be refused either by consumers or by merchants. In this framework, the interchange fee could be envisaged as a way of restoring the social optimality.
14. The Commission has initiated an inquiry into retail banking (European Commission, 2007). This sector inquiry suggests that several competition issues affect the banking industry.
15. See Rochet (2003) for a review of the literature on interchange fees.
16. For a detailed discussion of the methodological aspects involved in estimating these costs, see Humphrey et al. (2003).
17. This cost includes all fixed and variable costs to carry out a further transaction.
18. To the best of our knowledge, two further studies confirmed these figures. Bergman et al. (2007) estimated the social and private costs of cash, debit and credit card payments in Sweden in 2002 and Garcia Swartz et al. (2006) also analysed the social cost of cheque payments in the US in 2003.
19. Interpay is one of the largest European automated clearing houses; it covers the entire chain of giral and card-related processing, switching, clearing and settlement.
20. A payment card transaction depends on the individual structure of each payment card system. In particular, there are numerous differences between payment card systems which depend on the presence, or not, of issuing and acquiring processors operating on behalf of banks. We hereafter provide a simplified version of a payment card transaction without processors. This simplification is not fundamental for our overriding views.
21. In order to save costs, retail payment automated clearing house instructions are not executed individually but bundled and processed in batches at given times. Usually, the clearing of retail payments is a netting process, that is, only the net positions calculated will be settled.

REFERENCES

Asia Times Online (2007), 'China's Virtual Currency Threatens the Yuan', www.atimes.com/atimes/China_Business/HL05Cb01.html.

Baumol, W.J. (1952), 'The transaction demand for cash – an inventory theoretic approach', *Quarterly Journal of Economics*, **66**(4), 545–56.

Baxter, W. (1983), 'Bank interchange of transactional paper: legal and economic perspectives', *Journal of Law and Economics*, **26**(3), 541–88.

Berentsen, A. (1998), 'Monetary policy implications of digital money', *Kyklos*, **51**(1), 89–117.

Bergman, M., Guibourg, G. and Segendorf, B. (2007), 'The costs of paying – private and social costs of cash and card payments', Riksbank Research paper series no. 212, September.

Bounie, D. and François, A. (2006), 'Cash, cheque or debit card: the effects of transaction characteristics on the use of payment instruments', Telecom Paris Economics Working Paper, 06/05/ESS.

Bounie, D. and François, A. (2007), 'Economics of payment instruments: a survey of recent contributions', mimeo, Telecom ParisTech.

Bounie, D. and Gazé, P. (2007), 'Payment and the internet: issues and research perspectives in the economics of banking', in Brousseau, E. and Curien, N. (eds), *Internet and Digital Economics: Principles, Methods and Applications*, Cambridge: Cambridge University Press, pp. 569–87.

De Nederlandsche Bank (Dutch Central Bank) (2004), 'The cost of payments', *Quarterly Bulletin*, March, 57–64.

eMarketer (2006), 'Retail e-commerce (excluding travel) in the US, 2005–2011 (billions, % change vs. prior year and % of total US retail sales)', www.emarketer.com

European Commission (2006), 'Interim Report I, Banking Cards', Competition DG, April.

European Commission (2007), 'Report on the Retail Banking Sector Inquiry', Competition DG, January.

Garcia Swartz, D., Hahn, R. and Layne-Farrar, A. (2006), 'The move toward a cashless society: calculating the costs and benefits', *Review of Network Economics*, **5**, 199–228.

Ghose, A., Smith, M.D. and Telang, R. (2006), 'Internet exchanges for used books: an empirical analysis of product cannibalization and welfare impact', *Information Systems Research*, **17**(1), 3–19.

Goodhart, C.A.E. (1990), *The Evolution of Central Banks*, Cambridge, MA: MIT Press

Greenbaum, S. and Thakor, A. (1995), *Contemporary Financial Intermediation*, London: Dryden Press.

Hayek, F.A. (1978), *Denationalisation of Money. The Argument Refined: An Analysis of the Theory and Practice of Concurrent Currencies*, London: Institute of Economic Affairs.

Humphrey, D., Willesson, M., Lindblom, T. and Bergendahl, G. (2003), 'What does it cost to make a payment?', *Journal of Network Economics*, **2**(2), 159–74.

Kuttner, K.N. and McAndrews, J.J. (2001), 'Personal on-line payments', *Economic Policy Review*, Federal Reserve Bank of New York, December, 35–50.

Martin, A. and Schreft, S.L. (2006), 'Currency competition: a partial vindication of Hayek', *Journal of Monetary Economics*, **53**(8), 2085–111.

McGrath, J.C. (2006), 'Micropayments: the final frontier for electronic consumer payments', Federal Reserve Bank of Philadelphia Discussion Paper, June.

Mester, L.J., Nakamura, L.I. and Renault, M. (2005), 'Transaction accounts and loan monitoring', Federal Reserve Bank of Philadelphia Working Paper 05-14.

National Bank of Belgium (2006), 'Costs, advantages and drawbacks of the various means of payment', *Economic Review*, 41–7.

Pew Internet and American Life Project (2005), 'Reports: online activities & pursuits', www.pewinternet.org.

Rice, T. and Stanton, K. (2003), 'Estimating the volume of payments-driven revenues', Emerging Payments Occasional Papers Series, Federal Reserve Bank of Chicago, 2003-1C.

Rochet, J.-C. (2003), 'The theory of interchange fees: a synthesis of recent contributions', *Review of Network Economics*, **2**(2), 97–124.

Rochet, J.-C. and J. Tirole (2004), 'Two-sided markets: an overview', mimeo, IDET, Université de Toulouse.

Santomero, A. (1979), 'A model of the demand for money by households', *Journal of Finance*, **29**(1), 89–102.

Santomero, A. and Seater, J.J. (1996), 'Alternative monies and the demand for media of exchange', *Journal of Money, Credit, and Banking*, **28**(4), 942–60.
Shy, O. and Tarkka, J. (2002), 'The market for electronic cash cards', *Journal of Money, Credit, and Banking*, **34**(2), 299–314.
Steering Committee (2005), 'Costs, advantages and drawbacks of the various means of payment', Steering Committee on the future of the means of payment, National Bank of Belgium, December.
Tobin, J. (1956), 'The interest elasticity of transaction demand for cash', *Review of Economics and Statistics*, **38**(3), 241–7.
Van Hove, L. (2006), 'Why fighting cash is a worthy cause', *ProChip*, 8–13.
Weiner, S.E. and Wright, J. (2005), 'Interchange fees in credit and debit card industries: what role for public authorities?', Federal Reserve Bank of Kansas City, Proceedings – Payments System Research Conferences.
Whitesell, W.C. (1989), 'The demand for currency versus debitable accounts', *Journal of Money, Credit, and Banking*, **21**(2), 246–51.
Whitesell, W.C. (1992), 'Deposit banks and the market for payment media', *Journal of Money, Credit, and Banking*, **24**(4), 483–98.

7. Intellectual property rights and standard setting in financial services: the case of the Single European Payments Area*

Robert M. Hunt, Samuli Simojoki and Tuomas Takalo†

1 INTRODUCTION

Intellectual property is widely regarded as the main policy tool of modern societies for moulding private incentives to innovate and to diffuse innovations.[1] Alan Greenspan has frequently (for example, April 3, 2003, and February 27, 2004) pondered the question: 'If our objective is to maximize economic growth, are we striking the right balance in our protection of intellectual property rights?'. This is a difficult question for economists to answer in general. It is especially difficult to address this question in the context of financial services, including payment systems.[2]

One special feature of financial services is that, until recently, patents have only rarely been used to protect financial innovations as such (Tufano 2003; Frame and White 2004). In most other industries patents are common, providing their owners with strong and relatively broad protection of their technological innovations. But in the United States, at least, financial patents became commonplace after the landmark 1998 decision in *State Street Bank & Trust Co. v. Signature Financial Group*.[3] This decision made it clear that computer-implemented methods of doing business, including those involving finance, were indeed patentable subject matter (Hunt 2001; Lerner 2002).

The use of formal intellectual property rights to protect financial innovations is more limited in Europe than in the US. But most contemporary financial services rely on information technology. Unlike business methods *per se*, there is no doubt about the patentability of such technology.[4] Indeed, the information and communication technology (ICT) industries (for example, computers, communications, and electronics) are some of the most patent-intensive sectors of the economy (Bessen and Hunt 2007).

Intellectual property (IP) has already found its way to the European financial services sector in recent years, and it is likely to become ubiquitous in the future. Today, its role is often underappreciated by the management of financial companies and the staff of the government agencies that regulate them. In this chapter we argue that intellectual property is now an important facet of any effort in standard setting in financial services. Indeed, disputes over intellectual property pose a risk to the development of the Single Euro Payments Area (SEPA) and subsequent innovations in banking and retail payment media in Europe. This risk should be evaluated and carefully managed.

SEPA is a major public policy initiative to standardise non-cash payment methods in the euro area (see, for example, Kemppainen and Salo 2006).[5] The payments industry is a *network* industry, and, as such, it entails very large gains associated with standardisation. Without standardisation, many of the potential consumer benefits from the creation of the euro will not be realised. These benefits include, among other things, lower transaction costs, faster settlement, reduced risk, more transparency, and increased price competition. As part of the development of the European payment systems, a new Payment Services Directive (PSD) has been adopted in the European Union (EU) for providing a modern and comprehensive set of rules applicable to all electronic payment services in the EU and the necessary legal platform for SEPA.[6]

A conservative estimate of the direct cost savings achieved under full implementation of SEPA exceeds €20 billion a year (European Commission 2006). Two important sources of cost savings include the scale economies that can be attained by consolidating payment networks that currently operate at the national level and the substitution of electronic payments for paper transactions as the differences in their relative cost and convenience increase (Bolt and Humphrey 2008). But obtaining these benefits will require substantial investment. The cost to banks of implementing SEPA over its first five years is estimated to be in the range of €5–10 billion (Schmiedel 2007).

The intersection of standard setting and intellectual property rights is complicated and sometimes contentious. There is almost an inherent tension between the two: the goal of intellectual property is to stimulate the incentive to innovate by giving its owner a right to exclude others from using the innovation, whereas the goal of standardisation is to stimulate the use of innovations adopted as a standard. Standard-setting organisations (SSOs) must negotiate a compromise that is reasonably attractive to both the owners and the users of IP.

This is not always an easy task, as a number of scholars have recently documented (Shapiro 2001; Lemley 2002; Chiao et al. 2007). It is particularly difficult for industries where interoperability standards are required to make products or services compatible with each other in order to maximise the benefits of network externalities. It is further complicated by the potential for opportunistic behaviour by participants who own patents on a technology essential to the standard. There is a risk that without sufficient transparency and sufficiently strong mutual interests, network participants could make large investments to implement a standard only to be held up by a firm threatening to withhold a key piece of technology. In all likelihood some kind of agreement would be reached, but on terms substantially worse than the participants initially expected. Indeed, the risk of such an outcome may discourage firms from adopting a standard or even participating in the standard-setting process. In other instances, awareness of a key blocking patent might lead to the adoption of a standard that poses less risk to participants but which is also technologically inferior.

These externalities can also work in the opposite direction. If a financial SSO is sufficiently influential in coordinating the decisions of its member financial institutions and is able to require the sharing of technology at concessionary prices, the incentive to invest in these technologies could be significantly impaired. While financial institutions would be able to adopt a standard, the underlying technology would again be inferior when compared to a regime that offers better incentives for developers of new technologies.

Often SSOs have specific policies designed to mitigate these risks. But designing these policies and obtaining the acceptance of the relevant participants can be challenging. A well-designed IP policy should simultaneously provide incentives for firms to participate in the standard-setting process and encourage new innovations that would eventually lead to a better standard. The policy should also specify the rights enjoyed by owners of the relevant intellectual property and the licensing terms to be used. Often, these policies call for 'reasonable' royalties and access to the key technologies for all participants (for example, open or non-discriminatory licensing).[7] Of course, these terms must be acceptable to owners of the intellectual property, since their participation in a standard is typically voluntary. The difficulties in establishing a successful IP policy for a standard should not be discounted.

There are numerous historical examples of licensing disputes and allegations of hold-ups related to standards (see, for example, Bekkers et al. 2002; Blind et al. 2002; Lemley 2002).[8] By one estimate, patents covering an industry standard are 13 times more likely to be litigated than other US patents (Lemley 2007). This experience is relevant to the case of standard setting in financial services and to electronic payments in particular.

An additional complicating factor for SEPA is that legal treatment of financial innovations is evolving. In addition, modern payment systems rely extensively on ICT. The ownership of the relevant intellectual property is spread over many companies located in many countries. As result, there can be considerable variation in the IP strategies of these firms, which are influenced, in turn, by the historical and legal traditions of their home countries.

Each of these factors suggests that the development of SEPA should include a well-articulated IP policy. This is especially important given SEPA's objective of 'creating open and common standards that overcome technical and commercial barriers' for cashless payment services within the euro area. All electronic payments should 'migrate to common interoperable formats and processes'. SEPA should also be a 'forward-looking' process, 'both embracing and enabling the realisation of new technological opportunities'.[9]

The remainder of the chapter is organised as follows. We first review the law and economics of intellectual property in financial services and standard setting (Section 2). Our definition of financial innovation is broad, including technological innovations that facilitate financial services. We point out that such innovations are patentable in Europe and can also sometimes be protected through copyright and database rights. Based on the literature we explain why a well-defined IP policy is a key to successful standard setting in network industries.

In Section 3 we present some examples from the communications industry where IP disputes have jeopardised some standards, despite rigorous efforts to avoid them. We think that the experience of the communications industry is relevant for payment media, and we explain why: despite differences in the underlying technologies, the legal and economic problems are almost identical. We also point to the pattern of financial patenting and litigation in the US.

In Section 4 we argue that the lack of a proper IP policy may seriously hamper adoption of the new SEPA payment instruments and subsequent innovation in the European payment media industry. In particular, it seems likely that some patents encompassing future standards in SEPA payment methods will be owned by third-party suppliers rather than by European financial participants. This could make standardisation more complex and increase the risk of hold-up problems. Concluding remarks and policy recommendations are collected in Section 5.

2 THE LAW AND ECONOMICS OF INTELLECTUAL PROPERTY IN FINANCIAL SERVICES AND IN STANDARD-SETTING ORGANISATIONS

Intellectual Property and Innovations in Financial Services

It is widely believed that innovations in the European financial services industry are protected primarily by copyrights and trade secrets. The definition of financial innovation is often interpreted narrowly to encompass new financial market instruments or structures, such as collateralised debt obligations or hedge funds (see, for example, Tufano 2003). Financial formulas and methods are thought to be beyond the scope of patentable subject matter in Europe. Indeed, Article 52 of the European Patent Convention is typically interpreted to prohibit patents on methods of doing business, including financial ones, as such. This stands in contrast to the practice observed not only in the US (Hunt 2001, 2008) but also in other countries, including Australia, Japan, and South Korea.

But this view of the situation in Europe is not particularly accurate and is becoming less accurate every day. If we think about financial innovation more broadly, it certainly includes the inventions that enable new payment media to function. These would include features such as electronic record-keeping for bank and credit data, electronic communication and settlement of transactions, and their security solutions. They might also include enhancements of existing systems, such as improved ATM (automated teller machine) and ACH (automated clearing house) technologies, or mobile payments. Such inventions are surely technological in nature and hence have always been patentable in Europe and elsewhere.[10]

Moreover, while the European law, as it stands, makes obtaining a patent on a business method more difficult than in the US, it is hardly impossible. As the study by Wagner (2008) shows, business methods can be and are patented in Europe: the European Patent Office and national patent offices can legally award patents on financial and other business methods if these methods make a technical contribution; that is, they add something new to a technical field. For example, an apparatus for carrying out a financial method is not excluded from patentability. Similarly, a financial method is not excluded from patentability if the invention is not an abstract method *as such* but relates to technical means, such as computer networks, to carry out the method and the invention solves a technical problem in a non-obvious way.

Skilful patent lawyers can draft patent applications on 'softer' financial and business methods to emphasise their technical contribution. Sometimes a patent applicant adds a technical feature to a softer financial method to render it patentable.[11] In this respect, writing applications for business method patents in Europe today is similar to the way that software patents were drafted during the 1980s and early 1990s (Hunt 2001). Partially for these reasons, the European Patent Office recently changed its patent classification system to include a separate class (ECLA Class G06Q) for business methods with subclasses for payment schemes, architectures, or protocols (G06Q20); commerce, for example, marketing, shopping, billing, auctions, or e-commerce (G06Q40); and financial methods, for example, banking, investment, or tax processing (G06Q40).

The technical infrastructure of the payment industry is an extremely complex information technology system comprising a range of fields, including security technologies, data communications and data management (Evans and Schmalensee 2005). Many advanced solutions in the aforementioned fields are indeed patented, given the intense use of patents in the closely related fields of ICT on which these solutions rely.

Since one goal of the SEPA process is to promote technologically advanced standards for the European payment industry, it is likely that these standards will encompass one or more patented technologies.[12] Some of these patents may be essential for SEPA-compliant systems. For other patents, as long as the patent claims are known in advance, SEPA's standards could be designed to avoid infringement. In either case, it is clear that intellectual property is likely to influence the design and implementation of SEPA standards and it would be best to take this into account early in the planning stages.

The Impact of Interoperability Standards in Network Industries

It has been recognised at least since the seminal article by Katz and Shapiro (1985) that in network industries, coordination through interoperability standards offers substantial economic benefits.[13] These include larger markets with greater economies of scale and the greater ability to sell complementary goods. Simply agreeing on a standard has social value, irrespective of whether it is the best one. At the level of an individual company, being included or excluded from use of an interoperability standard can play a pivotal role in the company's fortunes.

Standards can be divided into two distinct varieties: *de facto* and *de jure* standards. De facto standards are not promulgated by a particular body but arise spontaneously in open markets. De facto standards are common in many network industries. That is because network effects often lead to 'market tipping', where most users adopt a dominant solution (as soon as one emerges) and most competing solutions disappear from the market. For example, Microsoft's operating system for personal computers emerged as a de facto standard in the 1990s. IBM abandoned its competing operating system, and the market share of Apple Computers fell precipitously. Apple was able to recover only when it made its operating system more compatible with applications designed for the Microsoft operating system.

When a firm's technology becomes a de facto standard, it often obtains a dominant position in the industry and may enjoy supra-normal profits.[14] In addition, the firm may enjoy significant influence over the technological development in the market, and this may in turn lead to significant strategic advantages.[15] Of course, competition law can be, and is, used to address questions about exercises of market power by the owners of a de facto standard.

Formal, that is, de jure, standardisation usually occurs when there is a perceived market failure that is preventing the emergence of a de facto standard (Blind et al. 2002). Although governments sometimes establish de jure interoperability standards, it is uncommon for these to be compulsory. Again, the market-tipping effect for network industries typically makes such coercion unnecessary. But we shall examine one counterexample – the mandatory technical standard for the global system for mobile communications (GSM) – later in this chapter.[16]

The European Commission examined the question of mandatory standards in the early 1990s and recommended that they reflect a consensus based on the views of all interested parties and that such standards should be available to all interested parties subject to the mandatory obligations (European Commission 1992). In short, the Commission strongly recommended the use of formalised standard setting in which all relevant parties could participate and an IP policy that would ensure open access to the standard. Today, mandatory standards within the EU framework are often used as common reference standards.

'Standard setting' is by definition a domain of de jure standardisation, where a standard is explicitly specified by an SSO or among a group of market participants. Since the SEPA initiative is an example of de jure standardisation, we focus on de jure standardisation and especially on the challenges that SSOs encounter. The standards developed under SEPA also fall into the category of mandatory technical standards (like GSM), since participation in the common market for the payment industry will require compliance with the standards developed under SEPA. These distinctions may be important when thinking about the role of intellectual property in the SEPA process.

The Role of Intellectual Property in Standard Setting

While there is a tension between standardisation and intellectual property, designing *optimal* IP laws and standard-setting policies involves common objectives. Economic theory suggests that an optimal IP law strikes a balance between the interests of inventors and creators on the one hand and the interests of consumers and other users of innovations on the other (Nordhaus 1969). Similarly, the optimal standard-setting policy must balance the interests of innovators and users. In other words, a good IP law and standard-setting policy both try to promote the use of innovations without stifling the incentive to make them in the first place.

Several factors explain the interaction between property rights and standard setting. First, intellectual property typically gives its owner an exclusive right to determine how it will be used. An SSO developing a standard that will rely on a patented technology must obtain the consent of the patent holder on terms that are agreeable to the likely users of the standard. In the process, the SSO may create substantial network effects that significantly increase the value of the patented technology, at least relative to an environment where no standard exists.[17] The question then is, who captures these benefits: the owners or the users of the technology and in what proportions?

Second, standard setting is designed to coordinate the adoption of particular technological solutions or processes. As a result, it tends to restrict the paths for future technological development and thus tends to concentrate the research and development (R&D) efforts of active participants. Thus, over time, standardisation is likely to increase the degree of technological overlap between firms. At the same time, so long as many firms remain active in their R&D, there can be a tendency for increased fragmentation of intellectual property rights (Rahnasto 2003; Ziedonis 2004; Kultti et al. 2006). This fragmentation of intellectual property rights, in turn, can complicate the implementation of better standards in the future.

Third, the standard-setting process is time-consuming and involves decisions subject to uncertainty and asymmetric information. It typically takes a long time to develop the consensus necessary to make the standard a commercial success. Some participants may have private information about the efficacy of a particular solution and the current or future owners of the relevant technology are not always known. These characteristics of the standard-setting environment create at least the potential for strategic behaviour for both users and owners of potentially relevant technologies. They also complicate the design of contracts or rules to prevent such behaviour.

For example, disclosing a pending patent application for a technology being contemplated for a standard may not be in the strategic interest of the firm seeking the patent. Other firms may anticipate the outcome of the standard-setting process and apply for patents that would be infringed by users conforming to the standard.[18] With incomplete disclosure of pending applications, technology users may underestimate the costs of complying with the standard, increasing the likelihood that they will agree to adopt the standard.

If compliance with the standard necessitates making significant fixed investments at an early stage, these participants may be 'locked in' to the standard. In other words, firms may object to paying royalties that are higher than they contemplated but choose to do so because the alternative would require making additional fixed investments that are even more costly. Understanding this, the owner of the intellectual property may insist on higher royalties. This is the basis for a potential 'hold-up' problem (see, for example, Williamson 1985; Hart 1995; Shapiro 2006; Lemley and Shapiro 2007). Indeed, the risk of a potential hold-up may dissuade participants from adopting the standard in the first place. That is why SSOs work hard to mitigate such risks.

The potential for strategic use of intellectual property is arguably one of the most challenging problems confronted by SSOs. This risk was described in academic papers decades ago, but a number of concrete examples have recently materialised (Iversen 1999). These include disputes arising from the GSM standard (Blind et al. 2002), recipes for clean burning gasoline (Mueller 2002), PC architecture (Shapiro 2001), and standards for computer memory chips, digital images, and HTML specifications (Chiao et al. 2007; Soininen, 2007).

The economic theory suggests that the ability to avoid hold-ups in standard setting hinges on the disclosure and licensing policies adopted by SSOs (Shapiro 2001; Lemley 2002; Chiao et al. 2007). Appendix 7A presents a simple model of a monopoly SSO that summarises the main results from the literature that are important for the case of SEPA. In this model, the SSO has two margins it can influence. The first is the 'quality' of the standard in the sense that a better standard will attract more users and hence generate larger network effects. These are the rents the SSO can use to induce users and IP owners to participate. The second margin is the terms by which essential intellectual property is obtained from its owners. The model also takes into account the relative bargaining power of the relevant constituents – users of the standard and the IP owners who provide at least some of the technology that makes the standard attractive in the first place.

Analysis of the model shows that, all else equal, an SSO where users of the standard (rather than owners of the relevant technology) have relatively more bargaining power will choose lower royalty rates and more open (for example, non-discriminatory) licensing terms. But SSOs generally seek to establish standards of the highest quality, in other words, ones that contribute to products and services that consumers really value. In that case, the SSO will be able to offer better terms to IP holders, since the large network effects will attract many users despite the higher prices implied by higher royalties. Indeed, if the high quality of the standard results from the contribution of high-value intellectual property, the SSO may have an incentive to offer attractive terms in order to obtain it

Chiao et al. (2007) also study disclosure policies adopted by SSOs. In practice, a disclosure policy means that SSOs can require their participants to notify others of the intellectual property that is relevant to a given standardisation effort. This may conflict with the interests of IP owners and so it can be difficult to form a consensus in favor of a strong disclosure policy.

In addition, SSOs have no legal force against third parties who are not participants in the standard-setting process. But this raises a related problem that SSOs encounter: the success of a standard depends on the ability to attract broad participation by parties who own technologies relevant to the standard. The disclosure and licensing policies of the SSO are likely to influence the willingness of these stakeholders to participate.

Outright hold-ups are less common than disputes over the terms of licensing intellectual property relevant to a standard. Often SSOs require patents to be licensed under fair, reasonable, and non-discriminatory terms ('FRAND or RAND terms'). In other words, SSOs usually seek a system of cross-licenses or royalty payments that are not too costly for users of the standards and which apply equally to all potential users. SSOs typically eschew *exclusive* licenses, which might limit the number of potential users according to the terms specified by the patent owners. To the extent that an SSO is successful in obtaining licenses on RAND terms, the result is a standard that is more 'open', since ownership of the underlying technology is not a precondition for participating in the standard.

But contracts in the standard-setting environment are almost inherently incomplete. Views on what constitutes RAND terms can vary substantially. Furthermore, the enforceability of such terms can prove to be difficult: who can file a complaint and under what regulations? Against whom should the complaint be filed if the patent has been assigned to a new owner who has not participated in the standard setting? Nevertheless, the scope for disagreements is likely to be smaller if the SSO has a well-crafted policy on intellectual property.

Even where an SSO has no IP policy, other laws and regulations may constrain strategic use of intellectual property in standard setting. For example, the US patent law recognises the *doctrine of estoppel* and the *doctrine of laches*, which aim at punishing a patent holder who delayed enforcing his/her patent (Carpentier 2006). The *doctrine of 'implied license'* in turn covers situations when a firm discloses its patent portfolio but then fails to comply with the restrictions on licensing with which it had concurred (Lemley 2002). In a recent decision, two patents owned by Qualcomm were found unenforceable due to waiver when a jury determined that the company had participated in the JVT (joint video team) standard-setting body without disclosing the pending patents.[19]

In the US, claims under antitrust law have usually been unsuccessful in cases involving allegations of patent hold-ups in standardisation. Suits alleging unfair or deceptive trade practices have also been generally unsuccessful in these cases. Other potential remedies against patent hold-ups in standardisation in the US include fraud, compulsory licensing, eminent domain, and patent misuse doctrine (Mueller 2002).

There is no case law in Europe related to patent exploitation in standard setting, and this limits the repertoire of legal remedies available for users and SSOs in instances of hold-ups. In the domain of competition law, in the recent *IMS Health* case (following the landmark case of *Magill*) the European Court of Justice concluded that in exceptional circumstances a dominant firm may be forced to license its intellectual property if it is attempting to monopolise a downstream market by refusing to license.[20] The prerequisite of market power, however, limits its applicability in standard setting, since companies holding essential patents are not automatically assumed to enjoy market power. Some scholars (for example, Näcke 1995), however, argue in favor of such a presumption.

At present, there are no decisions involving the application of EC competition law to disputes over patents in the context of standard setting, but this could change in the near future: Nokia, Ericsson, and several other mobile wireless technology companies have filed a complaint against Qualcomm's licensing practices with the European Commission. In particular, they allege that Qualcomm is not complying with an agreement to license certain patents essential to the WCDMA standard under RAND terms (Soininen 2007).[21] And in an unrelated decision, the European Commission required that Microsoft disclose, again on RAND terms, information necessary to ensuring the interoperability of certain kinds of third-party software applications with its operating systems.[22]

In summary, intellectual property has long been important to financial services if for no other reason than it is embedded in the technology it uses. More recently, financial services firms have been acquiring patent portfolios of their own. The financial services sector is also standards intensive and all the more so as it has become increasingly reliant on ICT. For a variety of reasons, adoption of standards increases the value of products and services (for example, network effects, scale economies, liquidity). But a high-quality standard is likely to rely on patented technology owned by a number of financial institutions and quite likely firms located outside the industry.

A successful standard-setting process is a careful balancing act, coordinating both users and producers of the relevant technology. The IP policy of an SSO typically requires the disclosure of any patents on technologies proposed for adoption in the standard and may also specify the licensing terms to be used by participants. These terms should be sufficiently generous to owners of the technology to induce them to disclose their patents and, quite often, to agree to licensing them on non-discriminatory terms. They should also be adequate to reward firms for their risky investments in R&D. On the other hand, excessively high royalty payments or other licensing restrictions may discourage potential users of the technology from adopting the standard.

While standard setting can significantly increase the size and value of a market, it can also create opportunities for hold-up problems. This can occur when adopting a standard entails significant irreversible investments by participants, which essentially locks them into a particular set of technologies. An opportunistic owner of a patented technology included in the standard may be able to exploit this lock-in effect to extract supra-normal rents from adopters of the standard. This is a difficult risk to mitigate, since most standard-setting arrangements lack the power to compel participation by technology providers or to dictate the terms of licenses on patents that were not voluntarily pledged to the standard during the deliberations.

Because of these risks, it is important that standard-setting organisations establish a consensus that enjoys the considerable good will of both users and producers and of patented technologies. Establishing a clear IP policy is a necessary ingredient in building such a consensus.

3 THE EXPERIENCE OF INTELLECTUAL PROPERTY RIGHTS IN STANDARD SETTING IN NETWORK AND FINANCIAL SERVICES INDUSTRIES

The Communications Industry

Network industries, where standardisation has played a pivotal role in the development of the market, include electronics, computing and telecommunications. All of these industries require interoperability. In the field of electronics and computing, public authorities have generally refrained from de jure standardisation, leaving companies and company alliances to compete in the formation of the industry standard.[23] In contrast, in the telecommunications industry, public authorities have actively participated in standard setting, using formal organisations. The history of the GSM standard serves as an example of the challenges posed by intellectual property rights in standard setting. Like the SEPA process, it involves European public authorities promoting a European interoperability standard for a network industry dominated by national incumbents.

In Europe, at least, a reliance on de jure standard setting in telecommunications was due in part to the industrial organisation of the industry. Until recent years, the European telecommunications market was dominated by national monopolies. These incumbents had to ensure conformity and coordination across their own networks, but they had little incentive to increase the interoperability of their networks. In the absence of robust private competition that could have created (de facto) standards, the

European Conference of Postal and Telecommunications Administrations (CEPT) was established in 1959. Its original members were the monopoly-holding postal and telecommunications administrations. CEPT's activities included cooperation on commercial, operational, regulatory and technical standardisation issues.

The gradual deregulation of European telecommunications, together with the introduction of new digital technologies, led to a restructuring of the standard-setting process for the industry.[24] CEPT was replaced by a new organisation, the European Telecommunications Standards Institute (ETSI). One reason for the establishment of ETSI was the perception that CEPT, which accepted only network operators as members, could not accommodate all of the relevant new actors in the market (Cunningham 2005). There was also a concern that strategic use of intellectual property in standard setting might impede liberalisation of the market (Prins and Schiessl, 1993).

The responsibility for the GSM standard was transferred to ETSI in 1988. By then it was clear that several patented technologies were essential for the implementation of the GSM standard. Motorola owned the largest number of these patents (Bekkers et al. 2002). Other patent holders indicated their willingness to license under RAND terms, but Motorola declined. It also continued to patent GSM-related technology extensively.

One plausible explanation for Motorola's different strategy was likely its experience in the US, where patent litigation was much more common in the industry. In contrast, Bekkers et al. (ibid.) describe how the European companies involved in the standardisation process believed that there was a 'gentleman's agreement' not to patent their contributions to the standard. A similar convention had been used successfully in the implementation of the prevailing NMT standard in the Nordic countries. Motorola also suspected that, as a US company, it would receive few contracts to produce equipment for the European market and thus expected patent licensing to become its main source of income from its GSM technology.

Motorola was able to license its GSM patents, but the practical result was not an open standard. By the end of 1993, Motorola had entered into cross-licensing agreements with four companies: Siemens, Alcatel, Nokia and Ericsson. For several other companies, Motorola's patents created a barrier for market entry. For example, a Danish manufacturer Dancall and all Japanese suppliers were left out of the market because the license fees for necessary patents were too high (ibid.).[25]

A separate dispute emerged in the mid-1990s when the company InterDigital began to assert a number of its patents after the GSM standard had already been widely adopted. In litigation in the US, nearly all of InterDigital's patent claims were eventually rejected on obviousness grounds and no infringement was found for the remaining ones.[26] Nevertheless, the firm had been successful in obtaining licensing income from these patents (Bekkers et al. 2006).

ETSI attempted to mitigate these conflicts with limited success, since it developed an IP policy only after the problems had become apparent. The first draft of the policy was forwarded by ETSI's Intellectual Property Rights Committee in 1989, but an actual policy was put in place only in March 1993, only to be replaced by a new policy in November 1994. The original proposal called for compulsory licensing of essential intellectual property, but opposition from US companies and authorities forced ETSI to adopt a more modest policy simply requiring the disclosure of essential patents (Iversen 1999).[27]

There is little doubt that the GSM standard has been a highly successful one. But the success of its IP policy was, at best, qualified. ETSI's goal was to establish an open, but not a royalty-free, standard available for all parties to use. This objective was not realised, since many companies were unable to obtain a license for the essential patents. In addition, some firms were exposed to potential liability for infringement after making substantial commitments to the GSM standard.

Financial Services in the US

A decade after the *State Street* decision in 1998, American financial services firms are adapting to the existence of business method patents. Many firms have added in-house patent counsel, developed internal processes for documenting their own innovations, and are regularly filing for patents. Financial patents are now commonplace in the US. At least 1500 patents are now granted for business methods annually (Figure 7.1). The number of applications for new business methods and financial patents is approaching 10,000 a year (Figure 7.2). The majority of these patents are obtained by firms in industries outside financial services. Many are obtained by computer and electronics manufacturers that are important suppliers of information technology to the industry.

Some firms have aggressively asserted their patents and have had some notable successes in obtaining licensing revenues. Demand letters are regularly sent, and dozens of financial institutions, including several Federal Reserve Banks, have been sued (Decker and Matthews 2007). A number of financial institutions have reached settlements, with significant licensing payments changing hands.

Lerner (2008) presents some preliminary evidence on the litigation experience of US financial patents. He finds that they are litigated at a rate 27 times higher than for US patents as a whole. According to Lerner, litigated

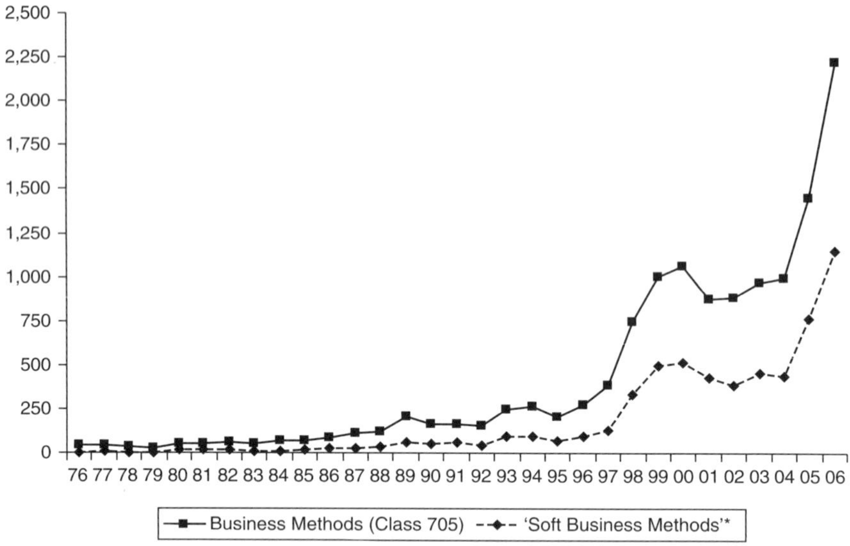

Note: * 'Soft Business Methods' counts only patents in the sub-classes of 705 that are most closely associated with financial services and which contain a smaller share of patents on mechanical inventions. For details, see Hunt (2008).

Source: US Patent and Trademark Office and authors' calculations.

Figure 7.1 Patents on computer-implemented methods of doing business in the US (by calendar grant year)

financial patents tend to be ones granted to individuals or smaller firms. But these owners are often not the plaintiffs in these cases; instead, the suits tend to be initiated by patent-holding companies. Financial patents acquired by foreigners are much less likely to be litigated. The defendants in these suits are typically larger financial firms or exchanges.

There are several notable examples of successful patent-licensing campaigns affecting US financial services firms. The first is Ronald A. Katz Technology Licensing, which, among other things, owns a portfolio of patents related to the technology used by telephone call centers. To date, Katz has struck approximately 150 licensing agreements. These include many large financial institutions and their processors, such as American Express, Bank of America, Capital One, Equifax, First Data Corporation, Merrill Lynch, Nationwide, OppenheimerFunds, Prudential Financial, T. Rowe Price, Vanguard Group, Wachovia Corporation and Wells Fargo.

A second leading example is that of DataTreasury Corporation, which owns at least six patents related to creating, processing and storing digital

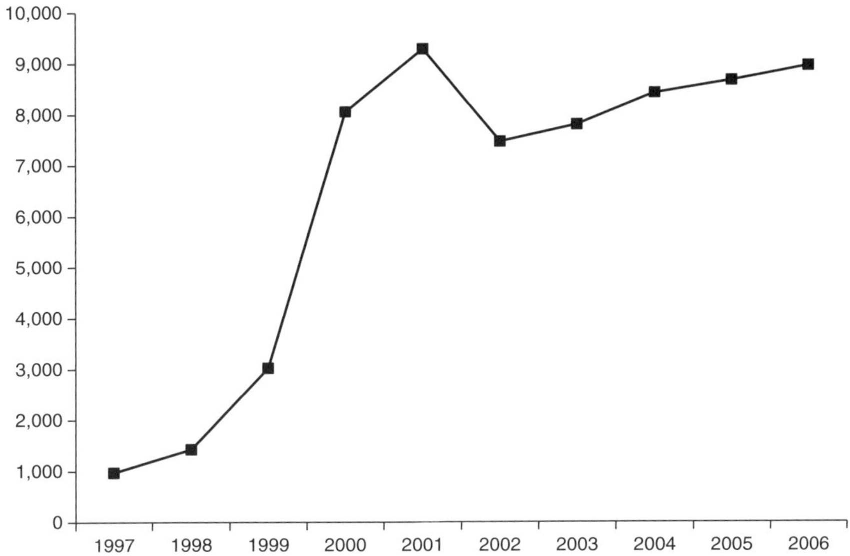

Note: Counts by fiscal year.

Source: US Patent and Trademark Office.

*Figure 7.2 Applications for business method patents**

images of paper checks. Check imaging and exchange technologies are especially important in the US at this time. Banks are in the process of eliminating the physical transportation of paper checks, which is generally required under the traditional law for these financial instruments. The Check Clearing for the 21st Century Act of 2003 permits banks to process check transactions without physically presenting the original check to the issuing bank, so long as certain standards are satisfied.[28] Financial institutions are currently making large information technology investments in order to take advantage of the efficiencies afforded by this reform.

In January 2006, DataTreasury sued 57 banks and other companies that participate in the check-image clearing process.[29] It has also sued the Clearing House Payments Co., which operates a check-image exchange network. In earlier years, it had sued a number of institutions and obtained licensing agreements with firms such as JP Morgan Chase, Merrill Lynch and ATM manufacturer NCR Corporation. More recently, the ATM manufacturer Diebold struck a licensing agreement with DataTreasury, in part to assuage bank customers who have grown increasingly concerned about their potential liability for patent infringement (Bills 2007a).

But the DataTreasury patents are not without controversy. In December 2006, the patent office invalidated 43 of 50 claims in one of DataTreasury's patents (no. 5,910,988) in a re-examination requested by a defendant firm – First Data Corporation – but then reversed itself in 2007 (Bills, 2007b). First Data argued DataTreasury's patents were anticipated in a standard (ANSI X9.46-1995) published more than a year prior to the application date of the patent. The patent claims were upheld because no printed copy of the standard could be located in a place that was accessible to the public, which is required to be considered as prior art.

Such developments are reminiscent of the dispute between Research in Motion (RIM), developer of the Blackberry, and NTP, a patent-holding company. In that case, RIM agreed to a $612 million settlement under threat of a court injunction after being found to infringe several NTP patents. Yet, prior to the announcement of this settlement, a patent office re-examination requested by RIM resulted in the preliminary rejection of every NTP patent relevant to the case.

In another case, LML Payment Systems sued First Data, U.S. Bancorp subsidiary Nova and the Electronic Clearing House for infringing its patent on a process for converting checks into ACH transactions at the point of sale. The firms reached a settlement in 2006 (Bills 2006). A number of other suits have involved several American financial exchanges and other firms developing advanced systems for trading stocks, bonds and derivatives (Hunt 2008).

To summarise, financial patents are now commonplace in the US. Some of these patents are being litigated and significant licensing revenues generated. There is some preliminary evidence that patents in this sector are relatively more prone to litigation than patents in general. The typical plaintiff is not a financial services firm, but the typical defendant is. There are already examples of litigation related to payment innovations and in particular ones that require significant coordination in order to ensure interoperability (for example, check imaging).

4 SETTING STANDARDS FOR SEPA: THE ROLE OF INTELLECTUAL PROPERTY

Since the introduction of euro banknotes and coins in 2002, citizens of the euro area have been able to make cash payments within all 13 countries from a single purse, as easily as with the previous national banknotes and coins. Yet, what is now reality for cash payments remains an aspiration for cashless payments, since these retail payment methods continue to vary from one country to another. Indeed, removing the national currencies from circulation proved to be a much easier task than establishing the legal, technical and economic infrastructure required for a modern, efficient cross-national consumer electronic payment network.

But efforts to create a fully unified payment area for the euro countries, that is, SEPA, have intensified over recent years (see, for example, Kemppainen and Salo 2006). A major step toward SEPA was Regulation 2560/2001 on cross-border payments in the euro area, adopted in December 2001. The regulation eliminated the difference in price between cross-border and national payments. After adoption of the regulation, the payment service provider sector (mainly the banking sector) established an SSO, the European Payments Council (EPC), to foster the development of SEPA. In 2002, the EPC published a white paper outlining a number of steps toward attaining SEPA. EPC expressed its conviction that a critical mass of transactions will have migrated to the SEPA payment instruments by 2010.

Another step forward will be the approval of the PSD, which will, among other things, establish licensing requirements for new payment institutions (which need not be banks) and provides for certain protections for consumers. Under the proposed PSD, these new payment institutions would enjoy certain rights of access to payment systems.[30] But those provisions do not address the question of access to the relevant intellectual property or technology.

But there are diverging views on how and when the goal of a unified (electronic) euro payment area will be achieved. Despite some progress in the preparatory work, the fruition of SEPA appears to be a long way off. In particular, there is still no harmonisation of standards in cashless retail payments, which remain predominantly based on national payment schemes, and consequently, national retail payment clearing and settlement infrastructures remain segmented by country. While many national retail payment systems function efficiently, this is not the case in cross-border retail payment systems. Improved cross-border payment systems would contribute to the process of deepening financial integration in the whole euro area. Some changes are required even in the most efficient national systems of today, since, by nature, the whole process is dynamic and forward looking.

As made clear in Sections 2–3, we think that policies that will assist in the management of any intellectual property essential to the interoperability standards adopted are crucial for the successful implementation of SEPA. To summarise the implications of the economic theory, we start with the observation that the EPC's members consist exclusively of banks, and banks are service providers in the retail market of payment media. The basic economics, as outlined in Section 2 (second subsection), suggests that an SSO controlled by service providers without a strong IP portfolio of their own have an incentive to implement an explicit but tough IP policy toward technology vendors.

But the GSM experience suggests a number of obvious concerns about the SEPA process. In that case, while involvement by public authorities prevented a standards war between two competing industry alliances, it did not succeed in establishing a truly open standard, since not all participants were able to license the essential patents. Public authorities have so far been unwilling to intervene in the standardisation process by requiring compulsory licensing or other legal instruments.[31] Second, European companies can be vulnerable to the foreign companies conditioned by a different culture of intellectual property.

Also, agreeing on effective IP policies in standard setting is not easy. Since compliance with an SSO's IP policy is almost always voluntary, these policies must be designed in order to obtain the consent of the relevant patent owners. The design of such policies is further complicated by the possibility that patents essential to compliance with the standard may be obtained by third parties who were not participants in the standard-setting process. In any case, the GSM experience underlies the importance of designing an IP policy early in the process rather than late, before the IP problems become acute.

The experience of the US financial services sector suggests that there are risks of potential hold-up problems and litigation is not uncommon. It would be particularly disappointing if costly patent disputes delay the migration away from more costly paper-based systems and toward more efficient forms of electronic payments. It is already apparent that the extension of patentable subject matter to financial methods has induced changes in the management of intellectual property in the US financial services sector. In particular, many large firms have added IP counsel to their in-house legal staff, and they are now regularly applying for their own patents.

There are also lessons common to both examples. In each instance, patentable inventions in ICT play an important role, and this suggests that a given standard may implicate dozens or even hundreds of patents. Similarly, in each instance, a significant share of the intellectual property is owned by firms in other industries – for example, by technology vendors serving the downstream industry. In addition, the ownership of ICT patents is cosmopolitan – licensing negotiations could involve firms headquartered around the world. Finally, while financial instruments themselves tend to be discrete, the systems and processes that make them work typically consist of many components (software and hardware) that are the product of cumulative innovation. It can be difficult to determine the contribution of a single patented component to the total value created by these new systems. Each of these factors suggests that obtaining the mutual consent of the essential parties may be complicated and time-consuming.

It is thus rather surprising to observe that the EPC has yet to publicly articulate an IP policy.[32] The EPC, the European Commission and the European Central Bank have clearly indicated that the objective is to create an open standard. For example, the opening paragraphs of the Eurosystem's vision statement (SEPA, The Single Euro Payment Area: An Introduction, 26 October 2006) states that 'by creating open and common standards that overcome technological and commercial barriers and by fostering competition and improving payments services, SEPA will lead to a more efficient and competitive payments industry'. However the precise meaning of open standard is not specified in the context of SEPA.[33]

Other SEPA documents suggest the intention to have the intellectual property related to SEPA payment schemes owned by a legal body established by the EPC:

> SEPA payment schemes/frameworks should be under the governance of a multi-scheme or a single scheme not-for-profit bank-owned vehicle to be further defined. Such vehicle(s) should be open to all banks and would have the *role of safeguarding intellectual property* and providing rule-making and change management procedures. (EPC Roadmap 2004–2010, p. 10, italics added)

In our view the idea of a bank-owned and -controlled organisation owning all intellectual property related to the payment schemes is not realistic, since a significant share of the relevant IP is likely to be owned by companies that are not financial institutions. And while the question has not been expressly discussed in any of the SEPA material we have consulted, some documents seem to suggest that the objective is to develop a standard unencumbered by any patent royalty payments. But sending such a message to potential patent holders could be a road to disaster, since it would discourage them from disclosing relevant patents to the EPC. It could be possible that here EPC merely refers to ownership of trademarks and not other intellectual property – this point is not elaborated in EPC documentation – but this would only underline the lack of transparency about the EPC's intentions concerning the organisation of industrial rights and copyrights.

The apparent lack of attention to intellectual property in the SEPA process is somewhat puzzling, especially given the European Commission's prior experience with these issues in matters involving standardisation. We can think of four potential explanations for the omission, but none is convincing. The first may be that the EPC assumes that SEPA relies on technologies not covered by patents. It is true that many of the technologies envisioned under SEPA are already in use. However it would be unwise to assume that this implies the technology does not enjoy at least some patent protection. Given the number of patents in the financial sector and the relevant ICT sectors, such a conclusion should only follow from a thorough analysis of the adopted technologies. It does not appear that such an analysis has been undertaken.

A second explanation is that the banks, or their associations, do not own essential intellectual property or do not think they will own such intellectual property in the future.[34] But, if this were the case, it would be in the EPC's interest to make an explicit and strict IP policy obligating extensive disclosures and free or RAND licenses for the relevant patents, perhaps after inviting major technology manufacturers to participate in the standard setting.

The third explanation is that the EPC has an IP policy but it is not public. If this were the case, the EPC could plan to have a tough IP policy toward patent holders but is not willing to announce it at this stage when political deliberations about SEPA are ongoing. An announcement now could induce an outcry from the public and technology manufacturers calling for a more lenient IP policy.

Finally, it is possible that the issue of IP policy has simply been neglected. Given that patenting in the European financial services industry is a relatively new phenomenon, it is possible that the IP policy design has not been a priority of the EPC or the public authorities. This also seems implausible, but nonetheless, it is our preferred explanation.

The ultimate explanation for the absence of an IP policy does not matter, however. The fact that there is no public IP policy is worrying in light of the examples from the previous section. It is possible that before or after SEPA enters into force, a party will emerge claiming to own an essential intellectual property to an interoperability standard that is a part of SEPA.

Although the design of an IP policy for the EPC is beyond the scope of this study, we briefly summarise the key lessons from economic theory and empirical evidence from other network industries. The ultimate challenge of an SSO is to create a policy that simultaneously encourages innovation, disclosure of relevant patents, and participation in the standard setting while ensuring access to the relevant intellectual property under acceptable terms, usually RAND terms. To reach this objective, SSOs should implement policies that would encourage disclosure of relevant intellectual property and participation in the standard setting. This is achieved through guaranteeing a reasonable remuneration for the patents and participation through attractive licensing schemes or other licensing practices. It appears that the EPC's approach has been to the contrary: the EPC documentation suggests a royalty-free standard owned by the EPC-established entity. No wonder patent holders have not lined up for the standard-setting process.

5 CONCLUSION

In this chapter we make three points. First, we argue that innovations related to financial services and payment media can be patented in Europe, although not as easily as in the US and other countries. Second, we review the law and economics literature and the actual experience of the telecommunications and the US financial services industries. This examination suggests that a well-designed IP policy is critical for successful standard setting in network industries such as payment media. Finally, we review the IP policy of the EPC, SEPA's standard-setting body. To our surprise, we find that they have none.

While it is difficult to imagine a convincing reason for the absence of the IP concerns in the SEPA project, one explanation might be that the European incumbents and policy makers in the financial services sector are relatively inexperienced in IP management. Such a situation prevailed in the GSM standardisation process in the communications industry. The GSM experience taught the European Commission and the European communications business and public authorities a lesson about the relevance of IP management. We hope that history does not repeat itself in the SEPA project.

NOTES

* We thank three anonymous referees for extensive comments. We would also like to thank Päivi Heikkinen, Ari Hyytinen, Kari Kemppainen, Pekka Sääskilahti, seminar participants at the Bank of Finland.

† The views expressed here are those of the authors and do not necessarily represent the views of the Bank of Finland, the Federal Reserve Bank of Philadelphia or the Federal Reserve System, or the firm of Borenius & Kemppinen.

1. We use the term 'intellectual property' generically. The issues raised are relevant to patents and other industrial rights, such as utility models and protection of topographies of semiconductor products. Sometimes, they also have a bearing on copyright and related rights, especially database rights. In contrast, trademarks, which differ in function and purpose, are not discussed.
2. See Hunt (2008) for a discussion of the measurement problem in the context of financial services in the US.
3. 149 F.3d 1368. See also the decision in *AT&T v. Excel Communications*, 172 F.3d 1352.
4. In other words, computer-implemented methods of doing business are more likely to satisfy the European Patent Office's 'technical effect' requirement of patentable subject matter than business methods in general.
5. As with the term intellectual property (cf. note 1), we use the term 'SEPA' generically. Our specific interest lies in the new pan-European payment instruments, infrastructures, regulation, and other standards that will make SEPA a reality, not in the concept of SEPA itself.
6. The deadline for the implementation of the Payment Service Directive (PSD2007/64/EC) is 1 November 2009.

7. In addition, a binding policy could, for example, stipulate that while a patent owner retains the right to obtain royalties, it has, under a binding contract, committed to forgo injunctive remedies or treble damages under patent law (Lemley 2007). Such terms would significantly reduce risks for the users of the patented technology, but they may not be acceptable to owners of that technology.
8. It should be noted, however, that the literature does not provide much in the way of concrete estimates of the social losses arising from these problems.
9. The quotations are from the European Commission's and the European Central Bank's joint statement 4 May 2006 (EC/ECB 2006) and the European Payments Council (2007).
10. For example, the first US patent on financial inventions was granted on 19 March 1799, for an invention for detecting counterfeit notes (USPTO 2000).
11. A famous example is Amazon's 'one-click' shopping method patent, which was granted in the US in 1999 (USPTO patent no. 5960511). As it turned out, in Europe the invention was not patentable, but a one-click shopping method with a gift option was patentable (EPO patent no. EP0927945).
12. See the joint the statement by the European Commission and the European Central Bank, 4 May 2006.
13. A network industry is one in which the value of a good or service to a consumer is an increasing function of the number of other consumers that use the same or a compatible product.
14. But this is not always the case. Some standards may commoditise a firm's product, causing margins to shrink.
15. Intel's ability to control the development of the standard for the USB interface is a prime example.
16. The technical standard was mandatory in the sense that licenses for the radio frequencies used by the mobile networks were conditioned on the requirement that equipment using those frequencies must be compliant.
17. As an example, Rambus was able to charge a royalty on patents included in an industry standard that was more than four times larger than the royalty charged for its other patents. See Patterson (2003).
18. In the US this strategy is facilitated by the use of *continuations*, which offer applicants a good deal of flexibility to amend their claims as the parameters of a proposed standard become more clear (Lemley 2007). The USPTO recently proposed a rule to limit continuations.
19. See *Qualcomm Inc., v. Broadcom Corp.*, 05-CV-1958-B (2007), decided by the US District Court for the Southern District of California. This case arose because Qualcomm sued Broadcom for infringement of the patents.
20. Decision ECJ 4/6/95; Case C-418/01, *IMS Health v. NDC Health*.
21. WCDMA stands for Wideband Code Division Multiple Access, a feature of next-generation (3G) mobile networks.
22. COMP/C-3/37.792 (2004).
23. Famous examples include the video cassette recorder (VCR), the compact disk (CD-ROM), and many different aspects of the design of personal computers (Grindley 1995).
24. For an early proposal for deregulation, see the European Commission (1987). For subsequent developments, see Nihoul and Rodford (2004).
25. It appears that these companies were at a disadvantage because they could not offer licenses to patents that Motorola found sufficiently appealing.
26. See *Motorola, Inc. v. InterDigital Technology Corp.*, 121 F.3d 1461 (1997). InterDigital has been more successful in obtaining licensing revenues from other patents related to GSM technology.
27. ETSI's intellectual property rights policy has been evolving since 1994 and has been subject to intense debate ever since. In 2005 the European Commission examined ETSI's new intellectual property rights policy in light of competition regulations and concluded

that the policy is in accordance with the regulations and underlined the importance of avoiding 'patent ambushes'.

28. Public Law 108-100, 12 U.S.C. 5001. If the issuing bank desires, it may insist on presentment of a 'substitute' check, an image of the original carrying certain information and satisfying standards set by the Board of Governors of the Federal Reserve System. Substitute checks can be sent electronically and then printed. Substitute checks are the legal equivalent of the original check.
29. *DataTreasury Corporation v. Wells Fargo & Co.*, E.D. Texas, No. 2:06-cv-00072-DF.
30. See Article 23 of the PSD proposal.
31. Mueller (2002) proposes that in government-mandated technology standards, entities holding patent rights in the subject matter should be required to license all users at reasonable commercial terms. Furthermore, in the case where the patent owner declines to comply, the government should exercise the principle of eminent domain, that is, the state's right under US law in certain cases to seize private property for public uses.
32. The EPC's website (www.europeanpaymentscouncil.eu), visited frequently from June 2006 to March 2007, includes no mention of an IP policy nor do the experts on SEPA at the Bank of Finland we have interviewed have knowledge that the EPC would have an IP policy.
33. It is usually defined as a standard fulfilling the following criteria: persons who are directly and materially affected by the activity in question are free to participate in the standard setting, and the standard is available for anyone to use (Caplan 2003).
34. In the communications industry, for example, the essential intellectual property is not always owned by telecommunications operators (service providers) but rather by technology vendors such as manufacturers of network equipment and handsets.

REFERENCES

Bekkers, R., E. Iversen and K. Blind (2006), 'Patent pools and non-assertion agreements: coordination mechanisms for multi-party IPR holders in standardisation', paper for the EASST 2006 Conference, Lausanne, Switzerland, 23–26 August.

Bekkers, R., B. Verspagen and J. Smits (2002), 'Intellectual property rights and standardisation: the case of GSM', *Telecommunications Policy*, **26**, 171–88.

Bessen, J. and R.M. Hunt (2007), 'An empirical look at software patents', *Journal of Economics and Management Strategy*, **16**, 157–89.

Bills, S. (2006), 'First Data, 2 others settle with holder of POP patent', *American Banker*, **171** (65), 5 April, 12.

Bills, S. (2007a), 'Diebold bids to lift image ATMs with patent deal', *American Banker*, **172** (16), 24 January, 13.

Bills, S. (2007b), 'Check image patent case gets a boost', *American Banker*, **172** (133), 12 July.

Blind, K., R. Bierhals, N. Thumm, K. Hossein, J. Sillwood, E. Iversen, R. van Reekum and B. Rixius (2002), 'Study on the interaction between standardisation and intellectual property rights', EC Contract No. G6MA-CT-2000-02001, Fraunhofer Institute.

Bolt, W. and D. Humphrey (2008), 'Reducing payment processing costs: scale economies and SEPA', *Journal of Payments Strategy & Systems*, **2**, 250–58.

Caplan, P. (2003), 'Patents and open standards', *Information Standards Quarterly* **14** (4), October.

Carpentier, X. (2006), *Essays on the Law and Economics of Intellectual Property,* Helsinki: Acta Universitatis Oeconomicae Helsingiensis, A-282.

Chiao, B., J. Lerner and J. Tirole (2007), 'The rules of standard setting organisations: an empirical analysis', *Rand Journal of Economics*, **38**, 905–30.
Council of the European Union (2007), 'Proposal for a Directive of the European Parliament and of the Council on Payment Services in the Internal Market and Amending Directives 97/7/EC, 2000/12/EC and 2002/65/EC – Outcome of the European Parliament's First Reading', http://register.consilium.europa.eu/pdf/en/07/ st08/st08718.en07.pdf, accessed 30 August.
Cunningham, A. (2005), 'Telecommunications, intellectual property, and standards', in I. Walden and J. Angel (eds), *Telecommunications Law and Regulation*, Oxford: Oxford University Press, pp. 341–75.
Decker, S. and S. Matthews (2007), 'Fiserv, Federal Reserve Banks face fraud patent suit', Bloomberg News Wire, 23 January.
European Commission (1987), 'Towards a dynamic European economy – Green Paper on the development of the common market for telecommunication services and equipment', COM(87)290final.
European Commission (1992), 'Intellectual property rights and standardisation', Communication from the Commission, COM (92)445.
European Commission (2006), 'Consultative paper on SEPA incentives', European Commission Internal Market and Services DG, 13 February.
European Commission and the European Central Bank (2006), 'Single Euro Payments Area. Joint Statement, 4 May 2006', http://www.ecb.int/press/pr/date/2006/html/pr0605041.en.html, accessed 7 October.
European Payments Council (EPC) (2007), 'Making SEPA a reality – implementing the Single Euro Payments Area', http://www.europeanpaymentscouncil.eu/documents/EPC066_06%20SEPA%20Overview%20v1.4.pdf, accessed 14 March.
Evans, D.S. and R. Schmalensee (2005), *Paying with Plastic*, 2nd edn, Cambridge, MA: MIT Press.
Frame, W.S. and L.J. White (2004), 'Empirical studies of financial innovations: lots of talk, little action?', *Journal of Economic Literature*, **47**, 116–44.
Greenspan, A. (2003), 'Market economies and rule of law', speech given at the 2003 Financial Markets Conference of the Federal Reserve Bank of Atlanta, Sea Island, Georgia, 4 April, http://www.federalreserve.gov/BoardDocs/Speeches/2003/20030404/default.htm.
Greenspan, A. (2004), 'Intellectual property rights', speech given at the Stanford Institute for Economic Policy Research Economic Summit, Stanford, California, 27 February, http://www.federalreserve.gov/BoardDocs/Speeches/2004/200402272/default.htm.
Grindley, P. (1995), *Standards, Strategy and Policy*, Oxford: Oxford University Press.
Hart, O. (1995), *Firm, Contracts, and Financial Structure*, Oxford: Oxford University Press.
Hunt, R.M. (2001), 'You can patent that? Are patents on computer programs and business methods good for the New Economy?', *Federal Reserve Bank of Philadelphia Business Review*, 5–15.
Hunt, R.M. (2008), 'Business method patents for U.S. financial services', Federal Reserve Bank of Philadelphia Working Paper 08-10.
Iversen, E.J. (1999), 'Standardization and intellectual property rights: ETSI's controversial search for new IPR procedures', Proceedings of the 1999 Standardization and Innovation in Information Technology (SIIT) conference, Aachen, Germany, 15–17 September.

Katz, M. and C. Shapiro (1985), 'Network externalities, competition and compatibility', *American Economic Review*, **75**, 424–44.

Kemppainen, K. and S. Salo (2006), 'Promoting integration of European retail payment systems: role of competition, cooperation and regulation', in M. Balling (ed.), *The Adoption of the Euro, Choice of Currency Regime and Integration of Payment Systems*, SUERF Studies 2006/5, Vienna.

Kultti, K., T. Takalo and J. Toikka (2006), 'Simultaneous model of innovation, secrecy, and patent policy', *American Economic Review, Papers and Proceedings*, **96**, 82–6.

Lemley, M.A. (2002), 'Intellectual property rights and standard setting organizations', *California Law Review*, **90**, 1889–980.

Lemley, M.A. (2007), 'Ten things to do about patent hold-up of standards (and one not to)', *Boston College Law Review*, **48**, 149–68.

Lemley, M.A. and C. Shapiro (2007), 'Patent hold-up and royalty stacking', mimeo, University of California at Berkeley.

Lerner, J. (2002), 'Where does State Street lead? A first look at finance patents 1971–2000', *Journal of Finance*, **57**, 901–30.

Lerner, J. (2008), 'The litigation of financial innovations', NBER Working Paper No. 14324.

Mueller, J.M. (2002), 'Patent misuse through the capture of industry standards', *Berkeley Technology Journal*, **17**, 623–84.

Näcke, T. (1995), 'Abuse of dominant positions', paper presented at the Symposium on Competition Policy in a Global Economy, Taipei, 19 April, http://ec.europa.eu/comm/competition/speeches/text/sp1995_025_en.html.

Nihoul, P. and P. Rodford (2004), *EU Electronic Communications Law. Competition and Regulation in the European Telecommunications Market*, Oxford: Oxford University Press.

Nordhaus, W. (1969), *Invention, Growth, and Welfare: A Theoretical Treatment of Technological Change*, Cambridge, MA: MIT Press

Patterson, M.R. (2003), 'Antitrust and the costs of standard setting', *Minnesota Law Review*, **87**, 1995–2017.

Prins, C. and M. Schiessl (1993), 'The new European telecommunications standards policy: conflicts between standardization and intellectual property rights', *European Intellectual Property Review*, **8**, 263–6.

Rahnasto, I. (2003), *Intellectual Property Rights, External Effects, and Antitrust Law: Leveraging IPRs in the Communications Industry*, Oxford: Oxford University Press.

Schmiedel, H. (2007), 'The economic impact of the Single Euro Payments Area', European Central Bank Occasional Paper No. 71, Frankfurt am Main.

Shapiro, C. (2001), 'Navigating the patent thicket: cross-licenses, patent pools, and standard setting', in A. Jaffe, J. Lerner and S. Stern (eds), *Innovation Policy and the Economy*, Vol. 1, Cambridge, MA: MIT Press, pp. 119–50.

Shapiro, C. (2006), 'Injunctions, hold-up and patent royalties', mimeo, University of California at Berkeley.

Soininen, A. (2007), *Patents in the Information and Communications Technology Sector – Development Trends, Problem Areas and Pressures for Change*, Lappeenranta, Finland: Acta Universitatis Lappeenrantaensis 262.

Tufano, P. (2003), 'Financial innovation', in G.M. Constantinides, M. Harris and R.M. Stulz (eds), *Handbook of Corporate Finance*, Vol. 1A, Amsterdam: Elsevier, North-Holland, pp. 307–31.

US Patent and Trademark Office (USPTO) (2000), 'Automated financial or management data processing methods (business methods), A White Paper', http://www.uspto.gov/web/menu/busmethp/whitepaper.pdf, accessed 14 March, 2007.

Wagner, S. (2008), 'Business method patents in Europe and their strategic use – evidence from franking device manufacturers', *Economics of Innovation and New Technology*, **17**, 173–94.

Williamson, O.E. (1985), *Economic Institutions of Capitalism*, New York: Free Press.

Ziedonis, R. (2004), 'Don't fence me in: fragmented markets for technology and the patent acquisition strategies of firms', *Management Science*, **50**, 804–20.

APPENDIX 7A A MODEL OF A MONOPOLY SSO

To summarise some of the main results from the literature that have implications for the case of SEPA, we consider a simple model of a monopoly SSO. Let us denote the quality of the standard by q and the SSO's IP policy by α. The higher α is, the tougher is the IP policy toward the parties that do not own essential intellectual property, such as service providers, users, and consumers. For example, a high α means that the price for a license is higher or that licensing contracts include more restrictions. Obviously, a tougher IP policy means that there will be less demand for the standard. The quality of the standard affects both users and IP holders positively. More formally, denoting the users' gross utility by $u(\alpha, q)$ and the IP holders' profits by $\pi(\alpha, q)$, it is natural to think that $u_\alpha < 0$, $u_q > 0$, and $\pi_q > 0$, where subscripts denote the partial derivatives with respect to α and q. We may further think that $\pi_\alpha(0, q) > 0$ but that $\pi_\alpha < 0$ for some α sufficiently high (so that $\pi_{\alpha\alpha} < 0$). In other words, the IP holders' profits are initially increasing in the toughness of the SSO's IP policy, but since a tough IP policy restricts the use of the standard, an overly tough IP policy will be harmful from the IP holder's point of view.

Following Chiao et al. (2007), let us assume that the SSO chooses the IP policy to maximise:

$$\Pi(\alpha) = \lambda u(\alpha, q) + (1 - \lambda)\pi(\alpha, q), \tag{7A.1}$$

putting weight λ on the users' utility. In other words, $1 - \lambda$ measures the extent to which the SSO is captured by the holders of the essential IP. If $\lambda = 0$, the SSO does not care about users at all, whereas if $\lambda = 1$, the SSO behaves as if it would only maximise the users' benefits.

The SSO's optimal IP policy is then implicitly given by:

$$\lambda u_\alpha(\alpha^*, q) + (1 - \lambda)\pi_\alpha(\alpha^*, q) \leq 0. \tag{7A.2}$$

From (7A.2) we immediately see that for high enough λ, we may have a corner solution where the optimal IP policy is as lenient as possible ($\alpha^* \to 0$), whereas otherwise we have an interior solution (recall that $\pi_{\alpha\alpha} < 0$). If we focus on the interior solution, a simple comparative-static exercise shows that:

$$\frac{d\alpha^*}{d\lambda} = -\frac{u_\alpha - \pi_\alpha}{\lambda u_{\alpha\alpha} + (1 - \lambda)\pi_{\alpha\alpha}} < 0. \tag{7A.3}$$

The sign follows from the second-order condition for the interior solution, which makes the denominator negative, and from the fact that at the interior solution $\pi_\alpha(\alpha^*, q) > 0$. Clearly, the more power the users have in the decision making of an SSO, the more lenient its IP policy. Similarly,

$$\frac{d\alpha^*}{dq} = -\frac{\lambda u_q + (1-\lambda)\pi_q}{\lambda u_{\alpha\alpha} + (1-\lambda)\pi_{\alpha\alpha}} > 0. \tag{7A.4}$$

In other words, the higher the quality of the standard, the tougher the IP policy. If the standard quality is high, there will be demand for the standard despite a tough IP policy.

REFERENCE

Chiao, B., J. Lerner and J. Tirole (2007), 'The rules of standard setting organizations: an empirical analysis', *Rand Journal of Economics*, **38**, 905–30.

8. The regulatory and market developments of covered bonds in Europe

Giuseppina Chesini and Monica Tamisari*

1 INTRODUCTION

Covered bonds have been one of the fastest-growing sectors of the fixed-income market in Europe over the past decade, continuing to expand with new jurisdictions and borrowers coming on-stream.

The rapid growth of the covered bond market has been driven by an accelerating demand for low-risk investment products as an alternative to government bonds. Covered bonds are secured bank obligations offering strong credit ratings, good liquidity and a higher yield compared to government bonds, together with a lower spread volatility. From an issuer's perspective, they represent a very cost-efficient instrument to raise long-term funding for financing low-profit businesses such as mortgage and public sector lending.

Originally issued in domestic markets and placed with local investors, covered bonds have become increasingly popular in Europe in the 1990s with the introduction of the new benchmark format designed to attract large institutional investors.

The launch of the benchmark format led to the internationalisation of formerly domestic markets. Germany started with large size issues under the name of 'jumbo' covered bonds in 1995. France and Spain followed in 1999. Since then, the covered bond market has expanded strongly within Europe. Almost all of the European countries have implemented new covered bond legislation or have updated existing rules to cover this development, while also responding to the considerable growth of mortgage lending in the European Union (EU).

In 2003 the first 'structured' covered bond was issued in the UK with the help of securitisation techniques, based on contractual agreements in the absence of a dedicated legal framework. The innovative product was widely accepted by the market and rapidly imitated by other lenders, not only in the UK but all across Europe, paving the way for a variety of new products to enter the arena.

Covered bonds have traditionally been characterised by a high degree of standardisation and homogeneity, which resulted in a limited analytical effort being required for investors. However, the impressive market growth increased diversity in the covered bond universe. New demand from investors as well as more stringent requirements from rating agencies led to an increased combination of traditional features with structured finance elements providing credit enhancement. The ever-broader range of products offers investors an enhanced degree of asset diversification, while requiring additional credit analysis. In any case, simplicity remains a key success factor of covered bonds.

With a total volume of €1.9 trillion in outstanding issuance from more than 20 countries at the end of 2006, covered bonds represent the second-largest bond market after sovereign debt in Europe. As one of the most dynamic segments of the European capital market, covered bonds are a main driver of the integration of European financial markets.

This chapter analyses the reasons behind the growing success of covered bonds in relation to the recent evolution in bank funding tools in Europe. It focuses on the mortgage markets' financing, where the effects of such a development are most evident. After a general description of the market and its evolution, it provides an overview of the different measures of credit risk, which is crucial, both for the issuers and for the investors. Then, attention is given to the regulatory developments and the problems arising when different legal frameworks coexist in a global financial market. The crucial points of the current debate concerning the appropriate regulatory response to market developments are examined. Finally, the efficiency implications of the adoption of covered bonds for banks are explored, together with the impact this has on the financial system as a whole.

2 THE COVERED BOND CONCEPT

Covered bonds are bank obligations collateralised by a dynamic pool of financial assets, to which bondholders have a priority claim ahead of unsecured creditors. Typical features include restrictions on the business activities of the issuer, eligibility criteria for the cover pool, specific asset valuation rules, asset–liability matching requirements and specific post-bankruptcy procedures.

As long as the credit institution is not insolvent or bankrupt, covered bonds behave as normal unsecured debt. Interest and principal on the outstanding bonds are paid by the credit institution out of its own funds, irrespective of the performance of the assets in the cover pool. Once the credit institution turns insolvent or bankrupt, covered bonds benefit from a direct claim against the cover pool similar to securitisations. The proceeds generated by the assets in the cover pool are used to satisfy the covered bondholders having priority over the unsecured creditors of the credit institution. In addition, should the cover pool prove insufficient to fully satisfy the claims of covered bondholders, the latter would rank *pari passu* with unsecured creditors of the insolvent estate.

Covered bonds issued by a single issuer are collateralised by the same cover pool, which is actively and conservatively managed by the issuer with new assets entering the pool as others mature or become ineligible. In the event of the credit institution becoming insolvent, the cover pool will turn static and will be separated from the insolvent estate. The cover pool and pertaining bonds will be managed as a separate entity, usually by a specifically appointed administrator, ensuring that investors will continue to receive the payments due according to contractual dates.

The covered bond issuance is generally subject to specific public supervision, with a legal framework specifying the key safety features such as the type and quality of eligible assets. In many frameworks, the composition and value of the cover pool is observed by an independent cover pool monitor, which usually reports to the banking supervisory authority. In the case of 'structured' covered bonds, the monitoring of the cover pool is mainly conducted by the rating agencies.

Due to their low-risk profile, covered bonds offer credit institutions a cost-efficient instrument to raise long-term funding for mortgage or public sector loans. Widely used in Germany under the name of 'pfandbrief',[1] covered bonds expanded throughout Europe in the 1990s, when the new benchmark product was introduced, which attracted large institutional investors.[2]

German mortgage banks introduced the so-called 'jumbo pfandbrief' in the mid-1990s with the purpose of internationalising their funding base. In contrast to traditional pfandbriefe, jumbo pfandbriefe were provided with a rating and even more importantly with a high degree of liquidity (Mastroeni 2001). The two main components used to bolster liquidity were a minimum issue size and a market-making obligation by the underwriting banks.

The new benchmark-format covered bond is a euro-denominated, bullet maturity, fixed annual coupon bond with a minimum size requirement of €1 billion. Quotations with narrow two-way prices are provided for by at least three market makers, enabling investors and market makers to easily execute rather large orders or unwind positions. Pricing transparency is enhanced through electronic trading on platforms such as

EuroCreditMTS. Benchmark covered bonds are primarily issued with maturities of between 5 and 10 years, but market segments with maturities of 15, 20 years or longer are gaining importance.

3 THE EXPANSION OF THE COVERED BOND MARKET

Since the launch of the first jumbo pfandbrief in 1995, the benchmark covered bond market has grown continuously, as shown in Figure 8.1, and has strongly increased international trade in covered bonds. Today, with a current outstanding volume of over €700 billion in 2006, the benchmark covered bond market is the second most liquid bond market after government bond markets and accounts for more than 40 per cent of the total outstanding volume of covered bonds in Europe.[3]

Following the overwhelming success of this innovative product, a number of countries across Europe have enacted their own covered bond legislation in the past few years. In other countries, such as the UK, in the absence of a specific legal framework, issuers started 'replicating' covered bonds via contractual agreements on the basis of the existing legislation.

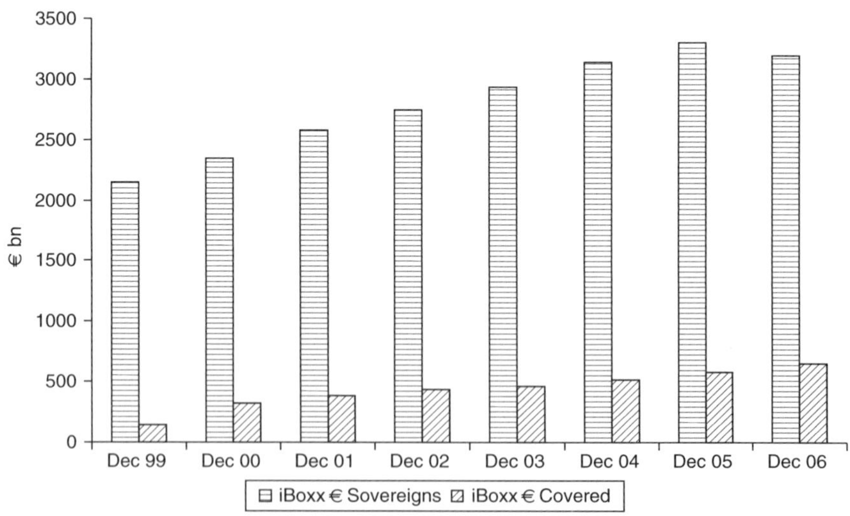

Source: Iboxx.

Figure 8.1 European sovereign debt outstanding versus jumbo covered bonds

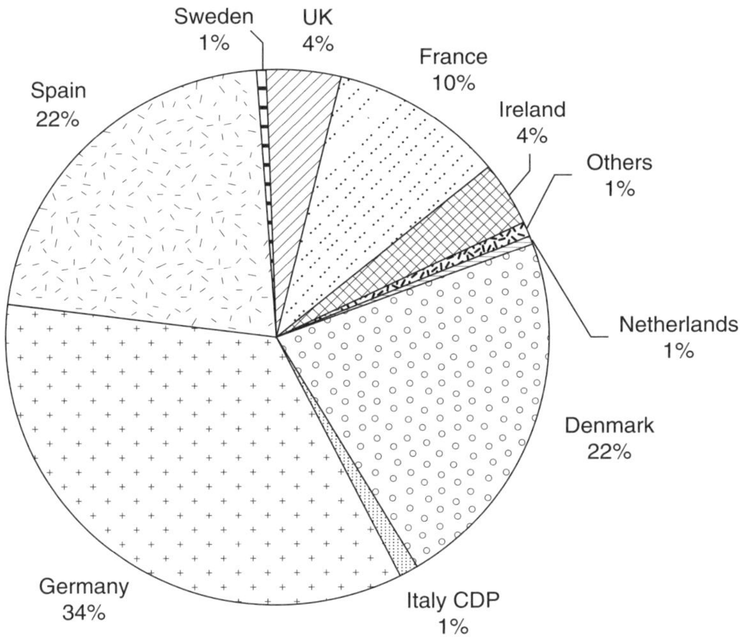

Source: Own elaboration from ECBC statistics.

Figure 8.2 Percentage of outstanding jumbo covered bonds by country in Europe, 2006

The market for covered bonds is now far more diversified than it was some years ago in terms of the geographical distribution of issuers. If in 2001 the German pfandbrief accounted for nearly 87 per cent of the outstanding jumbo covered bonds in the market, in 2003 the market share of German issuers was 59 per cent (ECBC 2006 [2007]), while at the end of 2006 it was only 34 per cent, as shown in Figure 8.2.

Looking ahead, the covered bond market shows no signs of growth slowing down in the near future. Demand for covered bonds continues to accelerate globally as new types of investors have started diversifying into asset classes for various reasons.

First, fiscal discipline within the government sector has deteriorated. The budget deficit/GDP ratios established by the Growth and Stability Pact are being exceeded in many countries, due to their economic conditions and the consequent lack of improvement in their fiscal positions. Compared to government bonds, the covered bond asset class allows a pick-up in yield and offers a high credit rating and a good liquidity. Moreover, cover bonds offer a wide, diversified risk (either public sector or mortgage), while government bonds offer a non-diversified risk of a government's finance policies.

Second, stock markets have become more unpredictable. Covered bonds, with their high credit ratings, good liquidity and solid performance in the secondary market have represented an attractive solution for traditional equity investors waiting for the next favourable equity opportunity.

Third, the euro's strength against the US dollar has been sustained. Covered bonds are issued in euros and this has allowed developing countries – with the majority of their reserves being in US dollars – to contain the risk of losses on their reserve positions by recourse to a more balanced currency mix. The market profited from the funds' shift from the dollar and gained increased liquidity and a good widespread performance against government bonds. This attitude could increase the recourse to covered bonds by central banks in the future. Moreover, many central banks possess far more reserves than needed in case of emergencies; as a consequence, some of them apply a similar approach to their portfolio management as mainstream fund managers.

Fourth, the US agency accounting problems have encouraged traditional agency investors to diversify more into covered bonds. Covered bond investors do not need to rely on an implicit government support mechanism as credit ratings are based on the profitability of the underlying business and the quality of the asset pool's backing issues.

Finally, many countries have adopted or plan to adopt covered bond legislation in the future. The local investors of a country which adopts covered bond legislation participate in the project, first by investing in the local brand of covered bond and then by investing in its foreign varieties also. For example, Irish investors showed signs of interest in covered bonds prior to the establishment of the Irish Asset Covered Securities (ACS) Act 2001,[4] and by 2005 the country represented a road stop show for Irish and non-Irish covered bond issuers alike. With many countries – also non-European ones – wishing to allow national credit institutions to issue covered bonds, the number of locally focused investors interested in all types of covered bonds is expected to rise significantly (Golin 2006, p. 20).

4 THE RELEVANCE OF COVERED BONDS IN THE MORTGAGE FUNDING CAPITAL MARKETS

Covered bonds have traditionally been issued by specialised banks whose scope of business was limited to mortgage or public sector lending and related activities. Now, universal banks are also allowed to issue covered bonds in different countries.

The specialist bank was the only possible issuer in Germany before July 2005[5] and this is still the case in Denmark,[6] Hungary, Poland, Luxembourg and Austria. By restricting the covered bond business to specialist banks, the regulator prevents the quality deterioration that cherry picking and segregation of high-quality assets entails for unsecured creditors and depositors.

In other frameworks, the issuer can be a universal bank without any business restrictions. In Russia, Sweden and Germany (since July 2005), a qualified covered bond licence based on specific requirements is necessary in order to issue covered bonds. In other countries, such as Spain, all banks are allowed to issue covered bonds without specific licences.

Indeed, covered bonds represent only a small part of the funding programme for universal banks, which usually have wide branch networks through which to collect retail deposits. Instead, they become pivotal to the core business model for specialised credit institutions with a limited distribution network presence. In particular, public sector or mortgage lenders find it advantageous to finance themselves in the long-term capital markets via covered bonds as they develop a virtuous circle of lower funding costs, which in turn enables them to onlend to their clients at more attractive levels.

In any case, covered bonds provide issuers – both deposit-taking and capital market financed – with a wide range of significant advantages including investor diversification, more efficient management of funding maturity, increased liquidity and stability of funding sources and cheaper funding.

Covered bonds are the most cost-efficient form of secured long-term funding available to banks, providing for a better asset–liability matching compared to retail deposits in connection with long-term assets such as mortgage and public sector loans (ECB, 2004).

Covered bonds allow the issuer to access the capital markets even in periods of stress. For covered bond issuers the ability to finance assets and thus offer more lending is less likely to be affected by external events (Packer et al. 2007, p. 53). Despite circumstances such as global political events or credit events that can cause wider spreads for lower rated credits, the market for AAA fixed income assets remains open as investors defensively tend to invest their money in the highest-quality products available.

Covered bonds also reach a well-diversified investor base in terms of types and countries. AAA assets enjoy the largest fixed income investor segment in the world, with investors ranging from big central banks to small retail investors. By accessing the AAA markets, the covered bond issuer profits from a continued flow of diversified financing.

Finally, given the relative simplicity of the instrument, it becomes easier to access the deepest and broadest investor demand in the world and to have frequent recourse to larger issuance volumes.

Over the last few years the level of competition in the European mortgage markets has substantially increased. One consequence of this is that mortgage lending margins have narrowed dramatically. The continuous introduction of new mortgage products is a clear indication of the high competitive pressure in mortgage markets (Issing 2005).

With respect to mortgage markets, financial innovation refers generally to both mortgage loans and funding mechanisms. In fact, the supply of mortgage credit products and the price at which they are offered rely heavily on the funding strategies of single institutions.

Mortgage loans have traditionally been financed by retail deposits. Retail deposits can be a relatively cheap form of funding, which nevertheless rely on large branch networks. The use of deposits for financing mortgage loans also creates issues in terms of asset and liability management, as deposits typically have short to medium periods of notice, whereas mortgage loans are typically medium- to long-term products.

In recent years, most European countries experienced a continuous decline in the volume of bank deposits as a result of consumers' search for alternative and better investments for their savings. Conversely, a relatively low interest rate environment, as well as house price rises, caused the demand for mortgage credit to grow constantly. Consequently, with the demand for mortgage credit increasingly outstripping the supply of deposits, mortgage lenders had to resort to capital markets to finance the funding gap (ECB 2005).

According to the most recent statistics, retail deposits continue to represent the predominant mortgage finance form for most EU member states, making up approximately 60 per cent of mortgage funding. However, the use of capital market products is rising. Covered bonds and mortgage backed securities (MBS) are the two main instruments for funding mortgages in the context of capital markets. In 2003, covered bonds were estimated to finance 17.5 per cent of outstanding EU mortgage loans, with MBS accounting for 11.6 per cent of newly issued mortgage loans (European Commission 2006).

The expansion of capital market products provides an alternative to retail deposits, giving lenders access to an international investor base which benefits both lenders and consumers. Even though the covered bond market remains the predominant European funding tool, recent data show European securitisation has steadily increased since 2001. In particular, in 2006 issuances were three times larger than in 2001 (ECB 2007b). The decision to use one type of capital market funding technique over another depends on a number of factors such as interest rate, term of interest rate fixing, accounting treatment, capital relief available, execution cost and funding costs. In many cases, the different funding techniques are complementary since they achieve different objectives and reach investors with different portfolio strategies.

When focusing on covered bonds and MBS as the main capital market funding tools for financing mortgage loans, it is worth comparing the two instruments in order to understand the reasons behind the choice of the funding mix for lenders.

Generally speaking, covered bonds constitute a more attractive funding tool for mortgage lending, allowing issuers to obtain large volumes of cheap long-dated funds, whereas securitisations are traditionally used for capital relief and risk transfer purposes.

Covered bonds are bank obligations collateralised by a revolving pool of financial assets, which typically remain on the balance sheet of the originator, whereas in the case of MBS the assets backing the bonds are taken off the balance sheet and transferred (together with the related risks) to a separate special purpose vehicle, which issues the bonds. Thus, there is no risk transfer from the originator to the investors in covered bonds. Moreover, covered bonds provide the lending institution with the necessary flexibility to deal with its customers, which also includes the modification of the terms of mortgages, which would not be possible if the mortgages were sold through a securitisation.

Obviously, for smaller not-rated banks with no access to the covered bond market, MBS remain an important funding tool. In addition, covered bonds can only be collateralised by high-quality assets, while there are no limits to the types of assets that can be securitised.

Apart from the different rationale, issuers are expected to continue to use both products for investor diversification purposes as covered bonds and MBS attract a very different investor base. Using a blended funding strategy would also facilitate better asset and liability matching, as covered bonds are issued at all maturities along the curve with fixed coupons, while MBS are floating-rate bonds with maturities ranging from less than one year to typically under seven years.

In relation to the two instruments, the funding mix has been observed to vary substantially among EU countries, due mainly to the different regulatory environments. Indeed, countries basically concentrate on either covered bonds or MBS, and only Spain appears to have mature markets in both instruments.[7] This evidence requires further investigation into the relevance of regulation for the development of covered bond markets.[8]

5 ASSESSING THE CREDIT RISK OF COVERED BONDS

The high rating generally attributed to covered bonds, combined with their preferential regulatory treatment, helps to explain the attractive funding levels that this instrument has achieved in recent years.

Rating agencies play an important role in assessing the credit risk of covered bonds. All outstanding jumbo covered bonds have at least one rating, and with more than 90 per cent of European jumbo covered bonds rated AAA and the remaining 10 per cent being rated in the AA area and no A ratings – the jumbo market is almost exclusively an AAA asset class (Deutsche Bank 2007).

The three major rating agencies (Moody's Investors Service, Standard & Poor's (S&P) and Fitch Ratings) adopted different methodologies to evaluate covered bonds for several years. Now, there is a certain degree of convergence in methods. What varies is the degree of emphasis given to each aspect of the evaluation process and the particular methods used to evaluate the credit quality of the cover pool and its dynamic nature.

More specifically, S&P concentrates on the asset quality of the cover pool and its cash flows and typically separates the covered bond rating from the senior unsecured rating of the issuer where the cover pools are legally insulated from the rest of the bank and will be continued after the default of the issuer. Moody's has recently revised its approach and is now focusing more on the attributes of the cover pool and the structural features of the issue than in the past, when rating assigned to the issue was assigned according to a notching-up approach (Moody's Investor Service 2005). Fitch announced a new rating methodology for covered bonds in July 2006 (Fitch Ratings 2006a), based on the calculation of the so-called 'discontinuity factor', which is used to determine the lowest achievable probability of default for covered bonds. According to this approach, the probability of default of a covered bond is the result of the probability of default of the individual issuer discounted by the discontinuity factor, which accounts for variables such as the asset segregation, the liquidity gap, the alternative management and the oversight of the cover pool.

The critical factors for the assessment of the credit quality of a covered bond issue, on which each rating agency puts different emphasis, can be summarised as follows (Golin 2006, pp. 27–8):

1. the strength of the investor protections embodied in the legal and regulatory framework;
2. the credit quality of the cover assets;

3. the creditworthiness of the issuer, separate and distinct from the particular features of the securities it has issued or intends to issue; and
4. the particular structural features of the issue, especially in so far as the issue is a 'structured' covered bond or structural enhancements are used in an attempt to improve the security's credit quality.

Generally speaking, the low-risk nature of the assets backing the bonds and the security features may result in a notably higher credit rating compared to the unsecured debt of the issuing bank. The implementation of a variety of self-restrictions and the provision of a degree of overcollateralisation also allow issuers to directly influence the rating assigned to the bonds. In particular, as the possibility of funding with a very high rated instrument can result in an improvement in profitability, this encourages a move towards covered bond issuers working with rating agencies on a set of structural enhancements and self-commitments that improves the rating and thereby the perceived safety of the issue for investors. Depending on the approach employed by the rating agencies, covered bonds can achieve ratings that are well above that of the issuer or even completely delinked from the latter. This leads to the vast majority of jumbo covered bonds currently outstanding being AAA rated.

Covered bonds also offer advantages in terms of regulatory treatment due to their low-risk profile. This is important for bank holders incorporated in the EU, who represent a significant segment of the market.

Following the acceptance of the first Basel Accord in 1988, internationally active banks concerned themselves with capital adequacy requirements and risk-weightings assigned to particular classes of instruments for capital allocation purposes.

The treatment of covered bonds for capital allocation purposes has become an interesting issue over the last several years as European regulators began to consider the implementation of the Basel Accord in the EU.

The Basel Accord in its global formulation did not address the matter of covered bonds, which were treated as ordinary bank debt. In the EU, where covered bonds were gaining more and more significance, it was felt by the banking industry that this asset class deserved a specific and more favourable capital treatment than other unsecured obligations against banks, in view of their lower risk nature. Thus, under EU law and regulations in member states, covered bonds were treated as a special case and supervisors could grant such securities preferential treatment on a discretionary basis.[9] In particular, this led to higher investment limits for regulated investment funds (up to 25 per cent instead of a maximal of 5 per cent) and lower capital requirements for banks (10 per cent risk-weighting instead of 20 per cent).

Following the implementation of the Capital Requirements Directive (CRD),[10] which brings the revised Basel Accord – known as Basel II[11] – into European law, the preferential treatment for covered bonds is confirmed.[12]

Under the Basel II framework, the required capital charge for bank investors is calculated under different approaches, based either on external or internal ratings. The Standardised Approach (SA) is based on rating agency assessments, while the Internal Ratings Based Approach (IRB) relies on internal risk management systems to produce more tailormade risk-weights. In principle, risk-weights under the IRB approach should be lower than the standardised ones so as to give banks an incentive to implement more advanced risk management tools.

Under the SA, risk-weights are set according to the asset type, similar to Basel I, which is based on credit ratings provided by external credit assessment institutions. For bank debt, there are two ways of obtaining risk-weights, linked either to the credit rating of the home country sovereign (option 1) or to that of the bank itself (option 2). The choice between the two options is at the discretion of national regulators, who apply one of them to all banks in their jurisdiction.

Under the IRB, risk-weights are calculated on the basis of certain formulae specified for different asset classes. Four parameters or risk components are required to calculate risk-weights, defined as follows:

1. probability of default (PD) is the one-year probability that a borrower will default, which must, however, not be lower than 0.03 per cent for bank debt;
2. loss given default (LGD) is a measure of the expected loss that a bank will experience in the event of borrower default, which may differ depending on the type of exposure, for instance if the exposure is secured or unsecured;
3. exposure at default (EAD) is a measure of the size of the exposure to a borrower in the event of default of the borrower; and
4. maturity (M) is a measure for the weighted-average length of time the bank is exposed to the borrower, which must, however, not be lower than one year and not longer than five years.

In particular, under the Foundation Internal Ratings Based Approach (FIRB), banks assess only the PD, while all other variables are given according to asset class. Under the Advanced Internal Ratings Based Approach (AIRB), banks must use their own data to provide inputs for all variables.

As far as covered bonds are concerned, under the SA they are assigned a discounted risk-weight on the basis of the risk-weight attributed to senior unsecured exposures of the credit institution which issues them, as in the existing regime. In particular, the adoption of option 1 by a national regulator determines equal treatment of all credit institutions and covered bonds from a given country, irrespective of any differences in the intrinsic worth of the institutions, the strength of the framework under which the covered bonds are issued, or the quality of the underlying collateral backing the covered bonds (Fitch Ratings 2006b, p. 3) and therefore nearly all EU covered bonds should maintain the 10 per cent risk weighting. Option 2 grants 10 per cent only to banks with AA– and above senior debt ratings. Conversely, A or BBB senior debt ratings banks obtain 20 per cent.

Under the IRB, risk-weights for covered bonds are based on the assessment of the different risk components, subject to the specific constraints set out in the CRD. By applying the FIRB, banks assess only the probability of default of the issuer, whereas all other variables are given. In particular, the loss given default is discounted to 11.25 per cent for covered bonds compliant with certain requirements set out in the EU legislation until 2010. Under the AIRB, banks internally compute the loss given default of the issue and the maturity of every asset in their portfolio, in addition to the probability of default of the issuer.

Preliminary simulations on outstanding covered bonds have indicated that the new Basel II regime will lead to an overall reduction in capital charges for investors, especially for those applying the IRB, together with an increased differentiation in risk-weightings with respect to issuer credit quality and maturity. Risk-weighting for MBS is also expected to decline, with highly rated notes benefiting the most.

With all the different scenarios considered, it seems that, on average, covered bonds will continue to benefit from a lower risk-weighting when compared to MBS (VDP 2006, p. 55). In any case, covered bonds and MBS are expected to continue to be complementary funding instruments, and consequently blended funding strategies will continue to be applied.

6 THE INTRODUCTION OF COMMON STANDARDS FOR COVERED BONDS

The growth in volume is accompanied by increasing diversity in the covered bond market as a large number of new issuers from different countries are entering the arena (Colomer 2006).

Legal frameworks and structures are being set up to replicate the successful features of the instrument, but the ways in which these features are implemented can differ significantly. In addition, new demand from investors, as well as more stringent requirements from rating agencies, are leading to an increased combination of traditional features with structured finance elements, paving the way for a variety of new products to come on-stream. Initially introduced by issuers in those countries without a specific legislation in place, so-called 'structured' covered bonds are now becoming a relevant segment of the market.

From an investor's perspective, the rising number of variations from the original product is conducive – especially for larger investors with commensurate research capabilities – to finding relative value, not only across issuers and maturities but also across differing legal and structural frameworks. On the other hand, the varying structures make for a much more research-intensive decision-making process in a market where simplicity has clearly been driving its expansion.

These developments challenge the analytical capacities of many investors. The analytical bottleneck is intensified as investors in the AAA benchmark segment tend to limit rather strictly the resources they dedicate to the analysis of the credit features of these products. This is not only because covered bonds are generally characterised by a high and rather stable quality, but also due to the fact that these investors typically focus strongly on managing interest rate risk and exposure to shifts in the yield curve.

In brief, while growing diversity and complexity in the market is clearly a sign of the success of covered bonds, it also raises the need to focus on the fundamentals of the covered bond concept in order to understand the differences between different products so that a uniform definition of covered bonds, based on a number of core features that covered bond instruments have in common, can eventually be formed.[13]

Given the increasing variety of products in the ever-expanding covered bond market, market players are becoming more and more sensitive to protecting the reputation of covered bonds as a safe instrument where investors do not need to overly concern themselves with credit analysis. Indeed, having a clear and overall accepted definition of covered bonds would help investors to think about them as a specific asset class different from other products in the market (for example, corporate bonds, asset-backed securities).

To date, the only available definition of covered bonds is that enshrined in the UCITS Directive. Article 22 (4) of this directive defines the minimum requirements that provide the basis for a privileged treatment of covered bonds in different areas of European financial market regulation (Hardt 2004). Covered bonds that comply with those requirements are considered to be particularly safe investments, which justify the easing of prudential investment limits for regulated investment funds, as well as the lower capital requirement for banks.

In particular, Article 22 (4) of the UCITS Directive requires that:

(i) the bonds are issued by a credit institution which has its registered office in a Member State;
(ii) the issuing credit institution is subject by law to special public supervision designed to protect bondholders;
(iii) the proceeds of issuance are reinvested in assets which are eligible for covering the bonds so that the amount of collateral covers the amount of outstanding bonds at all times;
(iv) the bondholders have a priority claim on cover assets in the event of failure of the issuer.

With the implementation of Basel II into EU law, the criteria set out in Article 22 (4) of the UCITS Directive remain the basis for the preferential regulatory treatment of covered bonds, with further provisions relating to the precise composition of the assets that underlie covered bonds. In particular, Paragraph 65 (a) to (f), Annex VI, Part 1, of the CRD introduces a comprehensive list of the classes of assets that can be eligible as collateral for covered bonds, as follows:

(i) exposures to public sector entities;
(ii) exposures to institutions;
(iii) mortgage loans (residential and commercial);
(iv) senior MBS issued by securitisation entities;
(v) loans secured by ships.

The definition assumed in the European legislation through these two European directives is clearly based on 'traditional' covered bonds, which reflect the German format. However, market developments demonstrate that there is also an acceptance of products as covered bonds even if the prerequisites of the mentioned directive are not fully fulfilled.[14] In most cases, protection for investors is the same or even better. The most prominent case is that of 'structured' covered bonds, which are excluded from the preferential treatment under the EU regulation in that they are not issued in accordance with law and special public supervision arrangements.

Currently, a lively debate is going on in Europe over what a proper definition of a covered bond should be. The most significant initiative in this respect is that made by the European Covered Bond Council, a platform for covered bond market participants created in November 2004 to represent and promote the interests of the industry.

The purpose of the definition would be to define the 'essence' of a covered bond, whereas the minimum requirements stipulated in UCITS 22 (4)/CRD aim only at identifying those products which are eligible for special regulatory treatment. In addition, the UCITS/CRD definition is also potentially misleading, since it indirectly incorporates non-essential features into its definition.

Thus, the debate is mainly focused on the question of whether or not to include in the common definition of covered bonds certain features that are explicitly mentioned in the UCITS Directive but which are not universally recognised as fundamental to the covered bond concept. Some of these include the status of 'credit institution' of the issuer, the occurrence of a specific supervision by the banking authority on covered bond issuance and the existence of a special legislation in place.

These prerequisites reflect typical features of 'traditional' covered bonds, which are not necessarily replicated in all covered bond models. The question is to what extent these prerequisites can be deemed to be crucial for a covered bond so as to be defined as such, or how they can be reformulated in order to embrace the various solutions adopted in different frameworks to obtain certain distinguishing features that can contribute to identify covered bonds as a specific asset class different from other products in the market.

However, attempts to define covered bonds seem to lead to results which are either too vague or too impractical. As expected, the most-established players in the market are in favour of a narrow definition in line with the UCITS Directive, while relative newcomers are in favour of a broad definition incorporating those covered bonds that do not fulfil the criteria of Article 22 (4) of the UCITS Directive but still have been accepted by the market.

A reasonable approach to tackle the increasing variety of covered bond programmes would be to focus on the relevant risk factors. According to this view, the definition should not only be based on purely legal features but should also encompass a series of economic features. In other words, the effort would be that of identifying those core features that most covered bonds have in common, thereby making sure that a high-quality product is issued.

In the definition proposed by the ECBC, which resulted from the current debate within the industry, covered bonds could be characterised by the following essential features:[15]

(i) the bond is issued by – or bondholders otherwise have full recourse to – a credit institution which is subject to public supervision and regulation;
(ii) bondholders have a claim against a cover pool of financial assets which gives them priority over unsecured creditors of the credit institution;
(iii) the credit institution has an ongoing obligation to maintain sufficient assets in the cover pool to satisfy the claims of covered bondholders at all times;
(iv) the obligations of the credit institution, in respect of the cover pool, are independently supervised.

This proposed definition has been formulated in order to encompass those products that provide recourse to (but are not issued by) credit institutions that are universally referred to in the market as 'covered bonds', namely the multi-seller *cédulas* structures, where the issuer is not formally a credit institution but a securitisation fund. 'Club' structures, similar to the multi-seller cédulas structure, may prove to be the only route to the covered bond market for smaller issuers in some jurisdictions. The new US issuer WaMu[16] has adopted a similar 'pass-through formula' (VDP 2007, p. 41). Such a definition excludes so-called 'corporate covered bonds', on the grounds that there is a material distinction to be made – in the form of public regulation and supervision, capital requirements, and so forth – between credit institutions and other entities. Since such instruments are in their infancy, it is too early to conclude that they have been accepted as true covered bonds by the market. This feature distinguishes covered bonds from other products issued by entities which are not under the same high level of public supervision as credit institutions, such as SPV in relation to securitisations.

Together with full recourse to the credit institution, bondholders need to benefit from a preferential claim on a segregated pool of assets in the event of insolvency of the credit institution. Of course, the cover pool has to be effectively ring-fenced from the insolvency estate of the credit institution, but the definition deliberately avoids specifying the method through which the proper ring-fencing has to be achieved. Independently of the specific solutions adopted in different frameworks to address the same issue, what matters is that the assets on which bondholders have a preferential claim are unequivocally identified and separated from the general bankruptcy estate in the event of insolvency of the issuer. In other words, there must be an effective security mechanism protecting investors which differentiates the product from an unsecured bond.

The classic form of asset segregation relies on the earmarking of cover assets, which remain on the balance sheet of the originator through a special cover register. The register is usually kept by an independent monitor which ensures that only eligible assets are entered into the register and that there is always enough collateral to secure the outstanding covered bonds. The cover assets are segregated only in the case of the issuer's bankruptcy. With the opening of the insolvency proceedings, the cover pool and the pertaining covered bonds will be run on a separate basis and the cash flows arising from the cover assets will be used exclusively to pay the bondholders on time. An alternative method is based on the segregation of assets outside the originator's balance sheet. The cover assets are transferred to a bankruptcy-remote subsidiary, which issues the covered bond itself (as in the case of the French *obligation foncières*) or issues a guarantee based on the transferred assets for a senior unsecured bond from the originating bank (as in the case of UK covered bonds).

The cover pool is actively managed by the credit institution issuing the bonds, to which the bondholders have full recourse, by replacing maturing and/or non-performing assets according to specific asset–liability guidelines and overcollateralisation requirements. Instead, in securitisations no asset adjustment can generally be made once the structure is finalised.

An independent supervision of the obligations of the credit institution, in relation to the cover pool, also exists in most of the covered bond frameworks, which can be executed by public bodies or private entities (such as trustees or auditors).

A long and controversial debate has arisen as to whether or not certain risk mitigating factors – ensuring the quality of the cover pool, the efficient neutralisation of asset–liability mismatches and protection against any counterparty exposures – are in place to protect bondholders. This is regardless of whether these features are enshrined in any laws or contractual agreements. In the end, special legislation was not deemed to be an essential feature of a covered bond. Instead, it was felt to be more of a method by which the essential features of covered bonds were to be put in place. In particular, it was argued that certain essential features, such as ring-fencing of the collateral assets in some contractually-based covered bonds, were somehow more robust than those achieved in legally-based covered bonds.

Missing acceleration,[17] upon default of the issuer – which typically distinguishes covered bonds from securitisations – has also been excluded from the proposed definition as the effects of a default vary from jurisdiction to jurisdiction. Thus, it has been recommended that the relevance of such a feature be left to the market.

7 REGULATORY AND MARKET DEVELOPMENTS IN THE COVERED BOND MARKET

The growing pressure for setting up common standards is clearly driven by the ever-increasing internationalisation of the market. The huge variety of covered bonds presents investors – especially those from outside Europe – with a great challenge in determining which structures are best to achieve geographical diversification. This in turn raises the issue of whether a certain degree of standardisation and homogeneity in the market would help further develop this market, resulting in a limited analysis effort for investors.

One main question that has arisen from the debate on a definition of covered bonds at industry level is whether or not minimum standards should be enshrined in law.[18] The benefit of such a move would be to protect the instrument's 'brand name', thereby preventing the risk of free riders entering the market and negative headlines spreading, unfiltered, across the entire sector. By contrast, a legal definition would be a disadvantage in terms of flexibility, since the market might be unable to react quickly enough to rapid market developments. The market drives financial innovations in the industry. Competition between different products enhances the quality of the covered bond instrument, stimulating continuous improvements and the development of new solutions that respond better to issuers' and investors' needs. Legislation helps to spread benefits throughout the entire system. But market changes are much faster than legislative changes.

In brief, both regulation and the market itself help the industry to grow. The interplay between regulatory and market developments in the covered bond universe is well represented by the dynamic between 'structure' and 'law'.

In this respect, an interesting case study is that offered by the UK experience in the field. In the early 2000s, in the absence of specific legislation at national level, UK issuers started issuing covered bonds via contractual agreements. The first covered bond in the UK was issued in July 2003 by HBOS. The deal was structured with the help of securitisation techniques on the basis of existing legislation, and succeeded in being accepted by the market as a covered bond even though the UK had no national covered bond legislation. Following the success of the new 'structured' covered bond, other UK lenders entered the market with similar products. Then, the covered bond market in the UK reached a certain thickness without being regulated for. At that point, the national banking regulatory body decided to acknowledge and recognise the existing covered bond structures and planned to implement a general regulation based on market practice, which is expected to incorporate the structured covered bonds that have been issued already. A similar pattern at national level can be observed in the Netherlands.

Both the UK and the Netherlands cases seem to underline the fact that there is a clear trend in the market to move from a structure-backed to a legislated system. In fact, it could be argued that there is a tendency towards transforming self-regulatory standards established by the industry itself into general rules, namely law-based prescriptions, with the purpose of achieving the objectives of systemic stability and investor protection.

However, rules easily become outdated by market developments. The recent cases of two new market entrants, namely BNP Paribas and HSBC, clearly illustrate the point. Both banks entered the market in 2006 with new innovative products.

The French bank designed a tailormade structured covered bond on the basis of the contractual methodology – even though there is a specific covered bond legislation in France – to better combine high investor protection with specific internal needs. HSBC set up an innovative programme that provides a unified platform to issue both covered bonds and residential mortgage backed securities (RMBS) notes backed by a single portfolio of residential mortgage-backed loans, thus helping to save fixed costs, as well as to promptly respond to the final implementation of Basel II and shifts in demand for both types of debt. In both cases, the search for efficiency and flexibility, in relation to market changes, was the main driver of innovation and led them to break with established rules.

These examples support expectations that as the covered bond market grows and develops there will be more variation and interpretations of what actually are the basic concepts of covered bonds. Although there is a clearly recognisable move from structured covered bonds back to a legal framework, this might not signal the end of the structured covered bond market and both markets could continue to grow in tandem.

In summary, once a financial innovation is successfully introduced into the market and starts spreading throughout the system as more and more players adopt it, a certain degree of regulation is required to achieve the objectives of systemic stability and investor protection.

In the financial industry, market standards and law-based prescriptions represent two equally valuable forms of governance. Market standards emerge endogenously from the prevailing industry practices, while law-based provisions stem from exogenous public intervention.

Sometimes, market standards emerge as a primary means of governance when no formal legal structures exist and are subsequently replaced by public regulation. In principle, market standards represent a more flexible tool than public regulation, as they are able to adjust more quickly and flexibly to financial innovation. Instead, the implementation of a set of formal rules might hinder further innovation in rapidly changing financial markets.

Interestingly, recent developments in the covered bond market confirm these dynamics. A clear desire to set up common standards is emerging at the international level as a result of the internationalisation of formerly domestic markets. This has led to various initiatives at the industry level being aimed at agreeing on common rules among market participants. Indeed, the establishment of these rules will possibly have an impact on the legislative process of the EU institutions in the future. For this reason, we can ask ourselves what are the appropriate regulatory responses to market developments.

8 THE CONTRIBUTION OF COVERED BONDS TO THE INTEGRATION OF EUROPEAN FINANCIAL MARKETS

Market forces play a key role in finding efficient and effective ways to fully exploit the opportunities offered by a more integrated capital market. A number of global forces seem to be working in this direction.

First, investor demand for better comparability is pushing for more homogeneity in the market, thus accelerating the creation of a single covered bond market. Rating agencies, which rate covered bond instruments across countries, also play an important role in setting common standards.

On the regulatory side, the Market Abuse Directive[19] further motivated the development of covered bond markets into accepting market-making in the jumbo covered bond market. Such measures assured liquidity, efficient price formation and gave investors confidence in the instrument (Gottlieb 2005).

Current developments towards a more integrated covered bond market are in turn expected to foster the integration of the European mortgage capital markets as a whole.

Covered bonds are emerging as the major funding tool for mortgage lending in Europe, gaining ground over the other alternative sources of funding, namely traditional retail deposits and MBS. First, the eroding deposit base forces lenders to diversify their funding sources, and accelerates the trend towards disintermediation. Second, regulatory changes coming into force are changing the attractiveness of MBS relative to covered bonds as an instrument to achieve regulatory capital relief:

1. new rules in Basel II will reduce the incentive to remove performing mortgages to improve capital adequacy ratios as capital requirements for residential mortgages will decrease significantly in order to better reflect the nature of the risks involved in mortgage lending; and
2. new criteria in IAS 39 will make it more complicated (and therefore more expensive) to obtain genuine off-balance-sheet treatment of securitisations.

In brief, a number of forces are leading to the integration of the European mortgage market, at least on the funding side. But indeed, as the US experience has shown, a more integrated market on the funding side will also help to promote the standardisation of the market for underlying mortgage products, which is currently highly fragmented.

Benefits arising from a more integrated, efficient and complete mortgage market will be substantial for both consumers and lenders. A better integration of the mortgage capital market will allow market participants to realise substantial economies of scale and may result in lower funding costs. In turn, an increased competition on the lending side will stimulate efficiency innovation on the funding side. Covered bonds allow lending institutions to finance their low-profit mortgage business on better terms and therefore allow them to face foreign competition on the domestic market and to penetrate foreign markets.

The economic impacts of such developments are potentially enormous. Mortgages are regarded as the key to unlocking the benefits of an integrated single market for financial services in Europe. Recent years have been exciting for the mortgage industry in Europe. Mortgage lending has been growing rapidly in most EU member states, particularly in those that joined more recently, where mortgage markets are expanding at exponential rates, and further developments are expected from the entry of 12 new member states.

Then, competition and regulation will ensure that the benefits of integration are shared right through the mortgage value chain. Consumers will have access to a wider product range at competitive rates while lenders will benefit from the opening up of new markets and new funding opportunities.

Rating agencies and regulators also agree that access to the covered bond market represents a stabilising influence on the banking market. Even in times of credit stress an issuer can command competitive terms, thereby reducing the threat of systemic risk and increasing the stability of the banking system overall.

9 CONCLUSION

One of the great recent innovations of the European bond market is undisputedly the development of the jumbo covered bond, which has proved to be the main driver of the internationalisation of the formerly domestic covered bond markets.

Covered bonds are increasingly used in the marketplace as a funding instrument, in addition to savings deposits and mortgage backed securities. Among the two capital market funding tools, the covered bond market is the most developed and the largest capital market, although MBS transactions have also experienced a remarkable growth over the past few years.

Covered bonds offer many relevant advantages to both issuers and investors. This accounts for their success and the ultimate development of the market during the last few years. The replication of the issuances in different jurisdictions has favoured the introduction of products with some differing characteristics from the original model, although a certain degree of standardisation has tended to be preserved within the global market.

In light of the changes introduced by the CRD adopting Basel II, issuers have started to rethink and reshape their securitisation and funding strategies. CRD defines covered bonds in more detail and maintains a favourable treatment with covered bond exposures if they fulfil certain eligibility criteria, which are specifically defined. Therefore, covered bonds should benefit from a lower risk weighting than MBS, even though uncertainty remains on some areas of application, due also to numerous national discretions. As a consequence, the issuance of covered bonds as a cheap financing tool for mortgages at the expense of MBS is likely to increase. Despite that, covered bonds and MBS will continue to be complementary funding instruments, mainly because they target different investor bases.

The spreading of financial innovation in the European marketplaces is deemed to produce positive effects at a systemic level. With regard to this, covered bonds play an important role in the financial system by contributing to the integration of the European mortgage markets. In fact, there is a close link between the origination and funding of mortgages. Indeed, financial innovation on the funding side heavily influences the supply and the price of mortgage credit products. In this respect, covered bonds may lead to increased efficiency, improved product diversity and a higher degree of competition in the EU mortgage markets. The consequent reduction in the cost of credit for end-customers may contribute to the efficient allocation of capital and ultimately to economic growth.

NOTES

* This chapter is the result of joint work between the authors. In the editing phase, Giuseppina Chesini wrote Sections 2, 3, 4, 5 and 9 and Monica Tamisari wrote Sections 1, 6, 7 and 8.

1. 'Although the German Pfandbrief market has a history dating back well over 200 years, its recognition as an asset class by international investors occurred only in the mid-1990s with the advent of jumbo Pfandbrief' (Cross 2004, p. 524).
2. 'While covered bonds such as Pfandbriefe or "Realkreditobligationer" have been used for several centuries in Germany and Denmark, they are nevertheless included as a financial "innovation" because these types of specific market-based funding instruments for mortgage loans have over recent years been introduced in other EU Member States' (European Central Bank 2007a, p. 20).
3. Own elaboration from ECBC statistics.
4. The 2001 Act laid down a statutory and regulatory framework for covered bond (or asset covered security, as they are referred to in the Irish legislation) issuance in Ireland. In April 2007 the Government had approved the publication of the Asset Covered Securities (Amendment) Act 2007 which amends and updates the Asset Covered Securities Act 2001.

5. On 19 July 2005 the new Pfandbrief Act came into force, replacing the previous three different legislations which regulated the issuance of pfandbriefe in Germany (the Mortgage Banking Act, the Pfandbrief Law for Public Sector Banks and the Ship Banking Act). The new regulation abolished the specialist banking principle so that all banks (universal banks) are allowed to issue pfandbriefe, provided that a special licence has been obtained from the German Federal Financial Supervisory Authority (BaFin).
6. A new regulatory framework on covered bonds entered into force on 1 July 2007 in Denmark, abolishing the special bank principle.
7. 'The EU's most active MBS markets were in the Netherlands, Spain, Italy, UK, Ireland and Belgium. By contrast, MBS activity was insignificant in other EU countries' (London Economics 2005, p. 124).
8. See Section 7.
9. See Directive 2001/108/EC of the European Parliament and of the Council of 21 January 2002 amending Council Directive 85/611/EEC relating to undertakings for collective investment in transferable securities (UCITS).
10. See Directive 2006/48/EC of the European Parliament and of the Council of 14 June 2006 relating to the taking up and pursuit of the business of credit institutions.
11. The Basel II framework was published in June 2004 and was last updated in November 2005.
12. For a more detailed analysis of CRD, see Credit Suisse (2006).
13. 'A unified approach to covered bonds in Europe would raise efficiencies and transparency in a market that suffers somewhat from certain disadvantages brought about by multiple systems. In the first instance, the market is highly complex' (Standard & Poor's 2006, p. 11).
14. 'The covered bond definition of the CRD was established for supervisory purposes, and therefore does not necessarily coincide with the market's definition of covered bonds. The future will show whether the covered bond definition of the CRD will be a sufficient base to set long-term standards for the European covered bond market, or whether new instruments and markets will go beyond those limits' (European Commission 2006, p. 26).
15. See current discussion within ECBC, Technical Issues Working Group.
16. Washington Mutual Inc. (WaMu), the largest US savings and loan institution, became the first US lender to tap the covered bond market in September 2006.
17. A general feature of most covered bonds is the fact that the insolvency of the issuer does not trigger the acceleration of the covered bond. The insolvent issuer will no longer substitute defaulting or maturing assets in the pool; consequently the pool will be exposed to credit deterioration and negative carry risks as well as cash flow mismatches until the last covered bonds has been repaid.
18. For a more detailed analysis of the relevance of the current debate, see Moore (2007).
19. See Directive 2003/6/EC of the European Parliament and of the Council of 28 January 2003 on insider dealing and market manipulation.

REFERENCES

Colomer, N. (2006), 'Covered bond flood euro market', Asset Securitization Report – SourceMedia, 23 October.

Credit Suisse (2006), *Covered Bonds and Basel II*, Basel, March.

Cross, Graham (2004), 'The German Pfandbrief and European covered bonds market', in Frank J. Fabozzi and Moorad Choudhry (eds), *The Handbook of European Fixed Income Securities*, New York: Wiley, pp. 523–49.

Deutsche Bank (2007), *The Covered Bond Market*, January.

European Central Bank (ECB) (2004), *The Euro Bond Market Study*, Frankfurt am Main, December.
European Central Bank (ECB) (2005), *EU Banking Structures*, Frankfurt am Main, October.
European Central Bank (ECB) (2007a), *The Dynamics of Bank Spreads and Financial Structure*, Working Paper Series, no. 714, Frankfurt am Main, January.
European Central Bank (ECB) (2007b), *The Euro Bonds and Derivatives Markets*, Frankfurt am Main, June.
European Commission (2006), *Report of the Mortgage Funding Experts Group*, Brussels, 22 December.
European Covered Bond Council (ECBC) (2006 [2007]), *European Covered Bond Fact Book*, Belgium: ECBC.
Fitch Ratings (2006a), 'Covered Bond Rating Criteria – Stop or Continue?', Criteria Report, New York, 13 July.
Fitch Ratings (2006b), 'Covered Bonds and Capital Requirements Directive', Special Report, New York, 8 December.
Golin, Jonathan (ed.) (2006), *Covered Bonds beyond Pfandbriefe. Innovations, Investment and Structures Alternatives*, London: Euromoney Institutional Investor.
Gottlieb, C. (2005), 'The European covered bond market: too big to ignore', *European Capital Markets Institute (ECMI) Commentaries*, no. 2.
Hardt, J. (2004), 'Covered bonds wake up to a new world', *The Banker*, November.
Issing, O. (2005), 'Mortgage markets and monetary policy: a central banker's view', Speech at the European Mortgage Federation Annual Conference, Brussels, November.
London Economics (2005), *The Costs and Benefits of Integration of EU Mortgage Markets*, Report for the Commission, DG-Internal Market and Services, August.
Mastroeni O. (2001), 'Pfandbrief-style products in Europe', *The Changing Shape of Fixed Income Markets: A Collection of Studies by Central Bank Economists*, BIS Papers, (5), October, 44–66.
Moody's Investor Service (2005), *Revisions to Moody's European Covered Bond Rating Methodology*, New York, 28 January.
Moore, P. (2007), 'Covered bonds debate: covered bond issuers take on the global market', *Euromoney*, June.
Packer, F., Stever, R. and C. Upper (2007), 'The covered bond market', *BIS Quarterly Review*, September, 43–55.
Standard & Poor's (2006), *Structured Finance View Point. Covered Bonds Expand Into New Areas*, New York: McGraw-Hill.
Verband Deutscher Pfandbriefbanken (VDP) (2006), *The Pfanbrief 2006. Facts and Figures about Europe's Covered Bond Benchmark*, Berlin: Verband Deutscher Pfandbriefbanken.
Verband Deutscher Pfandbriefbanken (VDP) (2007), *The Pfanbrief 2007/2008. Facts and Figures about Europe's Covered Bond Benchmark*, Berlin: Verband Deutscher Pfandbriefbanken.

9. Credit derivatives versus loan sales: evidence from the European banking market

Mascia Bedendo and Brunella Bruno

1 INTRODUCTION

Credit risk transfer (CRT) techniques such as securitisation, loan sales and credit derivatives (CDs) have been an important part of a wave of financial innovation during recent years. A fuller appreciation of these instruments and their implications for the banking industry requires some understanding of their role within the general framework of financial innovation.

There are various ways of looking at innovation. As far as the motivations for financial innovation are concerned, no general – or at least generally accepted – explanation exists, although there is a wide body of literature that addresses this issue. Given the multiplicity of theories, motivations for loan sales and CDs can be studied according to different perspectives. Adopting a taxonomic framework, loan sales and CDs help financial institutions to perform important functions, such as those of transferring credit risk and enhancing liquidity. Looking at the conditions that have stimulated financial innovation, improvements in both transaction and information technologies are considered fundamental incentives for both CDs and loan sales. Moreover, improvements in the ability to collect and elaborate information have made it easier to sell and buy assets subject to 'lemon-market' problems (that is, asymmetrical information between the seller and the potential buyer) such as loans. Finally, according to various authors, regulatory constraints represent one of the most important motivations for transferring credit risk (both via CDs and loan sales).

This chapter aims at comparing the role of CDs and loan sales in transferring credit risk away from banks, both from a theoretical and an empirical perspective. In this respect, we first attempt to investigate to what extent these instruments are complements and to what extent their functions overlap, from a theoretical point of view. Second, we analyse how a sample of European banks has been using these instruments in practice. In particular, we aim at assessing which banks act as financial innovators in the CRT market, and how they choose between loan sales and CDs.

The existing literature on the comparison between loan sales and CDs is quite small, and mainly theoretical. Under the assumption of no information asymmetries in the CD market, Duffee and Zhou (2001) analyse the consequences of introducing CDs and conclude that these instruments can help alleviate the lemons problem that affects the loan sales market. By relaxing this assumption, Thompson (2007) suggests that well-capitalised banks will prefer loan insurance contracts, whereas poorly capitalised banks will be forced into the loan sales market. The only empirical paper we are aware of that jointly examines the use of CDs and loan sales is by Minton et al. (2006). Based on a sample of US banks, the authors conclude that very few large banks use CDs, due to the significant asymmetric information problems in the CD market. Banks that act as protection buyers in the market normally engage in asset securitisation and loan sales as well, and are typically poorly capitalised.

Making reference to the literature on financial innovation, we first discuss the *raison d'être* of loan sales and CDs. We then move on to investigate similarities and differences between loan sales and CDs, in order to identify which instruments are more appropriate for trading credit risk, with respect to both the features of the innovator (protection buyer/originator) and the nature of the loan to be insured/sold. From this comparison we shall attempt to draw some conclusions on the preference that different banks are expected to show when choosing the most appropriate instrument for transferring credit risk.

These predictions will then be contrasted with the empirical evidence. We focus attention on a sample of European bank holding companies that have accessed the CD and/or loan sales markets over the 2003–05 period to reduce their credit risk. Information on the participation to the two markets is then cross-matched with balance-sheet information in order to investigate whether the preference shown by banks in accessing predominantly one of the two markets or both markets can be significantly linked to some measurable features such as: (i) bank size; (ii) bank capitalisation and liquidity; (iii) loan portfolio diversification; (iv) lending quality; and (v) profitability. Using basic panel econometric tools, we attempt to identify which of the above elements are more closely related to the use of CDs and/or loan sales.

As expected, we find that banks in our sample view CDs and loan sales mainly as complements, since most banks participate in both markets. In fact, the activity in the CD market seems to be mainly driven by trading purposes, whereas loan sales seem to be comparatively more used for credit risk management purposes. However, a minority of banks considers CDs and loan sales as substitutes, given that they take part primarily in only one of the two markets.

The chapter is structured as follows. Section 2 introduces CDs and loan sales within the financial innovation theory. Section 3 contrasts the two CRT techniques from a theoretical and practical perspective. Section 4 discusses the data and the methodology employed. Results from our empirical investigation follow in Section 5. Section 6 concludes.

2 LOAN SALES AND CDs WITHIN THE FINANCIAL INNOVATION THEORY

A large body of literature on loan sales addresses the question of why the loan sales market exists. According to this literature, some motivations for loan sales are consistent with explanations for financial innovations in general. Similarly to loan sales, CDs qualify as an instrument of financial innovation.

Adopting the classification scheme for innovations proposed by the BIS (1986), loan sales and CDs can be considered as either risk-transferring or liquidity-enhancing innovations. As risk-transferring innovations, loans sales and CDs allow banks to reduce credit risk and manage it 'actively'. If banks sell and purchase loans or buy/sell protection via CDs in order to increase the level of portfolio diversification, they are expected to manage their portfolio risk more efficiently. Several works focus on loan sales as active credit risk management tools. According to Pavel and Phillis (1987), Berger and Udell (1993) and Demsetz (2000) a bank may want to alter the diversification of its loan portfolio, selling certain types of loans in order to buy or originate other types of assets (diversification hypothesis). As for the relation between the seller's bank risk and loan sales, empirical results are ambiguous. According to Pavel (1989), on average, loan sales have little impact on bank risk. More recently, Cebenoyan and Strahan (2004) conclude that increasingly sophisticated risk management practices in banking such as selling and buying loans are likely to improve the availability of bank credit but not to reduce bank risk. The use of CDs by banks as instruments to improve portfolio diversification has been discussed by Das (2000). The impact of the introduction of CDs on the CRT market has been modelled by Duffee and Zhou (2001), who conclude that CDs can help alleviate the lemons problem in the loan sales market. Thompson (2007) also investigates the conditions under which credit risk can be effectively transferred via CDs and loan sales.

As liquidity-enhancing innovations, both loan sales and CDs can effectively promote liquidity in the underlying debt market, by turning bank loans, which are traditionally non-marketable, into negotiable assets. Loan sales also allow banks to free up alternative and (in some circumstances) cheaper funds than deposits and equity. Pennacchi (1988) shows that loan sales can provide lower-cost resources for those banks that face a competitive deposit market. On the contrary CDs, while transferring credit risk, do not generate financial resources.

Following the theory addressing the issue of financial innovation through a demand/supply perspective, demand and supply of innovation is strictly affected by factors such as: (i) regulation and (ii) advances in technology. As for the first factor, regulation leads to financial innovation by creating incentives for firms to skirt regulation requirements that restrict their ability to earn profits.[1] Within a dynamic framework, regulatory pressure is the basic factor of a continuative innovation process named 'regulatory dialectic' (Gardener, 1986). In essence, the regulatory dialectic theory suggests that financial innovation is the reaction to inappropriate regulation while re-regulation is the response. The cycle 'regulation → innovation → re-regulation → innovation' embodies the regulatory dialectic and suggests that innovation has often been a consequence of regulation. An important policy implication of this theory is that regulators may not always achieve their aims, since some apparent risk-reducing regulation may paradoxically be risk producing. Regulatory constraints matter also as motivations for loan sales and CDs. Pennacchi (1988) shows that banks may sell loans to avoid reserve requirements, capital requirements, and deposit insurance premiums. Among them, lowering capital requirements is the most often cited motivation for loan sales (Greenbaum and Thakor, 1987; Pavel, 1989). According to this body of literature, capital requirements in excess of what banks would hold in the absence of regulation make loans unprofitable. As a consequence, banks sell low-risk loans because they cannot afford to fund them (with the final effect of increasing portfolios' riskiness). In principle, capital relief represents an incentive for CDs too. In practice, this applies only to the extent that the derivative instrument constitutes a perfect hedge to a particular underlying reference obligation (bond or loan).

Besides regulatory pressure, improvements in both transaction and information technologies are considered important incentives for financial innovations.[2] In this regard, financial engineering used to create new derivatives and credit risk models employed for both loan pricing and portfolio management are all examples of financial technologies particularly useful for promoting CRT tools (Berger, 2003). According to Gorton and Haubrich (1990), Gorton and Pennacchi (1995) and Greenbaum and Thakor (1995), improvements in the ability to acquire, treat and transfer information have made it easier to sell and buy assets that are subject to lemon-market problems. From this point of view, developments in numerical analyses and simulation, hardware that enables faster processing and the internet are examples of those mechanisms that have arisen with the effect of allowing buyers to assess the quality of the loan and to avoid 'lemons'.

3 LOAN SALES VERSUS CDs: SIMILARITIES AND DIFFERENCES

Traditional CRT instruments such as loan sales have been available for some time, while new varieties of CRT mechanisms such as CDs have developed over the last decade and quickly expanded. Statistics from the British Bankers' Association show that the size of the market for CDs has grown dramatically in the last few years, going from $893 billion in 2000 to $20 trillion in 2006. Market surveys (see, for example, BBA, 2006) indicate that only one-third of banks' CD volume is related to their loan book. However, these instruments have rapidly gained a key role in the CRT market. More traditional loan sale instruments have also experienced an increase in recent years, doubling in size from $112 billion in 2002 to $238 billion in 2006 (LSTA, 2007).

While loan sales and CDs are both considered CRT mechanisms, some theoretical and practical differences arise, which will be important in determining the likelihood of choosing one instrument or the other for transferring credit risk. A typical loan sale contract is the simplest CRT mechanism through which the loan originator sells all or part of the payments from the underlying loan to a third party. Unlike securitisation, loan sales involve no creation of new securities. Loan sales come in three basic types (participations, assignments, and novations), which differ in the way they transfer rights and obligations.[3] Participations give the buyer only the right to receive future payments from the underlying contract, without transferring any of the rights and obligations of the original contract. Therefore the originator retains the relationship with the borrower. Assignments shift the direct debtor–creditor relationship from the originator bank to the loan buyer together with sellers' rights. In some cases, the contract may require the borrower to agree to the sale. Finally, a novation completely transfers all rights and obligations and implies a new contract stipulated between the buyer and the borrower. Currently, because of the higher monitoring costs and risks involved in participations and legal cost involved in novations, the bulk of loan sales occur in the form of assignments.

CDs are over-the-counter financial instruments whose payoffs are linked to a specific credit related event such as a default, debt restructuring, or credit downgrade of the obligor. The two main types of CDs traded on the market are credit default swaps (CDSs) and synthetic collateralised debt obligations (SCDOs). In a CDS, the credit protection seller agrees to pay the default payment to the protection buyer if a credit event has happened, in exchange for a fee to be paid at regular intervals until the credit event or maturity. In a CD contract the relationship between the protection buyer and the obligor is unaffected. CDSs can be written on individual names (single-name CDSs) or on baskets of names (CDS index), and overall they represent about 60 per cent of the CD volume (BBA, 2006). SCDOs in principle are very similar to debt securitisation, as a specialised entity (special purpose vehicle) transforms a pool of assets into various tranches of securities with different levels of risk (credit linked notes). However, in an SCDO, the pool of assets is given by a collection of CDS contracts, instead of a pool of bonds or loans. According to recent estimates, SCDOs account for about 15 per cent of the CD market size.

As far as the effectiveness in transferring credit risk is concerned, banks which sell loans/buy CDs obtain maximum benefit (for example, bypassing capital requirements) if they can entirely remove the credit risk of the underlying loan. For this purpose, two basic criteria must be met in the loan sales market: (i) the loan transferred and the original loan must have identical terms and conditions; (ii) loan sales must be without recourse. By doing so, the loan (and the related risk) can be removed from the bank's balance sheet. The higher the guarantee provided by the seller (through covenants or by transferring only a part of cash flows referred to the original loan), the lower the credit risk transferred and capital requirements bypassed. In practice, most loan transactions occur without any explicit or implicit recourse. As for CDs, credit risk can be removed only if the derivative instrument constitutes a perfect hedge to a particular underlying reference obligation. In most cases, CD trades do not fully meet the requirements of a hedging transaction and therefore, protection buyers do not benefit from a regulatory capital relief (BIS, 2005).

Different typologies of loans are transferred via loan sales. Two main segments can be identified (Saunders, 2000). In the first segment, loans transferred are very heterogeneous in terms of a borrower's characteristics and loan facilities. Consequently, these loans are not standardised – according to the terms defined above – and are mostly traded through online trading platforms. The second segment covers the majority of the deals and includes the most standardised transactions. Standardisation occurs with reference to facilities (mostly term loans), maturity (often three-to-six-year maturities), covenants and seniority (loans are usually senior secured and with strong covenant protection), facility rating (often speculative grade), and coupon (floating rate tied to Libor, with normally

250–400 basis points above these rates) (Fabozzi, 1998; Saunders, 2000). Loans meeting these criteria are highly leveraged transaction (HLT) loans, namely loans originated on the primary market through a syndication process in order to finance leveraged operations such as leveraged buyouts (LBOs) and mergers and acquisitions (M&As). Standardisation also occurs with reference to trading documents and market practices. As a consequence, a more liquid and transparent market has arisen, to such an extent that the HLT loan secondary market is now provided with daily dealer-quote-based mark-to-market pricing, similar to those existing in more efficient capital market segments.[4] As far as CDs are concerned, any type of loan or bond could potentially be apt as reference obligation. However, to enhance the liquidity of the market, the ISDA has released a set of standard terms and conditions for CD instruments (1999, 2003) concerning the definition of reference entity, reference obligation, credit event and default payment. A typical CD contract is normally written on the senior unsecured debt of the obligor, and has a maturity between one and 10 years, with five years being the most liquid maturity. Possible credit events include bankruptcy, failure to pay, obligation default, obligation acceleration, repudiation/moratorium and debt restructuring.

In the CRT market, the seller of credit protection has a clear information disadvantage with respect to the original lender. Therefore, CRT instruments give rise to agency problems, in terms of moral hazard and adverse selection (Pennacchi, 1988). Different mechanisms can be conceived in order to avoid such problems. With reference to the loan sales market, according to Pennacchi, and Gorton and Haubrich (1990), it could be possible to reduce lemon problems and increase the seller's incentive of monitoring through selling only a portion of the initial contract, by stripping the loan, or modelling incentive-compatible contracts. Mostly, loan contracting through the inclusion of borrowers' restrictive covenants seems to be an effective tool for mitigating agency problems (Drucker and Puri, 2007). With reference to CDs, agency problems are limited by the fact that the majority (around 60 per cent) of underlying assets in CDS contracts are rated investment grade, although the share of non-investment grade assets has expanded from 13 per cent in 2004 to 23 per cent in 2006 (BBA, 2006). Also, banks often retain the equity tranches of the structured credit products in their portfolio, providing a signalling effect. Poor-quality or non-performing loans are still channelled mainly via loan sales or securitisation (ECB, 2004).

CRT mechanisms can have major effects on the relationships between the original lender and the borrower. In a typical loan sale the borrower is notified of the sale and this may compromise future lending relationships with the selling bank. On the contrary, CDs allow banks to remove the credit risk of an asset without actually transferring the underlying credit, which remains on the balance sheet. This aspect is of crucial importance for protecting the special relationship that banks entertain with their borrowers. For certain types of loans, the relationship between borrowers and lenders is so important as to make a clean loan sales or securitisation undesirable for the bank. This is, for instance, the case of loans to small and medium-sized enterprises (SMEs) and more generally to borrowers that might want to keep the amount or even the existence of the relationship confidential. In these cases, CDs may represent, in principle, a more efficient way to transfer the underlying credit risk since the borrower is not aware of the transaction.[5] In fact, according to some empirical literature, the effect of loan sales on the relationship is ambiguous. Due to credit risk management, loan sales could be potentially beneficial to the relationship because they may actually increase the flexibility in future deals and provide the borrowers with additional sources of capital. In this respect, according to Drucker and Puri (2007), borrowers whose loans are sold are more likely to retain their relationship, by keeping the same lender in the future. Duffee and Zhou (2001) and Morrison (2005) investigate the effects of the introduction of CDs on relationship banking from a theoretical perspective. Duffee and Zhou claim that the introduction of CDs can help retaining the relationship with the borrower, but can shut down the loan sales market all together. Morrison suggests that CDs help to trade the credit risk away before monitoring by the protection buyer takes place, which may be undesirable.

4 DATA AND METHODOLOGY

Our purpose is to analyse the CD and loan sales activity of a sample of European banks for the 2003–05 period. The sample includes the 49 largest European bank holding companies in terms of total assets according to Bankscope.[6] A large number of bank groups are based in Germany (14 out of 49), whereas the remaining ones are equally spread in Europe (see Table 9A.1 for the geographical distribution of our sample). The banking groups in our sample are fairly representative of the European banking system as they account for around 70 per cent of the total assets and 66 per cent of the total loans of all the banks included in the EU25 plus Switzerland.[7] In order to investigate how the activity in those CRT markets is affected by bank characteristics, we construct a database using three different data sources. Loan data are collected from the Loan Pricing Corporation's (LPC) Dealscan database, which provides loan contract terms for all loans (mostly syndicated) originated globally. Given the unavailability of exact data on loan transactions on the secondary market for European banks, we use data on the loans originated by our sample banks as a proxy of their participation to the loan secondary market. We only include syndicated loans: (i) originated in the type of term loan and institutional term loan; and (ii) with covenants. This is consistent with both market practice (Fabozzi, 1998; Saunders, 2000) and recent empirical work (Drucker and Puri, 2007), according to which almost all of the loans sold on the secondary market are syndicated in the primary market, have additional covenants, and are term loans.[8] As a measure of annual loan sale volumes, we collect annual flows of loans originated from 31 July to 30 June of each year from 2002 to 2005 (for example, the 2003 loan sales volume is given by loans originated between 31 July 2002 and 30 June 2003). We gather loans originated in the July–June period (instead of January–December) as a proxy of loans sold in each year because of the common practice of selling loans within a few months after the date of origination.[9]

Data on the CD activity of individual European banks are very scarce, given that there are no common public disclosure requirements in this respect by individual institutions. Information on banks' use of CD instruments is mainly available at an aggregate level, through general surveys.[10] For our purposes, we gather information on the total notional amounts of CD instruments bought and sold by the bank holding companies in our sample during the 2003–05 period directly from the consolidated financial statements. The level of disclosure of the activity in the CD market greatly varies among the banks in the sample, although it has generally improved since 2003. In 2005, 33 bank groups (out of 49) report the notional amount of their CD transactions; seven banks claim to use CDs for hedging/trading purposes, but do not report figures, whereas nine banks do not mention CDs in their annual report. In line with previous empirical surveys (ECB, 2004), the largest volume of CD transactions seems to be for trading, rather than for hedging purposes, especially for the biggest bank groups in our sample. In general, banks are active both as credit risk protection buyers and as sellers,[11] and single-name CDS seems to be the most popular CD instrument.

Table 9.1 summarises the total volumes of CDs and loan sales recorded for our sample banks over the period under analysis.[12] In line with the explosive growth of the CD market, the notional amounts of CD instruments bought and sold have increased from €1,307 billion in 2003 to €7,543 billion in 2005. However, the increased popularity of CDs does not seem to have affected the activity in the loan sales market, which has increased over the 2003–05 period, consistently with the M&A trend.[13] These findings seem to suggest that CD and loan sales are perceived by banks as complements, rather than substitutes.

Table 9.1 Credit derivatives and loan sales activity for the sample

	2005	2004	2003
Credit derivatives			
Notional amount (€ million) of credit protection bought and sold	7,543,338	2,986,582	1,307,484
as a percentage of total assets	41.22%	20.27%	12.63%
as a percentage of total loans	108.87%	51.22%	32.15%
No. of bank holding companies disclosing figures on credit derivatives	33	31	26
Loan sales			
Volumes originated/sold (€ million)	111,792	114,554	56,963
as a percentage of total assets	0.45%	0.56%	0.33%
as a percentage of total loans	1.10%	1.34%	0.77%
No. of bank holding companies involved	46	48	47

Note: Volumes of CD and loan sales activity of the largest 49 European bank groups included in the sample. CD figures are taken from annual consolidated financial statements, when available. Loan sales volumes are proxies for the secondary market activity and include term loans and institutional term loans with covenants originated in the primary loan syndicated market, according to LPC.

Source: Figures for total assets and total loans are from Bankscope.

Our main purpose is to test whether and how the intensity of participation in CD and loan sales markets may be related to some banks characteristics, such as bank size, quality and diversification of the loan portfolio, capital structure and liquidity, and profitability. We have chosen the following indicators as measures of the bank features under analysis, since they have been widely used in several empirical studies and they are available for all bank groups in the sample:

Size Log of total assets.
Lending quality Loan loss reserves/gross loans.
Diversification of the loan portfolio

- total loans to retail customers/total loans to customers;
- Herfindahl–Hirschman index = $\sum_{i=1}^{3} L_i^2$ where L_i is the proportion of loans (over total loans to customers) for loan geographical category i, where each category includes loans grouped by the nationality of borrowers (Domestic, other European, Rest of the world).

Capital structure/liquidity

- Tier 1 ratio = (shareholders funds + perpetual non cumulative preference shares)/risk-weighted assets and off-balance-sheet risks;
- capital adequacy ratio = (Tier 1 + Tier 2 capital)/risk-weighted assets and off-balance-sheet risks, where Tier 2 capital includes subordinated debt, hybrid capital, and loan loss reserves;
- deposit run-off ratio = liquid assets/customer and short-term funds.

Profitability

- net interest income/total average assets (AA);
- other operation income/total average assets (AA);
- return on average assets (ROAA);
- return on average equity (ROAE).

Bank size (natural logarithm of total assets) may affect CRT transactions in many ways. In general, large banks might have comparatively stronger lending opportunities and comparatively higher funding costs, and therefore are more likely to buy credit protection/sell loans (Pennacchi, 1988). For loan sales, because of agency problems, it might be easier for higher reputation lenders – that is, larger banks – to sell or syndicate loans (Haubrich and Thomson, 1993; Dennis and Mullineaux, 2000; Drucker and Puri, 2007). Fixed costs associated with CRT techniques,[14] together with the high expertise required for pricing sophisticated CRT instruments (in particular, CDs) favour the participation of large banks. On the other hand, if small banks have limited opportunities for diversified lending, they may have an incentive to diversify their loan portfolio by selling credit risk protection via CDs or by buying loans on the secondary market. Alternatively, when small banks face binding legal lending limits, they are more likely to participate as loan sellers (Demsetz, 2000).

Our measure of loan quality (loan loss reserves/gross loans)[15] may help explain participation in the loan sales/CD markets in different ways. In principle, riskier banks – that is, banks with a lower loan portfolio quality – should sell more loans/buy credit protection in order to reduce potential distress and maintain their existing level of capital (Pavel and Phillis, 1987). On the other hand, considering the loan portfolio quality as a proxy of bank reputation and given that most loan sales occur without recourse, loan buyers may shy away from sellers with poor or unknown asset quality. This is consistent with a lemon-market problem associated with loan sales (Haubrich and Thomson, 1993; Demsetz, 2000). As for CDs, in practice, most of the underlying reference obligations are of the investment-grade type. Therefore, the loan quality indicator may not be significantly related to the activity in the CD market.

Diversification is one of the leading drivers of loan sales/CDs. Banks with poor opportunities for diversified lending can improve the mix of loans in their portfolio by using CDs or by participating in the secondary loan market (Pavel and Phillis, 1987; Demsetz, 2000; Minton et al., 2006). We use two measures of diversification. The first measure is the incidence of retail loans over total customer loans: the higher the ratio the lower the portfolio concentration, the lower the intensity of participation to loan sales/CD markets. This is consistent with the fact that retail loans are *per se* more numerous and diversified – for instance, in terms of loan types, maturity and location – than non-retail loans, and also more difficult to spin off via loan sales or CDs. The second ratio – a version of the Herfindahl–Hirschman index based on the nationality of borrowers – measures the degree of the loan portfolio geographical diversification. In this case, we expect banks with higher ratios – that is, banks geographically more concentrated – to access the CD/loan sales market more actively than banks with lower geographical concentration.

Funding and capital relief are among the main reasons for loan sales according to existing theoretical and empirical literature. In this respect, we would expect that more regulatory and liquidity constrained banks would sell loans in order to improve their existing level of capital and fund new loans instead of raising funds from the deposit and capital markets. As capital structure measures we use Tier 1 and capital adequacy ratios, both calculated under the Basel rules. As a liquidity measure, we use a deposit run-off ratio. For both capitalisation and liquidity measures, the higher the ratio, the more capitalised and liquid is the bank, the smaller the expected volume of loan sales. Unlike loan sales, CDs do not generate liquidity, therefore we do not expect the liquidity ratio to impact on the CD activity. On the other hand, previous empirical evidence (Minton et al., 2006) suggests an inverse relationship between capitalisation and participation in the CD market, given that less-capitalised banks are more likely to hedge.

To investigate the relation between profitability and participation in the CRT markets, we use four different measures of profitability. Besides the traditional measures of equity and asset profitability (ROAE and ROAA), we use net interest income ratio and other income ratio to gain insights into a bank's lending opportunities. Originating and servicing loans generate both interest income and fees. Consistently with the comparative advantage hypothesis, the more profitable the lending activity is, the more the bank sells loans, as originating and servicing loans becomes more profitable than warehousing them. As for CDs, given that the largest volumes of transactions are for trading purposes, we expect the most active

Table 9.2 Bank indicators: summary statistics

	Average	Std dev.	Max	Min
Size (log total assets)	12.85	0.74	14.11	11.76
Loan diversification	0.36	0.17	0.69	0.05
Geographic diversification	0.59	0.18	0.96	0.34
Loan quality	1.94	1.67	8.87	0.02
Tier 1 ratio	8.29	1.49	12.90	6.30
Total capital ratio	11.54	1.63	16.90	9.20
Net int. margin/AA	1.16	0.57	2.43	0.20
Other income/AA	0.99	0.53	2.06	0.05
ROAA	0.58	0.31	1.21	0.08
ROAE	15.26	6.41	34.43	3.37
Liquidity ratio	15.94	17.79	61.41	0.17

Note: Summary statistics for indicators of bank size, diversification, loan quality, capitalisation, liquidity, profitability. The summary statistics are computed on our sample of European banking groups for the year 2005.

Source: The indicators are authors' elaborations on data from Bankscope and annual consolidated reports.

participants in the CD market to display a high ratio of other income on average assets.

Some basic summary statistics of our bank indicators for the year 2005 are provided in Table 9.2.[16] We observe that the banks in our sample show sizes and capitalisation levels which are not too dissimilar, as highlighted by the small variation around their average levels. Instead, our banking groups differ more significantly in terms of diversification of the loan portfolio and profitability, whose standard deviation is about 50 per cent of the average levels. Finally, our sample is very heterogeneous in terms of quality of the loan portfolio and liquidity.

5 EMPIRICAL ANALYSIS

To investigate the distinctive features of the bank holding companies that act as top players in the CD and loan sales market, we proceed as follows. First, we select the top 15 players in each market (for each year under analysis) based on a proxy of market participation calculated respectively as:

- total notional amount of CDs bought or sold/total assets;[17] and
- annual flows of loan issues/total assets.

We then compute the average values of the banks' indicators for the top 15 players and compare them with the average values for all other players in the sample. A *t*-test for equality of means under the assumption of unequal variances is provided to formally check for significant differences in the average characteristics of the two subsamples (Table 9.3).

This preliminary analysis has been integrated with a more formal panel estimation of the impact of the various bank characteristics on the intensity of participation to CD and loan sales markets, respectively. For this purpose, we focus on only the 2004–05 period, to avoid potential distortions in the results induced by changes in the accounting standards since 2004. The dependent variables of the two panel regressions are the proxies for market participation to CD and loan sales market illustrated above. To avoid multicollinearity issues, we exclude from the analysis those explanatory variables which are more closely correlated with the other variables (proportion of retail loans, Tier 1 ratio, ROAA).[18] Random effects have been included in the panel specification and the Hausman test for model misspecification has been performed. The results are presented in Table 9.4 and confirm the preliminary analysis on the averages.

In the following we illustrate the main findings reported in Tables 9.3 and 9.4 for loan sales and CDs, respectively.

Loan Sales

The results in Table 9.3 and 9.4 suggest that bank size does not significantly affect the loan sales activity in our sample. Therefore, we do not find evidence of either a reputation effect or a presence of scale economies in the loan sales market. Geographic diversification appears to be a reason for selling loans. Our proxy for geographic diversification suggests that well-diversified banks sell more loans than concentrated banks. In fact, this result is not entirely surprising. Interpretation of the diversification coefficient may be confounded by the fact that the volume of loan sales may include transfers of loans among affiliates in a given bank holding company.[19] In this respect, transfers of loans among bank subsidiaries are more likely in geographically diversified entities, as the bank groups in our sample (Demsetz, 2000). The alternative diversification measure (total retail loans/total loans) is not significantly related to the loan sales activity, although the top players seem to be more diversified also according to this indicator.

The coefficient of the lending quality is negative, suggesting a lemons problem associated with loan sales, but not statistically significant.

As for capitalisation and liquidity, we do not find evidence of a capital and liquidity shortage as a motivation for loan sales. The results for liquidity

Table 9.3 Distinctive features of top players in credit derivatives and loan sales markets

	Credit derivatives			Loan sales		
	2005	2004	2003	2005	2004	2003
Size						
Mean top 15	13.477	13.276	13.160	13.093	12.912	12.808
Mean other banks	12.570	12.417	12.249	12.739	12.578	12.404
Mean equality test (*p*-values)	0.000*	0.000*	0.000*	0.126	0.130	0.052**
Loan diversification						
Mean top 15	0.379	0.373	0.393	0.397	0.415	0.420
Mean other banks	0.356	0.362	0.352	0.348	0.343	0.333
Mean equality test (*p*-values)	0.682	0.839	0.833	0.374	0.194	0.107
Geographic diversification						
Mean top 15	0.463	0.490	0.520	0.518	0.496	0.513
Mean other banks	0.644	0.659	0.648	0.619	0.656	0.661
Mean equality test (*p*-values)	0.001*	0.001*	0.004*	0.065**	0.002*	0.005*
Loan quality						
Mean top 15	1.881	2.485	2.573	1.739	2.129	2.516
Mean other banks	2.017	2.270	2.281	2.079	2.428	2.602
Mean equality test (*p*-values)	0.795	0.705	0.150	0.514	0.597	0.867
Tier 1 ratio						
Mean top 15	8.867	8.556	8.576	8.500	8.536	8.553
Mean other banks	7.909	8.029	8.118	8.071	8.038	7.950
Mean equality test (*p*-values)	0.024*	0.204	0.294	0.323	0.230	0.166
Total capital ratio						
Mean top 15	12.547	12.397	12.291	12.053	12.257	12.307
Mean other banks	10.944	11.306	11.412	11.162	11.368	11.138
Mean equality test (*p*-values)	0.000*	0.009*	0.000*	0.045*	0.036*	0.006*

Net int. margin/AA						
Mean top 15	0.973	1.083	1.228	1.363	1.436	1.525
Mean other banks	1.265	1.333	1.249	1.036	1.128	1.316
Mean equality test (*p*-values)	0.093**	0.085**	0.302	0.067**	0.070**	0.072**
Other income/AA						
Mean top 15	1.327	1.298	1.186	1.220	1.309	1.389
Mean other banks	0.872	0.919	0.926	0.919	0.870	0.953
Mean equality test (*p*-values)	0.004*	0.019*	0.076**	0.053**	0.005*	0.019*
ROAA						
Mean top 15	0.559	0.411	0.480	0.662	0.643	0.504
Mean other banks	0.598	0.514	0.463	0.553	0.412	0.405
Mean equality test (*p*-values)	0.691	0.351	0.109	0.263	0.033*	0.479
ROAE						
Mean top 15	16.141	9.875	10.266	16.431	12.032	8.009
Mean other banks	14.648	11.236	10.156	14.521	10.284	8.481
Mean equality test (*p*-values)	0.456	0.651	0.041*	0.340	0.561	0.897
Liquidity ratio						
Mean top 15	14.947	20.629	18.842	13.000	12.955	22.891
Mean other banks	16.847	16.514	16.887	17.706	19.899	25.096
Mean equality test (*p*-values)	0.735	0.450	0.606	0.400	0.200	0.620

Note: * Statistically significant at 5% confidence level; ** statistically significant at 10% confidence level.
Average values of the main characteristics of the bank holding companies of our sample that are very active in the credit derivatives and the loan sales markets (top 15 players). The top players have been chosen based on the ratio between credit derivative volumes and total assets and on the ratio between loan sales volumes and total assets, respectively. The average values for the top players are compared with the average values of the remaining banks in the sample. The test for equality of means between top players and other banks is a *t*-test under the assumption of unequal variances.

Table 9.4 Activity in credit derivatives and loan sales, and bank characteristics: panel estimation

	Credit derivatives		Loan sales	
	Coefficient	*p*-values	Coefficient	*p*-values
Constant	−183.666*	0.0212	1.166	0.3378
Size	12.642*	0.0251	−0.079	0.3301
Geographic diversification	−0.638*	0.0489	−1.183*	0.0010
Loan quality	−2.096	0.3402	−0.003	0.9083
Total capital ratio	5.593*	0.0370	0.058*	0.0406
Net int. margin/AA	−21.087*	0.0163	0.247*	0.0195
Other income/AA	33.380*	0.0018	0.231*	0.0421
ROAE	−0.132	0.7191	−0.007	0.0934
Liquidity ratio	−0.222	0.3888	−0.001	0.7982
Adj. R-squared	0.4188		0.3220	
Cross-sections included	33		49	
Hausman test (*p*-value)	0.5601		0.0672	

Note: * Statistically significant at 5% confidence level.
Estimates from panel regressions of a measure of bank activity in the credit derivatives and loan sales markets over the years 2004–05 on various bank characteristics. The ratio between notional amounts of credit derivatives and total assets and the ratio between loan sales volumes and total assets have been chosen as measures of bank activity in the two markets. Random effects have been included in the panel specification. The last row reports the results of the Hausman test of model misspecification (fixed vs. random effects, null hypothesis: no misspecification).

are consistent with the comparative advantage hypothesis, since banks affected by a liquidity shortage should sell more loans than liquid banks, but they are not statistically significant. On the contrary, the positive and significant coefficient on the capital ratio (Table 9.4) may reflect a reputation effect: buyers prefer loans from stronger, better-capitalised banks in order to avoid lemons (Haubrich and Thomson, 1993). Furthermore, a multi-country bank holding effect may occur. According to Cebenoyan and Strahan (2004), multi-state bank holding companies may be often overseen by multiple regulatory agencies, which may increase their need to hold regulatory capital. At the same time, it may be more difficult for multi-state banking companies to move capital among affiliates compared to multi-bank holding companies with subsidiaries in just one state.

As expected, banks with good lending opportunities are more active loan sellers than banks with less-profitable loans. Consistently with the comparative advantage hypothesis, high values of net interest margin/average assets (which is an indicator of profitable lending opportunities) are positively related with participation in the loan secondary market. Furthermore, the top participants in the loan sales market show high values of the other income/average assets ratio. This is consistent with the practice of originating loans with the intent of immediately placing them on the secondary market.[20] As for more general profitability measures (ROAA and ROAE), we do not find evidence of a significant relation to the loan trading activity.

Credit Derivatives

Our empirical findings from Tables 9.3 and 9.4 confirm our expectations on the relation between CD activity and bank size. In line with previous empirical results (Minton et al., 2006), the most active players in the CD market are significantly larger than other bank groups. Somewhat unexpectedly, bank groups with a better-diversified loan portfolio make greater use of CDs. When CDs are used for transferring credit risk of the banking book, we expect a positive relation between loan portfolio concentration and CD activity. However, in our case, most of the CD volume comes from trading book transactions, which are normally carried out by large bank holding companies that are usually well diversified. This can help to explain our 'counterintuitive' findings.

The quality of the loan portfolio does not seem to have a significant impact on the use of CD instruments. This can be explained by the fact that the most liquid CDs are written on investment grade obligors and, therefore, CDs are not routinely used as credit protection instruments for the riskiest loans. Again, contrary to previous empirical evidence, we find that better-capitalised bank groups access the CD markets more intensively. As previously mentioned, large bank groups operating in more than one country (which play a leading role in the CD markets) may be required to hold larger amounts of capital.[21]

Overall profitability measures (ROAA and ROAE) do not appear to be univocally related to the intensity of participation to the CD market. On the contrary, the top players in CDs display significantly lower margins from traditional financial intermediation and higher income from non-traditional operating activities, which are typical features of large and well-diversified bank groups. Again, this is in line with the fact that most of the CD transactions originate for trading, rather than for hedging purposes. As expected, the liquidity ratio does not play a significant role in explaining a bank's activity in CDs, which are unfunded CRT instruments.

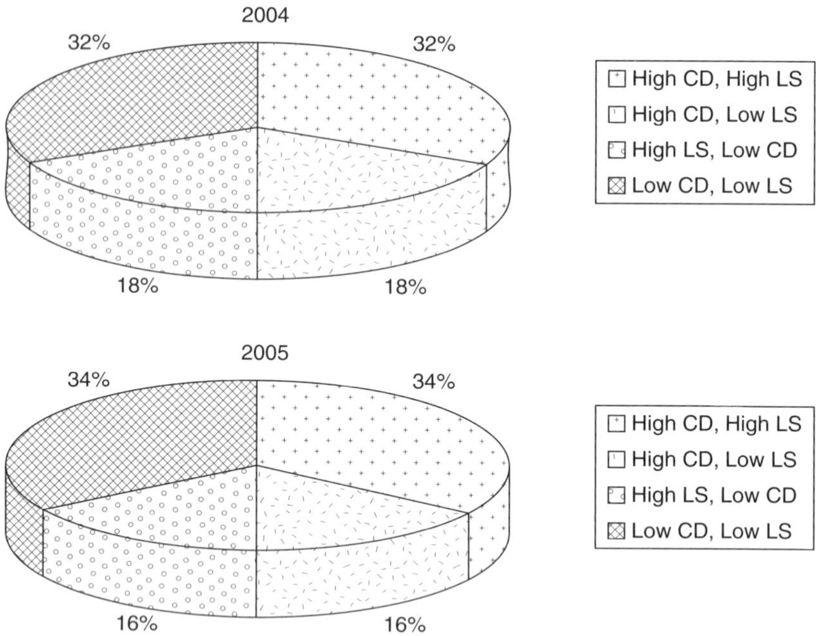

Note: Percentage of bank groups: (1) highly active in both CD and loan sales (LS) markets; (2) highly active in CDs but not in LS; (3) highly active in LS but not in CDs; (4) not very active in either CDs or LS. Participation rates are calculated with respect to the average activity of the banks in the sample. Activity in CDs and LS is measured as the ratio between CD volumes and total assets and the ratio between LS volumes and total assets, respectively.

Figure 9.1 Sample composition by intensity of participation to the CD and loan sales markets

Credit Derivatives versus Loan Sales: Complements or Substitutes?

At this stage, it is interesting to investigate whether the banks which are particularly active in the loan sales market are also active participants in the CD market. If banks perceive CDs and loan sales as complements, they would engage in both activities, whereas if they see them as substitutes, they would concentrate on one particular market. For this purpose we calculate the percentage of bank groups highly active in both markets, highly active in one market but not very active in the other market, and not very active in either market for the years 2004–05.[22] The composition of the sample is reported in Figure 9.1.

According to our findings, banks in our sample seem to consider CDs and loan sales mainly as complements, since around 66 per cent of the financial institutions take similar positions in both segments of the CRT market (high participation in both markets for 33 per cent of the sample and low participation for an equivalent proportion).[23] In fact, the bank groups in our sample access the CD market mainly for trading purposes given the high standardisation and liquidity of those instruments, whereas loan sales seem to be comparatively more used for credit risk management purposes. The most active players in both markets are typically very large and well-diversified bank holding companies having easy access to either market due to reputation effects and significant scale economies associated with CRT activities. On the contrary, a limited activity in the CRT market seems to be associated with less-sophisticated banks having smaller size and lower capital ratios. In addition, the propensity to adopt innovative CRT instruments may be linked to national factors such as the lending customer's base and the country-specific development of new financial market segments.[24]

It is interesting to note that around 34 per cent of the banks in our sample seem to consider CDs and loan sales as substitutes, given that they participate actively in only one of the two markets. In general, smaller banks with a higher proportion of retail loans in their portfolio tend to prefer loan sales, whereas banks with a higher percentage of corporate/public loans make more intensive use of CDs. This can be explained by considering that non-retail loans are less standardised and consequently more subject to relationship lending problems, for which CDs represent more appropriate instruments for transferring credit risk. On the other hand, retail loans are easier and less costly to sell on the secondary loan market, after appropriate bundling.

Before concluding, we should emphasise that our findings should be treated with caution, given the limitations of our sample. The limited sample size and the composition of the sample (large banking groups) may introduce some biases in our analysis. However, we believe that our results can provide some interesting insights on the characteristics of European banks accessing the CRT market, which is still a topic not sufficiently explored by the existing literature.

6 CONCLUSIONS

In this chapter we have investigated whether two very popular instruments, loan sales and CDs, are complements or substitutes for the purpose of transferring credit risk from both a theoretical and a practical perspective.

While similar in many aspects, loan sales and CDs differ in several respects. In particular, loan sales are funded instruments that allow transferring the credit risk via a true sale of the underlying loan. CDs are unfunded instruments that transfer the risk of the underlying obligation while retaining the ownership of the credit. Also, CDs are typically standardised and mainly written on investment-grade obligors, whereas loan sales can be more flexible and refer to speculative-grade borrowers.

Our empirical investigation is based upon the CD and loan sales activity of a sample of European banks for the 2003–05 period. The sample includes the 49 largest European bank holding companies in terms of total assets according to Bankscope. We tested whether and how, in line with theoretical predictions, the intensity of participation in CD and loan sales markets may be related to some bank characteristics, such as bank size, quality and diversification of the loan portfolio, capitalisation, liquidity, and profitability.

Bank size seems to be the main factor affecting participation in the CD market, which is mainly driven by trading-book, rather than banking-book, transactions. Large, well-capitalised and well-diversified banks are the top players in this market. As for loan sales, well-diversified banks with high capital ratios and good lending opportunities seem to be the major participants in the loan secondary market. Our findings suggest that, in general, banks have not substituted loan sales with CDs for credit risk management purposes. Therefore the two instruments are normally used as complements, rather than substitutes, in line with their distinguishing features as CRT tools. However, a non-negligible percentage of the bank groups in our sample tend to concentrate predominantly in one of the two CRT segments, suggesting that for some banks the two instruments might be considered quite close substitutes.

NOTES

1. Regulatory pressure is also a source of innovation for a sizeable body of literature that explains the innovation phenomenon through market imperfections such as taxes, regulation, information asymmetries, transaction costs, and moral hazard and incompleteness theories. See Tufano (2003) for a comprehensive review of such literature.
2. See the classic work by Schmookler (1967) and, more recently, White (2000).
3. About loan sales contract forms and legal issues, see Gorton and Haubrich (1990).
4. The growth of the HLT loan secondary market has highly improved after the formation of the Loan Syndication and Trading Association (LSTA), created with the primary aim of promoting a more liquid, efficient, and transparent market for C&I bank loans. See Bruno (2004) for a detailed analysis of the US loan secondary market structure.
5. The second key issue that arises in CRT activities, related to asymmetric information problems, remains, as the bank, acting as protection buyer, possesses a significant information advantage on the borrower over the protection seller.
6. The original sample included the 50 European largest bank groups. However, one group has been excluded given that its lending activity is almost entirely oriented towards the public sector. Therefore this bank presents very different features compared to the remaining banks in the sample.

7. Data on total assets and total loans for the European banking sector are taken from the general statistics provided by the European Banking Federation.
8. Syndicated loans are structured on the primary market in order to facilitate sale on the secondary market. Since selling loans can induce agency problems, loan contracting can increase the likelihood of selling loans. Term loans are more likely to be sold than credit lines because they require less ongoing information collection (Berger and Udell, 1995), while covenants can reduce reliance upon sellers' information (Drucker and Puri, 2007). According to LSTA (2007), almost 80 per cent of loans traded on the secondary market are term loans.
9. In this respect, Drucker and Puri (2007) find that over 60 per cent of the traded loans are sold within one month after the date of origination and nearly 90 per cent are sold within one year after origination.
10. See, for example, ECB (2004); Fitch Ratings (2004, 2005); BIS (2005).
11. Unfortunately, only a very limited number of banks report separate figures for credit risk protection bought/sold, and for CD transactions for hedging/trading purposes. A more detailed analysis of the activities of our sample banks in the credit derivatives market is therefore unfeasible, though desirable.
12. It is worth reminding that the figures for CDs underestimate the real activity in this segment, since some bank groups participate in CD markets, but do not report the relative figures in the annual reports. Similarly, the loan sales volumes are a proxy of the secondary loan market activity.
13. Typically, loan sales volumes follow the M&A trend, since a relevant part of loan trading is made up by loans originated on the primary market in order to finance highly leveraged deals such as M&As and LBOs.
14. For example, transaction, information technology, legal, and contracting costs.
15. Given a similar charge-off policy, the higher the ratio, the poorer the quality of the loan portfolio will be. Thus, other asset quality measures could have been chosen (for example, non-performing ratio and net charge-off ratio) but the one we use is the best proxy for loan quality we could construct, given data available on Bankscope.
16. Analogous statistics have been computed for the years 2003 and 2004, but have not been reported as the differences across the various years are negligible.
17. For credit derivatives, this indicator has been integrated with the League Tables of the main participants to the CD market.
18. See Table 9A.2 for correlation coefficients.
19. Membership in a multi-bank holding company may help explain participation to the secondary loan market, since transactions between holding company affiliates are not subject to agency problems. See Haubrich and Thomson (1993); Demsetz (2000); Cebenoyan and Strahan (2004).
20. A growing part of secondary market participants is constituted by banks acting as traders and market makers (Fabozzi, 1998; LSTA, 2007). Both these roles generate non-interest income, in the form of fees and bid–ask spreads.
21. It is worth noting that some findings may be distorted by the effect of the CRT activity on the bank's indicators. For example, banks with a large participation in loan sales and CD markets may be more diversified, more capitalised and more profitable as a consequence of their CRT activity. Unfortunately, given that data are available to us on an annual basis only and for a limited time period (especially for CDs), it is particularly difficult to assess the causality relationship between CRT activity and these variables.
22. High and low participation rates are calculated with respect to the average activity of the banks included in the sample.
23. Similar findings have been provided by Minton et al. (2006) on a sample of US bank holding companies.
24. For instance, Italian banks are not very active on either loan sales or CD markets. The majority of their loan portfolio includes small loans to unrated SMEs, which are not easily negotiable on the secondary market and do not represent adequate underlying reference obligations for liquid CD instruments.

REFERENCES

Bank for International Settlements (BIS) (1986), 'Recent Innovations in International Banking', Basel.

Bank for International Settlements (BIS) (2005), 'Credit Risk Transfer', Joint Forum, Basel Committee on Banking Supervision, Basel.

Berger, A.N. (2003), 'The economic effects of technological progress: evidence from the banking industry', *Journal of Money, Credit, and Banking*, **2** (35), 141–76.

Berger, A.N. and G.F. Udell (1993), 'Securitization, risk, and the liquidity problem in banking', in M. Klausner and L. White (eds), *Structural Change in Banking*, Irwin, Homewood, IL, pp. 227–91.

Berger, A.N. and G.F. Udell (1995), 'Lines of credit and relationship lending in small firm finance', *Journal of Business*, **68**, 351–81.

British Bankers' Association (BBA) (2006), 'Credit Derivatives Report 2006', London, September.

Bruno, B. (2004), *Il mercato secondario dei prestiti bancari*, Bancaria Editrice, Rome.

Cebenoyan, A.S. and P. Strahan (2004), 'Risk management, capital structure, and lending at banks', *Journal of Banking and Finance*, **28**, 19–43.

Das, S. (2000), *Credit Derivatives: Trading and Management of Credit and Default Risk*, John Wiley & Sons, Singapore.

Demsetz, R. (2000), 'Bank loan sales: a new look at the motivations for secondary market activities', *Journal of Financial Research*, **23**, 192–222.

Dennis, S.A. and D.J. Mullineaux (2000), 'Syndicated loans', *Journal of Financial Intermediation*, **9**, 404–26.

Drucker, S. and M. Puri (2007), 'On loan sales, loan contracting, and lending relationships', Working Paper 4, FDIC Center for Financial Research, Arlington, VA.

Duffee, G. and C. Zhou (2001), 'Credit derivatives in banking: useful tools for managing risk?', *Journal of Monetary Economics*, **48**, 25–54.

European Central Bank (ECB) (2004), 'Survey on Credit Risk Transfer in the European Market', Frankfurt am Main.

Fabozzi, F.J. (ed.) (1998), *Bank Loans: Secondary Market and Portfolio Management*, Frank J. Fabozzi Associates, New Hope, PA.

Fitch Ratings (2004), 'Global Credit Derivatives Survey: Single-Name CDS Fuel Growth', Fitch Ratings Special Report, September 2003, New York.

Fitch Ratings (2005), 'Global Credit Derivatives Survey: Risk Dispersion Accelerates', Fitch Ratings Special Report, November, New York.

Gardener, E.P.M. (1986), 'Securitisation and the banking firm', Research Papers in Banking and Finance 15, Institute of European Finance, University of Wales, Bangor.

Gorton, G.B. and J.G. Haubrich (1990), 'The loan sales market', in G.G. Kaufman (ed.), *Research in Financial Service: Private and Public Policy*, Vol. 2, JAI Press, Greenwich, CT, pp. 85–135.

Gorton, G.B. and G.G. Pennacchi (1995), 'Banks and loan sales: marketing non-marketable assets', *Journal of Monetary Economics*, **35**, 389–411.

Greenbaum, S.I. and A.V. Thakor (1987), 'Bank funding modes: securitisation versus deposits', *Journal of Banking and Finance*, **11**, 379–402.

Greenbaum, S.I. and A.V. Thakor (1995), *Contemporary Financial Intermediation*, Dryden Press, Harcourt Brace College Publishers, Fort Worth, TX.

Haubrich, J.G. and J.B. Thomson (1993), 'Loan sales, implicit contracts and bank structure', Federal Reserve Bank of Cleveland, Working Paper 7, Cleveland, OH.

International Swaps and Derivatives Association (ISDA) (1999), 'Credit Event Definitions', New York.

International Swaps and Derivatives Association (ISDA) (2003), 'Credit Event Definitions', New York.

Loan Syndication and Trading Association (LSTA) (2007), 'The LSTA Trade Data Study', New York, February.

Minton, B.A., R. Stultz and R. Williamson (2006), 'How much do banks use credit derivatives to reduce risk?', NBER Working Paper 11579, Cambridge, MA.

Morrison, A.D. (2005), 'Credit derivatives, disintermediation and investment decisions', *Journal of Business*, **78**, 621–48.

Pavel, C.A (1989), 'Loan sales have little effect on bank risk', Federal Reserve Bank of Chicago, *Economic Perspectives*, January/February, 23–31.

Pavel, C.A. and D. Phillis (1987), 'Why commercial banks sell loans: an empirical analysis', Federal Reserve Bank of Chicago, *Economic Perspectives*, May/June, 3–14.

Pennacchi, G.G. (1988), 'Loan sales and the cost of bank capital', *Journal of Finance*, **43**, 375–96.

Saunders, A. (2000), *Financial Institutions Management: A Modern Perspective*, Irwin McGraw-Hill, International Edition, Homewood, IL.

Schmookler, J.A. (1967), *Invention and Economic Growth*, Harvard University Press, Cambridge, MA.

Thompson, J.R. (2007), 'Credit risk transfer: to sell or to insure?', Working Paper 1131, Queen's University, Kingston, Ontario, Canada.

Tufano, P. (2003), 'Financial innovation', in G. Constantinides, M. Harris and R. Stultz (eds), *The Handbook of Economics of Finance*, Vol. 1, North-Holland, Amsterdam, pp. 307–35.

White, L.J. (2000), 'Technological change, financial innovation, and financial regulation in the U.S.: the challenge for public policy', in P. Harker and S. Zeniuos (eds), *Performance of Financial Institutions*, Cambridge University Press, Cambridge, pp. 388–415.

APPENDIX 9A

Table 9A.1 Sample of bank holding companies by country/geographical area

Country	Bank holding company
France	
Credit Agricole	BNP Paribas
Société Générale	Credit Mutuel – CIC
Groupe Caisse d'Epargne	Groupe Banques Populaires
Germany	
Deutsche Bank	WestLB
Dresdner Bank	Eurohypo
Commerzbank	Norddeutsche Landesbank Girozentrale
Landesbank Baden-Wuttenberg	HSH Nordbank
DZ Bank	Landesbank Hessen-Thuringen
Bayerische Landesbank	Hypo Real Estate Holding
Bankgesellschaft Berlin	Deutsche Postbank
United Kingdom	
Barclays Bank	HBOS
HSBC	Lloys TSB Group
Royal Bank of Scotland	Standard Chartered
Italy	
Unicredit	San Paolo IMI
Banca Intesa	Banca Monte dei Paschi di Siena
Capitalia Gruppo Bancario	
Switzerland	
UBS	Credit Suisse Groupe
Benelux	
ABN AMRO	Dexia
ING Bank	Rabobank Group
Fortis Bank	KBC Group
Spain	
Santander Central Hispano	Caja de Ahorros y Pen. De Barcelona (Caixa)
Banco Bilbao Vizcaya Argentaria	
Ireland	
Allied Irish Banks	Bank of Ireland
Scandinavia	
Danske Bank	Skandinaviska Enskilda Banken
Nordea Group	Svenska Handelsbanken
DnB NOR Group	

Table 9A.2 Pearson correlation coefficients of explanatory variables

	Size	Retail loans	Geographic divers.	Loan quality	Tier 1 ratio	Total capital ratio	Net int. margin/ AA	Other income/ AA	ROAA	ROAE	Liquidity
Size	1	0.450**	−0.313*	−0.182	0.365**	0.338*	−0.233	0.282	−0.090	0.224	−0.232
Retail loans		1	0.137	−0.409**	0.242	0.227	0.422**	0.437**	0.543**	0.339*	−0.603**
Geographic divers.			1	0.233	−0.197	−0.374**	0.511**	0.063	0.305*	−0.004	−0.167
Loan quality				1	−0.264	−0.253	0.082	0.061	−0.128	−0.299*	0.002
Tier 1 ratio					1	0.627**	−0.233	0.195	−0.085	0.096	−0.046
Total capital ratio					1	−0.197	0.281	−0.008	0.102	−0.016	
Net int. margin/ AA							1	0.488**	0.779**	0.242	−0.515**
Other income/ AA								1	0.633**	0.389**	−0.528**
ROAA									1	0.617**	−0.496**
ROAE										1	−0.316*
Liquidity											1

Note: * Statistically significant at 5% level; ** statistically significant at 1% level.

10. On the required regulatory support for credit derivative markets

Rym Ayadi and Patrick Behr

1 INTRODUCTION

Credit derivative markets have undergone a rapid growth in the last decade. According to figures from the British Bankers' Association, the global outstanding volume of credit derivatives was US$180 billion in 1996. Only 10 years later, at the end of 2006, the market size had expanded to a volume of more than US$20 trillion, roughly 112 times the market size of 1996. Yet, it seems that this growth has not come to an end. According to the same source, the market is expected to grow to a skyrocketing US$33 trillion by the end of 2008 (British Bankers' Association, 2006). This tremendous growth was accompanied by the invention of new, innovative products, therewith widening the diversity of credit derivative instruments. Nowadays, market participants can issue and trade in products such as single-name credit default swaps (CDSs), credit linked notes[1] (CLNs), credit spread options[2] (CSOs), collateralised debt obligations[3] (CDOs), equity-linked products, and portfolio products, to name just a few. The principal feature of these instruments is the separation and isolation of credit risk, which facilitates its trading and enables the replication, transfer and hedging of credit risk.

Credit derivatives are mainly used for credit risk management purposes, for example for credit risk diversification across sectors and geographical regions or regulatory capital relief. Banks and insurance companies use credit derivatives mostly for these purposes. In addition, there seems to be an increasing activity in trading in credit derivatives to create additional income resulting from the exploitation of pricing inefficiencies and asymmetrically distributed information. This is the driving factor behind the increasing participation of hedge funds in credit derivative markets.

Not surprisingly, the rapid growth of the market as well as of new credit derivative products and the increasing importance of new market players pose challenges to credit markets in particular and to the financial system as a whole. As credit derivative markets are still exceptionally opaque because market participants are not required to disclose their transactions, there are an increasing number of voices calling for more transparency and more regulation. An often-voiced argument is that the increasing volume of credit derivatives may threaten the stability of banks involved in credit derivative transactions and, ultimately, the stability of the financial system.[4]

Naturally, all financial innovations encompass advantages as well as risks and a core question associated with the increasing importance of credit derivatives is under what conditions do credit derivatives enhance the resilience of financial systems, and, under what conditions do they threaten the stability of financial systems? This chapter delivers a policy analysis with regard to the need for regulatory support for credit derivatives. We argue that the existing self-regulation by market participants should be accompanied by regulatory and supervisory actions in order to reduce the existing opacity of these markets and to minimise the risks associated with credit derivatives.

The chapter is structured as follows. In Section 2 we present some stylised facts and figures about global credit derivative markets and introduce CDS as the predominating credit derivative instrument. In the third section we describe how credit derivatives change the traditional lender–borrower relationship and discuss potential new incentive problems arising from credit derivative transactions. The fourth section examines whether and how credit derivatives impact on financial stability, and Section 5 discusses whether and what kind of regulatory support is needed for the functioning of credit derivative markets.

2 CREDIT DERIVATIVE MARKETS

Development of Credit Derivative Markets

The rapid expansion of credit derivative markets dates back to the mid-1990s. Since then, there has been a tremendous annual growth in the volume of the notional amount of outstanding credit derivatives. While this volume was only US$180 billion in 1996, it skyrocketed in the years thereafter, crossing the US$ one trillion threshold in 2001 and reaching a stunning US$20,207 trillion at the end of 2006. Yet, this rapid growth does not seem to have come to an end. For instance, the British Bankers' Association estimates the credit derivative markets volume to be around US$33 trillion by year-end 2008.[5] Figure 10.1 illustrates the exponential growth of credit derivative markets in the last decade.

The volume growth was accompanied by an increase in product complexity. The array of credit derivatives, which are mainly traded over the counter

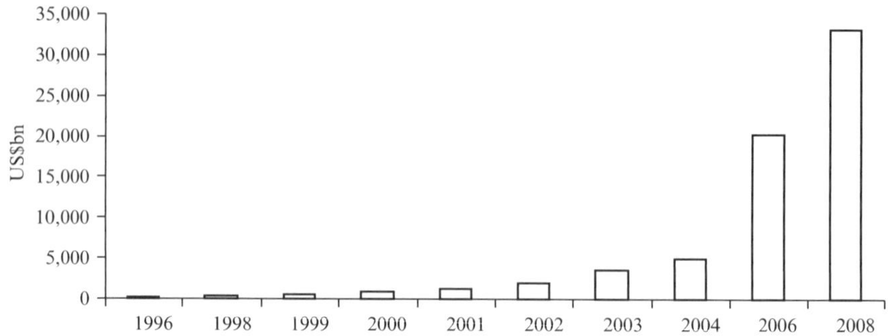

Note: The figure for 2008 is estimated.

Source: British Bankers' Association (2006).

Figure 10.1 Global outstanding volume of credit derivatives, 1996–2008

(OTC), nowadays ranges from CDSs, CSOs, CLNs, CDOs, and total return swaps, to portfolio products as well as loan-only CDSs and index-related products. The last, in particular, have recently experienced a boost in volume (Fitch, 2006). Notwithstanding the recent significant increase of highly complex instruments such as CDOs,[6] CDSs still seem to make up the lion's share of the credit derivative markets. Indeed, CDSs accounted for a market share of 67 per cent in 2002, 68 per cent in 2003, almost 70 per cent in 2004 and a more moderate 51 per cent in 2005 (ibid.). In the following subsection, we hence focus primarily on CDS functioning as this is still the most important credit derivative product in terms of market share. In addition, we briefly examine CDOs because of their recent gain in importance.

CDS Functioning[7]

A CDS is a transaction in which two counterparties enter into a swap transaction. One of the two parties is a loan originating bank that wants to swap the credit risk of a loan (reference instrument or reference entity) to a second party, which is usually, but not necessarily, another bank. The motive for the swap for the loan originator is to seek protection from the risk of a credit event occurrence. Credit events include bankruptcy, the restructuring of debt, or a failure of the reference entity to meet scheduled debt repayments. Consequently, the originating party is commonly referred to as the protection buyer. The swap counterparty is referred to as the protection seller because in the case of a credit event, which has to be precisely defined in the swap contract, the protection seller has to pay a lump sum to the protection

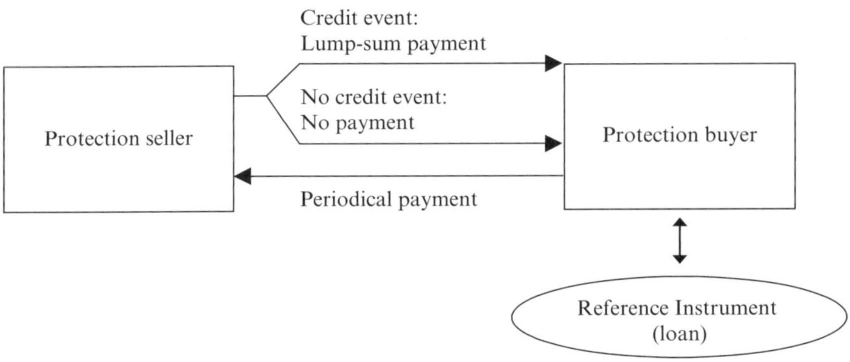

Figure 10.2 Functioning of a credit default swap

buyer. The lump sum is equal to the difference between the face and the market value of the reference entity's debt. In return, the protection buyer usually pays a periodical fee (often on a quarterly basis) to the protection seller. Figure 10.2 summarises the general structure of a CDS transaction. As the figure shows, in the case without a credit event the protection seller does not have to pay anything to the protection buyer. The receipt of the periodical payment to the protection seller remains unaffected by this.

Unlike other types of derivatives such as interest rate swaps, the risks assumed by the protection buyer and protection seller in a CDS transaction are not symmetrical. The protection buyer effectively takes on a short position in the credit risk of the reference entity, which thereby relieves the buyer of exposure to default. By giving up reference entity credit risk, the buyer effectively gives up the opportunity to profit from exposure to the reference entity. In return, the buyer takes on counterparty default exposure due to the possibility of a default of the protection seller, exposure to a simultaneous default of the reference entity and the protection seller, and so-called 'counterparty replacement risk'.[8] In addition, the protection buyer takes on basis risk to the extent that the reference entity specified in the CDS transaction does not precisely match the asset hedged through the acquisition of the credit risk. A bank hedging a loan, for example, might buy protection on a bond issued by the borrower instead of negotiating a more customised and potentially less liquid CDS linked directly to the loan.

The protection seller, in contrast, builds up a long position in the credit risk of the reference entity, which is essentially the same as the default risk assumed when lending directly to the reference entity. The protection seller also takes on counterparty risk because the seller will lose expected premium income if the protection buyer defaults.

One exception to the above risk allocation is the funded CDS (also called credit linked note), in which the protection seller lends the notional amount to the protection buyer in order to secure performance in the event of default. In a funded CDS, which requires an up-front payment by the protection seller, the protection buyer is relieved of the counterparty exposure to the protection seller but the seller has the exposure to the buyer along with the exposure to the reference entity. However, most CDS transactions are unfunded, which means that they do not involve up-front payments by the protection seller, but to circumvent counterparty credit risk, up-front payments and/or collateral may be required.

For the simplest (single-name) form of CDS, the reference entity is an individual corporation or government. If a corporate reference entity is taken over by another firm, the protection typically shifts over to the acquiring entity. If a reference entity de-merges or spins off a subsidiary, CDS market participants use a set of criteria, known as 'successor provisions', to determine the new reference entities.

A CDS with more than two or more reference entities is known as a 'basket' CDS. In the most common form of a basket CDS, the so-called first-to-default CDS, the protection seller compensates the buyer for losses associated with the first entity in the basket to default, after which the swap terminates and provides no further protection. CDSs referencing more than 10 entities are sometimes referred to as 'portfolio products'. Such products are generally used in connection with synthetic securitisations[9] in which a CDS transfers credit risk of loans or bonds to CDO note holders[10] instead of a true sale of the assets as in a cash securitisation (Mengle, 2007) (Figures 10.3a and 10.3b).

In a typical securitisation transaction where banks transfer the legal rights of the assets to an SPV, CDOs[11] involve the transfer of a portfolio of loans (collateralised loan obligation: CLO) or bonds (collateralised bond obligation: CBO) or a mixture of the two (CDO), and the tranching of the risk to attract investors. The use of tranching techniques enables the creation of highly structured types of credit risk profiles. Lower tranches bear the greatest risk of loss. The prospectuses in CDO issues typically contain information on the underlying obligations, diversity scores, and the ratings of the tranches. The underlying portfolio of a CDO can include various assets such as commercial loans or corporate bonds as well as asset-backed securities (ABSs), and may be static or actively managed. Holders of senior tranches have repayment priority over the more junior tranches and the transactions can be sliced into up to five or more tranches. The first loss tranche (also called an equity tranche) is unrated and carries the major share of risk in the structure. The senior tranche is normally structured in such a way that an AAA rating is assigned to it and accounts

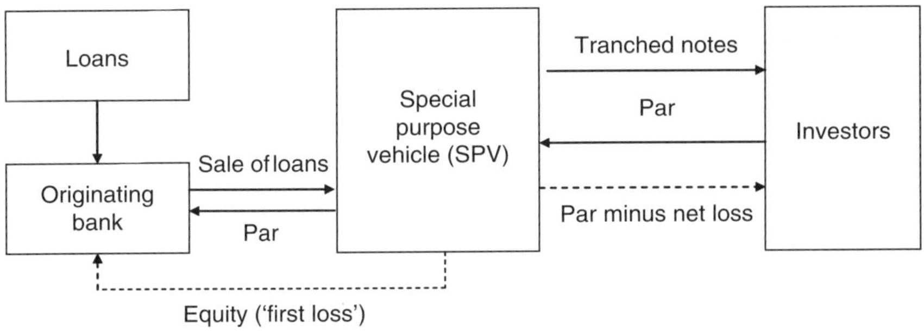

Figure 10.3a Cash securitisation

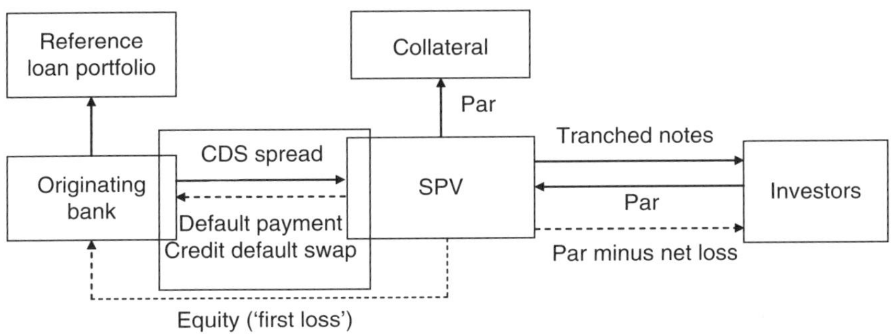

Figure 10.3b Synthetic securitisation

for most of the transaction volume – often it accounts for 70 to 90 per cent of the notional amount. The exact riskiness of the layers between the first loss and the senior tranches (known as mezzanine layers) depends on the structure – the size of the first loss tranche and the riskiness of the underlying portfolio. A distinction is also made between balance-sheet CDO and arbitrage CDO.

A major source of credit derivatives growth since 2004 has been the invention of index CDSs, in which the reference entity is an index comprising as many as 125 corporate entities. A CDS index offers protection on all entities in the index, and each entity has an equal share of the notional amount. The two main indices are the CDX[12] index, consisting of 125 North American investment grade rated firms, and the iTraxx[13] index, including 125 euro-based, mainly investment grade rated firms. In addition, there are indices for North American sub-investment grade rated firms, for European firms that have been downgraded from investment grade to junk status and for countries such as Japan, and regions such as Asia excluding Japan.

Recent innovations in CDS have extended protection to reference obligations instead of entities. A CDS on ABSs, for example, provides protection against credit events on securitised assets, usually securitised home equity lines of credit. In addition, a CDS can specify CDO notes as reference obligations. Finally, a loan CDS can reference leveraged loans to a specific entity.

Transaction Documentation and Settlement

The confirmation[14] of a CDS deal involves a standard set of credit events that must occur before the protection seller has to compensate the buyer for losses caused by the credit event. The deal counterparties decide which events they want to include and which not. The included events vary according to the type of reference entity. The five most often included ones are:

1. The most common credit event is failure to pay.
2. Bankruptcy is a credit event associated with corporate reference entities.
3. Restructuring, which refers to actions such as coupon reduction or maturity extension undertaken instead of default, is generally included as a credit event for corporate entities. Restructuring is sometimes referred to as a 'soft' credit event because, in contrast to failure to pay or bankruptcy, it is not always clear what constitutes a restructuring that should trigger compensation.
4. Repudiation or moratorium provides for compensation after specified actions of a government reference entity and is generally relevant only for emerging market governments.
5. Obligation acceleration and obligation default, which refer to technical defaults such as violation of a bond covenant, are rarely used.

In the event of default the protection seller compensates the buyer according to the settlement method chosen. There are two types of settlement: physical and cash settlement:

1. If a credit event occurs and the counterparties have opted for physical settlement, the protection buyer delivers the defaulted debt of the reference entity with a face value equal to the notional amount specified in the CDS to the protection seller. In return, the protection seller pays the par value, that is, the face amount of the debt.
2. If a credit event occurs and the counterparties have agreed on a cash settlement, an auction of the defaulted bonds takes place in order to determine the post-default market value. Once this value is deter-

mined, the protection seller pays the buyer the difference between the par value, which is equal to the CDS notional amount, and the post-default market value.

Table 10.1 summarises the main characteristics of CDS transactions.

Table 10.1 Main characteristics of CDS transactions

Characteristic	Description
Cash flows	• Protection buyer pays regular premiums over the life of the swap • Protection seller pays amount (depending on the agreed settlement procedures) following the credit event
Reference entity	• Generally investment grade rated corporations, banks and sovereigns from developed countries or emerging markets
Risks involved	• Counterparty credit risk – the risk that the transaction counterparty defaults before the final settlement of the transaction's cash flows – protection seller defaults on contingent payouts and protection buyer defaults on premiums • Legal or documentation risks – credit event definitions do not cover all potential risks • Market liquidity risk – associated with the decline in asset market liquidity resulting from the failure of winding down of one or more major participants in the CDS market • Operational risks
Types of CDS	• Unfunded or funded – whether the protection buyer receives funds in the transaction or whether the protection seller has to provide upfront funding in the transaction • Standardised contracts – corresponding to ISDA definitions • Contracts based on ISDA Master Agreements
Trigger events	• ISDA standard credit events – failure to pay, bankruptcy, restructuring, moratorium, obligation default
Settlement in the case of a credit event	• Physical settlement – the protection buyer delivers a bond issued by the reference entity or a bank claim that it holds on the entity in exchange for payment of the par value • Cash settlement – the reference entity's debt is valued at market price. The protection seller pays the protection buyer the difference between the security's nominal value and its market price, or the difference between its par value and the estimated recovery rate

Source: Own research and BIS (2003).

Participants (in) and Their Motives for Credit Derivative Transactions

An often-cited motive to enter into credit derivative transactions is the management of exposure to credit risk. This is particularly relevant *for banks* which face severe sectoral and geographical diversification constraints. Entering into credit derivative transactions allows such banks to diversify their credit portfolio by acquiring claims on firms that would otherwise not be accessible to them through regular client acquisition (European Central Bank, 2004). Managing credit risk is, however, not new to banks. They have managed credit risk long before the invention and rapid growth of credit derivatives, for instance, through syndicating loans or third-party guarantees and letters of credit. The novel aspect of credit derivatives is that their invention allowed the creation of a market for credit risk that is completely separated from the underlying reference obligation. This yielded a lot more opportunities than sheer default protection. For instance, investors who are confident that a given reference entity will not default can collect the premium payments in case they provide protection. On the other hand, arbitrageurs or market makers can exploit price discrepancies resulting from information asymmetries or market inefficiencies (Durbin, 2006). For the originators of credit risk transfer (CRT) transactions[15] motives such as regulatory capital relief, management of individual credit lines and concentration risks as well as the generation of additional fee income play a key role. The global derivatives survey by Fitch (2006) further cites that credit derivative markets participants increasingly use credit derivatives for trading purposes. Table 10.2 summarises some of the most-often-cited motives for credit derivative transactions for protection buyers and sellers.

A survey published in 2004 by the European Central Bank (ECB) revealed that large, globally operating universal banks mainly act as originators of CRT transactions while smaller, regionally oriented banks often act as protection sellers. The survey also reported that 80 per cent of the credit derivative transactions take place cross-border, therewith underlining the formerly mentioned regional diversification argument.[16]

According to the ECB survey, the market for CRT transactions is mainly a bank-to-bank market, that is, banks act not only as originators but are also the main counterparties of CRT transactions. Other market participants include insurance companies, pension funds, asset managers and hedge funds. The last, in particular, seem to have gained importance in recent years. Contrary to banks, the dominating motive for hedge funds in participating in credit derivative markets is to generate trading income.

The main originators of CRT transactions are large, globally operating

Table 10.2 Motives for using credit derivatives by type of financial institution

Type of financial institution	Buying protection for/ in the case of	Selling protection for/ in the case of
Banks	• Credit risk management • Regulatory capital relief • Balance-sheet management • Liquidity shortages (funding motive)	• Geographic/industry diversification of loan portfolio • Offsetting of costs of hedging other credits • Yield enhancement
Insurance companies	• Reduction or diversification of liability concentration in insurance portfolio without having to sell bond positions	• Diversification • Yield enhancement • Matching of maturity profile of liabilities
Securities dealers	• Market intermediation • Credit risk management • Regulatory capital relief	• Market intermediation • Geographical/industry diversification of loan portfolio • Offsetting of costs of hedging other credits
Asset managers	• Strategic trade construction • Exploitation of negative views on creditworthiness development	• Exploitation of positive views on creditworthiness (yield enhancement and diversification)
Hedge funds	• Exploitation of negative views on the credit quality • Packaging with bonds and/ or convertible bonds for basis trades	• Exploitation of positive views on a credit

Source: Own research and ECB (2004).

universal banks as well as investment banks, with relatively little variation in the group of the top 10 CRT transaction originators over the past four years. Table 10.3 illustrates this.

Whereas the share of reference entities with a rating below investment grade (worse than BBB– on Fitch's rating scale) was only 8 per cent in 2002, it increased to 31 per cent in 2005. At the same time the share of reference entities with an AAA rating decreased from 22 per cent in 2002

Table 10.3 Top 10 originators of CRT transactions, 2002–2005

Rank	2002	2003	2004	2005
1	JPMorgan Chase	JPMorgan Chase	Deutsche Bank	Morgan Stanley
2	Merril Lynch	Deutsche Bank	Morgan Stanley	Deutsche Bank
3	Deutsche Bank	Goldman Sachs	Goldman Sachs	Goldman Sachs
4	Morgan Stanley	Morgan Stanley	JPMorgan Chase	JPMorgan Chase
5	CSFB	Merril Lynch	UBS	UBS
6	Goldman Sachs	CSFB	CSFB	Lehman Brothers
7	UBS	UBS	Lehman Brothers	Barclays
8	Lehman Brothers	Lehman Brothers	Merril Lynch	Citigroup
9	Citigroup	Citigroup	Citigroup	CSFB
10	Commerzbank	Bear Stearns	Bear Stearns	BNP Paribas

Sources: Fitch (2003, 2004, 2005, 2006).

to 11 per cent in 2005. This might have been triggered by narrower credit spreads combined with an environment of low defaults (Fitch, 2006). Another reason might be that the degree of asymmetric information associated with non-investment grade rated borrowers decreased due to changes in the disclosure regimes.

All in all, in terms of players, the market for credit derivatives does not seem to have changed dramatically over the past few years. They are still largely dominated by banks, though particularly hedge funds are gaining importance, especially as protection sellers. Table 10.4 provides an overview of the composition of protection sellers from 2000 to 2006.

Credit derivative markets continue to be rather opaque and survey results are the only halfway reliable sources of information. Among other things, this opacity is fed by the change of the incentive structure of the underlying transaction with that of the derivative.

3 INCENTIVE ISSUES ASSOCIATED WITH CREDIT DERIVATIVES

It is well known that the borrower–lender relationship suffers from adverse selection and moral hazard problems, which screening and monitoring

Table 10.4 Protection sellers by institution type (in per cent), 2000–2006

Type of institution	2000	2002	2004	2006
Banks (including securities firms)	63	55	54	44
Banks – trading activities	–	–	–	35
Banks – loan portfolio	–	–	–	9
Insurers	23	33	20	17
Mono-line insurers	–	21	10	8
Re-insurers	–	–	7	4
Other insurance companies	–	12	3	5
Hedge funds	5	5	15	30
Pension funds	3	2	4	4
Mutual funds	2	3	4	3
Corporates	3	2	2	1
Other	1	0	1	1

Source: British Bankers' Association (2006).

by banks as delegated monitors help to mitigate.[17] However, with the introduction of CRT transactions the prevalent incentive structures in the borrower–lender relationship have changed by creating a new set of relationships among borrowers, lenders/protection buyers and protection sellers. For example, Morrison (2005) argues that the availability of credit derivatives could adversely affect banks by reducing their incentives to screen and to monitor borrowers. Furthermore, the use of credit derivatives could make bank loans less valuable to borrowers because the loans would entail a reduced certification effect.

Figure 10.4 provides a stylised summary of the traditional relationships between borrowers and lenders before and after the introduction of CRT transactions. According to the figure, the introduction of CRT transactions alters the borrower–lender relationships in several ways.

The relationship between the protection buyer and the protection seller (link A) suffers from: (a) the principal–agent problem which stems from the possibility for the lender to retain the relationship with the borrower and become the agent of the risk taker following the CRT. Since the protection buyer's monitoring efforts cannot be observed by the protection seller without a cost, there is an increasing incentive for the former to reduce its monitoring; (b) the incomplete contracting problem related to opportunistic behaviours by the contract parties, for instance, if the protection buyer is able to demand payments under the agreements that exceed credit losses actually incurred or if the protection seller is able to avoid payment following a genuine credit event; and (c) the asymmetric distribution of

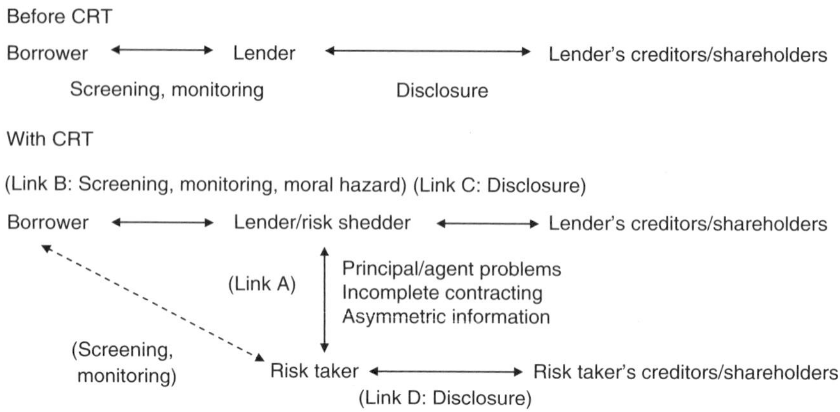

Source: BIS (2003).

Figure 10.4 Stylised summary of relationships affected by CRT transactions

information related to the information advantage of the lender (about the creditworthiness of the borrower) over the protection seller.

With regard to the relationship between the lender–protection buyer and the borrower (link B), the transfer of credit risk from a lender to a third party can have a knock-on effect on the borrower. Even if the lender–borrower relationship remains formally intact – for example, if the lender has used credit derivatives or insurance rather than selling the claim outright – the lender's behaviour towards the borrower may nevertheless be affected by the fact that it has reduced its exposure and by the precise terms on which it has transferred the risk.

Indeed, since the lender has transferred some or all of the credit risk on a given exposure, it might be expected to reduce its monitoring efforts.[18] Moreover, on the one hand, the use of CRT instruments should free up additional credit lines and thus benefit borrowers. On the other hand, some corporate borrowers have been reluctant to accept the transfer of their loans and this reluctance has impeded the development of secondary loan markets. One reason may be the concern that market participants interpret the risk transfer as a negative signal about a borrower's creditworthiness. The potential signalling effect depends on the visibility of the transactions to third parties, which is not equal for all CRT instruments. For instance, this visibility is rather low in the CDS market. Finally, the existence of credit risk protection might influence a lender's behaviour with respect to distressed borrowers because loss protection changes the risk/return profiles of various alternative actions. On the one hand, the existence of credit risk protection could encourage forbearance because there is no longer an incentive to try to reduce losses by early action. On the other hand, lenders who have shed credit risk by using credit derivatives – which include restructuring as a credit event – may be encouraged to agree to a debt restructuring, provided that it falls within the particular definition used, while if they have used instruments which exclude restructuring they may prefer to take a 'hard line' in the hope that the borrower will enter insolvency proceedings or default.

The relationships between the protection buyer, the protection seller and their creditors and shareholders, respectively (links C and D), can also be affected. As CRT instruments can alter institutions' risk profiles, their creditors and shareholders have an interest in such changes being properly reflected in disclosed statements/disclosure requirements. Since CRT may involve substantial counterparty, legal, operational and liquidity risk for protection buyers, the relevance of adequate disclosure is not limited to the protection seller.

Table 10.5 summarises the potential problems arising from CRT transactions and the relationships that CRT might affect.

As expected, the increasing importance of CRT transactions and their likely implications for credit markets and the real economy have led to a growing body of mostly theoretical works due to the lack of data in this area. The most notable ones are Gorton and Penacchi (1995), DeMarzo and Duffie (1999), Duffee and Zhou (2001), Arping (2005), Morrison (2005), Marsh and Wagner (2006), Chiesa (2006), Duffie (2007), and Franke and Krahnen (2007). These papers examine theoretically – from different angles and based on different underlying assumptions – how CRT transactions can change incentive structures, what the implications of these changes are, and how the real economy might be affected by the introduction of CRT transactions.

4 CREDIT DERIVATIVES AND FINANCIAL STABILITY

Consequences of Increasing Credit Derivative Activity for Financial Stability

There is growing consensus (IMF, 2006) that the flexibility provided by credit derivatives has the potential to facilitate risk sharing, to enhance the efficiency of risk management, and to promote market completeness.

Credit derivatives provide banks and other financial institutions access to a broader range of risk–return combinations and a wider pool of underlying risks. Importantly, credit derivatives enable banks to optimise

Table 10.5 Potential impacts of CRT transactions on the borrower–lender relationship

	Potential problem	Affected relationship
Adverse selection	Reduced incentives for lenders to screen out low-quality assets	Borrower–lender Lender–protection seller
	Lemons problem	Lender–protection seller
	Incentives for lenders to select low-quality assets	Lender–protection seller
Moral hazard	Reduced incentives for lenders to monitor borrowers	Borrower–lender Lender–protection seller
	Lender's purchase of credit protection against borrower's wishes	Borrower–lender
	Increased incentives for lenders to prematurely trigger default	Lender–protection seller Borrower–lender
	Protection seller reneges (partially or fully) on contingent payouts	Lender–protection seller

their overall risk profile and to improve their profitability and efficiency[19] thereby helping them to prevent situations of financial turmoil and to alleviate credit problems in specific sectors or regions. Credit risk – which traditionally has been warehoused primarily by banks – can nowadays be distributed more broadly, and other non-bank market participants such as insurance companies, investment trusts and increasingly hedge funds have access to exposures which were formerly not accessible to them (ibid.). A differently structured credit portfolio, which assumes the exposure at lower costs than the original lender, allows a more efficient allocation of risks within the economy. Economic shocks such as an economic recession or a crisis situation in specific business sectors or of a particular company can better be absorbed if the associated costs are lower in total and less concentrated. Credit derivatives can also supply important additional information on the borrower's creditworthiness through their market pricing[20] – provided that the risks incurred are accurately measured and priced and the markets are sufficiently liquid. They are thus likely to improve the information efficiency of financial markets.[21]

Credit derivative activity has also contributed to enhance the transferability of credit risks by allowing an increased specificity of credit exposures that can meet different investment demands, particularly in the 'primary' risk transfer markets.[22] The demand for trading and hedging tools has fostered the introduction and rapid growth of credit indices and standardised tranche products, resulting in an increasingly liquid market for such products. In particular, the increasing activity of hedge funds has been an important source of liquidity in credit derivative markets. This provides a twofold benefit for banks. First, it contributes to reducing banks' credit risks by allowing them to transfer assets[23] and/or credit risk[24] off their balance sheets,[25] and second, it improves their liquidity by providing secondary markets for credit risk.

Nevertheless, it should be borne in mind that in a period of relatively benign macroeconomic conditions – continued global economic growth, low inflation rates, high corporate profits combined with a low number of business failures and a more predictable monetary policy – the prices of financial assets often embody relatively low expected volatility and little reward for taking credit risk or for extending the duration of investor portfolios. With more risk traded in the market and more participants managing this risk through portfolio adjustments, the importance of market liquidity increases and the potential knock-on effects from an erosion of liquidity are multiplied. In some situations, asset price movements are exacerbated by the actions of market participants, including dynamic hedging strategies or forced liquidations (fire sales) of assets to meet margin calls. Most importantly, complex structured credit products, typically including CDOs whose risks and fair valuation are still difficult to be fully grasped by most investors, and rating agencies[26] could suffer a dramatic loss of liquidity in the event of stress scenarios.

Moreover, the multiplication of layers of intermediation between borrowers and lenders that increasingly characterises the financial system nowadays may create new channels for the transmission of shocks within the financial markets and into the economy at a global scale, therewith exacerbating contagion risks. The turbulences on credit markets in August/September 2007, triggered by the US 'sub-prime loan crisis', has (unexpectedly) spread much more widely in the global financial system, being fuelled by the loss of investors' and buyers' confidence in the quality of ABSs and in high-quality commercial papers, respectively, leading to an unprecedented drying-out of liquidity in the interbank market.[27] Packages of securities whose performance is tied to sub-prime mortgages have suffered unanticipated losses,[28] and as some originators went out of business and secondary markets were disrupted, institutions along the chain found themselves facing unexpected exposures from warehousing or financing the holding of loans before securitisation.[29] The impact of the dramatic widening of spreads on the riskier tranches of securitised sub-prime loans is difficult to quantify, though. A contagion effect can also adversely hit securitised loans of higher quality and may drive institutions, which are dependent on such instruments, to face a cessation of funding in the interbank market.[30] The consequences of such situations can escalate and cause a bank run.[31] Such severe 'stress scenarios' could entail large spillovers which pose a real threat to global financial stability and the real economy.

Risks Inherent in Credit Derivative Transactions

While risks can be dispersed in the financial system through the use of credit derivative instruments, credit derivatives entail a number of risks inherent in their nature. If improperly managed and priced, these risks may offset the benefits associated with credit derivatives.

1. *Counterparty credit risk* This is typically seen to be the most severe risk inherent in CDS transactions because the transactions are generally not funded. Measuring counterparty credit risk may prove to be complicated because of its two-way nature. In other words, the net exposure between two institutions involved in a CDS transaction may change with market price fluctuations and either party may become a net defaulter. A simple measure of counterparty credit risk is the current exposure, which is the net exposure at current market value. A more comprehensive measure is potential future exposure, defined as the maximum amount to which an exposure could grow over a future time period with a high degree of statistical confidence in case markets move against the counterparty. An additional issue that can arise when evaluating counterparty credit risk and the value of credit protection provided by all CRT instruments relates to the potential correlation between an underlying reference entity and the protection seller. This is referred to as 'wrong way risk'. Wrong way risk is highest when a perfect correlation between the reference entity and the protection seller exists – this is the case when the credit derivatives are sold by the reference entities themselves.

   The involved contractual parties may limit their counterparty credit risk exposures by using collateral agreements. However, systemic concerns remain, in particular in a crisis situation when credit risks are transmitted easily from one institution to another due to inter-linkages between credit exposures.

   The growth of unregulated hedge fund activities may exacerbate this danger in a crisis situation. Hedge funds managed an estimated

US$1,426 trillion in assets at the end of 2006, corresponding to over 700 per cent more than in 1995.[32] To a considerable extent, their activities consist in investments in CRT instruments. Initially, hedge funds participated primarily as protection buyers in the CDS market in order to take advantage of a lower-cost alternative to build up short positions in corporate bonds. More recently, their participation has broadened and now encompasses a wider variety of trading strategies and approaches that involve selling as well as buying protection (see Table 10.4).

Ever since the 'almost' collapse of Long Term Capital Management (LTCM) in 1998, regulators have showed interest in regulating hedge fund activities. Industry and financial supervisors agreed that excessive leverage and poor counterparty credit risk management as practiced by banks and other creditors raised concerns that market players seeking to sell large positions simultaneously could have negatively affected asset prices widely across markets, indirectly affecting other market participants such as mutual and pension funds. However, until now the hedge fund industry remains largely unregulated[33] and concerns about systemic risk associated with hedge fund activities in the CRT markets seem to rise steadily.

2. *Market liquidity risk* In addition to direct counterparty risks inherent in credit derivative transactions, there are indirect risks associated with a decline in asset market liquidity resulting from the failure or winding down of a major financial institution. A particular concern is that, in illiquid markets, market participants may be forced to sell positions to meet margin requirements (this is most imminent for hedge funds), thereby driving down market prices. In some severe cases, this may make it necessary for other market participants to sell their positions, which might eventually dry out liquidity. Such 'liquidity black holes' have diverse causes. When counterparties have concentrated positions, losses on these positions are more likely to lead to substantial decline in liquidity. According to a BIS survey (2005a), market participants noted that, particularly within the CDS market, liquidity varies widely between the first 50 to 200 and other reference entities, the former being substantially more liquid than the latter. Most importantly, it was indicated that there is liquidity in the CDS market even for reference entities that are close to default. However, severe market shocks, such as the default of a very large reference entity or a major market maker would certainly adversely affect liquidity in the CDS market.
3. *Documentation and legal risk* This risk can be defined as the risk that the legal effect of a transaction is different from what the involved

parties understand it to be. It is due to the relatively unrestricted range and scope of credit events covered by the instruments, poorly defined contract terms and the inappropriate identification of reference entities.

One case of legal documentation risk resulting from a CDS transaction arises when participants have a contractual relationship with the wrong legal entity. For example, as reported by the BIS (2005b), two major market participants entered into CDS contracts specifying the holding company of Armstrong World Industries as the reference entity. However, this legal entity did not have any debt outstanding and could thus not default, even though one of its subsidiaries went bankrupt. In other cases, there has been confusion between the buyer and the seller of the CDS regarding the specific legal entity on which the CDS was written. Documentation and legal risks were partly overcome by major market-making firms who commissioned the development of a common database of reference entities (RED) as well as a process to scrub the names which do not meet appropriate guidelines.

4. *Operational risk* This risk stems from operational shortcomings due to a rapid growth in trading volumes and the ever-increasing complexity of new products. Concerns were voiced over the mounting backlog of unconfirmed trades, the management of trade reassignments, and the weaknesses of settlement procedures. The backlog of unconfirmed trades may reflect inadequate investments in back-office capacity by the major market participants in recent years. With the entry of hedge funds as active traders on the scene, the issue of delays and/or incorrect notification procedures for reassignments of credit derivative contracts is likely to increase even further.
5. *Mispricing risk* Pricing models for credit derivatives are still at an early stage of development.[34] According to the BIS (2003), there is no generally accepted pricing model for credit derivatives and most of the existing models do not account for the true risks inherent in these transactions. In practice, this has resulted in oversimplistic approaches to assess the actual risk profile associated with CRT transactions (Duffie, 2007). A severe problem arises when market participants underestimate the actual risk profile of a CRT transaction and take on more risk than would be desirable. For instance, if credit risks were systematically wrongly priced, this would lead to a misallocation of resources in terms of capital efficiency. Price distortions may put the protection buyer at a disadvantage *vis-à-vis* the protection seller because he/she might have to pay an excess premium when prices are set too high and do not properly reflect the underlying risk. In practice it is very difficult

to investigate whether premiums on credit derivatives are appropriately set because it is not possible to observe the 'true' underlying credit risk and thus the amount of the 'correct', that is the fair, premium. The recent financial turmoil provides clear evidence of pricing weaknesses of credit derivatives and particularly synthetic CDOs. Rating agencies are believed to have provided adequate approximations for the underlying risk in CRT transactions. However, the evolving level of complexity of credit derivative instruments requires a serious revisiting of the rating agencies and other participants' risk assessment models. Last but not least, mispricing risks are also exacerbated by the inadequate knowledge of new market participants (for example, newly set up hedge funds) who lack experience in estimating and pricing default risk.

6. *Risks related to incentive problems* As discussed in Section 3 (see Figure 10.4), when credit risk is transferred by means of a credit derivative, the incentive structure of the underlying transaction is altered. The new incentives may lead to behaviours that could harm financial stability. In fact, it is often argued that using credit derivatives reduces incentives of lenders to screen borrowers and monitor credit quality because they transfer the credit risk in the case of synthetic securitisation and/or the asset in the case of fully funded CLNs away from the balance sheet to a third party. While facing less monitoring, the debtor may tend to behave in a way that threatens repayment of the loan. The generalisation of this behaviour may be detrimental to the overall economy. The severity of this problem relates closely to the extent to which the protection buyer is required to bear parts of the costs in the case of a credit event. However, the results of academic research analysing this potential moral hazard problem are not unambiguous; hence we abstain from passing final judgment on this issue.

   In practice, payment difficulties do not lead to a full default but only to a restructuring of the reference debt. The lender has fewer incentives in the case of a restructuring to seek a solution that is also acceptable for the debtor when a CDS on the reference entity exists. This implies that the lender may agree on terms that are disadvantageous for the debtor. The incentives crucially hinge on the chosen type of settlement. In the case of a physical settlement, the reference asset is transferred to the protection seller when a credit event occurs. The seller thus has an interest in ensuring that the company is restructured. While the problem of the altered incentive structure between the original lender and the reference debtor is not solved, a new, potentially functioning creditor–debtor relationship is created in which the protection seller is the new creditor. In the case of a cash settlement, the protection buyer receives the difference between the face value of the debt and its current market value from the seller. There are probably far fewer incentives in these cases for the protection buyer to work together with the debtor to agree on a way to restructure that is in the interest of both of them. If the protection buyer were to act opportunistically, he/she might even have an incentive to deliberately provoke a restructuring (for example, by refusing to grant further loans). As settlement is in cash he/she would suffer no loss from the restructuring, but rather have an incentive to negotiate the highest possible repayment later from the reference entity. This is because the cash settlement is based on the market value of the debt at a fixed point in time after the credit event, whereas the amount of the debt to be repaid to the protection buyer may be agreed upon at a later date.

All in all, our opinion is that the use of credit derivatives could improve the overall stability of the financial system if and only if the risks inherent in these transactions are properly measured and managed by all market participants.

5 REGULATION OF CREDIT DERIVATIVE MARKETS

It is sometimes argued that the emergence and development of derivative markets result from unintended consequences of government intervention (Miller, 1986). In fact, a large part of the early activity in derivative markets was motivated by regulatory arbitrage (ibid.). For instance, one key trigger for the global derivative market growth was the adoption of the Futures Trading Practice Act of 1992 in the US. This act fostered legal certainty in the derivative market and allowed the Commodity Futures Trading Commission (CFTC) to exempt OTC contracts from Commodity Exchange Act (CEA) regulation, which formerly was an obstacle for the growth of derivative trading. As laid down in Bergman et al. (2003), derivatives are subject to special protections during insolvency resolution, which tend to disproportionately favour creditors to the detriment of debtors. This gives banks incentives to outlay risks on their balance sheets by means of credit derivative transactions.

The one-size-fits-all, fairly simplistic 1988 Basel Accord, under which all bank assets were assigned a standardised risk weight for the calculation of the regulatory capital, motivated risk transfer activities and promoted regulatory arbitrage because of the capital requirement structure. Banks were intended to reduce their riskier portfolio holdings by complying with the regulatory framework, yet instead of low-risk assets they primarily sold high-risk assets to the market. This has led to increased securitization activity in order to achieve a more-efficient allocation of regulatory capital. However, credit derivative activity remained largely unregulated.

The growth and the complexity of required documentation associated with credit derivative transactions encouraged market participants to define their own terms and conditions. These self-regulatory initiatives, which could also be seen as market discipline, sought the standardization of credit derivative transactions while at the same time accommodating the instruments' inherent complexity. In the early days of credit derivative activity, market participants documented CDSs using individually developed confirmations within an International Swaps and Derivatives Association (ISDA) Master Documentation Framework. This created problems in negotiating transactions because the used confirmations differed heavily between the market participants. Delays in confirming and documenting transactions became problematic. The standardisation efforts of CDS contracts undertaken by the ISDA arose out of a process of consultation with the market participants, which led to the establishment of the first (standardised) documentation of 1999 followed by a second one in 2003. The review and standardisation process profited largely from the painful lessons learnt from the Russian[35] and Argentine[36] debt crises in 1998 and 2002. In particular, a more precise definition of what constitutes a credit event was worked out.

All efforts of the ISDA and market participants since 1998 have produced a fairly robust documentation determining the rights and obligations of credit derivative transactions. Despite these efforts, documentation, legal and operational risks still prevail and need to be continuously addressed by market participants and monitored by national regulators, particularly in light of the increasing role of hedge funds in credit derivative markets. Clearly, the role of market participants is important to reduce these risks. As rightly recommended by the Basel Committee on Banking Supervision in its report on CRT in March 2005,

> [A]ll market participants need to continue paying careful attention to the legal documentation relating to credit derivatives, such as the range of credit events covered by the instruments and the clear and unambiguous identification of the underlying reference. Standardization should also continue in a market where innovative financial instruments are mushrooming. Moreover, there is a need for market participants to encourage due diligence necessary to clearly identify their legal responsibilities to the counterparty or customer. It is crucial to foster further transparency when marketing structured and complex CRT products. Originators and dealers should foster a complete understanding of the nature and material terms, conditions and risks involved and should not solely rely on external ratings as a measure of risk associated with the transaction. Before

> entering in a CRT transaction, investors should ensure their capacity both on the outset and on an ongoing basis to obtain the necessary information to properly evaluate and manage the risks associated with their investment. Information on the risk profile of the investment should be accessible to them on a continuous basis . . .. (BIS, 2005a, pp. 7–8)

To reduce operational risk stemming from backlogs of unconfirmed trades and the management of trade reassignments, called 'novations',[37] and the weaknesses of settlement procedures, market participants already monitor the developments individually and at the industry level (ISDA, 2007). However, they should take further measures such as ensuring that credit derivative activity is undertaken by reputed professionals with the appropriate experience, skill levels and degree of specialisation and risk management systems' sophistication.

However, industry self-regulation has important downsides, as most regulatory efforts will necessarily foster the interests of the major market participants. Concerns have been raised as to whether ISDA's development of standardised documents actually created informational asymmetries and negative externalities (Partnoy, 2002). In particular, it seems clear that the major market makers represented through ISDA have no incentives to promote broader disclosure, as this would imply a loss of their informational advantage (Gottlieb, 2007). Moreover, given ISDA's monopoly position in formulating legal contracts and setting industry standards, these might be biased towards ISDA's largest stakeholders, that is, dealers. This implies that contractual frameworks established by the ISDA could have a pure dealer to dealer focus, which might go to the detriment of the end-users.[38] Consequently, end-users might have reduced incentives to participate in OTC derivative markets. Therefore, the industry-led self-regulatory measures may not suffice to ensure the stability of the market. They should thus be complemented by adequate regulatory and supervisory actions.

ISDA documentations and financial institutions' risk management systems continue to form the 'first line of defence' against the risks inherent in using credit derivatives. In addition, international regulators have been carefully watching the market developments, and provided recommendations to foster the transparency in the markets[39] as well as guidance on sound risk management of derivative activities (BIS, 2005a). A first step subsequent to the revision of the 1988 Capital Accord was taken in 1995 with the amendment of the treatment of market risk, introducing specific risk capital charges for positions hedged by credit derivatives (BIS, 1995). One of the main impacts of this amendment was the migration of the credit risk from the banking book to the trading book.

Although international regulators agreed on a set of prudential provisions for credit derivatives, national practices continued to differ, particularly as to whether these instruments are classified in the banking or trading book. In order to close the gap between supervisory requirements and credit derivative market developments and to ensure consistency in supervisory practices, the new capital adequacy guidelines issued by the Basel Committee for Banking Supervision (known as Basel II) in June 2004 (BIS, 2004) defined clearer and more sophisticated risk-sensitive provisions on risk mitigation techniques including credit derivatives – regardless of whether they are included in the trading or banking book. The new guidelines introduced extensive operational requirements for credit derivatives, ranging from eligibility criteria for protection sellers to an extensive list of credit events. A prudentially sound treatment of counterparty credit risk inherent in OTC derivatives and for double-default effects of covered transactions were also introduced in the new regulatory framework. Therefore, such regulatory framework is expected to improve the incentives for undertaking efficient CRT transactions. However, adjustments in regulatory capital standards for default correlation,[40] or at least granularity, seem to need further improvements.

The effectiveness of the Basel II guidelines with regard to credit derivative activity will crucially hinge on financial institutions' efforts to limit potential losses through setting the appropriate incentive structure for adequate risk management systems, including the use of stress tests. The latter, in particular, allow them to ascertain and appropriately limit their market and counterparty exposures in scenarios in which credit spreads widen rapidly and asset market liquidity decreases markedly as was the case in the recent sub-prime loan crisis.

National supervisors should focus on two priorities to ensure the success of their supervisory review and intervention: risk management and financial infrastructure.

With regard to risk management, supervisors will have to equip themselves with adequate analytical tools to understand and evaluate 'tail' events, that is, events that materialise with a low probability but a high impact. Supervisory efforts and need for resources are likely to increase with the complexity and the illiquidity of some financial instruments, the opacity of some counterparties (hedge funds), the rapidity with which large positions can change, and the potential feedback effects associated with leveraged positions. Stress testing and scenario analysis are central to the process of risk management.[41]

With regard to the financial infrastructure, national supervisors should ensure that clearing and settlement arrangements on which core institutions and other participants depend are safe and efficient. Weaknesses in such systems can be sources of systemic risks. The benefits of such supervisory initiatives can extend beyond the core regulated institutions themselves because improvements in their counterparty risk management practices will strengthen market discipline for their unregulated counterparties such as hedge funds.

International supervisors should also cooperate and coordinate their actions. A good example is the cooperation that the Federal Reserve Bank of New York, other prudential supervisors and industry representatives have entered into recently to encourage and support market participants' progress in addressing what were serious weaknesses in the infrastructure of the credit derivative markets. These supervisors are currently reviewing the core firms' management of counterparty exposures to hedge funds and other highly leveraged transaction partners (Federal Reserve Bank of New York, 2007). In particular, it is important to highlight that hedge funds and other institutional investors tend to rely on the ratings of structured credit products including CDOs when making investment decisions. Methodologies for rating CDOs, however, are still in their infancy, for instance correlation parameters used in ratings models tend to be based on rudimentary assumptions.[42]

All in all, there are good reasons to think that financial innovations over the past few decades, including the emergence and growth of the credit derivative markets, have increased the perception that financial systems are becoming more resilient. This perception may be true if:

1. inherent risks of credit derivatives are accurately measured and priced by all market participants;
2. financial institutions including hedge funds are armed with adequate risk management frameworks;
3. heterogeneity of investors' behaviours and risk appetite are preserved to ensure market liquidity; and
4. regulators are adequately equipped (early actions – stress testing) to face crisis situations, without increasing moral hazard.

However, in reality these innovations may not have eliminated systemic risk, and experience (recall the cases of LTCM, the Argentine crisis and others) has shown the weaknesses of derivative pricing and financial institutions' risk management frameworks, the incapacity to control aggressive investors' behaviours and the out-datedness of regulatory actions. The latest episode of the US sub-prime lending market is a vivid illustration of market disruptions leading to market liquidity dry-ups which forced central banks from both sides of the Atlantic to inject billions of dollars into the capital markets – together with the absence of effective early regulatory actions – that could jeopardise global financial stability practically overnight.

In this chapter, we argue in favour of a hybrid regulatory system that relies on market discipline and regulatory oversight, although we do not claim to know what exactly is the optimal mix between market self-regulation and policy initiatives. We rather argue that further market and regulatory measures should be taken to ensure a more viable financial system where credit derivatives are traded efficiently. These are:

1. Need for continuous promotion of market standards and mitigation of legal, documentation, operational, pricing and incentives-related risks.
2. Need to increase transparency of credit derivative markets – clear principles and guidelines should serve as a basis towards the construction of an adequate transparency framework.
3. Regulators are urged to produce a global regulatory framework for liquidity management and to enhance their capabilities in terms of scenario and stress testing.
4. Basel II provisions for counterparty risk and double default should be adequately enforced and if necessary strengthened.
5. Given the hedge funds' growing influence in the global financial markets and the potential systemic risk they pose, a code of practice – to enhance transparency of hedge funds' activities particularly in credit derivative markets and give them the right incentives to strengthen their risk management abilities – seems to be necessary at this stage.

The implementation of these measures will require strong regulatory efforts (and resources) and a great deal of international harmonisation and it remains to be seen whether the increasing activity on credit derivative markets fosters or harms the stability of financial systems across the globe.

NOTES

1. CLNs are designed to enable investors to capture returns on a single reference entity (underlying bond or loan).
2. Credit spread products are options or forwards on the credit spread of bonds, loans or other credit assets. These instruments allow the separate trading of the credit spread for the purpose of risk reduction, speculation or return enhancement.
3. CDO is the generic term used for credit portfolio securitisation. It entails repackaging credit portfolios (loans/bonds and/or derivatives) for sale to investors, hence, it can be described as a combination of a fixed income security with an embedded credit derivative.
4. In March 2003 the *Financial Times* quoted Warren Buffett as follows: 'Derivatives are financial weapons of mass destruction, carrying dangers that, while now latent, are potentially lethal to the financial system'. In a letter to the shareholders of his company

Berkshire Hathaway, Inc., he added: 'derivatives are wildly mispriced, but continue to generate hundreds of millions of dollars'. This quote nicely reflects the fear of (some) market participants and observers that credit derivatives threaten the stability of financial systems.

5. Although the market volume figures vary from source to source (Fitch, ISDA, British Bankers' Association) they all show the same trend of a continued rapid growth. The variation is due to the fact that most stylized facts stem from surveys and survey participants vary markedly from source to source.
6. According to recent figures, the aggregate European CDO issuance hit US$46.8 billion in 2005, reflecting an increase of 85.6 per cent from the US$25.3 billion issued in 2004.
7. This subsection draws on Rule (2001), Das (2005) and Mengle (2007).
8. According to the Bank for International Settlements (BIS, 1998) replacement cost risk is the risk that a default of a counterparty will require the non-defaulting counterparty to incur a cost to replace the contract or a portfolio of contracts.
9. A synthetic securitisation is a structured transaction that involves the transfer of risk on a portfolio of assets through a CDS or a CLN. The originating bank packages more than 10 reference loan entities into a portfolio product. The package is subsequently sold to an independent special purpose vehicle (SPV) formed for the specific purpose of funding the loans. The SPV is a separate company and must not be owned by the originator. In a classical or cash securitisation transaction, the SPV issues tradable securities to fund its purchase of the loan portfolio from the originator. The performance of these securities is directly linked to the performance of the loan portfolio. The securities are then sold to investors. In a synthetic securitisation transaction, a CDS on the reference portfolio is created between the originating bank and the SPV. The originating bank pays a premium to the SPV and in the case of a credit event the SPV ensures the default payment to the originating bank.
10. The characteristics of this transaction type are the following: (i) only credit risk is transferred, (ii) assets remain on the balance sheet, and (iii) there is no generated funding.
11. More details on CDO design can be found in Duffie (2007).
12. CDX is a brand name for the family of CDS index products covering North America and emerging markets. They are owned, managed, compiled and published by Markit Group Limited, the leading industry source of independent pricing, reference data and valuations.
13. iTraxx is the brand name for the family of CDS index products covering European and Asian markets. These indices were launched in 2004 in conjunction with a consortium of leading global investment banks. The rules-based indices comprise the most liquid entities in the European and Asian credit markets, and consist of iTraxx Europe, iTraxx Hivol, iTraxx Crossover, iTraxx Asia ex-Japan, iTraxx Japan, iTraxx Australia, iTraxx SDI-75, and various sub-indices. The iTraxx indices were owned, managed, compiled and published by International Index Company (IIC), a leading independent provider of credit derivative and fixed income indices that also licenses market makers. In April 2006, IIC and Markit announced that they had signed an agreement governing the calculation and publication of IIC's iTraxx indices, the benchmark for the European and Asian credit markets.
14. Leading market participants recognised the need for documentation standardisation and worked with the ISDA to develop a standard documentation format for CDS, the so-called 'ISDA Master Agreement'. The first attempt to standardise documentation resulted in the development of the confirmation for an OTC credit swap transaction (single-reference entity, non-sovereign). This confirmation, entitled the Long Form Documentation, was published in 1998. However, the structure of this document was very complex and caused delays and misunderstandings among market participants. It therewith increased the risk of operational errors. In July 1999, the ISDA published a revised standard documentary framework for privately negotiated CDSs. The revised format consisted of (i) a standard definition for CDSs (the 1999 Definition); and (ii) a shorter confirmation for individual CDSs, the so-called 'short form' confirmation. In

2002, the ISDA reviewed the 1999 credit definitions, and in February 2003 it adopted the new credit derivatives definitions.

15. We shall henceforth use the terms 'CRT transaction' and 'credit derivative transaction' interchangeably as credit risk is usually transferred by means of a credit derivative transaction.
16. The survey further reported that small German public banks – the so-called 'Sparkassen' – often act as protection sellers. Sparkassen are geographically restricted with regard to their loan business. They are allowed to do business only in the very region where they are operating. For such banks the only way to geographically diversify their loan portfolio is to participate in CRT transactions. These enable them to include credit risks in their portfolios to which they would otherwise not have access.
17. Diamond (1984) was the first to point out the delegated monitoring role of banks.
18. Note, however, that the academic literature analysing this issue is not unambiguous with regard to the impact of CRT on the monitoring efforts of the loan originator.
19. According to Wagner and Marsh (2006), 'The diversification it brings about reduces the risk premiums required by financial institutions for financing firms, which lowers firms financing costs and increases output in the economy'. However, they point out that the main limit of CRT activities is the decrease of banks' incentives to monitor their borrowers.
20. For instance, the premiums for CDSs are now an important indicator of an enterprise's or even a bank's credit quality.
21. A discussion of the information content of CDS index tranches for financial stability is provided in ECB (2006).
22. But, as the IMF (2006, p. 66) points out: 'However, once transferred, secondary market liquidity risks remain, and may constitute the most significant stability risks emanating from the structured credit markets'.
23. Through a traditional fully funded credit linked note (CLN).
24. Through synthetic securitization, for instance.
25. However, Wagner (2007) showed that the benefits of increased liquidity through risk transfers in good times and enhanced power of liquidation in a crisis are counterbalanced by hefty increases in banks' risk taking. Overall, stability is reduced because the enhanced liquidation in a crisis reduces banks' incentives to avoid a crisis. Banks therefore take on an amount of new risk that leads to a higher probability of default.
26. As pointed out in Duffie (2007, p. 4), 'Even specialists in collateralized debt obligations (CDOs) are currently ill equipped to measure the risks and fair valuation of tranches that are sensitive to default correlation. This is currently the weakest link in CRT markets, which could suffer a dramatic loss of liquidity in the event of a sudden failure of a large specialty investor or a surprise cluster of corporate defaults'.
27. A discussion on the US sub-prime mortgage loan problems spillover to CRT markets is provided in ECB (2007).
28. These securities may include risky CDO tranches. Such assets can be particularly illiquid and vulnerable to macroeconomic performance and may be used as an argument against credit risk transfer by banks.
29. A vivid example is the near collapse of the German IKB Bank which suffered heavy losses due to the US sub-prime crisis. Only with the help of the mostly government-owned Kreditanstalt für Wiederaufbau and some other public and private German banks, which together injected more than €8 billion into IKB, could the collapse be averted.
30. The key dependency of the UK's mortgage bank Northern Rock was its use of securitisation although that was based on high-quality assets. The market disruption did not affect the bank's existing securitised assets but, due to the liquidity crisis, the market for new issuances had largely dried out.
31. On September 13, Northern Rock actually experienced a bank run 'obliging' the UK government to intervene by safeguarding depositors and change their previous stance

about the adverse impact (increasing moral hazard and sowing seeds for future financial crisis) of bailing out risky behaviours of aggressive lenders.

32. Figure taken from Hedge funds research, Inc., www.hedgefundresearch.com, 27 August 2007.
33. An industry-led UK initiative to regulate hedge funds is underway. A hedge fund working group headed by Andrew Large, former deputy governor of the Bank of England, will look at existing principles, standards and guidelines, will evaluate areas that may require strengthening and will suggest workable solutions that may include voluntary adherence to voluntary standards.
34. There are two basic ways to determine a CDS spread, namely, from asset swap spreads and from the calculation of expected CDS cash flows.
35. On 17 August 1998, the Russian government announced the restructuring of its sovereign bond debt and suspended transactions on those securities. In response to this announcement, the foreign currency-denominated external debt depreciated strongly, in spite of the fact that it had not been ascertained that Russia would also default on this asset class. The diverse nature of Russia's debt highlighted the gaps in the existing documentation covering CDS contracts. The complex structure of Russia's debt and the litigation arising from it prompted the ISDA to tighten up certain aspects of their documentation. More specific details were included regarding the issuer's identity, subordination clauses and the creditor's status.
36. Following the moratorium on Argentina's external debt declared on 23 December 2001, the settlement of CDS contracts did not encounter many difficulties given that at mid-February 2002, 95 per cent of outstanding CDS contracts had been settled. Nonetheless, the settlement of CDS in this context provided an opportunity to define contracts more precisely with regard to three main aspects: (i) definition of a credit event: debt swaps executed on a voluntary basis were no longer considered as credit events. Protection buyers wanted to include in the moratorium the exchange of debt that had taken place in November 2001, arguing that it constituted a restructuring linked to the default; (ii) definition of deliverables: zero-coupon bonds that satisfy the criterion of non-contingence were accepted as deliverables; and (iii) option of partial cash settlement: partial cash settlement was permitted when the protection buyer is unable, either out of technical or legal reasons, to deliver securities.
37. To reduce backlogs, the ISDA completed a solution known as the ISDA Novations Protocol in 2005.
38. In fact, within the ISDA, end-users have no voting rights. Consequently their role in policy making is marginal.
39. Among the initiatives, in February 1995 a working group established by the central banks of the group of 10 countries published a report on macro-prudential risks from derivative activity. They mainly recommended enhancing the transparency in the market by expanding national central banks' data collection efforts consistently across countries. In 1996, they published concrete proposals to improve and enhance data collection of global derivative markets. In 1998, another report on the settlement procedures and counterparty credit risk management in OTC derivatives recommended prudential supervisors to review the backlogs and associated risks at institutions they supervise (especially derivative dealers), to assess the effectiveness of the institutions' policies and procedures for limiting the associated risks, and to encourage improvements in practices where appropriate. The report also urged supervisors to develop supervisory guidance on the use of collateral as a means of reducing credit risk, including guidance on operational risks and on legal due diligence and to take action where necessary to reduce legal uncertainty about the enforceability of collateral agreements. (For more details on the sequence of regulatory initiatives, see www.bis.org.)
40. Default correlation across a pool of loans forming the collateral of a CDO can have a significant impact on the risks and market values of individual CDO tranches. Currently, the weakest link in the risk measurement and pricing of CDOs is the modelling of default correlation. There is relatively little emphasis in practice on data or

analysis bearing on default correlation. When valuing a CDO, somewhat arbitrary 'copula' default correlation models are typically calibrated to the observed prices of CDS-index tranches, a class of derivatives that behave much like CDOs. See Duffie (2007).

41. These tools are expected to capture, on a high frequency basis, the full exposure of the firm to a sufficiently broad range of adverse conditions, the aggregate exposure to specific types of different risk factors and types of counterparties, the potential interactions among those factors, the effects of a general loss of liquidity and confidence in markets, and the constraints on the ability of the firm to move to reduce its exposure to further losses.
42. For example, treating all pairs of names within a given industrial sector as if they have the same default correlation, and treating all pairs of names not within the same industrial sector as if they have the same default correlation. See Duffie (2007).

REFERENCES

Arping, S. (2005), 'Credit protection and lending relationships', Working Paper, University of Amsterdam.

Bank for International Settlements (BIS) (1995), 'Issues of Measurements Related to Market Size and Macro-prudential Risks in Derivatives Markets', Report prepared by a working group established by the central banks of the Group of Ten countries, Basel, February.

Bank for International Settlements (BIS) (1998), 'OTC Derivatives: Settlement Procedures and Counterparty Risk Management', Report prepared by the Committee on Payment and Settlement Systems and the Euro-currency Standing Committee of the central banks of the Group of Ten countries, Basel, September.

Bank for International Settlements (BIS) (2003), 'Credit Risk Transfer', Report prepared by the Committee on the Global Financial System, Basel, January.

Bank for International Settlements (BIS) (2004), 'Basel II: International Convergence of Capital Measurement and Capital Standards: A Revised Framework', Basel Committee on Banking Supervision, Basel, June.

Bank for International Settlements (BIS) (2005a), 'Credit Risk Transfer', Basel Committee on Banking Supervision, Joint Forum, Basel, March.

Bank for International Settlements (BIS) (2005b), 'The Application of Basel II to Trading Activities and Treatment of Double Default', Basel Committee on Banking Supervision, Basel, July.

Bergman, W.J., R.R. Bliss, C.A. Johnson and G.G. Kaufman (2003), 'Netting, financial contracts, and banks: the economic implications', in G. Kaufman (ed.), *Research in Financial Services*, Vol. 15, *Market Discipline in Banking: Theory and Evidence*, Amsterdam: Elsevier.

British Bankers' Association (2006), 'Credit Derivatives Report 2006', London, September.

Chiesa, G. (2006), 'Risk transfer, lending capacity, and real investment activity', Working Paper, University of Bologna.

Das, S. (2005), *Credit Derivatives, CDO and Structured Credit Products*, 3rd edn, New York: Wiley Finance.

DeMarzo, P. and D. Duffie (1999), 'A liquidity-based model of security design', *Econometrica*, **67** (1), 65–99.

Diamond, D. (1984), 'Financial intermediation and delegated monitoring', *Review of Economic Studies*, **51**, 393–414.

Duffee, G.R. and C. Zhou (2001), 'Credit derivatives in banking: useful tools for managing risk?', *Journal of Monetary Economics*, **48**, 25–54.

Duffie, D. (2007), 'Innovations in credit risk transfer: implications for financial stability', Working Paper, Stanford University.

Durbin, M.P. (2006), *All About Derivatives*, New York: McGraw-Hill.

European Central Bank (2004), 'Credit Risk Transfer by EU Banks: Activities, Risks and Risk Management', Frankfurt am Main, May.

European Central Bank (2006), 'Financial Stability Review', Frankfurt am Main, December.

European Central Bank (2007), 'Financial Stability Review', Frankfurt am Main, June.

Federal Reserve Bank of New York (2007), 'Statement Regarding progress in credit derivatives markets', September.

Fitch Ratings (2003), 'Global Credit Derivatives: A Qualified Success', Special Report, New York, September.

Fitch Ratings (2004), 'Global Credit Derivatives Survey: Single-Name CDS Fuel Growth', Special Report, New York, September.

Fitch Ratings (2005), 'Global Credit Derivatives Survey: Risk Dispersion Accelerates', Special Report, New York, November.

Fitch Ratings (2006), 'Global Credit Derivatives Survey: Indices Dominate Growth as Banks' Risk Position Shifts', Special Report, New York, September.

Franke, G. and J.P. Krahnen (2007), 'Default risk sharing between banks and markets: the case of collateralized debt obligation', in M. Carey and R. Stulz (eds), *Risks of Financial Institutions*, National Bureau of Economic Research, Chicago, IL: Chicago University Press, pp. 603–34.

Gorton, G.B. and G. Pennacchi (1995), 'Banks and loan sales: marketing nonmarketable assets', *Journal of Monetary Economics*, **35**, 389–411.

Gottlieb, C. (2007), 'Derivative markets: background note for CEPS', Harvard Law School Symposium, Louveciennes, 29–31 March.

International Monetary Fund (IMF) (2006), 'The Influence of Credit Derivative and Structured Credit Markets on Financial Stability', Global Financial Stability Report, Chapter II, Washington, DC, April.

International Swaps and Derivatives Association (ISDA) (2007), 'Annual Operations Benchmarking Survey', www.isda.org.

Marsh, I. and W. Wagner (2006), 'Credit risk transfer and financial sector stability', *Journal of Financial Stability*, **2**, 173–93.

Mengle, D. (2007), 'Credit derivatives: an overview', paper presented at the ISDA 2007 Financial Markets Conference, Federal Reserve Bank of Atlanta, 15 May.

Miller, M. (1986), 'Financial innovation: the last twenty years and the next', *Journal of Financial and Quantitative Analysis*, **21**, 459–71.

Miller, M. (1991), *Financial Innovations and Market Volatility*, Oxford: Blackwell.

Morrison, A.D. (2005), 'Credit derivatives, disintermediation and investment decisions', *Journal of Business*, **78**, 621–47.

Partnoy, F. (2002), 'ISDA, NASD, CFMA, and SDNY: the four horsemen of derivatives regulation', *Brookings–Wharton Papers on Financial Services 2002*, 213–52.

Rule, D. (2001), 'The credit derivative market: its development and possible implications for financial stability', Bank of England, Financial Stability Review, London, June.
Wagner, W. (2007), 'The liquidity of bank assets and banking stability', *Journal of Banking and Finance*, **31**, 121–39.
Wagner, W. and I.W. Marsh (2006), 'Credit risk transfer and financial sector stability', *Journal of Financial Stability*, **2** (2), 173–93.

11. Innovation in trading activity: should stock markets be more transparent?*

Caterina Lucarelli, Camilla Mazzoli and Merlin Rothfeld**

1 INTRODUCTION

Direct access trading (DAT) represents one of the most important financial innovations in the last 20 years related to stock market activity. DAT gives market participants direct access to the stock exchanges, in terms of submissions of orders and, above all, in terms of the amount of information available directly and in real time. These main features make DAT particularly suitable for short-term (or intraday) traders, as their economic results can be strongly linked to the speed of their order execution and to the available real-time information. In fact, DAT platforms give traders the possibility of displaying in their order books information about buying and selling orders (pre-trade transparency: PTT) and about trades (post-trade transparency). In this study we shall focus on PTT and its three main dimensions: (i) the identification of the trader who sends the order to the market (level 1 of PTT, or PTT1), (ii) the desegregation of price levels (or PTT2) and (iii) the number of price levels displayed in the order book (or PTT3).

From an international perspective, the pre-trade information *actually* disclosed may differ significantly within stock exchanges and this information also depends upon the typology of the traders to which it is disclosed (for example, retail or institutional traders). In fact, the general DAT infrastructure is made up of a chain of interconnections between market authorities and participants (data vendors, institutional traders and retail traders). Nevertheless, each national market shows different barriers that customise these interconnections and may interfere with the complete disclosure of the pre-trade information for DAT users. We refer to regulatory barriers and commercial barriers.

Regulatory barriers deal with the institutional choices of local authorities concerning the discipline of their domestic stock markets. In some cases, even if the platforms of stock exchanges technically allow a high level of PTT, in practice local authorities may restrain its full application. Commercial barriers increase the complexity of the relationship between market authorities and participants. The general rules are: (i) whoever has information requires an economic reward (fee) in order to distribute it, (ii) the available information is broken up and packaged into different samples of data services with specific fee structures, and (iii) samples of data services are created and sold by each market operator (stock exchange and data vendors) according to their customers' requests and to their competitors' offers.

Depending upon the attitude of the stock exchange authorities within a stock market, as well as the complexity of DAT infrastructure, these regulatory and commercial barriers can be strengthened or weakened. As a consequence, the use of a financial and technological innovation, such as DAT, can be limited in serving its best role.

This chapter describes the DAT financial innovation and depicts how PTT is disclosed in various stock exchanges. Stronger or weaker barriers in different stock markets determine different PTT dimensions and levels of pre-trade global information. The aim of the chapter is to test whether different PTT levels are able to affect the *volatility* and *liquidity* of a stock exchange. Much research carried out over the last few years has attempted to describe these relationships, yet their empirical results have sometimes contradicted one another (see Section 2). Nevertheless, the innovative contribution of this chapter is to study, on a large international scale and through a wide set of indicators, each of the three different PTT dimensions (specifically PTT1, PTT2 and PTT3) in relation to liquidity, on the one hand, and to volatility, on the other. Our attention is focused upon the equity division of the following 18 stock exchanges: the Hong Kong Stock Exchange, the Singapore Stock Exchange, the Australian Stock Exchange, the Toronto Stock Exchange, the New York Stock Exchange (NYSE), the NASDAQ, the American Stock Exchange (AMEX), the London Stock Exchange, Euronext (Paris, Amsterdam, Brussels and Lisbon), Deutsche Bourse (Xetra), the Madrid Stock Exchange, Borsa Italia, the Stockholm Stock Exchange, the Copenhagen Stock Exchange and the Helsinki Stock Exchange. All these stock markets are electronic order driven or hybrid markets. Pure quote-driven stock exchanges are not typically attended by high-frequency traders, because they admit orders sent only by market makers.

The remainder of this chapter is organised into six further sections. Section 2 provides a short review of the literature concerning the financial innovation for trading activities. Section 3 outlines the general model of the market microstructure suitable for short-term trading and depicts its main features for the stock exchanges belonging to our sample, with a focus on their DAT services. Section 4 describes the different levels of PTT, within the international context, given the regulatory and commercial barriers we find relevant in each stock exchange. Section 5 summarises our data and methodology and Section 6 shows the empirical analysis and answers to the research question of this study. Section 7 presents our conclusions.

2 FINANCIAL INNOVATION AND TRADING: THE THEORETICAL BACKGROUND

For the last decade, the financial industry has been facing a remarkable revolution in the way trading is conducted within international markets. The trading process has been largely automated and information technology has led to a restructuring of the whole securities trading activity. As a consequence, many stock exchanges have replaced their open outcry systems (floor trading) with electronic trading systems. In particular, with reference to the dissemination of PTT, open outcry systems immediately provide traders with information about the name and the intentions (bid or ask orders) of all the participants, as they can directly observe each other, on the floor. On the contrary, on electronic trading systems, the identity of the trader can be anonymous and bid–ask orders can be hidden.

The different PTT received by traders in an open outcry or in an electronic system can influence their behaviour. This aspect has been examined in the literature since the beginning. Previous studies have focused upon the different effects that floor and electronic trading have upon the liquidity and volatility of the stock exchange. As far as liquidity is concerned, Miller (1991) and Fung et al. (2005) suggest that factors such as anonymity and faster execution provided by electronic trading attract more investors to the market thus increasing its liquidity as witnessed by lower bid–ask spreads. Moreover, Blennerhassett and Bowman (1998) suggest the possibility of an enhancement of liquidity in the electronic exchange due to a decrease in transaction costs.[1] In contrast, Frino et al. (1998) suppose that the anonymous nature of electronic trading limits the transmission of information that floor traders might otherwise observe in an open outcry; as a consequence, this raises concerns for adverse selection that should produce a wider bid–ask spread, as a form of liquidity reduction. Nevertheless, the results provide empirical support to show that electronic trading markets usually produce lower spreads compared to floor trading markets. Furthermore, Tse and Zabotina (2001) assume a cautious attitude towards the innovation of electronic trading; they find that stock exchanges which move from floor to automated trading show lower spreads after the transitin, thus providing support for an increase in liquidity; nevertheless, at the same time they make use of the Hasbrouck model and show that trades in the open outcry market have higher information content and suggest that electronic trading should complement, rather than replace, open outcry in stock exchanges.

In general, however, there is a widespread consensus within the literature that the financial innovations introduced through electronic trading bring about benefits for investors in terms of both enhanced liquidity and lower transaction costs.

As far as volatility is concerned, there is little literature specifically dealing with the relationship between electronic trading and the volatility of stock markets, although some studies have analysed the relationship between volatility and the factors that are related to the transition from floor trading to electronic trading, such as transaction costs and trading execution. As far as the latter is concerned, Hasbrouck and Saar (2002) find that faster execution of orders brings about market vivacity and, therefore, quicker and larger price movements; in this sense, as electronic trading reduces the execution time, we could say that somehow it increases market volatility. With reference to the transaction cost, Haud (2002) provides empirical support to show that an increase in trading costs, such as a taxation, would increase the level of volatility in the market. Therefore, as electronic trading reduces trading costs, we could state that the introduction of electronic trading potentially reduces volatility in the market, even if this contradicts the findings of Hasbrouck and Saar. Consequently, we can conclude that in the case of volatility there is no general consensus in the literature about the effects that electronic trading produces as a financial innovation.

Subsequent studies focus on how different pre-trade information levels, provided by electronic trading devices, influence the liquidity and volatility of the market.

Comerton-Forde et al. (2005) study the impact of order anonymity upon the liquidity of the Paris, Tokyo and Korea stock exchanges. In particular, Paris and Tokyo introduced anonymity in 2001 and 2003, respectively, while Korea removed anonymity in 1999. Liquidity is measured through the bid–ask spread. The results provide evidence that anonymity has an impact upon liquidity. In particular, Paris and Tokyo show higher liquidity (lower bid–ask spread) after 2001 and 2003, and Korea reduces its attractiveness towards investors after becoming more transparent. Similarly, Simaan et al. (2003) measure the impact of different levels of PTT on the behaviour of market makers in the NASDAQ Stock Exchange. They demonstrate that as market makers prefer being anonymous, a higher level of PTT reduces their competitiveness and so reduces liquidity in the market as measured by larger bid–ask spreads. Madhavan et al. (2005) conduct their analysis on the Toronto Stock Exchange, examining its transition from floor trading to electronic trading. They demonstrate that, contrary to the common presumption among policy makers and regulators, greater transparency might not increase market quality; instead, it can increase execution costs and volatility and hence cause a reduction in market makers' profits, thereby upholding the authors' opposition to any increase in transparency. In contrast to the previous literature, Boehmer et al. (2005) show that disclosing more information about limit orders in the order book is beneficial in terms of enhanced liquidity and reduced volatility. Focault et al. (2004) analyse changes in liquidity and volatility in the Euronext Paris Stock Exchange after the transition to an anonymous order book. They find evidence that after this transition, bid–ask spreads decrease significantly, and this provides support for an increase in liquidity. With reference to the volatility, they find that this reduction in the spread can be considered a predictor of a future decrease in volatility, even if after the transition to anonymity these results appear less clear.

To sum up, it is quite evident that, despite increased research attention being devoted to the subject, there is little consensus on the overall effects that different PTT levels produce upon the main features of a stock exchange. All of the previous studies focus on just a few stock exchanges and may therefore be sample specific. Moreover, these studies take few indicators into consideration (sometimes only the bid–ask spread) and fail to consider all the three different PTT dimensions (PTT1, PTT2 and PTT3). This is why we are now enriching the debate by using of a wider range of liquidity and volatility indicators, and conducting an analysis on a large international scale involving the comparison of 18 different stock exchanges. Moreover, we consider the results for each of the distinct PTT dimensions.

3 SOME FEATURES OF EQUITY STOCK MARKET MICROSTRUCTURE SUITABLE FOR SHORT-TERM TRADERS

We focus on market microstructures that are suitable for short-term traders, as these investors are the most interested in the pre-trade information. PTT features (identification of counterparties, desegregation and number of price levels) could be less valuable for long-term investors, as they should be driven mostly by other information, such as the economic fundamentals of the stocks (Allen and Taylor, 1992; Marshall et al. 2008).

Table 11.1 Organised multilateral trading venues suitable for short-term traders: some key features

	Regulated markets	MTF
Trading tools[1]	Phone trading Online trading Direct access trading (DAT)	Direct access trading (DAT)
Market making	Yes/no according to market microstructure (order driven, quote driven, hybrid)	Generally not[2]
Pre-trade info	It depends on the trading tool	It depends on the stock exchange's rules
Post-trade info[3]	It depends on the trading tool	It depends on the stock exchange's rules[4]

Notes:
1. We do not consider the tools that are not coherent with a short-term horizon.
2. In the US, traders on ECNs (the most developed ATS (alternative trading system), and in a way, MTF) may anonymously submit orders and trade with one another directly rather than place orders with a specialist or a dealer. Brokers working on this communication network act on an agency basis. In Europe, the two most prominent ECNs (Tradepoint and Jiway) combine an anonymous limit order book with market makers (see Degryse and Van Achter 2003).
3. Post-trade information refers to the dissemination of data about trades.
4. For example, pre- and post-trade information concerning off-market orders and trades is usually available on ECNs in the USA but it is usually not, for example, on the German ECNs.

Short-term investors usually trade stocks through organised multilateral trading venues.[2] Depending on their specific features, these venues can be either official (regulated market[3]) or unofficial (off-market multilateral trading facilities: MTFs[4]). Investors interested in listed shares may easily access the stock exchange where the security is listed, and trade according to its rules. However, in some cases, MTFs offer price improvements and better liquidity than traditional stock exchanges. These MTFs include electronic communication networks (ECNs).[5]

The trading tools, the market microstructure and the pre- and post-trade information change significantly among regulated markets and MTFs, as shown in Table 11.1.

The trading tools allowing short-term investors to trade in the organised multilateral trading venues are: phone trading, online trading and DAT. Online trading (OLT) is simply the technological evolution of phone trading (PT). In fact, an OLT contract allows the investor to send buying and selling orders through the bank's web page instead of doing it on the phone. Once the bank receives the order, it sends it to the market[6] because investors do not have any direct connection with the stock exchange. This means that they have no guarantee about the execution time. As far as the pre-trade information is concerned, investors receive data from the market but *not in real time* (generally with some minutes delay), as the information is transferred through a 'pull' technology.

DAT represents a revolution in the way investors can trade, because it provides traders with a direct connection to the market. DAT allows investors to directly address their orders, without any substantial intermediation. Intermediaries are only technological 'vehicles'.[7] Moreover, as far as the pre-trade information is concerned, investors have real-time information through a 'push' (*real-time*) technology. In Figure 11.1 we provide a description of DAT with reference to the order entry and to the pre-trade information processes.

Therefore, there are two main features distinguishing DAT from the other two trading tools. First, making use of OLT and PT, investors inform banks only of the name and the amount of the stocks they wish to trade, together with the price and the type of order. The order execution time is totally unpredictable because it depends on how long it takes the bank to send the order to the market. In contrast, DAT allows investors to directly control the execution time. Second, with reference to the pre-trade information, in PT and OLT, there is no possibility for investors to select stocks making use of a complete set of information coming from the market, except for that which they are able to get from newspapers or other media (TV, internet and so on). DAT, on the contrary, provides traders with the maximum level of order-book transparency according to the national regulatory barriers and to the commercial ones.

With reference to the investors involved in short-term trading we must distinguish between retail traders, institutional traders that are registered at the stock exchange (registered members: RMs) and institutional traders that are not registered (non-registered members: NRMs). In fact, RMs, because of their agreement with the stock exchange, are allowed to send orders through specific platforms not available for NRMs. Moreover, they receive full information about PTT directly from the stock exchange of which they are members. On the contrary, NRMs send their orders as dealers through the DAT platforms they buy from one of the different providers and they receive pre-trade information according to the commercial solutions offered by data vendors.[8] Retail traders wishing to trade through DAT are forced to open accounts with intermediaries (for example, banks) thus being allowed to send their orders directly to the market through their trading platform. In this case, the orders pass through both the server of the bank and the platform provider (simple electronic vehicles). The electronic

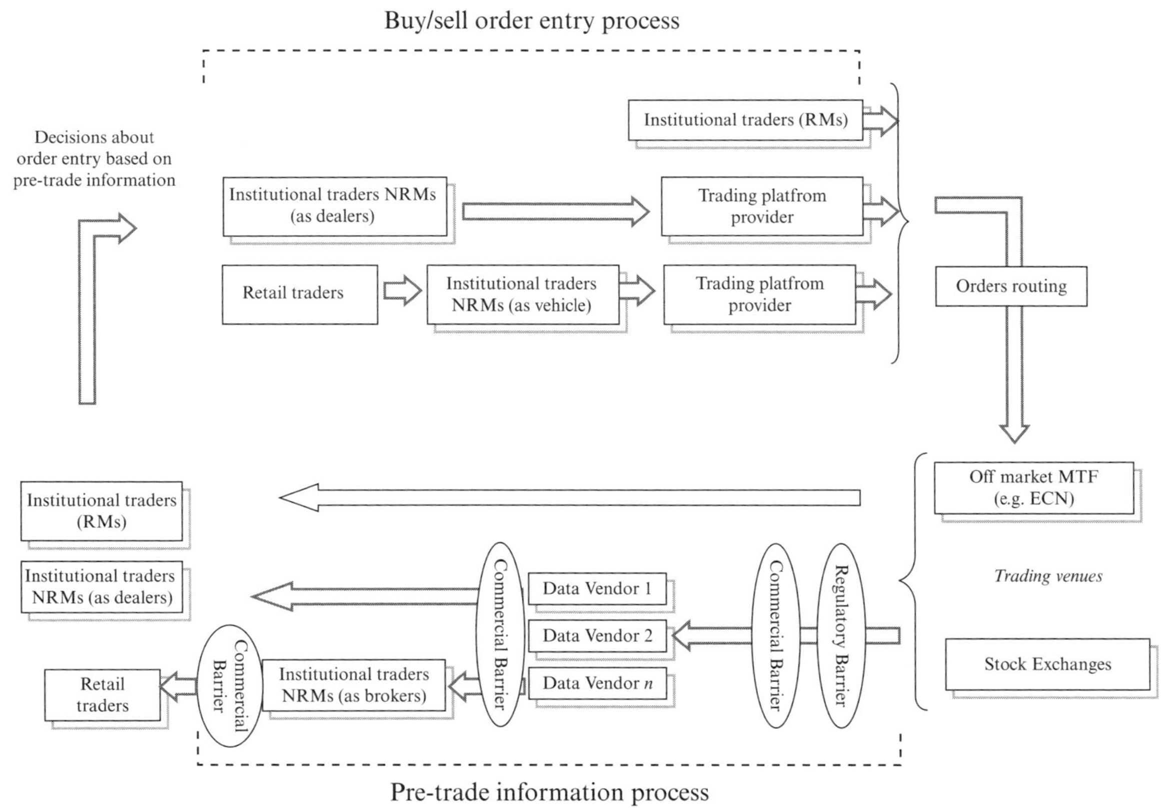

Figure 11.1 Order entry and pre-trade processes in DAT

access of the order to the market is technically called 'order routing' and it refers both to regulated stock exchanges and to MTFs (as ECNs).[9]

Once the order is collected electronically in the order book of the stock market, or MTF, it becomes pre-trade information for other investors and it is disseminated according to the regulatory and commercial barriers. As far as ECNs are concerned, this process depends upon the ECN and upon the stock exchange considered. In fact, some stock exchanges do not provide investors with pre- and post-trade information about the orders matched out of the regulated exchange.[10] This is the reason why we only focus upon the PTT provided by regulated markets.

4 THE REGULATORY AND COMMERCIAL BARRIER OF PRE-TRADE TRANSPARENCY

The regulatory barrier refers to the political choice of each stock exchange regarding the information to be disclosed to the public through data vendors. It may depend upon the technological and institutional features of the exchange. The commercial barrier consists of the different information packages that the exchange offers to data vendors wishing to buy its PTT.[11] Once the data vendor buys the information from the exchange, it is broken up and unbundled into different samples of data services, with a specific fee structure. These different packages of pre-trade information are sold to institutional NRM traders depending on their commercial agreements. At the end of the chain, retail traders receive information through their DAT account, with an amount of PTT coherent with their economic affordability and the regulation of market authorities.[12] All this means that, depending on regulatory and commercial barriers, NRMs and, even more, retail traders are allowed to receive a limited amount of pre-trade information compared to RMs. This can influence the liquidity and volatility of the market.

As far as the regulatory barrier is concerned, the rules of each stock exchange dictate what is considered *private* information, which can be disseminated only to RMs. On the contrary, *public* information is what can be given to all the other market participants. This barrier interferes with all the three dimensions of the pre-trade information: identification of the trader that sends the order (PTT1), desegregation of price levels (PTT2) and the number of visible price levels (PTT3). In Table 11.2 we provide a description of what each of the 18 stock exchanges considers public information with respect to the three PTT dimensions.

The public information represents the maximum level of PTT that data vendors can buy from each stock exchange. If no commercial barrier

Table 11.2 Regulatory barriers for the PTT dimensions

Stock exchange	Identification (PTT1)	Desegregation (PTT2)	Price levels (PTT3)
Borsa Italia[1]	No	Yes	All
Euronext (Paris, Lisbon, Amsterdam, Brussels)	No	Yes	All
Xetra	No	No	All
OMX (Copenhagen, Helsinki, Stockholm)	No	No	20
Madrid	No	Yes	20
Nasdaq	Yes	Yes	All
Amex	Yes	Yes	All
Nyse	Yes	Yes	All
London	With code[2]	Yes	All
Hong Kong	Yes	No	5
Singapore	No	Yes	All
Toronto	Yes	Yes	All
Australian	No	Yes	All

Notes:
1. Borsa Italia imposes the condition that retail investors and institutional NRM investors can see only the first five aggregated levels of the order book anonymously. Nevertheless, on 21 March 2007 Borsa Italia announced the forthcoming introduction of 'Book Profondo', which will enable all investors to see up to 20 disaggregated anonymous price levels in the order book according to the commercial barriers.
2. Identity is displayed only on SEAQ, SETSmm IOB and SEAT-plus. SETS is totally anonymous.

Sources: Rules and Regulation of Borsa Italia, Xetra, Euronext, OMX, LSE, Toronto, Madrid, NASDAQ, NYSE and AMEX. For Hong Kong, Australia and Singapore, see Comerton-Forde and Rydge (2006).

existed, every trader would have complete access to this information. On the contrary, retail traders face a double commercial barrier; the first depends upon what the stock exchange offers to vendors, while the second depends upon the information packages offered by these vendors to the final users. These commercial complexities lead us to suppose that institutional NRM traders, above all, have the economic power to bear the financial costs of full public information (the PTT allowed by the market authorities). On the contrary, retail traders generally find it convenient to buy a limited amount of pre-trade information, with fees resembling the scale of their trading activity.[13] With reference to Euronext, for example, public information consists of all the disaggregated price levels.[14] As regards the traders' identification, Euronext modified its market rules (on

23 April 2001), imposing the condition of the anonymity of market participants. This event, together with the technological improvement of the trading platform, allowed this stock exchange to enlarge its data feed offer, including a full cash market depth as public information (cash premium). This product is obviously addressed to both retail and institutional NRM traders. Nevertheless, our survey of mass market (retail) solutions, offered by worldwide data vendors, shows that reduced PTT is disclosed, including only the first five levels of the Euronext order books. This is mainly due to the low demand coming from retail traders for the full set of information in relation to its costs. The same happens within OMX exchanges. In fact, the regulatory public information includes 20 price levels, with aggregated volumes and anonymity of traders. Nevertheless, the retail trader's packages for most of the data vendors include only five aggregated and anonymous levels.

Table 11.3 offers a reasonable description of the pre-trade information available for retail and institutional NRM traders. We assume that the latter can afford the cost of buying the public information a stock exchange chooses to sell (see Table 11.2), while retail investors could receive a lower amount of PTT, due to commercial barriers.[15] That is why the left-hand column of Table 11.3 refers to 'partially informed traders', who are investors with no economic power to overcome the commercial barrier; in contrast, the right-hand column refers to 'fully informed traders', both institutional and retail NRMs, who buy all the public information available in that market.

A comparison between the two columns, for each stock exchange, shows in which cases partially and fully informed traders hold the same PTT. It occurs in the Anglo Saxon area (NASDAQ, NYSE, AMEX, Toronto SE and London SE), while the Eurozone (Euronext, Borsa Italia, OMX, Madrid SE and Xetra) shows an information gap, to the detriment of partially informed traders. Culture and competition are likely to be the reasons for these differences between the two regions. As far as culture is concerned, the attitude of the North American markets towards a large PTT comes from the conviction that 'pre trade transparency improves not just price discovery, but also the fairness, competitiveness, and attractiveness of U.S. markets' (see U.S. SEC, 1994). Moreover, US markets feature high levels of competition and the National Association of Securities Dealers (NASD) itself avoids 'any unfairly discriminatory terms that prevent or inhibit any person from obtaining efficient access to quotations'.[16]

Moreover, the commercial attitudes of stock exchanges towards data vendors also affect the cost of partially informed traders' PTT. In general, the cheaper a stock exchange sells its data to vendors, the better the prices those vendors can offer to partially informed traders. This regularity is

Table 11.3 Cross-country survey of PTT

Stock exchange	Partially informed traders			Fully informed traders (NRM)		
	Identification (PTT1)*	Desegregation (PTT2)	Price levels (PTT3)	Identification (PTT1)	Desegregation (PTT2)	Price levels (PTT3)
Amex	Yes	Yes	All	Yes	Yes	All
Australian	No	Yes	All	No	Yes	All
Madrid	No	No	5	No	Yes	20
Borsa Italia	No	No	5	No	Yes	All
Copenhagen	No	No	5	No	No	20
Euronext Amsterdam	No	No	5	No	Yes	All
Euronext Brussels	No	No	5	No	Yes	All
Euronext Lisbon	No	No	5	No	Yes	All
Euronext Paris	No	No	5	No	Yes	All
Helsinki	No	No	5	No	No	20
Hong Kong	No	No	5	Yes	No	5
London	With code	Yes	All	With code	Yes	All
Nasdaq	Yes	Yes	All	Yes	Yes	All
Nyse	Yes	Yes	All	Yes	Yes	All
Singapore	No	Yes	All	No	Yes	All
Stockholm	No	No	5	No	No	20
Toronto	Yes	Yes	All	Yes	Yes	All
Xetra	No	No	10	No	No	All

Note: * 'With code' means that the name of the trader is not visible but he/she can be recognised through a specific code.

Source: Estimations obtained from data vendors' commercial offers.

strengthened when MTFs are relevant trading venues, as occurs in the Anglo Saxon area. In fact, ECNs tend to offer to their subscribers PTT about their order books at costs affordable to both partially and fully informed traders, in order to enlarge their market share. As a consequence, regulated stock exchanges compete with the aggressive ECN commercial policies and are forced to lower their fees. Moreover, data vendors compete with each other for their own market share, especially in highly developed capital markets, such as the Anglo Saxon ones, and this leads to a further reduction in the fees they impose upon partially informed traders.

5 DATA AND METHODOLOGY

The sampling process is based on monthly data on the volumes of stocks making up the constituents of the most important national stock indexes, from November 2005 to November 2006 (source: Thompson DataStream). We select the most traded shares, as they are normally negotiated by a large range of traders, who are both fully and partially informed. As far as the latter are concerned, studies about behavioural finance demonstrate that retail traders (generally, partially informed) are used to pick stocks that 'glitter' and somehow catch their attention through the trading volume, the news and so on (Barber and Odean, 2007). So, the most traded shares seem suitable for those kinds of traders, even if they can obviously be picked by institutional (fully informed) investors, as well.

The sample is made up of the 10 shares with the highest average trading volumes, within each stock index,[17] during the year before the observation period. So the set of shares includes 180 stocks traded on 18 European, North American and Australasian stock exchanges (see Appendix 11A1).

The dataset is made up of tick by tick data of quotes and volumes downloaded for each stock, from the Digital Data Exchange (DDE) function of Realtick® Trading Platform for the European and North American Stock Exchanges, and from the Historical Tools' function of Bloomberg Trading Platform,[18] for the Australasian markets (Singapore, Hong Kong and Australia). The period we chose for the observations goes from 29 November 2006 to 20 December 2006 and from 8 January 2007 to 26 January 2007 (around 30 trading days, for each stock). In Appendix 11A1 we provide an accurate summary of the days' data we collected for every stock.[19] Within the described period, we downloaded tick by tick data, from the opening to the closing time of each stock exchange.[20] The final dataset, made up of more than 70,000,000 observations, is managed through specific queries based on the Structured Query Language (SQL) Software.

As far as the methodology is concerned, the first step involves the transformation of qualitative information about PTT collected in Table 11.3 into quantitative data necessary to carry out the analysis. Subjectivity is necessary in order to carry out this process. We attribute a score to each of the three PTT dimensions, assigning 0 to the lowest level of PTT and 1 to the highest, as shown in Table 11.4.

The PTT differences for fully and partially informed traders, shown in Table 11.3, induce us to weight their respective influence through the amount of their trading activity when computing the PTT dimensions for each stock exchange; so we obtain a national specific PTT1, PTT2 and PTT3. The few and partial data available[21] on this trading activity lead us to cautiously presume that the two categories contribute equally (weights 0.5

Table 11.4 PTT dimensions scoring

Dimension 1: PTT1 Traders' identification		Dimension 2: PTT2 Orders desegregation		Dimension 3: PTT3 Number of visible levels	
Identification	Score	Desegregation	Score	Price levels	Score
Yes	1.00	Yes	1	5	0.25
No	0	No	0	10	0.5
With code	0.75			20	0.75
				All	1.00

and 0.5) to the value of shares trading. Nevertheless, as the full PPT dimensions can also be bought by retail traders, we show the results obtained by overweighting the fully informed traders (weights 0.25 and 0.75).

To give an example, let us consider the pre-trade information related exclusively to the *traders' identification* dimension (PTT1). The weight 1 is assigned to PTT1 if the identity of traders is completely disclosed, 0.75 is given if an identification code is provided for each market participant and 0 is assigned to those stock exchanges allowing trades to be completely anonymous. To obtain the PTT1 of each stock exchange we calculate the weighted average of PTT1 levels assigned to partially and to fully informed traders, using both a 0.5 and 0.5 weight and a 0.25 and 0.75 one. Finally, we also calculate a global PTT (PTTG) as a simple average of the three scores of the PTT dimensions. As a consequence of the whole process, both singular dimensions (PTT1, PTT2 and PTT3) and the global PTT indicator go from 0 to 1.

The second step consists of the calculation of three volatility and three liquidity variables for each of the 18 stock exchanges belonging to the sample. This is done in order to establish whether any relationship exists between the different PTT dimensions of each market and the relative liquidity and volatility features.

As far as the liquidity variables are concerned, we provide in the observation period on a one-minute basis and for each of the 18 stock exchanges:

1. the average trading volume (*V*);
2. the number of book orders, as a sum of the best bid and best ask changes (*ON*);
3. the relative bid–ask spread (*BAS*).

As volatility variables, we provide in the observation period on a one-minute basis and for each of the 18 stock exchanges:

4. the relative open–close range (*OCR*);
5. the relative high–low range (*R*);
6. the realised volatility (*RV*).

In Appendix 11A2 we offer a detailed description of how the variables are calculated. In order to rank the 18 stock exchanges with liquidity/volatility indicators going from 0 to 1, we carried out a normalisation process. This normalisation is realised, for each indicator, by dividing each of the 18 values by the highest value among them.[22]

6 THE EMPIRICAL RESULTS

Preliminary Descriptive Statistics

The observation period for the empirical analysis, as specified in Section 5, goes from the end of November 2006 to the end of January 2007. Nevertheless, it is important to consider this period *in context*, observing the immediately preceding and following months. Hence, we consider the market performances of the stock exchanges from January 2006 to March 2007.

Two features are evident from Figure 11.2. First, one can see the general uncertainty of stock indexes' performances (returns), shown before and during the observation period. In fact, after the slide of June 2006, all stock indexes show a general recovery trend during the summer/autumn months of 2006, with the exception of the NASDAQ, which falls in August, and of the Toronto SE and the AMEX, in October. November and December 2006 (the first part of our observation period) present a reversal in the trend of the previous bullish period; in January 2007 markets seem to recover, even if February confirms the general uncertainty.

The second relevant feature from Figure 11.2 is the high correlation among all the stock indexes. In order to deepen this aspect, Table 11.5 shows the correlation coefficients within these markets and depicts how they are strongly interconnected. Apart from the Australian SE, all the other stock markets show a positive linear correlation (high and positive coefficients). This is important because it allows us to consider most of the analysed stock exchanges as a relatively homogeneous area with reference to the investors' sentiment.

As far as the sampled stocks are concerned, we calculate their 'beta', as the covariance of their returns in relation to the relative stock index volatility. The beta is a well-known measure of the stocks' systematic risk. The simple average of the beta, within the stocks of every stock exchange, is a

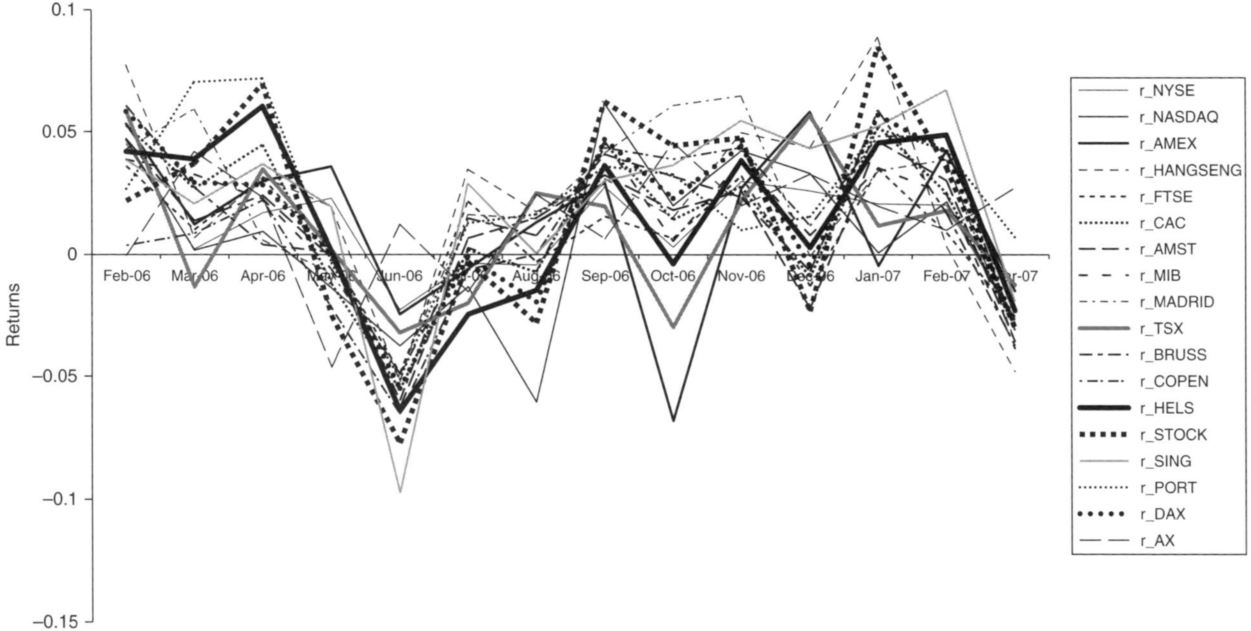

Note: *List of Indexes: Nyse Composite; Nasdaq Composite; Amex Composite; Hang Seng Composite; Ftse All Share; France Cac All Shares; Amsterdam Se All Share; Milan Mibtel; Madrid Se General; S&P/Tsx Composite Index; Brussels All Share; Omx Copenhagen (Omxc); Omx Helsinki (Omxh); Omx Stockholm (Omxs); Singapore All Sing Equities; Portugal Psi General; CDax General Index; Asx/All Ordinaries.

Source: Thompson DataStream Advance.

Figure 11.2 Monthly returns of stock indexes, [*] *January 2006 to March 2007*

Table 11.5 Correlation matrix of the stock indexes return, January 2006 to March 2007

	1	2	3	4	5	6	7	8	9	10	11	12	13	14	15	16	17	18
1	1.00																	
2	0.78	1.00																
3	0.69	0.41	1.00															
4	0.82	0.53	0.41	1.00														
5	0.71	0.54	0.30	0.84	1.00													
6	0.74	0.67	0.33	0.78	0.92	1.00												
7	0.72	0.52	0.29	0.79	0.92	0.94	1.00											
8	0.82	0.76	0.46	0.79	0.87	0.94	0.89	1.00										
9	0.60	0.60	0.09	0.61	0.76	0.77	0.83	0.85	1.00									
10	0.75	0.48	0.84	0.62	0.43	0.49	0.44	0.53	0.19	1.00								
11	0.72	0.58	0.21	0.84	0.87	0.90	0.94	0.88	0.86	0.38	1.00							
12	0.63	0.66	0.18	0.64	0.74	0.82	0.82	0.84	0.82	0.37	0.77	1.00						
13	0.75	0.65	0.52	0.64	0.81	0.91	0.83	0.89	0.68	0.57	0.73	0.79	1.00					
14	0.56	0.62	0.09	0.63	0.84	0.93	0.84	0.86	0.76	0.25	0.79	0.88	0.86	1.00				
15	0.74	0.63	0.41	0.74	0.81	0.78	0.81	0.82	0.75	0.51	0.77	0.87	0.79	0.75	1.00			
16	0.39	0.38	0.19	0.47	0.69	0.80	0.72	0.73	0.62	0.30	0.65	0.71	0.83	0.83	0.70	1.00		
17	0.80	0.76	0.34	0.76	0.89	0.96	0.92	0.95	0.83	0.45	0.91	0.85	0.91	0.90	0.82	0.71	1.00	
18	–0.24	0.07	–0.34	–0.12	–0.09	0.09	–0.02	0.07	0.21	–0.03	0.00	0.29	0.11	0.24	0.02	0.36	0.03	1.00

Legend to Table 11.5 Stock exchange code

No.	Index	No.	Index	No.	Index
1	Nyse Composite	7	Amsterdam Se All Share	13	Omx Helsinki (Omxh)
2	Nasdaq Composite	8	Milan Mibtel	14	Omx Stockholm (Omxs)
3	Amex Composite	9	Madrid Se General	15	Singapore All Sing Equities
4	Hang Seng Composite	10	S&P/Tsx Composite Index	16	Portugal Psi General
5	Ftse All Share	11	Brussels All Share	17	CDax General'perf' Index
6	France Cac All Shares	12	Omx Copenhagen (Omxc)	18	Asx/All Ordinaries

Table 11.6 Systematic risk for sampled stocks by market

Market	Beta of the sampled stocks by market
Amex	1.7
Amsterdam	1.0
Australia	1.1
Borsa Italia	0.8
Brussels	0.9
Copenhagen	0.9
Helsinki	0.8
Hong Kong	1.1
Lisbon	0.7
London	1.0
Madrid	0.6
Nasdaq	1.2
Nyse	1.4
Paris	1.0
Singapore	1.2
Stockholm	1.0
Toronto	1.5
Xetra	0.9

synthetic measure of the reaction (aggressive or defensive) of the sampled shares to the stock index movements. Table 11.6 shows that the sampled stocks are mainly aggressive.

Further preliminary statistics refer to the overall results for our liquidity and volatility indicators, introduced in Section 5 and analytically described in Appendix 11A2. So we build up the indicators of the average one-minute basis volume, orders number and bid–ask spread as far as the liquidity is concerned. Furthermore, we calculated the value of the three volatility indicators (open–close range, range high–low and realised volatility). The results are shown in Table 11.7.

Regional peculiarities are clear. Average volume (*V*), on a one-minute basis, appears much greater for Australasian stock exchanges than for Western markets. On the contrary, as far as the average orders number on a one-minute basis (*ON*) is concerned, North American stock exchanges appear the most dynamic. Average bid–ask spread on a one-minute basis (*BAS*) shows considerable differences between markets, but this cannot be attributed to homogeneous geographical areas, as in the previous cases.

As far as the volatility indicators are concerned, the absolute open–close range (*OCR*) informs us about the so-called 'trend volatility'. This indicator is low (or 0) if the share closing price matches the opening price and it is

Table 11.7 Liquidity and volatility indicators

Market	*V*	Market	*ON*	Market	*BAS**	Market	*OCR**	Market	*R**	Market	*RV**
Hong Kong	808943.71	Nasdaq	449.40	Australia	−2.2014	Lisbon	0.0235	Lisbon	0.0943	Xetra	0.0004
Singapore	167945.75	Nyse	301.69	Nyse	0.4438	Xetra	0.0241	Australia	0.1608	Brussels	0.0005
Nasdaq	108934.49	Toronto	142.48	Xetra	0.5825	Paris	0.0242	Brusselles	0.2292	Paris	0.0006
Borsa Italia	82353.95	Paris	52.45	Nasdaq	0.6004	Brussels	0.0250	Singapore	0.2492	Nyse	0.0006
London	74410.30	Borsa Italia	45.80	Paris	0.7434	Borsa Italia	0.0260	Helsinki	0.2756	Amsterdam	0.0006
Nyse	70347.45	Amsterdam	35.67	Borsa Italia	0.8420	London	0.0268	Copenhagen	0.3214	Borsa Italia	0.0006
Australia	40188.04	London	28.57	Amsterdam	0.9282	Helsinki	0.0279	London	0.3898	London	0.0006
Stockholm	33756.61	Amex	26.78	Brussels	1.1026	Amsterdam	0.0287	Hong Kong	0.4562	Helsinki	0.0009
Madrid	29495.17	Xetra	17.58	London	1.2329	Hong Kong	0.0319	Amsterdam	0.4947	Nasdaq	0.0011
Amsterdam	17171.97	Australia	17.57	Toronto	1.3935	Copenhagen	0.0355	Xetra	0.5340	Toronto	0.0017
Paris	14783.33	Hong Kong	17.46	Helsinki	1.6636	Nyse	0.0365	Stockholm	0.5563	Lisbon	0.0044
Xetra	12350.78	Madrid	16.75	Hong Kong	1.7056	Australia	0.0401	Borsa Italia	0.6496	Madrid	0.0126
Toronto	8697.61	Brussels	15.87	Copenhagen	2.2703	Nasdaq	0.0488	Paris	0.6673	Amex	0.0202
Helsinki	8680.01	Singapore	12.80	Stockholm	2.4397	Toronto	0.0526	Toronto	0.8239	Australia	0.0228

Table 11.7 (continued)

Market	*V*	Market	*ON*	Market	*BAS**	Market	*OCR**	Market	*R**	Market	*RV**
Amex	5793.65	Helsinki	11.22	Madrid	5.4822	Madrid	0.0570	Madrid	0.8598	Copenhagen	0.0251
Lisbon	3581.53	Stockholm	10.44	Lisbon	7.2759	Singapore	0.0586	Nyse	0.9519	Stockholm	0.1429
Copenhagen	2133.13	Copenhagen	4.85	Amex	8.4427	Stockholm	0.1049	Amex	1.2566	Hong Kong	0.8100
Brussels	1118.43	Lisbon	4.50	Singapore	10.5283	Amex	0.1250	Nasdaq	1.3316	Singapore	1.0290

Note: *= values × 1.000.

high (close to 1) if the share closing price is very different (higher or lower) from the opening price. The high–low range (*R*) is a 'fluctuating volatility' indicator because it informs us about the distance between the highest and the lowest price reached by the share in the 60 seconds making up each minute. The fluctuating volatility may be high even if the trend volatility is zero, because stock prices can change rapidly within the 60 seconds of each minute, despite the closing prices matching the opening ones. The realised volatility (*RV*) is a more traditional speculative risk indicator, and it tells us about how one-minute closing prices change within a trading day.

Observing volatility indicators in Table 11.7, regional peculiarities are clear as well and show Asian markets as being much riskier than the other ones, at least for the realised volatility. Nevertheless, North American stock exchanges feature a higher level of fluctuating volatility (high–low range).

RELATIONSHIP BETWEEN PTT AND LIQUIDITY/VOLATILITY INDICATORS

Studying all three dimensions of PTT in relation to liquidity and volatility, on a large international scale and through a wide set of indicators, is what makes our research unique. The conceptual framework of our analysis is shown in Figure 11.3. In brief:

1. we consider the regulatory and commercial barriers interfering with the complete disclosure of the information technologically available thanks to the DAT innovation;
2. we collect from both market authorities and data vendors the information about the characteristics of the PTT dimensions (traders' identification, order desegregation and price levels), for traders that have all public information available (fully informed traders) and for those affected by restrictions (partially informed traders);
3. we score these levels of PTT, from the best (value = 1) to the worst (value = 0) and we obtain the three national-specific PTT dimensions, weighting properly the relevance of fully informed traders and partially informed ones; and
4. we look for any relationship, in a cross-border comparison, between these PTT dimensions and a series of liquidity (volume, orders number and bid–ask spread) and volatility indicators (open–close range, high–low range and realised volatility).

Both PTT levels and liquidity/volatility indicators are measured within the 0–1 spectrum, as described in Section 5. We build up a chart where the

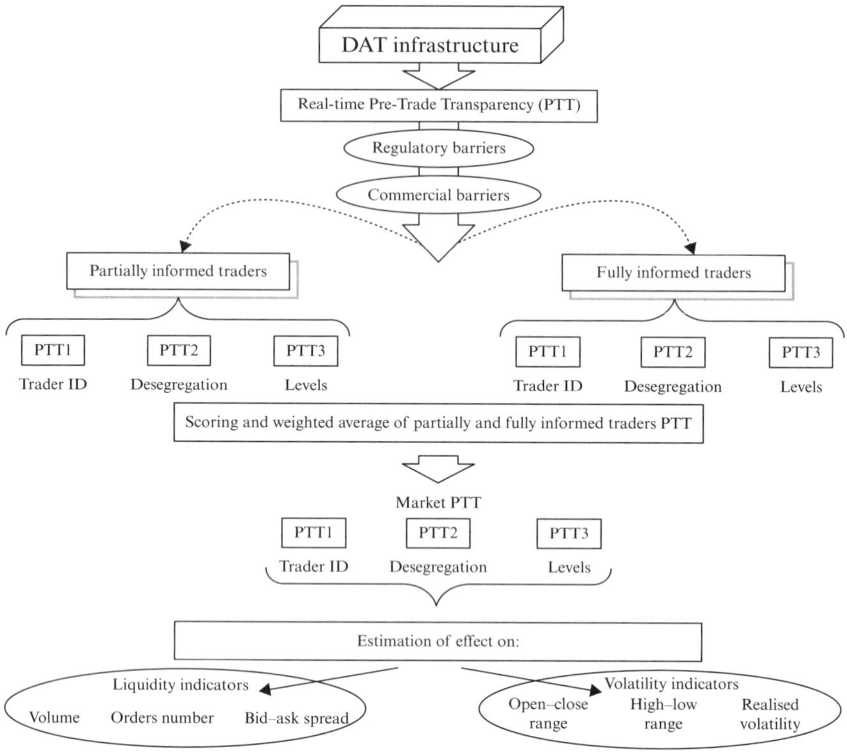

Figure 11.3 The conceptual framework of the empirical analysis

PTT are the independent variables and the liquidity (or volatility) indicators are dependent ones, in order to compare transparency with market quality. Every stock exchange is represented by two plotted coordinates, with each coordinate representing its relative market. More precisely an XY dispersion graph is built for each PTT dimension and each indicator, thereby enabling us to look for an interpolation of these crosses through an ordinary least squares (OLS) method. The straight line corresponding to the interpolation is drawn only if its slope coefficient has a p-value lower than 10 per cent.[23]

Figure 11.4 shows an example of our findings. At first sight, this set of charts indicates that the relationship between PTTG, the aggregate indicator for all the three PTT dimensions, and our liquidity and volatility indicators does not always show statistical significance. We are aware that the liquidity (and volatility) of a market depends upon something more than the amount of pre-trade information provided to investors.

Furthermore, some stock exchanges experience the same level of PTT but are characterised by different levels of liquidity/volatility. Geographical

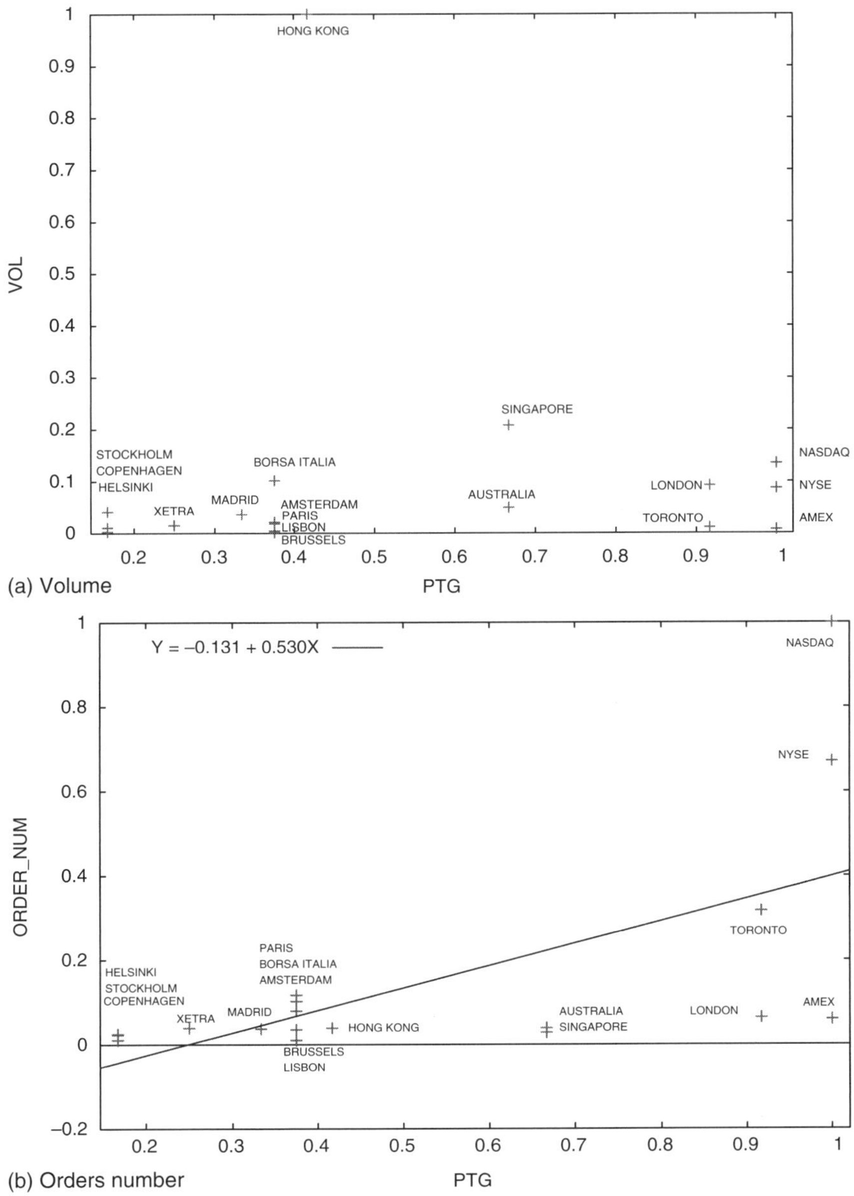

Note: Weight of partially and fully informed traders: 0.5 and 0.5.

Figure 11.4 The relationships between the PTTG and the liquidity/volatility indicators

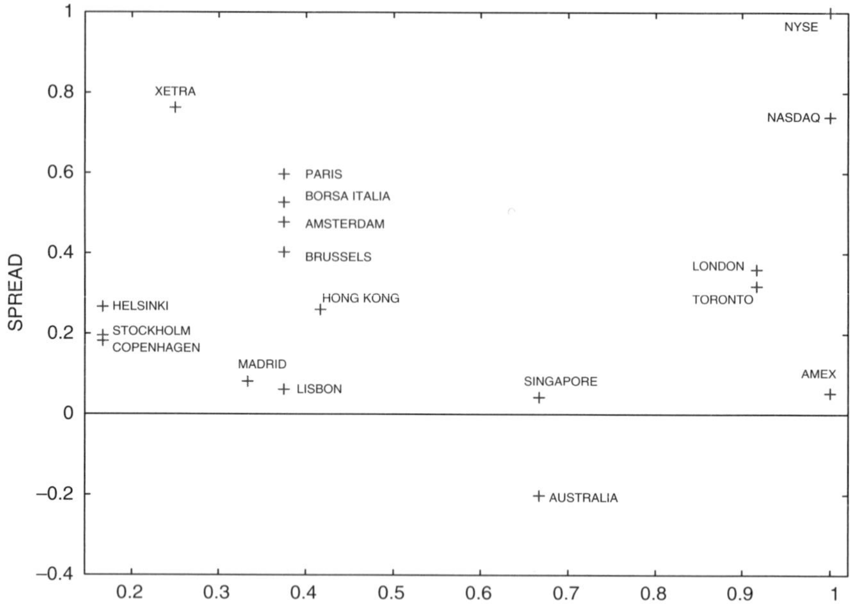

(c) Bid–ask spread

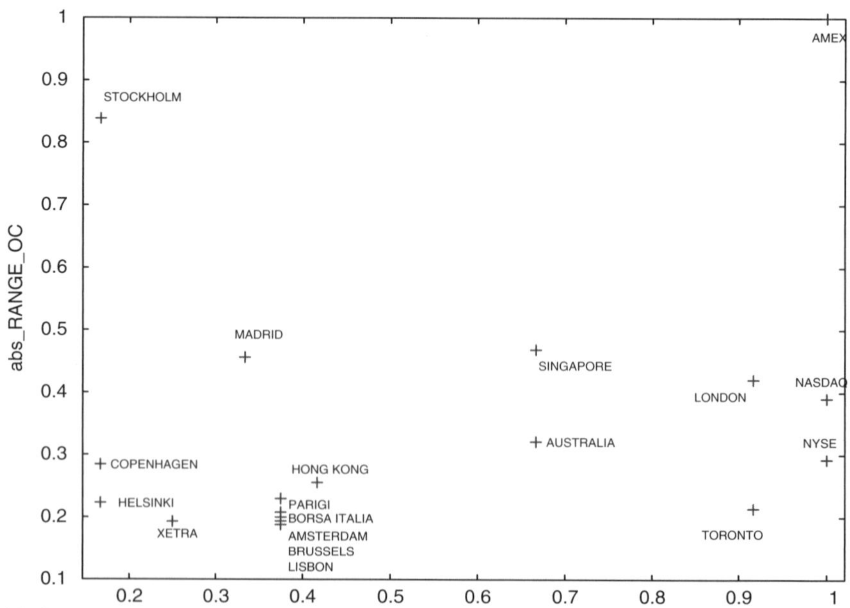

(d) Open–close range

Figure 11.4 (continued)

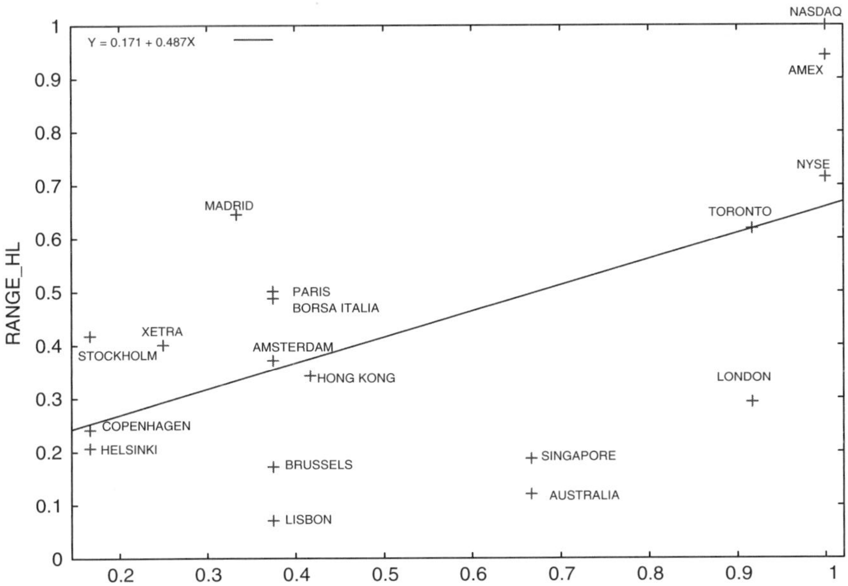

(e) High–low range

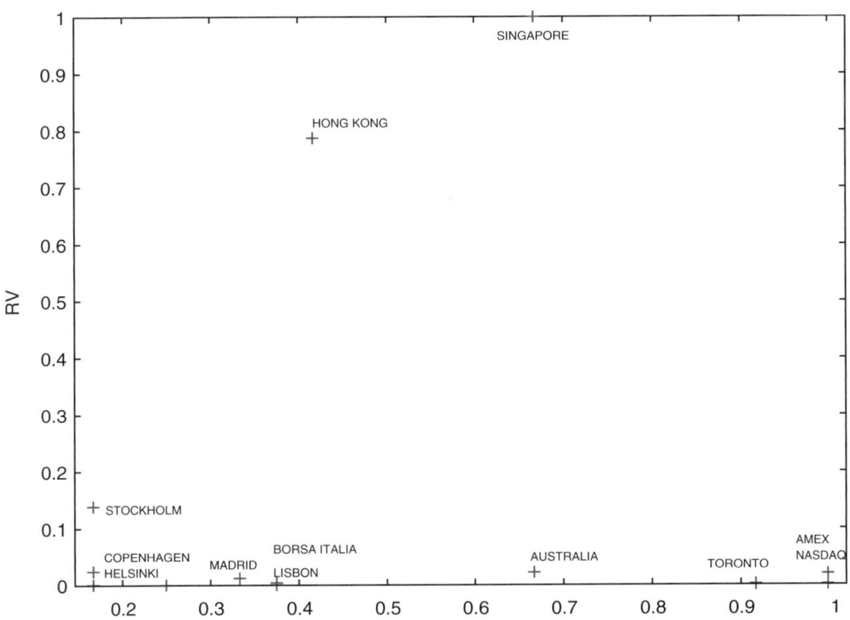

(f) Realised volatility

Figure 11.4 (continued)

and cultural peculiarities, together with both market microstructure and share-specific features, may exhibit a *noise* effect. Future research will attempt to understand the role played by PTT together with other variables in explaining the liquidity and volatility of stock exchanges in a multivariate framework. Nevertheless, the results of this research represent the first fundamental step in understanding these relationships.

We indicate in Tables 11.8 and 11.9 the global outcomes of our analysis, with the 0.5 and 0.5, and the 0.25 and 0.75 weights for, respectively, partially and fully informed traders. We show only the relationships with statistical significance. The results consider both the full sample of 18 stock exchanges and a subsample obtained excluding Australasian markets. In fact, the descriptive statistics listed above reveal geographical peculiarities of these exchanges (for correlation, volumes and risk) which lead us to focus our analysis also upon the more homogeneous Western area.

These outcomes allow a double-way interpretation of Tables 11.8 and 11.9: by *row*, we catch the different relationships between each PTT dimension, plus PTT globally, and our indicators; by *column*, we find out which indicator(s) is (are) linked with PTT, and how.

Results by row

The traders' identification dimension (PTT1) is strongly related to the liveliness of intraday trades. The outcomes show a positive slope coefficient, with a p-value of less than 10 per cent between the PTT1 and the average orders number, on a one-minute basis, for all the tests conducted: including and excluding Australasian stock exchanges and changing the relevance of partially/fully informed traders. This allows us to assume that the identification of market participants is connected with a higher average orders number on a one-minute basis. At the same time, the identification of market participants is always linked with a higher level of fluctuating volatility, given the positive relationship shown in Tables 11.8 and 11.9 between PTT1 and the high–low range volatility indicator. The co-relevance of these specific indicators (orders number and high–low range) appears reasonable; in fact, both of them represent proxies of the market intra-minute liveliness. In other words, a higher number of orders, within every minute, may easily be associated with a larger gap between the highest price and the lowest price, within the same time frame. Moreover, excluding the Australasian markets, the traders' identification dimension is also positively related to the average volume on a one-minute basis, confirming the relevance of PTT1 to the market intra-minute liveliness. Results regarding the other two PTT dimensions (PTT2 and PTT3) do not differ[24] remarkably from the PTT1 when considering the 0.5 and 0.5

Table 11.8 Outcomes with weight 0.5 and 0.5 (partially versus fully informed traders)

	PT info level	Volume	Orders number	Bid–ask spread	Open–close range	High–low range	Realised volatility
Full sample of stock exchanges	PTT1 (t. identification)	–	0.431	–	–	0.457	–
	PTT2 (offers desegregation)	–	0.311	–	–	–	–
	PTT3 (N. visible levels)	–	0.511	–	–	–	–
	PTT globally	–	0.530	–	–	0.487	–
Stock exchanges, Australasian stock markets excluded	PTT1 (t. identification)	0.348	0.447	–	–	0.438	–
	PTT2 (offers desegregation)	0.369	0.412	–	–	0.410	–
	PTT3 (N. visible levels)	–	0.833	–	–	0.778	–
	PTT globally	0.462	0.562	–	–	0.549	–

Note: The value of the slope coefficient is exposed if the relative *p*-value is lower than 10%.

Table 11.9 Outcomes with weight 0.25 and 0.75 (partially versus fully informed traders)

	PT info level	Volume	Orders number	Bid–ask spread	Open–close range	High–low range	Realised volatility
Full sample of stock exchanges	PTT1 (t. identification)	–	0.399	–	–	0.425	–
	PTT2 (offers desegregation)	–	–	–	–	–	
	PTT3 (N. visible levels)	−0.672	–	–	–	–	–
	PTT globally	–	$\beta = 0.586$	–	–	0.552	–
Stock exchanges, Australasian stock markets excluded	PTT1 (t. identification)	0.348	0.447	–	–	0.438	–
	PTT2 (offers desegregation)	–	0.321	–	–	0.326	$\beta = -0.285$
	PTT3 (N. visible levels)	–	0.107	–	–	0.926	–
	PTT globally	0.510	0.605	–	–	0.591	–

Note: The value of the slope coefficient is exposed if the relative *p*-value is lower than 10%.

weight, as shown in Table 11.8, and the 0.25 and 0.75 weight, as shown in Table 11.9 (particularly excluding Australasian markets). Nevertheless, we find a negative relationship between PTT2 and the realised volatility. This means that higher orders desegregation is also related to intraday price stability. So, even if PTT2 is positively linked to market liveliness (orders number and fluctuating volatility) this does not necessarily cause a shift into a larger variability of one-minute closing prices[25] (realised volatility) that paradoxically decreases. The global PTT always shows a positive relationship with both the orders number and the high–low range indicator, thus remarking the solid and persistent link with the stock market intra-minute vivacity. If we exclude Australasian exchanges, we also find a positive relationship with the average one-minute basis volume. This confirms that higher levels of global PTT are related, *ceteris paribus*, to the liveliness of intraday trades.

Results by column

As far as *liquidity* indicators are concerned, PTT is often positively related to the one-minute basis average volume. This happens either when changing the weight of partially and fully informed traders or when excluding Australasian markets. Similarly, PTT has a remarkably positive effect on the one-minute orders number (both bid and ask orders). All the three PTT dimensions contribute to these results, even if PTT1 plays a much stronger role. On the contrary, the bid–ask spread, in our research, is never significantly affected by any PTT dimensions.

With reference to the *volatility* indicators, no relevance is found as regards the so-called 'trend volatility' (the open–close range). PTT is positively related to the fluctuating volatility, confirming the already mentioned relationship with market liveliness. Within the full sample of stock exchanges, this connection is held only by PTT1. Realised volatility is negatively related to PTT when fully informed traders' activity is overweighed and when Australasian markets are excluded. PTT2 holds this relationship.

7 CONCLUDING REMARKS

DAT represents a financial and technological innovation that has changed the worldwide trading activity dramatically over the last years. Nevertheless, the attitude of national stock exchange authorities, as well as the relationships within market operators (data vendors, dealers, brokers and so on) raise regulatory and commercial barriers. These barriers can interfere with DAT full application, at least as far as pre-trade information is concerned.

In fact, DAT technology allows direct access to the stock exchanges and, above all, provides traders with real-time pre-trade transparency. Nevertheless, regulation and fees may customise the PTT that is given to investors. In this chapter, we evaluate the relevant relationships between different levels of PTT and some stock markets' features in order to deduce whether and how any limitation in the application of DAT is able to affect the market quality, in terms of both liquidity and volatility.

Although previous literature addressed the issue of the relationship between pre-trade information and the liquidity or volatility of a stock exchange, this chapter is original for the breadth of the empirical set (18 stock exchanges), for the variety of market indicators (three for liquidity and three for volatility), for the consideration of a wide range of PTT dimensions (traders' identification, desegregation and number of price levels) and, finally, for the set of traders potentially influenced by PTT (partially and fully informed traders).

Our main findings reveal a positive link between the pre-trade information and the vivacity of the stock exchange; in particular, the higher the PTT within a stock market, the more the bid–ask orders number within each trading minute and the higher the fluctuating volatility (in terms of one-minute basis high–low range). Sometimes, we also observe a positive relationship between PTT and the average one-minute volume, even if this link is weaker compared to the previous ones. The *traders' identification* (PTT1) shows this evidence more clearly. Moreover, when overweighting the trading activity of fully informed traders, we find a positive relationship between the *orders desegregation* (PTT2) and the *intraday price stability*. So, even if PTT2 is positively linked to market liveliness (number of bid orders and fluctuating volatility) this does not necessarily result in a shift to a larger variability of one-minute closing prices (realised volatility), which paradoxically decreases.

These general results are coherent with Boehmer et al. (2005) who reveal that higher pre-trade information is related to enhanced liquidity and reduced volatility. Moreover, our results about the link between a trader's identification and market liveliness are not comparable with a large part of the previous literature because it only uses the bid–ask spread as a measure of the market liquidity (Simaan et al., 2003; Foucault et al., 2007; Comerton-Forde et al., 2005). In our analysis, the bid–ask spread indicator is never statistically related to PTT. Nevertheless, our two further liquidity indicators (volume and number of orders) reveal a divergent result in terms of a positive relationship between transparency and liquidity.

Our research represents the first step in understanding the relationship between pre-trade transparency and market features through cross-country comparisons. Future analysis will endeavour to understand the role played by PTT together with other variables (market microstructure, stock fundamentals and so on) in explaining the liquidity and volatility of stock exchanges, in a multivariate framework.

The outcomes of this research may also have an institutional use: DAT infrastructure can be customised by regulatory authorities to adjust the public information in order to have a hold over the main features of a stock exchange. For example, authorities may decide to manipulate PTT1 if the vivacity of the market is to be increased, or it may modify PTT2 if the market volatility needs to be controlled. In this sense, recent reforms addressed to enhance the financial market integration and the investors' safeguards within the European Union[26] are likely to produce considerable effects upon stock market features. First of all, they should help to control the commercial barriers.

MiFID, at art. 44, dictates that regulated markets must disclose public information on '*reasonable commercial terms and on a non discriminatory basis*'.[27] This is strengthened by the foreseeable higher competition between trading venues '*which should increase investors' choice, encourage innovation, lower transaction costs, and increase the efficiency of the price formation process on a pan Community basis*'.[28] This new regulatory framework should play a relevant role in reducing dissimilarities of PTT for different kinds of traders.

Furthermore, these European reforms specifically dictate a minimum PTT obligation for all the trading venues that investors can choose (regulated markets, MTFs, systematic internalisers, or others). The harmonised *minimum* public information, for continuous auction order-book trading systems, is made up of '*the aggregate number of orders, at each price level, for at least the five best bid and offer price levels*'.[29] The identification of traders and the desegregation of orders, together with a wider minimum order-book depth, are not openly imposed. These limits may confirm dissimilarities compared to North American stock exchanges and may also maintain relevant differences within European stock markets. Ultimately, according to our outcomes, these missed measures may also fail to foster the vivacity of European stock exchanges.

NOTES

* Sections 1, 6 and 7 are attributed to Caterina Lucarelli; Sections 2, 4 and 5 are attributed to Camilla Mazzoli; Section 3 is attributed to both Merlin Rothfeld and Camilla Mazzoli.

** We are grateful both to Melissa Morgan (Townsend Analytics Chicago, USA) and to OMX, Euronext, Xetra, Singapore SE, NYSE and the Australia SE for the market information they provided as well as to Carole Comerton-Forde (University of

Sydney) for providing us with some of her published and unpublished papers about the microstructure of Asian stock exchanges.

We would also like to thank GL and SIA (Italy) for the valuable information they provided about worldwide pre-trade transparency and to InvestNet Italia spa, 'L. Bocconi' University and Fano BCC for providing us with access to Realtick® and Bloomberg data, respectively. Special thanks go to Mr Danilo Cerroni for his informatics support, which was vital for creating and managing the SQL database.

Finally, we are grateful to all the anonymous referees for their accurate work in providing us with comments and suggestions.

1. This reduction would occur through a decline in the information processing costs. Blennerhassett and Bowman (1998) study the level of trading and the bid–ask spread on electronic stock exchanges versus other floor markets. In fact, if the cost of transacting decreases on the electronic market they expect a migration of transactions to this market from other locations. The ratio of trades done within the market relative to trades done off the market and the bid–ask spread are analysed; both of these indicators suggest that liquidity increases in the electronic exchange, thus providing strong evidence for the positive effects of electronic trading.
2. We exclude from our analysis bilateral trading venues such as systematic internalisers. We use the terminology of recent European reforms about financial markets to codify more general concepts. Article 4.7, Directive 2004/39/EC states: 'Systematic internaliser means an investment firm which, on an organised, frequent and systematic basis, deals on own account by executing client orders outside a regulated market or an MTF'.
3. Article 4.14, Directive 2004/39/EC: 'Regulated market means a multilateral system operated and/or managed by a market operator, which brings together or facilitates the bringing together of multiple third-party buying and selling interests in financial instruments – in the system and in accordance with its non-discretionary rules – in a way that results in a contract, in respect of the financial instruments admitted to trading under its rules and/or systems, and which is authorized and functions regularly and in accordance with the provisions of Title III'.
4. Article 4.15, Directive 2004/39/EC: '*Multilateral trading facility (MTF) means a multilateral system, operated by an investment firm or a market operator, which brings together multiple third-party buying and selling interests in financial instruments – in the system and in accordance with non-discretionary rules – in a way that results in a contract in accordance with the provisions of Title II*'.
5. MTF is similar to the US alternative trading system (ATS), which is a trading mechanism developed independently from the established marketplaces and designed to match buyers and sellers on an agency basis. ATS may be an electronic communication network (ECN), crossing networks or smart order routing technology (SORT). See Degryse and Van Achter (2003).
6. Nevertheless, orders that are sent on the phone or through OLT can also be directly executed by the bank as a systematic internaliser, in those markets where there is no mandatory concentration rule.
7. This is due to regulatory restrictions that allow only banks and investment companies to directly access the stock markets.
8. It is necessary to distinguish between platform providers and data vendors. Platform providers sell the technological tool to trade; data vendors sell information about pre- and post-trade transparency. Thus, even if platform providers are usually data vendors, investors can subscribe only to the trading services and/or to the information flows.
9. ECNs are the most suitable MTF for direct access traders.
10. This is the case of Xetra, for example, where, according to the information we obtained from data vendors, around 50 per cent of the trades are executed out of the regulated stock exchange.
11. Generally, post-trade information is also included; we do not consider this aspect of the process.
12. In some cases, partially informed traders can buy information directly from the data vendors. Nevertheless, by doing so, they do not open any trading account and are not

allowed to send orders to the market. To do this, they have to subscribe to the service with an institutional investor.

13. This information comes directly from a survey we carried out among data vendors.
14. Euronext Cask Markets Trading Manual, issued on February 2007, Article 5.2: 'Market by orders (not available for warrants): The market by orders show all buy orders (listed from highest to lowest) and sell orders (listed low to high). For each order, the Euronext Trading Platform reports the disclosed quantity and the price entered. During the order accumulation periods, the theoretical price is disseminated as soon as it can be calculated. For buy orders with prices higher than the theoretical price and for sell orders with prices lower than the theoretical price, the price limit displayed is the theoretical price. A fast-market procedure is applied in the event of extreme activity in the market in one or more Securities (e.g. in a privatisation). In a fast market, the messages that would normally allow a cumulative update of the outstanding-orders market are no longer disseminated ("market by orders")'. Article 5.3: 'The market by limit's information disseminated is composed of the five best limits of buy orders (listed from highest to lowest) and the five best limits of sell orders (listed low to high). For each limit, the system reports the number of orders and total disclosed quantity displayed in the order book at that price. During the order accumulation periods, the theoretical price is disseminated as soon as it can be calculated'.
15. Obviously, this is a representation of the PTT commercial offer of the data vendors. Nevertheless, at the moment there is no collected data on what every trader really buys; so the affordability of each PTT level seems a sensible criterion to distinguish the different information available to partially and fully informed traders.
16. NASD marketplace rules, 4300A. Quote and Order Access Requirements.
17. More specifically: for AMEX it is ALL AMEX; for the Australian SE it is ASX 100; for Madrid SE it is ALL MADRID; for Borsa Italia it is the S&P/MIB; for Copenhagen SE it is the OMX COPENHAGEN 20; for Euronext Amsterdam it is the AEX; for Euronext Brussels it is the BEL 20; for Euronext Lisbon it is the PSI 30; for Euronext Paris it is the CAC 40; for Helsinki SE it is the ALL HELSINKI; for Hong Kong SE it is the HANG SENG; for London SE it is the FTSE 100; for NASDAQ it is the NASDAQ100; for NYSE it is the ALL NYSE; for Singapore SE it is the ALL SINGAPORE; for Stockholm SE it is the OMX STOCKHOLM 30; for Toronto SE it is the TSX COMPOSITE INDEX; for Xetra it is the DAX 30.
18. It has been necessary to download the data for the Asian stock exchanges from Bloomberg Platform as they are not yet available on the Realtick® Platform.
19. This is because some stocks are not traded every day due to holidays or extraordinary events that affect the company.
20. For the US markets, as they feature a higher level of ticks, we are forced to select only a few hours of the day; in particular, we sample data from 9:30 am, 12:00 pm and 3:00 pm, downloading the maximum amount of data Realtick® DDE memory can bear. This way, even if the datasheet is not able to contain all the data of the day, we are able to observe different market moments.
21. See KPMG (2006). Unfortunately, we have no information about similar studies for other stock markets. The data collected in the survey, together with those provided by the World Federation of Exchanges (WFE), enable us to estimate the weight of the retail and institutional traders within the Italian Electronic Stock Exchange (in terms of both the number and value of shares traded in 2005). We take the WFE data on the electronic transactions of shares in the Italian Stock Exchange and, through the KPMG data on the electronic trading of retail traders, we calculate the weight of this category of operators. The weights for the year 2005 are, respectively, 60 per cent for retail traders and 40 per cent for institutional traders. Nevertheless, there is no information about the real PTT used by traders to negotiate. Consequently, the only definite information we have is that fully informed traders account for at least 40 per cent of the weights, even if we are aware that an uncertain percentage of partially informed traders may buy the full PTT levels. That is why we consider a weight 0.5 and 0.5 or higher, in favour of the full PTT dimensions.

22. For the bid–ask spread ratio the normalisation process is carried out with the lowest value. For details, see Appendix 11A2.
23. Note that the significance of the slope coefficient reveals the presence of a 'relationship'. Also, if we consider the PTT as independent variables, nothing can be said on the real 'direction' of the relationship. In other words, we cannot conclude that the PTT 'causes' effects on the liquidity and volatility indicators, but only that the considered PTT levels are associated with particular levels of liquidity and volatility. Further research will attempt to deal with this specific research question.
24. With regard to the number of visible levels (PTT3) we do not pay much attention to the negative relationship with the average volume indicator, in Table 11.9, because this may be a typical noise effect due to Australasian peculiarities, especially shown for the average one-minute base volumes (see Table 11.7).
25. The one-minute base close prices are the points of reference for the realised volatility calculation.
26. We refer to Directive 2004/39/EC of 21 April 2004 on markets in financial instruments (MiFID) and the Commission Regulation (EC) No. 1287/2006 implementing Directive 2004/39/EC with regard to, among other things, the market transparency.
27. MiFID, Article 44, paras 1 and 2.
28. Commission Regulation (EC) No.1287/2006, p. 2.
29. Commission Regulation (EC) No. 1287/2006, Article 17 implementing Articles 29 and 44 of Directive 004/39/EC, para. 2, together with Annex II, Table 1.

REFERENCES

Allen, H. and Taylor, M.P. (1992), 'The use of technical analysis in the foreign exchange market', *Journal of International Money and Finance*, **113**, 301–14.

Barber, B. and Odean, T. (2007), 'All that glitters: the effect of attention and news on the buying behaviour of individual and institutional investors', *Review of Financial Studies*, **21** (2), 785–818.

Blennerhassett, M. and Bowman, D.G. (1998), 'A change in market microstructure: the switch from electronic screen trading on the New Zealand Stock Exchange', *Journal of International Financial Markets*, **8**, 261–76.

Boehmer, E., Saar, G. and Yu, L. (2005), 'Lifting the veil: an analysis of pre trade transparency at the NYSE', Working Paper, New York Stock Exchange.

Comerton-Forde, C. and Rydge, J. (2006), 'The current state of Asia–Pacific stock exchanges: a critical review of market design', *Pacific-Basin Finance Journal*, **14**, 1–32.

Comerton-Forde, C., Frino, A. and Mollica, V. (2005), 'The impact of limit order anonymity on liquidity: evidence from Paris, Tokyo and Korea', *Journal of Economics and Business*, **57**, 528–40.

Commission Regulation (EC) No. 1287/2006 of 10 August 2006 implementing Directive 2004/39/EC of the European Parliament and of the Council as regards record keeping obligations for investment firms, transaction reporting, market transparency, admission of financial instruments to trading, and defined terms for the purposes of that Directive.

Degryse, H. and Van Achter, M. (2003) 'Alternative trading systems and liquidity', in M. Balling, F. Lierman and A. Mullineux (eds), *Technology and Finance: Challenges for Financial Markets, Business Strategies and Policy Makers*, London: Routledge, pp. 171–89.

Directive 2004/39/EC of the European Parliament and of the Council of 21 April

2004 on markets in financial instruments amending Council Directives 85/611/EEC and 93/6/EEC and Directive 2000/12/EC of the European Parliament and of the Council and repealing Council Directive 93/22/EEC.
Focault, T., Moinas, S. and Theissen, E. (2007), 'Does anonymity matter in electronic limit order markets?', *Review of Financial Studies*, **20** (5), 1707–47.
Frino, A., McInish, T. and Toner, M. (1998), 'The liquidity of automated exchanges: new evidence from German Bund futures', *Journal of International Financial Markets, Institutions and Money*, **8** (3–4), 225–41.
Fung, K.W., Lien, D. and Tse, Y.K. (2005), 'Effects of electronic trading on the Hang Seng Index futures market', *International Review of Economics and Finance*, **14**, 415–25.
Hasbrouck, J. and Saar, G. (2002), 'Limit orders and volatility in a hybrid market: the island ECN', Department of Finance Working Paper FIN-01-025, Stern School of Business, New York University.
Haud, H. (2002), 'The role of transaction costs for financial volatility: evidence from the Paris Bourse', CEPR Discussion Paper 3651, London, Centre for Economic and Policy Research.
KPMG (2006), 'E-retail Finance in Italy', Milan, Italy, May.
Madhavan, A., Porter, D. and Weaver, D. (2005), 'Should securities markets be more transparent?', *Journal of Financial Markets*, **8**, 266–88.
Marshall, B.R., Cahan, R.H. and Cahan, J.M. (2008), 'Does intraday technical analysis in the U.S. equity market have value?', *Journal of Empirical Finance*, **15** (2), 199–210.
Miller, M. (1991), *Financial Innovation and Market Volatility*, Oxford: Blackwell.
Simaan, Y., Weaver, D. and Whitcomb, D. (2003), 'Market maker quotation behaviour and pre trade transparency', *Journal of Finance*, **50**, 1247–67.
Tse, Y. and Zabotina, T. (2001), 'Transaction costs and market quality: open-outcry versus electronic trading', *Journal of Futures Markets*, **21**, 713–35.
US Securities and Exchange Commission (SEC) (1994), *An Examination of Current Equity Market Developments*, Washington, DC: Government Printing Office.

Rules and Regulations of the Stock Exchanges

Australian Stock Exchange, 'Enhancing the Liquidity of the Australian Equity Market', January 2005.
Borsa Italia, 'Regolamento di Borsa Italia', April 2007.
Deutsche Borse, 'Deutsche Borse Group Xetra Release 7.1: Market Model Equities', September 2004.
Euronext, 'Euronext Cash Markets Trading Manual', February 2007.
London Stock Exchange, 'Rules of the London Stock Exchange', January 2007.
NASDAQ, 'NASD market place rule 4300A'.
Norex, 'Norex Member Rules', March 2007.
Toronto Stock Exchange, 'The Rules of Toronto Stock Exchange', June 2006.

APPENDIX 11A1

Table 11A1.1 Summary of stocks, tickers and trading days in the observation period for European markets

	BORSA ITALIA			LONDON	
Symbol	Name	Days	Symbol	Name	Days
AZA.MIL	ALITALIA	29	BARC.LSE	BARCLAYS	31
CAP.MIL	CAPITALIA	29	BP.LSE	BP	31
ENEL.MIL	ENEL	29	BT.A.LSE	BT GROUP	31
ENI.MIL	ENI	29	HSBA.LSE	HSBC HDG.	31
F.MIL	FIAT	29	ITV.LSE	ITV	31
PC.MIL	PIRELLI	29	LGEN.LSE	LEGAL & GENERAL	31
PG.MIL	SEAT PAGINE GIALLE	29	LLOY.LSE	LLOYDS TSB GROUP	31
TIT.MIL	TELECOM ITALIA	29	OML.LSE	OLD MUTUAL	31
TRN.MIL	TERNA	29	TSCO.LSE	TESCO	31
UC.MIL	UNICREDITO ITALIANO	26	VOD.LSE	VODAFONE GROUP	31
	MADRID			XETRA	
Symbol	Name	Days	Symbol	Name	Days
AVZ.MAD	AVANZIT	31	ALV.ETR	ALLIANZ	31
BBVA.MAD	BBV ARGENTARIA	31	BAY.ETR	BAYER	31
ECR.MAD	ERCROS	31	CBK.ETR	COMMERZBANK	31
ELE.MAD	ENDESA	31	DBK.ETR	DEUTSCHE BANK	31
IBLA.MAD	IBERIA	31	DCX.ETR	DAIMLER-CHRYSLER	31
JAZ.MAD	JAZZTEL	31	DPW.ETR	DEUTSCHE POST	31
POP.MAD	BANCO POPULAR ESPANOL	31	DTE.ETR	DEUTSCHE TELEKOM	31
REP.MAD	REPSOL YPF	31	SIE.ETR	SIEMENS	31
TEF.MAD	TELEFONICA	31	TKA.ETR	THYSSENKRUPP	31
XSBP.MAD	BNC. SANTANDER CTL.HISP.	31	TUI1.ETR	TUI	31

Table 11A1.1 (continued)

COPENHAGEN			HELSINKI		
Symbol	Name	Days	Symbol	Name	Days
CARLB.	CARLSBERG 'B'	31	ELI1V.HEL	ELISA	30
CPH		31	MEO1V.	METSO	30
DANSKE.	DANSKE BANK	31	HEL		
CPH		31	MRLBV.	M REAL 'B'	30
DCO.CPH	DANISCO	31	HEL		
EAC.CPH	OSTASIATISKE	31	NOK1V.	NOKIA	30
	KOM	31	HEL		
GN.CPH	GN STORE NORD	31	OTE1V.HEL	OUTOKUMPU 'A'	30
GR4SEC.	GROUP 4	31	POS1V.HEL	PERLOS	30
CPH	SECURICOR		SAMAS.	SAMPO 'A'	30
NOVOB.	NOVO NORDISK		HEL		
CPH	'B'		STERV.	STORA ENSO 'R'	30
TRYG.CPH	TRYGVESTA		HEL		
VWS.CPH	VESTAS		TIE1V.HEL	TIETOENATOR	30
	WINDSYSTEMS		UPM1V.	UPM KYMMENE	30
BOB.CPH	BANG&-	31	HEL		
	OLUFSEN 'B'				

STOCKHOLM			AMSTERDAM		
Symbol	Name	Days	Symbol	Name	Days
ABB.STO	ABB (OME)	31	AABA.AMS	ABN AMRO	31
ATCOA.	ATLAS COPCO	31		HOLDING	
STO	'A'		AGN.AMS	AEGON	31
BOL.STO	BOLIDEN	31	AH.AMS	AHOLD KON.	31
ERICB.STO	ERICSSON 'B'	31	ASML.AMS	ASML HOLDING	31
HMB.STO	HENNES &	31	HGM.AMS	HAGEMEYER	31
	MAURITZ 'B'		INGA.AMS	ING GROEP	31
NDASEK.	NORDEA BANK	16		CERTS.	
STO			KPN.AMS	KPN KON	31
SAND.STO	SANDVIK	31	PHIA.AMS	PHILIPS ELTN.	31
SECUB.STO	SECURITAS 'B'	31		KON	
TEL2B.STO	TELE2 'B'	31	RDSA.AMS	ROYAL DUTCH	31
TLSN.STO	TELIASONERA	31		SHELL A	
			UNA.AMS	UNILEVER	31
				CERTS.	

Table 11A1.1 (continued)

BRUSSELS			LISBON		
Symbol	Name	Days	Symbol	Name	Days
AGFB.BRU	AGFA GEVAERT	31	BES.LIS	BANCO ESPR. SANTO	31
DELB.BRU	DELHAIZE	31	BPI.LIS	BANCO BPI	31
DEXB.BRU	DEXIA	31	CPR.LIS	CIMPOR	31
FORB.BRU	FORTIS	31	EGL.LIS	MOTA ENGIL SGPS	31
GBLB.BRU	GBL NEW	31	IPR.LIS	IMPRESA SGPS	31
KBC.BRU	KBC GROUPE	31	PAD.LIS	PARAREDE	31
MOBB.BRU	MOBISTAR	31	PTC.LIS	PORTUGAL TELECOM SGPS	31
OME.BRU	OMEGA PHARMA	31	PTI.LIS	PORTUCEL EMPRESA	31
UCB.BRU	UCB	31	SCOAE.LIS	SOARES DA COSTA	31
UMI.BRU	UMICORE	31	SON.LIS	SONAE SGPS	31

PARIS		
Symbol	Name	Days
ACA.PAR	CREDIT AGRICOLE	31
BNP.PAR	BNP PARIBAS	31
CS.PAR	AXA	31
EAD.PAR	EADS	31
FP.PAR	TOTAL	31
FTE.PAR	FRANCE TELECOM	31
SAN.PAR	SANOFI AVENTIS	31
STM.PAR	STMICRO-ELECTRONICS	31
SZE.PAR	SUEZ	31
VIV.PAR	VIVENDI	31

Table 11A1.2 Summary of stocks, tickers and trading days in the observation period for North American markets

AMEX			NASDAQ		
Symbol	Name	Days	Symbol	Name	Days
AUY	YAMANA GOLD	30	AMAT	APPLIED MATS.	30
BQI	OILSANDS QUEST	30	CSCO	CISCO SYSTEMS	30
			DELL	DELL	30
CUP	PERU COPPER	30	EBAY	EBAY	30
DVW	COVAD COMMS. GP.	30	INTC	INTEL	30
			MSFT	MICROSOFT	30
HEC	HARKEN ENERGY	30	ORCL	ORACLE	30
			SIRI	SIRIUS SATELLITE RADIO	30
KRY	CRYSTALLEX INTL.	30			
NXG	NORTHGATE MRLS	30	SUNW	SUN MICROSYSTEMS	30
QEE	QUEENSTAKE RES.	30	YHOO	YAHOO	30
TGB	TASEKO MINES	30			
UPL	ULTRA PTL.	30			

NYSE			TORONTO		
Symbol	Name	Days	Symbol	Name	Days
AMD	ADVANCED MICRO DEVC.	30	ABX.CAT	BARRICK GOLD	31
			BBD.B.CAT	BOMBARDIER 'B'	31
GE	GENERAL ELECTRIC	30	ECA.CAT	ENCANA	31
			ELD.CAT	ELDORADO GOLD	31
MOT	MOTOROLA	30			
NT	NORTEL NETWORKS	30	G.CAT	GOLDCORP	31
			NT.CAT	NORTEL NETWORKS	31
PFE	PFIZER	30			
S	SPRINT NEXTEL	30	TLM.CAT	TALISMAN EN.	31
T	AT&T	30	UTS.CAT	UTS ENERGY	31
TWX	TIME WARNER	30	A.CAT	ABITIBI CONSOLIDATED	31
XOM	EXXON MOBIL	30			
BIG	BIG LOTS	30	AGA.CAT	ALGOMA STL.	31

Table 11A1.3 Summary of stocks, tickers and trading days in the observation period for Australasian markets

AUSTRALIA			HONG KONG		
Symbol	Name	Days	Symbol	Name	Days
ANN	ANSELL	14	BOC	BOC HONG KONG	11
COH	COCHLEAR	14	CBANK	CHINA CON. BANK 'H'	9
LLC	LEND LEASE	14	CMOB	CHINA MOBILE	11
MAP	MACQUARIE AIRPORTS	14	CNET	CHINA NETCOM GP.	11
MBL	MACQUARIE BANK	14	CUNIC	CHINA UNICOM	11
MOF	MACQUARIE OYCE	14	FOX	FOXXCONN	11
ORI	ORICA	12	HSBC	HSBC HOLDINGS	11
PPX	PAPERLINX	14	HUTCH	HUTCHISON WHAMPOA	11
WES	WESFARMERS	14	CATHAY	CATHAY PACIFIC AIRWAYS	32
WPL	WOODSIDE	14	CNOOC	CNOOC	32

SINGAPORE		
Symbol	Name	Days
CAPL	CAPITALAND	15
COS	COSCO	15
CSM	CHARTERED SEMICON.	15
ST	SINGAPORE TELECOM	15
STAT	STATS CHIPPAC	15
UFS	UNITED FIBER SYSTEM	15
UTAC	UNITED TEST & ASSB.CTR.	14
BH_ GLOBAL	BH GLOBAL MARINE	32
FED_INTL	FEDERAL INTL (2000)	32
MEDIA-RING	MEDIARING	32

APPENDIX 11A2

Average Volume (V)

Starting from the intraday one-minute data, we obtain the daily average volume for each of the 180 stocks in the 18 stock exchanges. Through another average for the daily volume in the entire observation period we obtain a volume data for all of the 180 stocks over the period, as follows:

$$\overline{V}_{\psi,i} = \frac{1}{n}\frac{1}{d}\sum_{j=1}^{n}\sum_{k=1}^{d} V_{\psi,i,j,k}, \tag{11A2.1}$$

where:

$\overline{V}_{\psi,i}$ is the average volume for the stock ψ in the market i in the observation period;
n is the number of minutes in the day k (depending on the stock, market and day we are considering);
d is the number of days making up the observation period;

Then, we obtain the average volume over the observation period for each of the stock exchanges in the sample, as follows:

$$\overline{V}_i = \sum_{\psi=1}^{m} \frac{\overline{V}_{\psi,i}}{m} \tag{11A2.2}$$

where:

$\overline{V}_i$ is the average volume of all the stocks in the market i in the observation period;
m is the number of sampled stocks in every stock exchange.

The normalisation of the average volume indicator is carried out as follows:

$$N\overline{V}_i = \frac{\overline{V}_i}{\max(i = 1...18)\,\overline{V}_i} \tag{11A2.3}$$

where:

$N\overline{V}_i$ is the normalised average volume in the market i;
max (i = 1. . .18) is the maximum average volume among the 18 stock exchanges belonging to the sample and, so, the normalisation parameter.

Order Number (*ON*)

Making use of tick by tick data, we provide the average daily order number for each of the 180 stocks in the 18 stock exchanges. A further average of the daily value allows us to obtain the average order number for each stock in the sample over the entire period, as follows:

$$\overline{ON}_{\psi,i} = \frac{1}{p}\frac{1}{n}\frac{1}{d}\sum_{z=1}^{p}\sum_{j=1}^{n}\sum_{k=1}^{d}(bid_z + ask_z)_{\psi,i,j,k} \tag{11A2.4}$$

where:

$\overline{ON}_{\psi,i}$ is the average number of orders for the stock ψ, in the market i;
p is the number of new bids and ask orders recorded in the order book within every minute in the sample;
bid_z and ask_z are every new bid order and ask order recorded in the order book.

Then we calculate the average order number over the observation period for each stock exchange in the sample, as done in (11A2.2) and we carry on the normalisation process, as in (11A2.3).

Bid–Ask Spread (*BAS*)

Based on tick by tick data, we obtain the average daily bid–ask spread for each of the 180 stocks in the 18 stock exchanges. Another average process on the daily value allows us to obtain the average bid–ask spread for each stock over the whole period, as follows:

$$\overline{BAS}_{\psi,i} = \frac{1}{n}\frac{1}{d}\sum_{j=1}^{n}\sum_{k=1}^{d}\frac{\overline{A}_{\psi,i,j,k} - \overline{B}_{\psi,i,j,k}}{\left(\frac{\overline{A}_{\psi,i,j,k} + \overline{B}_{\psi,i,j,k}}{2}\right)} \tag{11A2.5}$$

where:

$\overline{BAS}_{\psi,i}$ is the average bid–ask spread for the stock ψ in the market i over the observation period;
$\overline{A} = \sum_{z=1}^{t}\frac{A_z}{z}$ is the average best ask within every minute;
$\overline{B} = \sum_{z=1}^{t}\frac{B_z}{z}$ is the average best bid within every minute;
$\overline{B}_{\psi,i,j,k}$ is the average best bid in the day k on a one-minute basis for the stock ψ in the market i;

$\overline{A}_{\psi,i,j,k}$ is the average best ask in the day k on a one-minute basis for the stock ψ in the market i.

We calculate the average bid–ask spread over the observation period for each stock exchange in the sample, as done in (11A2.2). Then we carry out a normalisation in order to ascribe higher values to lower bid–ask spreads (as they are examples of liquidity). This is the reason why, in this case, the normalisation parameter is above the line and not under it, as it was previously.

$$\overline{NBAS_i} = \frac{\max(i = 1\ldots 18)\overline{BAS_i}}{\overline{BAS_i}} \tag{11A2.6}$$

where:

$NBAS_i$ is the normalised bid–ask spread over the period;
max(i = 1. . .18) is the maximum average bid–ask spread among the 18 stock exchanges belonging to the sample and, so, the normalisation parameter.

Nevertheless, this normalisation process is not able to return 0–1 values. A further normalisation, as in (11A2.3), is necessary to reach this goal.

Open–Close Range (*OCR*)

We make use of intraday one-minute data, to compute the daily average open–close range for each of the 180 stocks in the 18 stock exchanges. As a result, we get the average *OCR* for each stock over the period:

$$\overline{OCR_{\psi,i}} = \frac{1}{n}\frac{1}{d}\sum_{j=1}^{n}\sum_{k=1}^{d}\frac{CP_{\psi,i,j,k} - OP_{\psi,i,j,k}}{\left(\frac{CP_{\psi,i,j,k} + OP_{\psi,i,j,k}}{2}\right)} \tag{11A2.7}$$

where:

$\overline{OCR_{\psi,i}}$ is the average open–close range for the stock ψ in the market i over the observation period;
CP is the one-minute closing price;
OP is the one-minute opening price.

Then we calculate the average open–close range over the observation period for each stock exchange in the sample, as done in (11A2.2) and we carry on the normalisation process, as in (11A2.3).

High–Low Range (*R*)

Starting from the intraday one-minute data, we find the daily average high–low range for each of the 180 stocks in the 18 stock exchanges over the period:

$$\overline{R}_{i,\psi} = \frac{1}{n}\frac{1}{d}\sum_{j=1}^{n}\sum_{k=1}^{d}\frac{HP_{\psi,i,j,k} - LP_{\psi,i,j,k}}{\left(\frac{HP_{\psi,i,j,k} + LP_{\psi,i,j,k}}{2}\right)} \qquad (11A2.8)$$

where:

$\overline{R}_{i,\psi}$ is the average high–low range for the stock ψ in the market i in the observation period;
HP is the one-minute highest price;
LP is the one-minute lowest price;

Then we calculate the average high–low range over the observation period for each stock exchange in the sample, as done in (11A2.2) and we carry on the normalisation process, as in (11A2.3).

Realised Volatility (*RV*)

On the intraday one-minute data, we get the realised daily volatility for each of the 180 stocks in the 18 stock exchanges.

$$RV_{\psi,i} = \frac{1}{n}\frac{1}{d}\sum_{j=1}^{n}\sum_{k=1}^{d}\left(\frac{\ln P_{\psi,i,j,k}}{\ln P_{\psi,i,j-1,k}}\right)^2 \qquad (11A2.9)$$

where:

RV is the realised volatility on a one-minute basis over the observation period for each stock in the sample;
$P_{\psi,i,j,k}$ is the closing price for the minute j in the day k of every stock in every market in the sample.

Then we calculate the average realised volatility over the observation period for each stock exchange in the sample, as done in (11A2.2) and we carry on the normalisation process, as in (11A2.3).

Index